Digital Degrowth

"*Digital Degrowth* addresses new challenges emerging from the digitalisation of every sector of our lives, impacting our sovereignty and democracy. A vital book for anyone concerned about justice and equality, and about the limitless extraction of the Earth's resources to support the technologies of limitless greed and limitless growth."

—Vandana Shiva, environmental activist

"This book is a must-read for anyone who wants to know the brutal truth of digital colonialism driven by the American Empire. Don't get deceived by the American tech 'left' who is actually funded by billionaires. The true left vision of the future is digital degrowth."

—Kohei Saito, author of *Slow Down: The Degrowth Manifesto*

"*Digital Degrowth* pulls back the curtain to reveal the starkly naked machinery of imperial wizards and corporations that lack care and compassion. Our collective battles for 'ecosocialist degrowth' will reflect war resistance that protects our contaminated lives and challenges corporate extraction preying upon biological, mineral, and spiritual life. This text is a must-read manual for upgrading your security zones."

—Joy James, author of *New Bones Abolition* and editor of *Beyond Cop Cities: Dismantling State and Corporate-Funded Armies and Prisons*

"Synthetic and encyclopedic, Michael Kwet surveys the landscape of US monopoly power in the global technology sector, traces the capillaries containing the capital and cobalt flowing from core to periphery, periphery to core, required to fuel that power and the way of life it accompanies, and delivers a map to ending it. A must-read."

—Max Ajl, author of *A People's Green New Deal*

"As resistance movements around the world evolve, the question of 'resistance against what and who' has gained renewed importance. *Digital Degrowth* forces us to look at America's tech empire critically to inform a new wave of resistance led by today's youth. Kwet explains the problems clearly and provides solutions that directly impact the climate change debate. It's a must-read and call to action for activists and activist communities in all sectors of society."

—Itumeleng Moabi, Fees Must Fall activist and resistance movement archivist

Digital Degrowth

Technology in the Age of Survival

Michael Kwet

In loving memory of my Yiayia and Papou,
Edward and Lillian Basel.

First published 2024 by Pluto Press
New Wing, Somerset House, Strand, London WC2R 1LA
and Pluto Press, Inc.
1930 Village Center Circle, 3-834, Las Vegas, NV 89134

www.plutobooks.com

British Library Cataloguing in Publication Data
A catalogue record for this book is available from the British Library

ISBN   978 0 7453 4986 2   Paperback
ISBN   978 0 7453 4988 6   PDF
ISBN   978 0 7453 4987 9   EPUB

This book is printed on paper suitable for recycling and made from fully managed
and sustained forest sources. Logging, pulping and manufacturing processes are
expected to conform to the environmental standards of the country of origin.

Typeset by Stanford DTP Services, Northampton, England

Simultaneously printed in the United Kingdom and United States of America

Contents

List of Figures and Tables

FIGURES

TABLES

Acknowledgments

This book extends back half a decade. At the time, I had just completed my doctoral dissertation, *Digital Colonialism: South Africa's Education Transformation in the Shadow of Silicon Valley,* at Rhodes University in South Africa. I began to think about how degrowth—the notion that planetary boundaries require us to abandon a way of life premised on the domination of nature and limitless growth—relates to the digital society. For me, this was a game-changer: everything about society has to be re-designed, quickly. We have a limited window of opportunity to push for radical equality, which must be achieved in this lifetime, or we're toast.

This book's narrative challenges the status quo at the core of our being, from big corporations and nation-states all the way down to the relationships we have with each other in our everyday lives. At present, we live in a world of bosses and subordinates, owners and the dispossessed. The bosses include members of the self-professed radical "left". They accumulate and command the power and wealth in every major institution, from the corporate retail chain to the university. And they are intent on keeping it that way.

In this book, I've chosen to do what I'm responsible to do—tell the truth. As someone new to be being a "professional intellectual," I've quickly seen how the "professional" part can all-too-easily take over people's minds and ambitions. I learned that a small minority of intellectuals make big money, while most others are struggling to get by. There are pressures to sell out, to kiss up to bigger names, to suppress your speech and behavior. Writings become a commodity for sale in a marketplace where the more popular you are, the more perks you receive. Colleagues start chasing influence. They want citations and followers, tied to the perks, including salaries reaching several hundred thousand dollars or more. Opinions about politics become sports commentary on the lives of the poor and oppressed. Many (especially Western) professional intellectuals across the identity spectrum have lives of privilege with little or no skin in the game.

Every day, I try to stay as far away from this thinking as possible. What is written in this book is serious. We are in a real, deep emergency, and we need to tell the truth with no filter.

Swimming against the tide is no easy task. This is why I want to thank, first and foremost, my loving parents, Linda Basel Kwet and Fred Kwet, for their support over the years. We are from a middle class background. Without their gracious and ongoing financial and emotional support, I wouldn't have been able to survive as an academic to this point. I also want to thank my friends, too numerous to list. Some of them include Sohrob Kazerounian, Jonathan Oronzo, Itumeleng Moabi, Grace Nyambosi, Sanele Khakhu, Thabo Motshweni, and my kind and loving dog, Lily Kwet. I want to give special thanks my mother, Linda Basel Kwet, for her daily conversations with me about the topic, as well as Agnes Oberauer, who reviewed the manuscript in detail with outstanding feedback. Last but not least, I want to thank the Centre for Social Change at the University of Johannesburg for supporting this work, as well as Pluto Press for bringing the book to publication.

People are rebelling against injustice across the world. I hope this book can add some clarity to the struggle and inspire even more rebellion. Now is the time.

We must rapidly begin the shift from a thing-oriented society to a person-oriented society. When machines and computers, profit motives and property rights, are considered more important than people, the giant triplets of racism, extreme materialism, and militarism are incapable of being conquered.

—Martin Luther King, Jr.

We are not just in a climate emergency. We are in the foothills of the sixth mass extinction, and [environmental defenders] are some of the few people standing in the way. They don't just deserve protection for basic moral reasons. The future of our species, and our planet, depends upon it.

—Vandana Shiva

If you [intellectuals and activists] show more peerage with wealthy conservatives and progressives than you do with the working class, stand down. If you accumulate hundreds of thousands and millions of dollars and nobody even knows… then stand down… You have to have limits on your accumulation… *do not discipline the radicals.* And that's what I mean by "stand down."

—Joy James

Introduction

The famous biologist, Ernst Mayr, once had a debate with the legendary physicist, Carl Sagan, about why humans have not discovered life in outer space. After all, there are likely trillions of other planets. How could it be that we haven't encountered other living beings?[1]

Of course, to communicate with extraterrestrial life, we need to be able to send signals to each other that can be perceived and understood. This, in turn, requires what we call "higher intelligence." Mayr, a towering figure in biology central to the biological species concept, argued that "lower intelligence" life forms, such as bacteria, survive for long periods and proliferate. Species with "higher intelligence" are smaller in number and seem to die off faster. Just one—Homo sapiens—has the ability to communicate with life on other stars. Perhaps "higher intelligence" is a "lethal mutation," as Noam Chomsky put it, reflecting on the debate.[2]

With the environmental crisis heating up, humanity needs to decide quickly whether it's better to be smart or stupid. Right now, it looks like we are choosing to be stupid. If we don't drive ourselves to extinction, we're on the fast track to a permanent nightmare.

For starters, we are overheating the planet, which is now 1.2°C above the pre-industrial level, and growing. Studies show that global heating has already produced more numerous and intense extreme weather events—hurricanes, monsoons, floods, wildfires, and droughts—because of anthropogenic (human-caused) climate change. If we keep pushing the global temperature up, we will trigger irreversible *tipping points*—catastrophic events, like the melting of the glacial ice sheets, the mass die-off of coral reefs, and the conversion of the Amazon rainforest into a savanna. These events cannot be undone once they're set in motion. Like falling dominoes, tipping points set off cascading effects that spiral out of control. Some environmental scientists believe that we've already triggered several tipping points. Even if that's true, it's absolutely essential to keep from triggering more.

In addition to overheating the planet, we are destroying the biodiversity and habitats that sustain the web of life. Humans are killing off species at approximately 1,000 times the typical "background" rate in evolutionary history, and we are dramatically reducing the population size of many other species, putting them at existential risk. Scholars call this the "Sixth Mass Extinction." We are overfarming the soils and transforming arable land into desert. We are clearing tropical rain forests for livestock grazing, primarily to feed wealthier consumers, because they find beef tasty. We are ruining the oceans, polluting them with plastics while depleting the stocks of fish. Our good friends, the South African penguins, are facing extinction, thanks to human economic expansion.

We need to take a look in the mirror and ask ourselves, are we going to be smart, or are we going to be stupid? What kinds of changes are needed to avert a permanent catastrophe? Can we build a global society that respects Mother Nature, and that is also fair and just? And what does any of this have to do with digital technology? This book addresses these questions.

DIGITAL DEGROWTH

If we're going to be smart, then we need to understand what is causing this unfolding disaster—before it's too late. That requires us to take a deep look at human society. As we'll see throughout this book, digital technology is central to the state of the environment. It not only alters how we conduct our day-to-day lives, it also drives the global economy. The digital economy is not only overheating the planet and destroying biodiversity, it increases inequality within and between countries, stimulates consumerism, enhances surveillance and technologies of violence, boosts the power of militaries, and strengthens propaganda. All of this undermines the environment.

Before we launch into the digital connection, let's start with the basics. The global economy is organized through *capitalism*, a system that is predicated on *limitless growth* that is destroying the planet. As we will see, the solution to this is *degrowth*—the re-engineering of society to produce a good life for everyone within planetary boundaries.

Capitalists arrange economic activity by investing resources into enterprises that grow. The more growth, the more wealth and return on investment. Capitalism also produces high degrees of inequality. Those in favor of capitalism argue that inequality can be justified because total growth makes everyone wealthier, even if some people are richer than others.

2

Yet as we will see in Chapter 2, the scientific literature is clear that we cannot continue growing the global economy without overshooting planetary boundaries. If we keep using more and more resources, we're likely to overheat the planet and collapse the environment. You can't burn the walls of your house to keep yourself warm. Capitalism is just one of several societies humanity has created, and it has to be drawn to a close.

A growing consensus around degrowth is developing as the evidence piles up. Scores of studies and reports are demonstrating that worldwide economic growth is no longer viable. In 2023, a survey of nearly 800 climate policy researchers from around the world found that 73% of respondents deem worldwide economic growth to be incompatible with environmental sustainability.[3]

But capping economic growth leaves us with a moral problem. How do we alleviate global poverty if we stop growing the global economy? Over half the world's people live *under* a meager poverty line of $7.40 per day—the amount needed to achieve normal life expectancy. What do those of us with a decent standard of living say to the billions living under the poverty line, or those living in shacks? You're stuck with this life forever?

As we'll see in later chapters, there *is* enough to go around for everyone, but only if we spread it equally. There are 8 billion people alive today, and the global economy produces a little over $100 trillion per year. Under perfect equality, that leaves about $80,000 of income for a family of four. However, according to environmental scientists, we likely need to *reduce* the present level of material consumption, which would leave us with even less. If we want all 8 billion people to enjoy a decent standard of living that stays within planetary boundaries, we need to get rid of inequality between and within countries. The environment and human equality are fundamentally linked, and we need to stop treating people and nature like objects for self-gratification.

Thus, we need to reconstruct our societies so that they are *designed* to produce economic, political, and social equality. That means temporary growth in consumption for the global poor and a reduction in standards of living for those above the fair and sustainable limit, accompanied by a change in lifestyle based on less consumption, fewer working hours, and a more pleasant, socially harmonious society.

To get rid of inequality, we have to identify and contend with the actors responsible for global inequality and planetary destruction.

This book demonstrates that the United States of America holds the greatest degree of responsibility for the present crisis. It has burned more carbon and consumed more of the Earth's finite resources to build its wealth than any other country on the planet. And it obtains its riches in large part through the violent exploitation of the world's people. The US houses just 4% of the world's population, but holds 31% of the world's wealth and 45% of the world's financial assets. This concentration of wealth and power needs to be dramatically reversed *fast* if humanity is to build a just and sustainable transition. And there is no fixing the environment without seriously re-engineering the digital economy and society.

Indeed, if we look closely, American tech giants are at the center of this disparity. Of the top 100 global corporations, over 31% are transnational tech corporations—about twice that of the second-largest sector. Sixty percent of those tech firms are American, just 10% are Chinese.

This book is the first and only to assess, in detail, who owns the global digital economy and its connection to environmental costs. In doing so, it sets the record straight, establishing that one country *alone*—the United States—completely dominates the global digital economy. The popular belief that China has close parity with the Americans is pure fantasy.

Of the top 1,000 or so digital technology corporations, the United States accounts for 55% of the companies, 77% of the market cap (akin to wealth), and 59% of the revenue. China, by contrast, has just 6% of the companies and market cap, and 11% of the revenue. The Global North has 89% of the companies, 94% of the market cap, and 88% of the revenue.

In fact, the Big Tech giants have more accumulated wealth than the annual gross domestic product (GDP) of most countries. It would take a country like South Africa—with a labor force of 22 million people—almost three *decades* to produce the wealth of the top five American tech giants, which employ less than a million workers.

Added to this, Americans have the world's largest share of billionaires and millionaires, thanks in large part to the tech sector. People like Bill Gates (Microsoft), Jeff Bezos (Amazon), and Elon Musk (Tesla, Twitter/X, SpaceX) top the charts of the world's richest people. This extends down to the non-celebrity set of smaller billionaires and millionaires, and even the

4

average white-collar tech engineers with salaries of \$250,000 to \$300,000 per year.

Through the process of *digital colonialism*, the Americans have taken control of the global digital society. American tech supremacy supercharges the *ecologically unequal exchange* and *division of labor* created through classic colonialism over the past few centuries. Rich tech giants in the Global North monopolize the means of computation and knowledge while the poor countries perform the menial labor, like digging in the dirt for metal, picking coffee beans, labeling data to train artificial intelligence models, or cleansing social media networks of disturbing content.

Through the ownership and control of the digital economy, Americans utilize tech for the economic, political, and social domination of sovereign nations. US corporations dominate the world's social media networks, search engines, semiconductors, cloud computing systems, operating systems, business networking, office productivity software, and more.

Anyone who challenges the American Empire faces the prospect of economic sanctions, armed intervention, and authoritarian repression by the US and its allies across the world. Environmental defenders on the front lines—mostly in the Global South—are disproportionately subjected to dystopian digital surveillance, most of which has been engineered by the West. The same can be said for other marginalized groups, alongside anyone seriously challenging US power, irrespective of their identity.

Added to this, the digital economy is contributing mightily to environmental breakdown. The Information and Communications Technology (ICT) sector emits 2–5% of global carbon emissions, depending on the estimate, and its physical infrastructure for devices and batteries requires mining operations that destroy local habitats and poison surrounding environments. Industrial agriculture is extraordinarily carbon-intensive and ecologically destructive, yet tech giants like Microsoft and Amazon (as well as agribusiness behemoths like Bayer-Monsanto and John Deere) are digitalizing agriculture. Fast fashion is spreading like wildfire, while e-waste from the rich countries is dumped on the global poor. Through all of this, Global South laborers are exploited inside the factory sweatshops, mines, and farms. They are left to endure the devastation of extreme weather alongside chronic health problems from pollution and toxic waste.

Instead of helping the South, the US plunders it, doing everything it can to maintain the disparity between the rich and the poor so that it can sustain its global power and benefit from cheap labor and raw materials. As a result, each year, a net transfer of raw materials flows from the South to the North. Instead of trying to create world peace and sanity, the US is maintaining its 750+ foreign military bases, now with a ring of bases encircling China. (By comparison, China has one military base on foreign soil, in the African country of Djibouti.) Instead of trying to save the environment and build a decent life for everyone, the US is extracting record amounts of fossil fuels and plowing ahead with its system of limitless economic growth, devouring everything in its path—all to feed its super-rich and appease its middle class.

As we'll see in the pages that follow, it's no exaggeration to say that the United States is the greatest threat to life in human history. And yet, very few people walking the planet see the situation clearly. If we're going to survive, or at least have a decent future ahead of us, the people of the world are going to have to demand global equality. That makes the US ruling class and its tech empire public enemy #1.

Those who dominate other people think of themselves as "good" and those they dominate as "bad." Indigenous Americans and Africans were called "savages" by those enslaving them and committing genocide against them. But who was the "savage" in this relationship—the enslaver or the enslaved, colonizer or colonized? Most Americans still think of themselves as the "good guys" who bring "democracy" and "human rights" to the rest of the world, while they bomb them, arm dictators friendly to US corporations, and exploit their labor for pennies. In this sense, the US is still "civilizing the savages." I hope that Americans—of which I am one—will see the facts presented in the coming chapters and open their mind to a different story. Time is running out, but we can still save the day by fighting for equality.

SEEING THE BIG PICTURE

In his introduction to *This is Biology*, Mayr noted how many of his fellow biologists take a narrow approach to the study of biology. Regrettably, Mayr wrote:

... many biologists themselves have an obsolete notion of the life sciences. Modern biologists tend to be extreme specialists ... they are often uninformed about developments outside their field of expertise. Rarely do biologists have the time to stand back from the advances of their own specialty and look at the life sciences as a whole. Geneticists, embryologists, taxonomists, and ecologists all consider themselves to be biologists, but most of them have little appreciation of what these various specialties have in common and how they differ fundamentally from the physical sciences. To shed some light on these issues is a major purpose of this book.[4]

The goal of this book is very similar. It brings together aspects of society which are often studied in silos, such as software development, degrowth, industrial agriculture, cloud computing, artificial intelligence, semiconductors, ecologically unequal exchange, American Empire, resistance movements, social media, anti-apartheid, police, the military, race relations, radical unions, and more. Bringing a wide variety of topics together into a coherent whole, it offers a big-picture analysis of the digital age viewed in the context of the environmental crisis.

While I cover a lot of ground, I wrote this book for the global public—not specialists, technologists, or academics. Over the years, I ran the ideas and stories by family members and friends who aren't heavily tuned into politics. This book can be read by a mom, a high school student, or an everyday worker listening to an audiobook. I assume the reader knows almost nothing about digital technology, the environment, the United States, or politics. Everything is explained from scratch, with references at the back of the book should the reader want to learn more.

While this book can be read by a general audience, it also addresses intellectuals and activists. On that score, let me mention a few words about the two major camps of "intellectuals" writing about the two core topics of the book—digital politics and degrowth.

As for the first (digital politics) I argue that the common understanding of digital technology needs to be reframed around degrowth in a global context. In this book, I offer a new paradigm, *digital degrowth*, that lays out the needed theoretical framework for all digital politics. This stems from the degrowth *science*. By the time you get through this book, you will never see the world the same way again.

The framework in this book is missing from tech, I argue, because digital politics is dominated by a US-centered tech "left" that has shaped the narrative in most of the world. This *American School* of digital politics erases or trivializes the American Empire, digital colonialism, and degrowth, while instead focusing on things like Big Tech's surveillance of internet activity (e.g., surveillance capitalism), moderate reforms to make digital capitalism more "fair" and "competitive" (e.g., antitrust), and narrow human rights (e.g., racial bias in algorithms).

Here I put "left" in scare quotes to label these individuals who exploit social justice to get rich and famous. Like politicians, they pretend to stand for the people, but instead service the power elites they work for. Genuine leftists are internationalists who stand for full economic, political, and social equality across the world. They do not use social justice movements to get wealthy and build extravagant lifestyles. At a bare minimum, they tell the plain truth about power. Many of them take it further and endure low income, joblessness, imprisonment, torture, or death as a penalty for taking a stand.

As we'll see in the coming chapters, it makes no sense to even *think* about digital tech without framing it around degrowth and digital colonialism, with a focus on the American Empire as the central actor. Imagine trying to explain the motion of the planets without accounting for the sun, or trying to explain global politics in the nineteenth century without ever speaking about the British Empire, as if it doesn't exist. Imagine trying to discuss Israeli politics without mentioning the occupation of Palestine, or writing a book on South African history while only mentioning colonialism, apartheid, and white supremacy in a single paragraph. People might say, "wow, these people are morally and intellectually bankrupt." In the closing chapter, I argue that the American tech "left" is actually this bad, and that they operate within a racist, imperialist framework required by their connections to money and power.

Having spent years at Yale Law School and reviewing the works of scholars and journalists, I can say confidently that the American Empire and degrowth have been erased or trivialized across the board by the "thought leaders" from the top universities (especially the Ivy League), legacy media, NGOs, think tanks, government agencies, and Big Tech corporations themselves—most of whom are taking money from Big Tech, Big Foundation capitalists, and the government. This network receives accolades from the big corporate media, films streaming on Netflix, jobs at moneyed institutions, and top positions in the US government. Many of them are striking it rich manufacturing consent for the American Empire.

But it's more than just the theoretical framework that needs to be changed. That's just the start. More importantly, we need to change our *behavior*— our activism, our strategies and tactics for social justice, our policies, our workplaces, our ways of life. I believe we the people can save the day, but we need two things to happen. *First*, the mass majority needs to strongly desire full equality, and *second*, the masses need to create it themselves by working together as equals. The idea that there are saviors—be they charismatic leaders or political parties on the right or left—will always empower a minority that oppresses us. We, the common folk, have to liberate ourselves.

* * *

As for the second camp of intellectuals, degrowth advocates are much better than the US tech "left," but they have a few areas for improvement. In particular, degrowth advocates have hardly interrogated how the digital society connects to degrowth. When it comes to technology, most degrowth research and activism focuses on *green technologies* like solar panels and wind turbines, not the relationship between companies like Google, Microsoft, and Facebook to degrowth. This book is the first to do this. For that reason, I am hoping it will widely appeal to environmentalists.

Moreover, degrowth advocates typically speak of a future society where everybody is "flourishing"—one where we spread the wealth equally, work fewer hours, and live in harmony with each other and the environment. It sounds awesome, until you think about the transition process to make it a reality.

To be sure, we should all want this kind of society. More than that, we *need* it. But the scale of transformation from inequality to equality is not only unprecedented in human history, attempts to create it will almost certainly be met with extreme violence and repression. The minorities holding onto their wealth and power will oppose a movement for equality with every tool of violence and repression at their disposal. In the digital era, this means they will be using the most advanced tools of surveillance and violence ever developed. That's one of many connections between degrowth and the digital society. This book deepens our understanding of degrowth by addressing major themes like these that have not previously been discussed.

Right now, we're at a fork in the road. If we continue with business as usual, the rich and powerful will bury us all underground, or at least damage our planet beyond repair for future generations. If we resist, they're going to bury *some* of us underground, anyway, for trying to appropriate their wealth and power. We're either going to build a new and better world (ecosocialist degrowth) or we're going to be plunged into a permanent abyss by ruling-class elites who refuse to stop plundering the planet. Either way, *business as usual is coming to an end.*

* * *

Here's how the book will flow. Chapters 1 and 2 set the stage for how to understand digital degrowth. This can't be done by jumping right in the middle of the idea, because you have to know about both digital technology and degrowth at the same time. So I explain each topic in its own chapter, and then I merge them in Chapters 3–5.

Chapter 1 explains digital colonialism, demonstrating in detail that the United States completely dominates the global digital economy. The tables and numbers I produce have never been presented before, and the data is pretty shocking. I also explain some of the core concepts and history explaining *how* digital colonialism works and *why* the United States became so dominant.

Chapter 2 jumps away from digital politics into a seemingly different world. I explain the theory of degrowth, including the core environmental science of climate change, biodiversity, and its connection to capitalism and economic growth. We see that aggregate (total) global growth is environmentally unsustainable. Our only ethical option is to reduce growth in the rich countries and increase growth in the poor ones. This requires a radical redistribution of wealth and income between and within all countries. There is enough wealth to provide a decent life for everyone on the planet, but only if it's distributed equally across the world.

Chapter 3 begins connecting the dots by deepening the discussion of digital colonialism and degrowth, putting two and two together. I explain the notions of climate and ecological debts owed by the US and Europe to the Global South, based on historical and contemporary disparities in carbon emissions and material resource use. I also introduce the concept of ecologically unequal exchange, whereby the rich countries dominate the most lucrative part of the global economy—digital tech—and consume the lion's share of the world's material wealth, while the poor do the menial labor for pennies. Here I begin connecting degrowth to the digital economy. The rich American tech corporations monopolize the high-tech economy, while the poor dig in the dirt for minerals like cobalt to power our devices, work in sweatshops to assemble our iPhones, and more. The Big Tech corporations and their rich elites plunder the material wealth of the South, emit the most carbon, and consume many times more than their fair share of Earth's finite resources.

Chapter 4 continues this line of analysis, extending it to cloud computing and data centers. I start off with a story about indigenous resistance to the opening of a cloud center in Cape Town, South Africa as an evolution of colonial conquest. I then assess the American dominance of cloud computing, its connection to ecologically unequal exchange, as well as controversies behind the environmental footprint of data centers and artificial intelligence.

Chapter 5 deepens the conversation of digital ecocide. I explain how industrial agriculture works and its relationship to the environment before diving into the digitalization of agriculture through projects like Microsoft Azure Data Manager for Agriculture (formerly known as FarmBeats). I then cover the issues of digital consumerism, including advertising, e-commerce, fast fashion, and e-waste.

Chapter 6 changes things up. After concluding that digital colonialism and capitalism cannot be sustained, I dig into the means of coercion. I show that anyone trying to stop this crazy, violent, ecocidal world order—from social justice advocates to environmental activists—now faces dystopian technologies of violence harnessed by the US military and its allies. I also cover the

11

environmental impact of the US military, which damages the environment more than any organization in the world.

Chapter 7 explores the use of digital technology to police activists and environmental defenders. It covers the #FeesMustFall protests in South Africa, which I participated in while studying for my PhD at Rhodes University, as well as the sophisticated technologies now being deployed by police, prisons, legal systems, and border patrols.

Chapter 8 takes us in yet another direction, this time to digital degrowth *solutions*. The world is a big place, and there are people trying to build a better society. First, I explore People's Technologies built for democracy and equality. I explain alternatives based on freedom-respecting software for many of the core technologies we use, from operating systems and texting apps to email and social media. In the second half of the chapter, I propose a more comprehensive overhaul of the digital society through a Digital Tech Deal. This details a ten-point program to build an ecosocialist digital economy that is fair and just for everyone.

Chapter 9 closes the book out with suggestions on how to fight back. With a different worldview, digital degrowth, having been laid out in Chapters 1–8, I begin by offering some explanations on why everything detailed in the book is so obvious, but missing from the conversation in digital politics. This chapter explains what elites say (or omit) about the core themes of digital degrowth. I argue that the common narrative—including among the tech "left"—is dominated by American intellectuals employed by wealthy institutions representing the interests of American power. I argue that we need to redistribute wealth and power within and between our knowledge institutions if we're going to get the word out to the mass majority. In the last two sections, I suggest a boycott, divestment, and sanctions campaign against the American tech giants (#BigTechBDS), as well as an argument for revolution.

Taken as a whole, this book presents a radically different picture of digital politics and new insights into the environmental crisis. Like Ernst Mayr did in *This is Biology*, I hope I can help people understand the broad variety of issues covered and how they relate to each other. And I hope by making the big picture clear, I can inspire confidence in you, the reader, to push for a radically better world, in *this life*, not future generations.

As I write these words, people are protesting the unfolding Israeli genocide against Palestinians in Gaza. However, the United States is the Godfather in the background not only enabling Israel, but destroying the planet we live on. We need this kind of action against the American Empire itself, not just Israel, and it needs to be sustained. The only thing worse than genocide is ecocide, which is really genocide against other species and ourselves—especially the most vulnerable among us. Our window of opportunity is rapidly closing. The time to act is now.

Johannesburg, South Africa, May 2024

1
Digital Colonialism

In July 2023, South African Uber and Bolt drivers embarked on a national strike to protest against low pay and unsafe working conditions. Uber first showed up on South African shores in 2013 with promises of creating jobs with fair pay. Instead, the company made tensions in the local taxi industry worse, provoking violent conflict. In July 2017, a handful of taxi drivers petrol bombed the car of Uber driver Lindelani Mashua. He died of serious burn wounds.

Meanwhile, Facebook and Google have sucked the money out of online advertising, forcing many South African news outlets to put up paywalls while starving them of much-needed revenues.[1] And in May 2023, Amazon defeated resistance to the construction of their new African headquarters on a vital ecological floodplain that is also sacred indigenous land. The company now threatens to devour the local online e-commerce space while imposing surveillance and low pay on workers it claims to support. The indigenous-led Liesbeek Action Campaign, which spearheaded the protest, quipped: "same colonists, different ships."[2]

WHAT IS DIGITAL COLONIALISM?

Digital colonialism is the use of digital technology for political, economic, and social domination of another sovereign country or people.[3]

Under classic colonialism, infrastructure like railroads and canals were built through labor exploitation to service European colonizers. Notorious symbols of empire, railways bypassed local villages to connect sites of labor exploitation, military outposts, and sea ports. Corporations like the East India companies stole land, waged wars, and imprisoned natives. Slaves were imported to conduct back-breaking labor, while indigenous persons were massacred and forced off their land to clear the way for European settlement.

Science, technology, and infrastructure were central to colonial conquest. Heavy machinery and advanced manufacturing processes were monopolized by the *core* (the colonial countries in the Global North*), and they became necessary for material extraction and processing. Indigenous knowledge of manufacturing and medicine was appropriated, while Western engineers (e.g., chemists) migrated to the *periphery* (the colonized countries in the Global South) to help mining companies extract minerals. Other raw materials like cotton were extracted and exported for European manufacturers, who in turn flooded the Global South with cheap textiles, undermining the capacity for local industries to compete. A worldwide *unequal exchange* and *division of labor* ensued. The Global South became *dependent* upon the North, and its people were forced to conduct menial labor on the cheap for the European core.

Colonial conquest was a violent affair. Militaries administered violence, and new technologies like gunboats were utilized to penetrate the periphery. By the late nineteenth century, submarine cables facilitated telegraphic communications in service of the British Empire, while cutting-edge developments in recording, archiving, and organizing information were exploited for surveillance by US military intelligence to subjugate the Philippines. These technologies were then brought back to the United States for use by police and intelligence agencies. Meanwhile, colonialists built panoptic (surveillance-based) structures to police labor and prisons.

Colonization necessarily included psychological warfare and manipulation. Europeans spun deceptive narratives to justify conquest abroad (often through missionaries, in the name of religion) and at home (often by intellectuals, in the name of science). In their minds, the people they were brutalizing were "savage" inferiors, but they were also "civilizing" them and "saving their souls." The West imbued the world with a pernicious and manipulative ideological framework that causes immense suffering to this day.

In short, classic colonialism depended upon ownership and control of territory, infrastructure, and knowledge by states and corporations, as well as the deception of the people to manufacture consent. This process evolved over centuries, with new technologies and doctrines added into the mix.

---

* In this book, I use the term "West" and "Global North" interchangeably for word variety.

Today, the United States is at the helm of the contemporary colonial world order.[4] The "open veins" of the Global South are the "digital veins" crossing the oceans, wiring up a tech ecosystem owned and controlled by a handful of mostly US-based corporations. Some of the transoceanic fiber-optic cables are fitted with strands owned or leased by the likes of Google and Facebook to further their data extraction and service monopolization. The cloud server farms are heavy machinery dominated by Amazon and Microsoft used to store, pool, and process big data, proliferating across the world like military bases for US Empire. The engineers are the corporate armies of elite computer technologists with upper-class salaries of $300,000 or more. The exploited laborers are the people of color extracting the minerals in the Congo and Latin America, the armies of cheap labor annotating artificial intelligence data in China and Africa, and the workers suffering from post-traumatic stress disorder (PTSD) after cleansing social media platforms of disturbing content. The platforms and spy centers (like the National Security Agency (NSA)) are the present-day panopticons, while data is the raw material processed for artificial intelligence-based services. The governments in the North set imperialist policies like antitrust ("fair" and "competitive" capitalism), with poor countries unable to extricate themselves from the rules of the game benefiting their imperial masters. The Big Social Media networks are used to concentrate elite voices and manufacture consent.

Digital colonialism further entrenches the unequal exchange and division of labor established under classic colonialism. The dominant powers use their ownership of digital infrastructure, knowledge, means of computation, and command of the supply chain to subjugate the South, which remains in a state of perpetual dependency. Under this new division of labor, manufacturing has moved down the hierarchy of value, displaced by an advanced high-tech economy in which American Big Tech corporations are firmly in charge.

THE UNITED STATES OWNS THE GLOBAL DIGITAL ECONOMY

The first step to understanding digital colonialism—and the digital society in general—is to get a clear picture of who owns the international digital economy. Almost all intellectuals assume that the United States and China are waging an epic battle for global digital supremacy, as if there is close parity between the two countries. Yet they haven't run the numbers. This book sets the record straight: one country, and one country *only*—the United States—dominates the global digital economy, with no close competitor in sight.

Before we move forward, we should put the question of national economic power in greater perspective. As of 2024, there are 8 billion people in the world. The United States has 340 million, about 4% of the world's total. China, by contrast, has 1.4 billion people—about 18% of the world's population. India also has 1.4 billion people. Home to one third of the world's population, both China and India have *four times* the amount of people as the US. Yet, as we will see, the US dominates the global economy—especially the digital sector—as well as the world's wealth.

Those arguing for US–China parity present a general picture of the global economy measured by GDP—the annual monetary or market value of all finished goods and services produced within a country's borders. China's official GDP is $17.9 trillion as of 2022, they note, which is nearly as large as that of the United States ($25.5 trillion), or even larger if we adjust for the purchasing power of our currencies.[5]

Yet, as will be shown, this approach is flawed. It not only ignores that China likely overstates the size of its GDP, but it does not account for overseas production by a country's own corporations. For example, in the *Fortune* Global 500 Index, which lists the top 500 companies by revenue (sales), China edges out the United States when accounting for all sectors. This is sometimes used to suggest China is overtaking, or threatening, US economic dominance. However, unlike US corporations, most of the Chinese companies in the Fortune 500 are not *internationally* competitive, as the bulk of their business takes place *inside* China's borders, while overseas operations are *negligible*. Moreover, as *Fortune* magazine itself notes, Chinese firms in its Global 500 are much less productive than their US counterparts and they are much less profitable. *Fortune's* Global 500 simply tells us that China has many (often state-owned) oligopolies mostly generating money within the confines of the Chinese market.[6]

As political economist Sean Starrs notes, these kinds of approaches to measuring national economic power are misleading.[7] GDP and business activity within a country's borders wrongly treat states as self-contained units, "interacting as billiard balls on a table." If we broaden our outlook to account for transnational ownership, Starrs argues, then we find that American economic dominance "hasn't declined, it globalized."[8]

Starrs profiled the world's top 2,000 publicly traded companies, as ranked by *Forbes* Global 2000, and organized them according to 25 sectors. For profit share, US transnational corporations are singularly dominant. As of 2013, American transnationals led in 18 of the top 25 sectors, with especially high levels of dominance in the digital sector. That dominance still holds a decade later, as we'll see in a moment.

Portraying the US and China as equal contenders in the battle for global tech supremacy—the near-universal narrative—is a neocolonial fantasy of the West. As a matter of hard empirical fact, I will demonstrate in this chapter and throughout the book that the United States is in a league of its own as the only tech empire.

There are several ways to measure this. First, borrowing from Starrs's approach, we will detail the *aggregate* ownership of US and Chinese tech corporations—as well as others (e.g., Europe, the Global North, the Global South)—among top tech corporations worldwide. By "aggregate" I mean accounting for all business activity, including inside each country's own borders.

Second, since many Chinese corporations operate primarily *inside* mainland China, we will go beyond Starrs's approach by evaluating revenues generated *outside* of each country's borders—which further demonstrates the overwhelming dominance of the Americans. Third, we will measure who owns the core products and services in the digital economy. And finally, we will evaluate other factors, like startups, investment, and ownership of knowledge.

Part of this data—especially that about core products and services—will be presented in other chapters. However, the data necessary to establish an approximation of national ownership and power are set out in this chapter as a foundation for the rest of the book. Let us begin with the first approach: measuring ownership of the world's leading tech corporations. The next few sections of this chapter are data-heavy, in order to provide the factual basis for core claims in this book.

THE WEALTH OF TECH TRANSNATIONALS

Digital technology occupies a large share of the global economy. At present, the top 20 tech giants hold at least 36% of the top 500 companies listed on the US stock exchange (the S&P 500).[9] They also make up 31% of the world's 100 largest public corporations (valued collectively at $29.748 trillion in 2022). That's almost twice the size of the next largest sector.

Table 1.1   100 Largest Public Corporations by Sector and Country

Sector	# Co's	US	%	Ch	%	Mcap*	%*	US ($)	%	Ch ($)	%
Technology	20	12	60	2	10	9.221 (tr)	31.2	7.306	79.2	0.537	5.8
Consumer Discretionary	17	10	58.8	2	11.8	4.676	15.9	3.21	68.6	0.390	8.3
Health Care	17	13	76.5	0	0	4.402	14.6	3.432	78.0	0	0
Energy	8	3	37.5	1	12.5	3.398	11.5	0.904	26.6	0.127	3.7
Financial	14	7	50	3	21.4	2.91	10.2	1.948	65.6	0.631	21.2
Industrials	9	8	88.9	0	0	1.822	6.1	1.638	90.0	0	0
Consumer Staples	7	5	71.4	1	14.3	1.815	6.1	1.05	57.9	0.313	17.2
Telecommunications	5	4	80	1	20.0	0.842	2.9	0.697	82.8	0.145	17.2
Basic Materials	2	0	0	0	0	0	0	0	0	0	0
Utilities	1	1	100	0	0	0.172	0.4	0.172	0	0	0
TOTAL	100	63	63	10	10	29.748	100	20.357	68.4	2.143	7.2
Global North	86	—	—	—	—	*25.316*	*85.1*	—	—	—	—
Global South	14	—	—	—	—	*4.432*	*14.9*	—	—	—	—

* Total for all countries in the dataset.
Author's table and calculations. Source for data: Dorothy Neufeld and Bhabna Banerjee, 2022.[10]

This table gives us a first snapshot of corporate power at the global level across all sectors, as measured by market cap. *Market cap* approximates a company's total value, and is calculated by multiplying the value of a company's individual shares by the total number of shares. This is different than *revenue*, which measures a company's total income generated before expenses are subtracted. *Profit* is the amount a company earns after its expenses are subtracted.

In Table 1.1, we can see the following:

- The US has twelve tech companies (60%) compared to China's two (10%) with about 80% of the market cap compared to China's 6%.
- The US has many times more companies and market cap than China (and everyone else) in every category (except "basic materials," which is not lucrative).
- The Global North has 86% of the companies and 85% of the market cap.

We also see that transnational tech giants top the ranks of corporate power. At present, eight of the top ten publicly listed corporations are now tech giants (America's Apple, Microsoft, Alphabet/Google, Amazon, Nvidia, Tesla, Meta, plus Taiwan's TSMC). The world's largest corporations, led by Big Tech, now have more wealth than the annual GDP of most of the world's countries.[11]

Table 1.2 Top 943 Tech Corporations by Country†

Country	Companies	%	Market Cap*	%	Revenue*	%
United States	519	55.0	17.632	76.7	3.212	58.9
Global North (other)	189	20.6	2.305	11.2	1.201	22.0
Europe	129	12.5	1.258	5.7	0.395	7.2
China	60	6.3	1.239	5.7	0.605	11.1
India	25	2.7	0.059	2.2	0.008	0.1
Global South (other)	21	2.0	0.145	0.5	0.031	0.6
TOTAL	**943**	**100**	**$22.642**	**100**	**5.452**	**100**
Global North (total)	*837*	*89.4*	*21.195*	*93.6*	*4.808*	*88.2*
Global South (total)	*106*	*11.1*	*1.447*	*6.4*	*0.644*	*11.8*

† *Numbers and percentages are rounded.*
* *In trillions of dollars.*
Author's table and calculations. Source for data: Companiesmarketcap.com, 2023.[12]

Extending our data set to the top 943 tech corporations, once again we find the US remains overwhelmingly dominant:

- Of the largest 943 tech corporations by market cap (collectively worth $22.7 trillion), 519 are US-based (55.0%) with a combined value of $17.63 trillion (76.7%).

- China, by contrast, has 60 corporations (6.4%) and $1.26 trillion (5.5%). Taken together, the Global North has 837 corporations (88.8%) and holds $21.2 trillion (93.6%) by comparison to the Global South's 94 corporations (11.2%) and $1.45 trillion (6.4%).
- Of the top 100 tech companies on the list, 60 are from the US—including the top eight—while 13 are from Europe and ten are from China.[13]
- The numbers are similar if we index the data according to other categories, where India has a modest increase in market share relative to other countries.

As for profits, in an email, Starrs shared his 2020 numbers from his forthcoming book, *American Power Globalized: Rethinking National Power in the Age of Globalization*, from Oxford University Press:

1. *IT Software & Services* → US profit share is 76% vs China 10%.
2. *Technology Hardware & Equipment* → US is 63%, South Korea 14%, Japan 7.9%, China 6%, and Taiwan 5.7%.
3. *Electronics* → US is 43%, Japan 15%, Taiwan 12%, South Korea 12%, China 10%.

Starting from a low base, "China has increased its profit share by over 300% [over about a decade]," Starrs remarks, "but the US has also increased and China still has only the *fifth* highest profit share in the world in 2020, after being the largest electronics exporter continuously from 2004."[14]

To deepen our analysis, we will next observe that the numbers presented so far actually *understate* the extreme dominance of US transnational tech giants, as most Chinese tech is sold *inside* of mainland China. The data I compiled in Tables 1.1 and 1.2, in addition to those by Starrs, measure *aggregate* numbers. This includes each country's economic activity *both* inside *and* outside of its own borders. However, Chinese corporations typically do most of their business *inside* mainland China, with little market share *outside* of China. US corporations, by contrast, are predominantly transnational and hold substantive market share in foreign countries.

Table 1.3 separates domestic from international economic activity. If we look into tech corporations based in the US and in China, we confirm that the US has a much greater market share *outside* of its own borders than China does.

Table 1.3 Domestic vs Foreign Revenue Among Top US and Chinese Tech Corporations*†

Company	Domestic Revenue	%	Foreign Revenue*	%
†Apple[15]	169.66	43.2	222.63	56.8
Microsoft[16]	83.953	49.9	84.135	50.1
Alphabet (Google)[17]	135.761	48.0	147.075	52.0
Amazon[18]	338.95	65.9	175.0	34.1
Nvidia[19]	8.292	30.7	18.682	69.3
Meta (Facebook)[20]	48.4	41.1	69.5	58.6
Tesla[21]	40.553	49.8	40.909	50.2
Broadcom[22]	5.92	20.3	23.29	79.7
Oracle[23]	31.226	62.5	18.728	37.5
Adobe[24]	10.25	58.2	7.35	41.8
AMD	7.84	34.6	14.84	65.4
Salesforce	19.76	63.0	11.59	37.0
Netflix	13.8	40.9	19.92	59.1
Cisco	29.9	52.5	27.1	47.5
Intel	14.85	27.4	39.37	72.6
TOTAL (US)	**959.115**	**51.0**	**920.119**	**49.0**
Tencent	74.72	90.6	7.73	9.4
ByteDance[25]	85.2	90.0	9.4	10.0
Alibaba[26]	114.286	90.2	12.418	9.8
Lenovo	17.19	24.0	54.43	76.0
Huawei[27]	55.796	62.9	32.862	37.1
Pinduoduo[28]	17.44	74.4	6.00	25.6
Meituan[29]	27.60	100.0	0.0	0.0
NetEase (games)[30]	12.158	90.0	1.216	10.0
Xiaomi	21.152	50.8	20.487	49.2
Jingdong Mall (JD)	155.373	100.0	0.0	0.0
Baidu	17.931	100.0	0.0	0.0
SMIC	5.380	74.0	1.890	26.0
Kuaishou	13.911	99.3	0.093	0.7
Trip.com	2.425	81.4	0.554	18.6
Didi	20.038	95.8	0.871	4.2
TOTAL (China)	**640.6**	**81.24**	**147.951**	**18.76**

* In billions of dollars.
† Author's table and calculations. Numbers in this table are rounded and culled from publicly available data. Revenue is in billions of dollars; year of revenues are within the last 1–3 years (2021–2023); currency conversions from yuan or Hong Kong dollars to US dollars were carried out on November 15, 2023.

As we can see, among the top 15 tech companies for each country, revenues in foreign markets are larger and proportionally greater for the US (about half) than for China (about 20%). Moreover, China's tech economy thins out as you move down the list of the top 1,000 tech companies: the US has an additional 504 companies on the list, whereas China has just 45.

There are also a few key points about market share and global power we should observe. First, US market share abroad often devastates foreign countries. For instance, even though Google and Meta only get a small portion of their online ad revenue from a country like South Africa, they undermine its local media by taking close to 80% of the country's total online advertising market.[31] Thus even when the sum of revenue obtained from a poor country appears trivial for a US tech giant, it is a major problem for that country. Second, because the Big Tech giants dominate foreign markets across the world, what seems to be small slivers of revenue from each country adds up to a large fraction of total revenues. Put another way, American Big Tech giants are so big precisely because they are *global* colonizers.

WHO OWNS THE PRODUCTS AND SERVICES?

As noted earlier, a second way to measure who owns the global digital economy is by looking at core products and services. The tech giants tower over the rest of the industry because they offer things that the masses of people—i.e., everyone across the world—depend upon. This is the core stuff of the digital ecosystem that people require to use their devices—computer chips (semiconductors), operating systems, cloud server farms, and so on.

In this regard, China also fares poorly against the United States. To be sure, there are exceptions in global markets where China does have substantial foreign market share, such as 5G base stations (Huawei), social media (TikTok), e-retail (Shein, Temu), commercial drones (DJI), CCTV cameras (Hikvision, Dahua), and mobile phones (Oppo, Huawei, Xiaomi). That said, some of these providers source parts (such as computer processors or memory) from the Global North or sell products based on hyper-exploited Chinese labor to Western consumers—hardly a condition of parity. Even without those caveats, US corporations dominate or have substantial market share in most digital products and industries in the global economy, including, among others:

- Search engines (Google)
- Semiconductors (Nvidia, Intel, AMD, Qualcomm, Broadcom)
- Web browsers (Google, Apple)
- Smartphone and tablet operating systems (Google, Apple)
- Mobile app stores (Google, Apple)
- Online advertising (Meta, Google, Amazon)
- Desktop and laptop operating systems (Microsoft, Apple)
- Office software (Microsoft, Google)
- Video conferencing (Zoom, Google, Microsoft)
- Email (Apple, Google, Microsoft, Yahoo)
- Cloud computing (Amazon, Microsoft, Google, IBM)
- Social media platforms (Meta, YouTube, X/Twitter, Reddit)
- E-hailing/taxi platforms (Uber, Lyft)
- Business networking (Microsoft)
- Streaming video (Google, Amazon, Netflix, Disney+, Hulu)
- Streaming audio (Google, Apple, SiriusXM)[32]

In short, anyone using a computer across the planet is paying multiple American tech corporations a cut all day long. To be sure, there are many thousands of tech companies that make up the rest of the digital economy. These firms form a "long tail"—meaning they offer products that aren't widely used or lucrative. While they collectively offer millions of apps and services, most of them don't have many users and don't make much money. The tech giants, on the other hand, offer products required for computers to carry out *basic functions* (like processing and storing data) or perform *basic services* on those computers (such as posting a photo, fetching a taxi, or streaming a series).

These segments are broken down in later chapters, where we'll see that the United States dominates every category.

WHO OWNS TECH STARTUPS AND INVESTMENT?

So far we've observed the number, value, and revenue of top tech corporations, and we've noted that the US dominates the core products and services—which is empirically documented in subsequent chapters. The United States also runs the show in the other major parts of the digital economy. Take a look at the ownership share of tech startups by city and country, for example, in Table 1.4.

Table 1.4   Ownership of Global Technology Startup Economy by Country*†

Location	Unicorns	%	Value	%	Vc Funding	%
United States	477	63.7	4,205	62.4	718	57.8
Global North (other)	116	15.5	790	11.7	162.1	13.0
Europe	92	13.1	684	10.1	187	15.0
China	64	8.5	1,063	15.8	176	14.1
Global South (other)	0	0	0	0	0	0
TOTAL	**749**	**100**	**6,742**	**100**	**1,243.1**	**100**
Global North (total)	*685*	*91.5*	*5679*	*84.2*	*1,067.1*	*85.8*
Global South (total)	*64*	*8.5*	*1,063*	*15.8*	*176*	*14.2*

Author's table and calculations. Source for data: Startup Genome, 2023.[33]
* In billions of dollars.
† Percentages are rounded. "Value" is in billions of dollars and defined as the value of exits and startup valuations.

As of 2023, the US holds eight of the top 20 cities for tech unicorns (startups valued at $1 billion or more) compared to China's two. Those eight American cities have 477 startups worth $4.205 trillion compared to China's 64 startups worth $1.063, giving the US about 7.5 times more startup ecosystems than China and four times the value.

Outside of China, cities from the entire Global South failed to produce even one tech unicorn in the top 20. This includes India, with 18% of the world's population. As for newer developments, Europe is home to 41% of the top 100 emerging (i.e., not yet mature) tech startup cities. By comparison, North America has 29% and Asia 16%. The rest of the world has 9%. Africa has essentially nothing. The recipients of venture capital funding—small companies with promising growth potential—are also overwhelmingly led by the US (57.8%) and the Global North as a whole (85.8%).

We can see in Table 1.4 that US tech startups receive the most venture capital investment, which helps them grow and develop their companies. However, the database provided by the source, Startup Genome, didn't tabulate which countries are the leading *investors*, who rake in the profits from that growth. Compiling data on which country's firms lead investment in tech startups outside of both the United States and China would help us understand how China fares against the US in global tech investments. Yet the data on this isn't publicly available, as startups are not required to disclose their investors, so obtaining that level of detail would be impossible.

We can instead start by looking at *aggregate* investment data compiled by research institutes. This will deepen our understanding of which countries dominate *general* investment, and thereby collect the returns on investment and command financial ownership of firms. Such an approach helps us see beyond potential exceptions where foreign investors own a specific company. For example, Arm Holdings, a British semiconductor and software design company based in the UK, designs the computer chips in nearly every mobile phone. However, a Japanese investment holding company, Softbank, owns over 90% of the company's shares. We want to get a sense of how common this kind of scenario exists so we can get a more precise picture of which countries dominate tech investment.

Sean Starrs found that at the most general level, spanning all sectors—from retail and energy to construction and tech—"American investors are not only the predominant owners of American corporations, but also the largest owners of top European corporations and significant owners of top corporations domiciled in the rest of the world." Therefore, American investors "own *and thus profit* from the world's top [firms] (whether US-domiciled or not) more than any other nationality."[34] If tech follows this general trend, then we should expect US investors to dominate.

A review of the *aggregate* data confirms that the United States dominates information technology (IT) investments worldwide. Of the top ten countries, the US invests $1.065 trillion (50.1%) in IT compared to China's $333 billion (15.7%).[35]

However, we can take this further, as this doesn't separate out investments by the US and China outside of their borders. We want to understand who dominates *global* tech investment. Studies on tech investment covering broad geographical landscapes demonstrate that American firms do in fact hold the lion's share of global investment in the digital economy.

In Europe, 69% of foreign direct investment (FDI) is sourced from the United States, with software and IT services the largest segment. Asia is the second-largest investor, accounting for just 18% of FDI. In Asia itself, 70% of investment comes from within the region.[36]

According to a 2022 study of venture capital deals in Africa, 81% of VC deals were in technology or technology-enabled companies. Of those, $5.2 billion was raised by 604 companies in 650 deals. Forty percent of the investment came from North America, the largest share by far. Just 9% came from all of Asia-Pacific (which includes China).[37] Another study of foreign investment in Africa found that of the top 20 deals—which accounted for 65% of the investment deployed on the continent—62.5% came from the United States. The next largest contributor came from the UK (7.5%); China invested less than 4%.[38]

In Latin America, where tech occupies the largest share of foreign investment projects, the United States and Europe were the largest investors in the region.[39] In 2022, Crunchbase reported on the top 14 most active early- and late-stage investors in Latin American companies. Of the 380 deals, 121 came from the US (32%), with the remainder spread across Latin America (26%), Japan (10%), and Europe (6%).[40]

It's important to identify *which country* does the investing in tech startups because venture capitalists typically take 25–50% of a new company's ownership.[41] This not only sets them up to profit off the companies themselves, but it also gives them power to direct the orientation of the companies. Venture capitalists operate on a model where they shower money across a variety of startups, and they pressure those companies to grow into unicorns to become the "next big thing," contributing to severe market concentration.[42] Think of Uber and Lyft for e-hailing services or Spotify and Pandora for streaming music. More than any other country or region, then, American investors are profiting from and directing the goals and initiatives of the global tech sector—all to turn a buck for themselves.

Finally, we can look at research and development (R&D). The European Commission (EC) publishes an annual R&D scoreboard that breaks down investment by region. According to the 2022 report:

- The top 2,500 firms spent €1.0938 trillion on R&D. The US accounts for the majority of companies (822) and R&D invested (40.2%), followed by China (678 and 17.9%) and the EU (361 and 17.6%).[43]

Its 2021 report published the spending amounts:

- For total spending (including all sectors), the US's 821 firms dished out €463.1 billion, or 42.3% of the total. The US accounted for 315 ICT firms (38.3%) to China's 236 (28.7%) and the EU's 72 (8.8%).
- In the ICT sector, the US spent €194.5 billion on ICT (51.6%) to China's €64.4 billion (17.1%) and the EU's €39.6 billion (10.5%).[44]

We can conclude, then, that the United States dominates the financing to generate wealth in the global tech sector. It has more startups, receives more money to develop its companies and knowledge, and invests more money into the digital economy than any other country. This makes sense when considering the dominance of the United States at large and the outrageous size of Wall Street and US tech giants on the global stage.

WHO OWNS THE KNOWLEDGE?

The private ownership of knowledge—in the form of intellectual property, data, and digital intelligence derived from data—is another major component of the global digital economy. Here, too, the United States is king.

Patents give inventors a temporary monopoly on their inventions—e.g., 20 years—in return for disclosure of how the invention works. If you register a patent on, say, an electronic mousetrap, you are required to disclose it to the public for the benefit of public knowledge, and others cannot use or copy that design unless you let them. Very often, patent holders will prevent someone from using their patented monopoly unless the user pays them.

A *copyright*, by contrast, grants a temporary monopoly on a specific instance of a creative artifact. If you record a song, for example, you own the copyright on that song, and you can set a paywall so that others cannot obtain, copy, or sell that song unless they purchase it as an individual unit or through a paid license to share (say, on a radio broadcast through a "compulsory license"). Patents cover inventions, processes, or scientific creations, whereas copyrights cover an author's specific *works*. While other forms of intellectual property, such as *trademarks* and *trade secrets*,[45] impact the economy, we have good metrics to approximate the value and role of patents and copyrights in the digital economy. Therefore, we will be reviewing those two elements of the intellectual property ecosystem.

Who owns the patents?

Sometimes the number of patents a country registers is taken to indicate its level of ownership power and innovation. However, adding up total patents by country is highly misleading. For example, China has led the world in the number of patent filings since 2011. Yet China's patents are widely considered of poor quality, as they are primarily registered inside of China, where standards for granting the patents are low and the government rewards patentees with money (thereby incentivizing junk patents). Chinese patents have a low rate of registration and acceptance in patent offices abroad, and they have a comparatively low commercialization and industrialization rate—meaning they aren't typically useful. Between 1985 and 2000, 81–91% of Chinese patents were for utility models and industrial design, while only 11–19% were for inventions—a stronger marker of innovation. Of these, 91% of design and 61% of utility patents were invalid during 2013–2017 because the holders didn't pay the annual fee. An estimated 90% of China's patents have no market value, meaning they are trash.[46]

To create a more accurate approximation of value, the Organization of Economic Cooperation and Development (OECD) measures "triadic" patents—those registered in at least three of the largest patent offices— the European Patent Office, the Japan Patent Office, and the US Patent and Trademark Office. Triadic patents are considered the "gold standard," as those three offices have a high bar for acceptance. Passing all three therefore indicates high quality. As of 2020, Japan leads all countries with 35.1% of the world's triadic patents, followed by the US (26.2%). China lags well behind in third (11.9%).[47] A more pointed measure—number of world-class patents in advanced digital technologies—indicates a correlation between patents and market share in the *digital* economy. Here, the US leads with 49,248 patents compared to China's 27,928, Japan's 12,763, and the EU's 9,883.

In general, because patents are typically granted to those with the formal education and skills to create them, they reinforce social inequality. In the United States, women hold less than 20% of all patents, African American and Hispanic college graduates hold less than half the patents as their white counterparts, and a person born under the median income line is ten times less likely to receive a patent than a person born in the top 1%. This tracks with the typical pattern under capitalism, which divides people by group identities and confers advantages on some at the expense of others.[48]

Who owns the copyrights?

The fruits of copyright accrue to the United States, followed by Europe. In one study based on over 20 countries covering books in the trade and educational sectors, the United States held the largest sales revenues at $26.8 billion, followed by Germany ($11.4 billion), Japan ($11.3 billion), and the UK ($5.4 billion). Sales data was not available for China, but ISBN registrations—the top international standard to identify a book which serves as a proxy for the size of a publishing market in a country—are also topped by the US, which had 3.93 million titles to China's 0.26 in 2020.[49]

Video games comprise the largest share of digital media revenue in the world. For first quarter revenues among the top ten gaming companies in 2023, the US took $14.67 billion (47.4%) to China's $10.27 billion (33.1%). For filmed entertainment, the US market generated $23.8 billion in 2021; China was a distant second at $11.5 billion. Streaming music now accounts for 67% of the overall recorded music market, and here, too, the US generates the most revenue, with 41.6% of the global market compared to Asia's 22.9%. The American music industry took in $15.9 billion in 2022, while one study found Africa's music revenue stood at just $94 million that same year—a reminder of how far the Global South lags behind its rich counterparts.[50]

Revenue from software copyrights is difficult to obtain (as opposed to customer support, renting services like data storage, etc.), but of the world's top ten software companies, the US rakes in $347.42 billion (89.4%) of the total ($388.53 billion).[51]

Who owns the data?

In addition to copyrights and patents, ownership and access to large troves of data—often called "big data"—is a critical asset. Big data is used to build the artificial intelligence algorithms that sort and produce information for services like chatbots, search engines, social media news feeds, language translations, image recognition, and speech-to-text transcriptions, as well as "generative AI" that creates images, videos, music, and more. What's called "artificial intelligence" essentially has two branches. The first is *logical AI*, which attempts to understand things in the world by programming logic into AI software. The second is *statistical AI*, which essentially attempts to predict and discern patterns about things in the world by evaluating enormous amounts of content—text, images, videos, and so on—for statistical regularities.

Statistical AI is presently dominant and the engine behind AI engineering feats of the past couple of decades. With statistical AI, a computer program may be fed a million pictures of a letter—say the letter "T"—so that when it tries to recognize letters, the software can identify the letter "T." In many instances, AI software is stupidly wrong about the patterns it is supposed to recognize. For instance, AI may identify a yellow school bus as an "ostrich."

Those kinds of failures illustrate that it is misleading to call this "intelligence"—a point the eminent scientist and social critic, Noam Chomsky, has been making for decades.[52] A human doesn't need to see a million pictures of a school bus to know that it's a school bus, and it doesn't mistakenly think a school bus is an ostrich. In reality, computer programs aren't sentient, and they don't "know" anything. An AI software that can beat a human chess master doesn't "know" it's playing chess any more than a printer "knows" what it is "writing" when it prints a document. A computer is not a chess player and a printer is not an author. Using the word "intelligence" to describe current forms of "artificial intelligence" software misleads and confuses the public.

Some "AI" gurus believe that "artificial general intelligence" (AGI)—a form of AI that can perform a multitude of *general* tasks, from playing chess to evaluating the stock market—will be invented in the near future. However, leading experts critical of this view contend that these kinds of strong claims have been made for almost a century, and that statistical AI offers no path to AGI.[53]

In any event, big data feeds today's dominant form of "artificial intelligence," statistical AI, which, despite its limitations (and hype), is increasingly used for many major tech services.

Information on data ownership by country does not appear to be indexed in a study, and the evaluation of who leads the data economy is complex and contested. A 2019 study claimed China generated 23.4% of the "Datasphere" (the collection of data in digital form), slightly more than the US, and will continue to lead the world in data generation.[54] Another 2019 study came to a different conclusion. It assessed which countries lead the data economy, based on four criteria: volume (broadband consumed by the country), usage (number of users active on the internet), accessibility (openness of data flows that can be accessed by researchers, innovators, and apps), and complexity (volume of broadband consumption per capita). The US comes out on top, followed by the UK and China.[55]

It should be noted that owning lots of data does not ensure a market advantage. The idea of "data" itself is too generic. The first study above noted that "video surveillance is a common driver of content," which has limited use cases. For example, video surveillance data doesn't help you develop AI that will translate language or produce a chatbot relevant to different users across the world.

Moreover, the mere possession of data has limited value if it cannot be used as effectively as competitors. Only those who have access to large troves of data—*as well as* the human talent (programmers), computer processing power to build AI models, and, in many cases, a service, such as a social media or cloud computing platform to pull in that data and generate the revenue to make use of it—have an upper hand on those who don't have the data or resources to offer high-quality data-driven features. China lags behind the US in these categories—especially with respect to its global market share in core products and services—and so it remains to be seen to what extent China can eat into US market share for data-driven products and services outside of its own market.

MARKETS AND GOVERNANCE: HOW THE US ACHIEVES DOMINATION

So far, we've seen that American Big Tech corporations thoroughly dominate the global digital economy. They own the lion's share of the large tech corporations, many of which hold more wealth than the GDP of entire countries. China has a sizable digital economy, but it is tiny compared to the US. Contrary to popular opinion, in the tech space, the US is the undisputed king, with no competitor in sight. How, then, did it become so dominant?

For starters, the American government spent decades building up its tech industry. The research that produced inventions like the computer, the internet, artificial intelligence, GPS, and Google's search engine were all heavily subsidized by the state. Once a core foundation was in place, corporations began privatizing the technologies, securing ownership first through intellectual property rights, and then through internet-based platforms and data-driven services made possible by the spread of personal computers, the internet, mobile phones, and cloud computing to store and process big data.

Contemporary developments began in earnest during the 1980s, when corporations began extending personal computers to Global North markets and privatizing knowledge as intellectual property. Prior to this time period, computers were giant, refrigerator-sized mainframes that cost millions of dollars, and the computer programming community shared their code freely. Shortly after the US legal system extended copyright to software, corporations began locking up their code as private property. This laid the foundation for the rise of Microsoft—the leading tech behemoth of the 1990s and early 2000s—to monopolize the software industry. If code were free and open source, Microsoft wouldn't have been able to take command of the market.[56]

As the internet spread, the online platform economy emerged.[57] Tech platforms produce incredible market concentration due to design choices, mutually reinforcing market mechanisms, and government regulation. That may sound like a mouthful, but the core elements are easy to understand. Let's use social media as a case example to see how it works.[58]

Social media networks are very concentrated—meaning, there are just a few networks that have many millions of users—in large part because they are designed to exploit what scholars call *network effects*. With network effects, the more people use a network, the more valuable it becomes.

For example, imagine there was a small town called Phoneless Town with no telephones. Pretend a new company, the Red Company, starts rolling out telephones to the neighborhood. Then another company, the Green Company, starts doing the same a year later. Let's say the Red Company sells its phones to 80% of the people living in Phoneless Town, and that the Red Phone was designed only to work with other Red Phone users. Let's

33

also pretend that 10% of the town bought a Green Phone, because the Red Phone sold out.

Now let's say the Red Phone comes back in stock. If the remaining 10% of the people are going to purchase a phone, they are better off buying a Red Phone because more people use Red Phones, so they are able to call more people. You would only buy a Green Phone if there is some special reason—for example, all your friends were among the 10% who bought a Green Phone, or you really like the color Green. Exceptions notwithstanding, the more people using the Red Phone network, the more *valuable* the Red Phone network becomes.

You might say that people may be willing to buy a Red Phone *and* a Green Phone. But they will never want to buy, say, 20 different phones—a Blue Phone, an Orange Phone, a Pink Phone, a Purple Phone, and so on—because nobody wants to have 20 phones to call 20 sub-sets of people on 20 different phone networks. Imagine your home had 20 phones! It just wouldn't work. In this scenario, the only way to make room for a wider variety of phone companies is to force them to *interoperate*—to make laws forcing the phone companies to make their calls work with each other's networks so that a person with a Red Phone can call someone with a Green Phone, or any other phone. Nobody is stuck inside a single phone network. (Being locked into a single company's product is called a *walled garden*—a situation where you can access the fruits of a technology, but only from inside the walls of the platform.)

In the early days of social media, there were many different networks, but they didn't interoperate. Due to network effects, people congregated into a few networks, and eventually the market hit a *tipping point*—a point at which it became extremely difficult for competitors to enter the market. Scholars call this dynamic a *winner-takes-all* marketplace. MySpace became the first major social media network, followed by Facebook and Twitter. Facebook eventually acquired a major competitor, Instagram—what economists call *horizontal integration*—and then TikTok came along.[59] MySpace is mostly dead, but the others have consolidated the market.

Of course, social media is a bit more complex than a phone, which simply makes calls to people. TikTok was able to carve out a space because it offered something catchy and different—unlike its competitors at the time, it featured videos as its primary product and used algorithms to show you

34

content you may like from people you don't know. Nevertheless, without interoperability, only a few networks will ever be popular. Like the Red and Green Phone companies, Facebook users can only interact with and follow Facebook users, TikTok users can only interact with and follow other TikTok users, and so on.

Many other platforms feature these winner-takes-all dynamics. For instance, the e-hailing (online taxi) industry features network effects—drivers don't want to drive for 20 different companies, and riders don't want to search through 20 different apps to catch a taxi. Uber took advantage of this dynamic. Moreover, because it operated at a loss—thanks to the deep pockets of rich investors—it could offer users a personal chauffeur at an artificially low price, undermining local taxi industries.[60] Uber also took advantage of a marketplace ill-equipped for fast technological changes. It declared its workers "contractors," denied them benefits and fair wages, and tweaked its algorithms to manipulate prices in its favor. Using these market mechanisms, it beat its competition to the spot—called a *first mover advantage*—and began colonizing the public transportation market across the world.

Economies of scale is another core element leading to market concentration in the platform economy. Companies like YouTube, Facebook, and Twitter are responsible for keeping copyrighted work off their networks. Any platform allowing users to post content like videos and music could be sued by rightsholders if they don't remove copyrighted content within a reasonable time period. To avoid lawsuits, YouTube has invested $100 million to build Content ID, a system that scans content and identifies copyrighted content in uploaded videos. When the system identifies a copyrighted work, it asks the rightsholders if they would like to monetize it with ads or have the video blocked. YouTube also has to pay enormous sums to store its videos on the cloud, it can afford lawyers to deal with lawsuits, and it can pay out high salaries to top-notch computer engineers that make its system work smoothly, with visually pleasing features that appeal to its user base. Factors like these make it extremely expensive to host a video platform or run a social media network, and only those with deep pockets can afford to enter the market and compete.

Some companies also exploit *vertical integration*, where they design, manufacture, and sell their own products, with parts that are often built to work together. Apple is the iconic example of vertical integration. If you purchase an iPhone, you have to use the iPhone operating system, which comes pre-loaded with an array of Apple products, such as iTunes and iCloud. Apple designs its products to work together and keep its users inside "Apple World" as much as possible.

While the above-mentioned dynamics are widely discussed in academic literature, less discussed is the fact that many US Big Tech companies support each other because they rely on each other's products. If Amazon wants to build a cloud center, for example, it needs to purchase a wide variety of products, including semiconductors (e.g., from US companies like Intel or AMD), hard drives to store data (from US companies like Seagate or Western Digital), server hardware (from companies like Cisco and Dell), and so on. These other companies, in turn, may use Amazon Web Services for cloud computing, list their consumer products on the Amazon Marketplace platform, sell ads through Amazon Ads, and so on. The intersectional co-dependency of Big Tech helps to secure the collective dominance of American tech corporations. We will detail how this works, and its ecological consequences, in Chapter 4.

AMERICAN SUPREMACY AND THE NEW COLD WAR

The digital society has grown fast. Today, we take our computer-mediated existence for granted. But a short time ago, it wasn't like this. Believe it or not, in the early 2000s, it was actually a big deal for a company to have a ".com" affixed to their brand. Media outlets didn't have special "tech" sections until recently, and the intellectual classes didn't pay much attention to digital politics. Some intellectuals have long recognized the importance of computers to geopolitical power, but they were in the extreme minority.[61]

For most of its existence, Big Tech was actually viewed as "hip" and "progressive" by most academics and journalists. Despite the extensive abuses of Big Tech corporations from the outset, the Global North's intellectual classes only began regularly publishing a (narrow) set of negative things about today's tech giants around 2016—less than a decade ago. (We'll revisit these tech "critics" in Chapter 9.)

The United States government, by contrast, recognized the strategic importance of advanced technology to its global power early on, and it has fashioned tech policy as a tool for American supremacy. In the early twentieth century, it funded the creation of computers (for military warfare); subsidized the development of the internet (for military, scientific, and commercial purposes, and as a decentralized communications network that could withstand nuclear war); extended intellectual property rights to software; and commercialized the internet, for American interests, as computers and the internet spread to middle- and upper-class households.[62] By 2001, Bill Clinton remarked, "Advances in computer technology and the Internet have changed the way America works, learns, and communicates. The Internet has become an integral part of America's economic, political, and social life." Most mainstream intellectuals were asleep to this reality at the time.[63]

More recently, in a bid to maintain global technological supremacy, the US has waged a "New Cold War" against China. As we saw earlier, China's tech sector has minimal global market share, but Washington is unwilling to tolerate even minor encroachments on its hegemony. In 2021, US President Joe Biden told the press, "[China has] an overall goal to become the leading country in the world, the wealthiest country in the world, and the most powerful country in the world. That's not gonna happen on my watch."[64] Ostensibly referencing the anachronistic misconception that GDP measures national economic power, Biden is extending and intensifying previous administrations' measures to contain China, with digital supremacy as the cornerstone of his strategy.

To be sure, the United States is no longer at the apex of its global power, which arguably peaked at the end of World War II. It cannot bark orders to China, which makes heavy use of protectionist "industrial policies" and has become the leading trade partner in the Global South—to the dismay of Washington.[65] Over the past two years, the US was unable to cajole support from the South for its war efforts in Ukraine. As Noam Chomsky and Vijay Prashad put it, American power is fragile—but it's still the world's sole superpower, as measured by its economic, political, and military supremacy.[66]

It would be a mistake to simply express American economic dominance in terms of the wealth of its transnational corporations, financial institutions, and ruling-class elites. Rather, it's imperative to understand that as the supreme global hegemon, the US *organizes* global capitalism through its economic, political, and social power.[67] For the most part, everyone plays by the rules framed by and for the American ruling classes. In the domain of tech, the US imposes its core economic interests on the rest of the world through its intellectual property regime, corporate lobbying, economic trade policies, and broad capitalist framework.

The US set the rules of the game early. The "private sector should lead," read Bill Clinton's 1997 Framework for Global Electronic Governance. "The Internet should develop as a market-driven arena not a regulated industry ... parties should be able to ... buy and sell products and services across the Internet with minimal government involvement or intervention."[68] This light-touch "neoliberal" approach to internet regulation helped American tech giants colonize the global tech economy. The internet is largely borderless, and the world's countries have effectively become digital colonies of the United States.

Around that time, China developed its "Golden Shield"—also called the "Great Firewall of China"—to screen out foreign corporations that wouldn't enact its censorship regime. Some view this as a prescient attempt to protect its budding tech corporations, while others plausibly argue that many US tech corporations failed in China on their own merits, in part because Chinese citizens preferred their own country's products.[69] In a relatively short time, China was able to build up its own native tech industry, with giants like TikTok springing up seemingly overnight.

The rapid growth of the Chinese economy sparked xenophobic fears in the West, which pointed to the Chinese Communist Party's authoritarian governance as a justification for aggressive action. In 2011, the Obama administration famously "pivoted" attention to Asia, strengthening economic, diplomatic, and military alliances in the region. At present, China is surrounded by several hundred US military bases.[70]

As one can imagine, this is worrying to China. There are no Chinese military bases stationed in Canada or in Central America. In fact, the US has over 750 foreign military bases; China has one.[71] In the nineteenth century, Britain and France forced opium down the throats of China at the barrel of a gun during the infamous Opium Wars. China's crime was trying to ban the import of opium, which was destroying its people's health.

For over a hundred years, Western powers, along with Japan, invaded and looted China—what it calls the "century of humiliation." After World War II, the US pursued an aggressive Cold War policy to "contain" China through trade sanctions, military alliances, and efforts to isolate the country from its regional neighbors.[72] Relations thawed starting in 1979 with Nixon's visit to China, as Beijing turned toward capitalism and famously "opened" itself up to Western trade and investment. China offered up millions of cheap laborers for American manufacturers to exploit in sweatshops. In exchange, its own comprador capitalists amassed fortunes, also based on the exploitation of their own labor force.

Over time, Chinese growth began to worry Washington. As part of its "pivot to Asia," the Obama administration began restricting US government purchases of Chinese IT equipment, citing hypocritical concerns about Chinese espionage.[73] A slew of new sanctions targeting China's digital economy soon followed. In 2015, the US placed export restrictions on the sale of semiconductors for China's supercomputers, on grounds that they could be used for nuclear weapons testing.[74] The Trump administration followed suit, escalating the trade war by setting trade barriers against China as part of his "America First" policy.

Under Trump, the number of Chinese persons and tech companies on the US Entity List—a trade restriction list consisting of foreign persons, entities (such as companies), and governments—increased dramatically. As a result of US sanctions, China's Huawei fell from the world's second-largest smartphone company to ninth—a hole it's now trying to climb out of.[75] With approval from American intellectuals, Trump rationalized sanctions against Chinese tech companies on grounds that they might share data with the Chinese Communist Party (CCP)—precisely what US corporations do for Washington—an issue we detail in Chapter 5.

The Biden administration further deepened the trade war against China through restrictions on the semiconductor industry, with bipartisan support. Semiconductors are the engines powering the digital economy. Because less advanced semiconductors are slower than their high-end counterparts, they increase the cost of processing data and slow down business and consumer devices, making the latter less preferable to competitor products. To justify the sanctions, Washington argues that Beijing could use advanced computer chips for military purposes and human rights abuses, and therefore the Americans need to block China's access to high-end processors as a matter of "national security."

The bans are designed to weaken China's broad economy, which relies on advanced microchips. During the pandemic, chip shortages cost the US

1% of its GDP, amounting to hundreds of billions of dollars. If they work, the chip sanctions could set China back decades.[76] The Americans own 48% of the global semiconductor market; China owns just 7%, which comprises lower-end parts of the industry.[77] The effects will also likely impact semiconductor firms in the US, Europe, and Asia that sell to China at high volumes. US allies such as the Netherlands, Japan, Taiwan, and South Korea have all expressed reservations about the chip sanctions, though they have largely complied with American demands to participate, in part due to their reliance on US military support. In retaliation, China has put into place its own sanctions.[78]

The United States is also looking to restrict Chinese access to American cloud computing companies. Like semiconductors, cloud computing is a core technology used to process data and perform artificial intelligence. If America blocks China's access then it will further weaken its ability to use advanced artificial intelligence chips. Another measure, the RESTRICT Act, is in the pipes. If passed, it will ban technology supplied by "foreign adversaries"—i.e., any country that challenges American supremacy. Under RESTRICT, the press reported:

> Information or communications products or services with more than 1,000,000 US users—like ByteDance's TikTok app—as well as internet hosting services, cloud-based data storage, machine learning services, and other apps that are found to pose "an undue or unacceptable risk to the national security" would be subject to such regulation.[79]

In April 2024, President Biden signed a bill forcing ByteDance to sell off TikTok or face a ban in the US. ByteDance is appealing the law in the courts.

In addition to restrictions and bans on Chinese tech companies, the US is heavily subsidizing its own semiconductor industry. While America dominates the sector as a whole, it fell behind Taiwan in the *manufacturing* of advanced semiconductors. In 2022, the Biden administration enacted two major bills that subsidize US industry: the CHIPS and Science Act of 2022 (which provides $280 billion in subsidies to domestic semiconductor manufacturing, R&D, and other high-tech industries)[80] and the Inflation Reduction Act (which provides $20 billion in green energy subsidies to US industry). *The Wall Street Journal* called the former "one of the most significant acts of government intervention since World War II."[81] Together, the two laws offer more than $400 billion in tax credits.[82]

Other countries object to these "industrial policies" condemned by American "free trade" ideologues, but to no avail. "It's like a declaration of war," said Robert Habeck, Germany's vice-chancellor and economics minister, of the US subsidies. "The [Americans] want to have the semiconductors, they want the solar industry, they want the hydrogen industry, they want the electrolysers." However, Europe has little recourse. "People were saying: let's go to the WTO [World Trade Organization], make a big fuss,' [said] one senior official in Berlin" to the *Financial Times*. "I said: we're in the middle of a war [with Russia]. Now's not the time to pick a fight with our biggest ally."

European competitors are far from innocent, having already "adopted the politics of if you cannot beat them, join them [by enacting your own state subsidies]. 'If we don't keep up, they'll have them [the key industries] and we won't. That's the brutal reality,'" Habeck remarked.[83] American subsidization of high-tech South Korean industry illustrates another instance aimed to shift Korean commerce from China to the US. Over the past year, the United States has expanded its trade war against China in the Global South, where it is applying pressure to cut ties with Chinese companies.[84]

Of course, Washington's policies contradict its self-professed commitments to "free trade." Nevertheless, the Americans have been pushing international policies that protect intellectual property, oppose internet taxes, prohibit customs duties on digital products, prohibit forced software source code transfers, oppose net neutrality, and promote (already limited) privacy standards to ensure cross-border flows of data to American corporations.[85] These policies are designed to block protectionist measures desired by smaller and less-developed countries for their own development, even though such protections are quite weak. Indeed, the "brutal reality" of "really existing capitalism" has always been one in which "the strong do what they can, the weak do what they must."

* * *

In this chapter, I introduced the idea of digital colonialism—the use of technology for political, economic, and social domination of a sovereign country or people. It is a foundational theme throughout this book.

Next, we're going to address this book's other foundational concept, *degrowth*. As we'll see in the following chapter, a just and sustainable economy under degrowth requires a radical redistribution of wealth and power between and within countries. Digital colonialism is *central* to this, as we can't have one country using digital technology for ruling-class power and wealth accumulation. But before we unpack that, we first need to understand what degrowth is, so that we can relate it to the digital economy and build a theory of digital degrowth.

So on to the next question: what is degrowth?

2
What is Degrowth?

A long time ago, there was an inventor who built chessboards for a living. One day, he was given the opportunity to speak with the king. The king said he would give the inventor any reward in return for the chessboard. The inventor responded with a proposition: the king will place one grain of rice on the first square, two on the second, four on the third, eight on the fourth, doubling the number of grains on each square, until he reached the end.

"As you wish," the king said, perplexed by the tiny sum. But the king was unaware of how fast this doubling—or *exponential*—growth of rice would add up. By the fifth square, there were only 32 grains to pay out. Pennies. By the tenth, the king owed 1,024 grains. Still not bad. By the 15th square, he owed 32,768 grains (getting big), and by the 20th, the king owed over a million! By the 32nd square—half the chessboard, the king owed over 4 billion grains of rice. And there was still another 32 squares to go. Filling the board would quickly exceed more rice than the entire kingdom possessed. In the end, the inventor was executed for trolling the king.

This fable is frequently told by people explaining the nature of *exponential* growth. Most people are more familiar with *linear* growth, which is easier to visualize: increments of growth increase equally over time. With linear growth, if you add by two, you get "two, four, six, eight, ten, twelve," and so on. We can picture how it carries on forever in our heads.

Exponential growth is very different. It keeps doubling upon the previous doubling. Because it starts small—one grain, two grains, four grains, then eight—exponential growth seems small, much like linear growth. But if you keep doubling, the growth eventually becomes so enormous that the human mind can barely comprehend it.

Capitalism is an economic system predicated on *exponential* growth. Capitalists plan economies by pumping their money into businesses that grow. As companies grow, a portion of the surplus produced is reinvested in production. Investors purchase shares in companies and make earnings from profits (called *dividends*), while banks lend money to borrowers who pay back the original sum plus a small percent extra to reward the lender (called *interest*). The more companies grow, the more money they make, which signals to investors that they are a good place to invest, so they can make money for themselves. The larger and faster the growth, the better the investment. Capitalism is a growth system.

Government policymakers create policies to grow their economy, so that there is more "stuff" to be consumed each year that goes by. This is advertised as the method to make society just and prosperous. Even if there is rich and poor, as long as everyone has something more at the end of the year, then life is getting better. This thinking drives government policy and rationalizes inequality under capitalism.[1]

Even if we believed this system was just, it cannot last forever. Just like the rice on the chessboard, the amount of resources used to produce new things expands astronomically as time marches on. Under capitalism, the amount of material resources required to keep growing the economy would eventually exceed the mass of the planet. For this reason, *everyone* has to agree there are limits to economic growth, and that capitalism must eventually come to an end. The only question is *how much* we can grow our economies before we begin to push the environment beyond its sustainable limit.

As we will see in this chapter, the science strongly suggests we have *already* breached that limit. We need to reduce and cap *total* (aggregate) annual material resource use in order to avoid permanently destroying our one and only habitat, planet Earth. But if we reduce and cap material resource use, we would have to use less than the total amount of material resources presently consumed by humans today. This leaves us with a terrible scenario. Over half the world's people are living in squalor, and about 20% of the world's population enjoys a Westernized middle-class lifestyle or better. The problem, then, is obvious: when material wealth is *fixed*, there needs to be an equitable distribution of resources to ensure a decent life for everyone.

Let's put it this way: imagine the world's wealth is a ten-slice pizza pie produced in a town of 100 people. A few rich people own the dough, oven, restaurant, guns, and houses, and they force the majority to cook the pie. One person (representing the upper class) takes five of the slices and the next nine people (representing the middle class) take another four. The last slice is divided among the remaining 90 people (representing the global poor). This is how wealth is divided across the world. Socialists have long argued that this arrangement is totally unjust, and have been trying for over a century to make a fair and equitable alternative. Defenders of capitalism argue that it is ethical. Instead of sharing the pizza equally, we can keep growing the total size of the pie, and one day everyone will have enough.

But if you can't grow the economy, then you have to count up the number of people, figure out how much there is to go around, and come up with a fair distribution. Or you just let the wealthy people keep eating the nine slices, and everyone else can have little to nothing. As we will see by the end of this chapter, this is essentially our situation. There are 8 billion people on planet Earth, and the global economy produces about $20,000 per person. The majority of the world's people don't have that much money because the rich people appropriate most of the pie. As we'll see later, if we can't keep growing the economy, we have to divide up the pie equally within and between every country in order to provide each person with a decent standard of living. There's not enough wealth for there to be rich and poor. A fair and just environmentally sustainable global economy therefore requires universal class abolition.

The digital economy may seem detached from this process. We are accustomed to thinking of the "digital" in abstract terms, disconnected from physical things as if there is a "digital" economy and a "physical" economy. A music album used to be purchased as a physical item, like a vinyl record or CD. But now we stream or download albums to our computers. There's no physical unit. We spend time on the "internet," but we don't actually go anywhere. There are no buildings to enter or streets to travel. Small devices, like laptops or smartphones, are the only physical things we use when we visit "cyberspace."

We'll see in the following three chapters that this is a mirage. The digital economy is not only made of physical stuff, it is deeply *connected* to the rest of the physical economy. It's impossible to separate the two. One might already see where this going, per the previous chapter: the process of digital colonialism concentrates resources into the hands of ruling-class Americans (among others), which prevents people from getting a fair share of the pie in an economy that caps material resource use. So we need *digital degrowth*.

Before we get to *digital* degrowth, we need to understand the basics of degrowth—the subject of this chapter.

THE SCIENCE OF DEGROWTH

The idea of a degrowth has roots at least as far back as the nineteenth century, when John Stuart Mill discussed a "stationary economy" that focused on improving the quality of economic life instead of quantitative expansion. Socialists like Karl Marx (especially in his later works published posthumously), Rosa Luxemburg, and Peter Kropotkin raised the issue that the capitalist growth machine inherently destroys the environment, what some now call "degrowth communism." But it wasn't until 1972, when a collection of scientists from the Club of Rome published a report, *The Limits to Growth*, that environmental scientists took up the issue in earnest.[2]

The Limits to Growth predicted that on the current trajectory, population growth and material resource use would become unsustainable within the next century, likely leading to "a rather sudden and uncontrollable decline in both population and industrial capacity." Alternatively, they argued, "a global equilibrium could be designed so that the basic material needs of each person on earth are satisfied," allowing each person the opportunity to reach their potential without overshooting planetary boundaries. If people opt for the second, "the sooner they begin working to attain it, the greater will be their chances of success."

In parallel, André Gorz—who coined degrowth—made the case for the limits to growth on socialist grounds, while economist Nicholas Georgescu-Roegen began integrating ecological considerations into economic theory. Yet the environmental and social scientists centering the issue of growth were small in number and mostly ignored.[3]

In the past decade, several studies have generally affirmed Club of Rome's projections of population growth and material resource use.[4] Of course, not every single prediction was accurate. But our understanding of the environment has improved since then, and the issue has regained scientific and popular attention under the moniker "degrowth." This is because as we move further along the chessboard, environmental pressures on the planet intensify, forcing us to confront root causes.

According to degrowth science, the present level of aggregate material resource use—the sum total of all human consumption across all societies—is completely unsustainable. Recent studies focus on two central problems with continuing *aggregate* economic growth. First, it is accelerating the pace

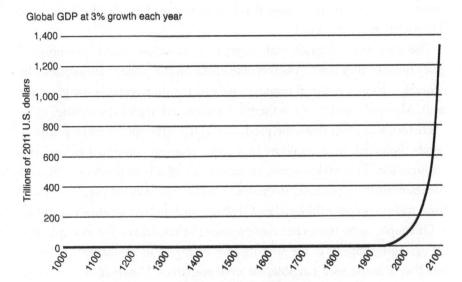

Global GDP at 3% growth each year

Figure 2.1   Continuous GDP growth is irrational

A graph depicting exponential GDP growth. Source: Kallis, 2021.[5]

of climate change due to anthropogenic (human-caused) global warming, which threatens to breach "tipping points" that will create irreversible environmental catastrophes. Second, it is contributing to equally catastrophic biodiversity and habitat loss. Let's start with the first.

Climate change

Producing material things requires energy. Fossil fuels, such as oil, coal, and natural gas, are used to create most of the products we produce. Burning fossil fuels emits gases into the atmosphere, which absorb and radiate heat, making the planet warmer. Other production processes, detailed in Chapter 4, contribute mightily to global heating, especially industrial farming. Because trees absorb carbon, when we cut down forests (deforestation)—the vast majority of which is for livestock grazing and agricultural expansion—we make the planet warmer, as there are fewer trees to suck carbon out of the air. Climate change also displaces and reshapes planetary tree cover, which kills off primary (old-growth) forests, thereby disrupting habitats of rich biodiversity while leading to mass species extinctions. In other words, forests aren't generic tree zones that can be replaced by planting new ones. They need to be preserved.[6]

The collection of gases that warm the planet are called "greenhouse" gases because they have a blanket-like effect on the planet's atmosphere. In general, the more material resources we use, the more greenhouse gases we emit. Material resource use is therefore connected to global warming.

Historically, gross domestic product (GDP)—the total sum of prices of goods produced in an economy in a given year—is connected to material resource use. This makes sense: an economy's goal is to produce stuff, and the more stuff we produce, the more material resources we use. If we burn fossil fuels to produce things, then GDP is connected to fossil fuel emissions.

Of course, some things use more resources than others. For example, the act of singing appears to use nothing (it is *intangible* or *immaterial*), whereas building a house uses tangible, material resources. However, singers need to consume things—such as furniture, clothes, etc.—as a reward for their efforts. Being a singer, then, is *connected* to the material economy. Given that

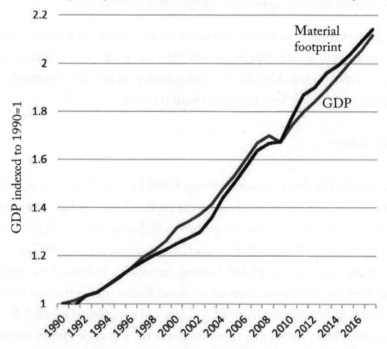

Figure 2.2   GDP and material footprint (courtesy of Jason Hickel)

GDP tracks closely with global material footprint. Source: Hickel and Hallegatte, 2022.[7]

we all want things (not just songs) and songs can only provide so much value (in terms of quantity and quality)—aggregate GDP growth will increase material resource use over time.

At present, humans collectively consume about 100 billion tons of material resources each year. This is a major jump from two decades ago: in the year 2000, we used just 54 billion tons of resources per year. That doubling is connected to our rate of growth.[8] For decades, the global economy has been growing by 3% per year. At that rate, the economy doubles every 23.5 years. On the current trajectory, by 2043, we'll be consuming 200 billion tons of material resources per year, by 2067, 400 billion tons, by 2090, 800 billion, and by the early twenty-second century, 1,600 billion tons.

Each day that goes by, the *rate* of growth is increasing—meaning, growth is intensifying over time. At present, fossil fuels account for about 82% of global energy use.[9] It takes time to transition to "green" renewable energy sources like solar and wind, so we have to keep using fossil fuels until we make a full transition to green energy. Since we can't turn off fossil fuels overnight, the more the global economy grows as we're making that transition, the more fossil fuels we will have to burn.

The question then becomes: how much extra heating will occur if we keep growing the economies as we're making the transition to green energy? And is this amount of temperature increase compatible with climate change (overheating the planet) goals?

According to climate scientists, humans have heated the planet by 1.2°C above the pre-industrial level (1850–1900). This has already increased the frequency and intensity of wildfires, floods, droughts, and other extreme weather events across the world.[10] But if we keep warming the planet, things will get *much* worse, because we will trigger irreversible *tipping points*. As we will see, if we keep growing, we're unlikely to prevent triggering those tipping points. But before we get there, let's examine what tipping points are and why they are so important.

Tipping points

Tipping points are irreversible, catastrophic events that occur when global temperatures exceed a certain threshold. We typically think of warming the environment in linear terms: if we make the planet one unit warmer, then we will make things one unit worse. But this isn't how tipping points work. Instead, when a tipping point is breached, it causes *qualitative shifts* in the environment. If we overheat the oceans and destroy all the coral reefs, they won't come back. If we turn the Amazon rainforest into a savanna, it's gone forever.

But it's even worse than this. With tipping points, changes in the climate system can become self-perpetuating. *Feedback loops*—a change that gives rise to an additional change at least as large as the initial change, leading to additional changes, and so on—can set in, triggering other tipping points that may cause widespread Earth system impacts. Think of tipping points as permanent changes to climate systems that can cause chain reactions which spiral out of control.

The melting of major ice sheets can kickstart tipping cascades. Scientists believe the Western Antarctic ice sheet is already in a permanent state of collapse—a major warning that climate mitigation needs urgent action. The melting of the Greenland ice sheet could trigger changes to the Atlantic Meridional Overturning Circulation (AMOC) stream critical to stable weather patterns, which would in turn warm the Southern Ocean, thereby destabilizing the Antarctic ice sheets, pushing up the global sea level, further melting the Greenland ice sheet.

The 2015 Paris Agreement, an international treaty on climate mitigation which includes 195 United Nations signatories, aims to keep long-term mean temperature rise to "well below" 2°C (3.6°F), with a preferable limit below 1.5°C (2.7°F). We want to keep the temperature below 1.5°C in part because we want to avoid triggering tipping points at all costs.

A 2022 study in a leading academic journal, *Science*, assessed hundreds of previous studies on tipping points and found that several tipping points may have already been breached.[11] These include Greenland ice sheet collapse (GrIS), West Antarctic ice sheet collapse (WAIS), tropical coral reef die-off (REEF), and abrupt permafrost thaw (PFAT). At 1.5°C heating—the minimum level of warming now expected by the 2030s even with rapid emissions cuts—the four tipping points will move from "possible" to "likely." In that scenario, major changes to northern forests will occur, and much of the mountain glaciers will melt, leading to the release of pathogenic microbes, among other effects. Warming of 2°C further increases the likelihood of near complete warm-water coral die-off, abrupt permafrost thaw, heavy glacier loss, land carbon sink weakening, Boreal forest shifts, and the triggering of AMOC collapse.

The impacts will be devastating: thawing the permafrost—soil that remains below the freezing point throughout the year—will release massive amounts of GHGs (CO_2 and methane). Killing off the coral reefs will be a complete nightmare: coral reefs harbor the highest biodiversity of any eco-system, housing a quarter of the ocean's marine species while supporting over 500 million people worldwide (especially in poor countries). Melting the glaciers will raise the sea level, displace millions and elevate storm surges, further warm the planet, and slow down or collapse the AMOC stream. The Earth's boreal forests, located just south of the northern Arctic, absorb carbon and house numerous species of mammals, fish, plants, insects, and birds. Warming imperils the southern parts of the boreal forests while shifting the tree line north into warming areas at a pace that likely cannot keep up with losses in the south. Southern boreal habitats will be destroyed and there will be a total reduction in tree cover.

Clearly, overheating the planet would be a total disaster that *we cannot reverse*.

The insane effects of climate change

While tipping points are major disasters, the extreme effects of climate change are already here. In 2022, a massive flood put one third of Pakistan under water, killing 1,700 and displacing 7.9 million people. Hurricane Ian shredded Florida up to the Carolinas, causing $115 billion in damages. A megadrought hammered the Horn of Africa, killing nearly 9 million live-stock while devastating crops. In Baidoa, Somalia, 230 children were buried in a single grave site after dying from malnutrition.

In 2023 climate records tumbled. Ocean temperatures were completely off the charts, smashing previous seasonal records. June was by far the hottest month ever recorded.[12] And despite the urgent need to reduce greenhouse emissions, global fossil fuel emissions hit a record high while the US extracted more oil and gas than any year before.

Other developments also are taking place faster than anticipated. With 400 billion trees and about 10% of the world's species, the Amazon is the largest rainforest in the world. However, it is at risk of drying out. Twenty percent has already been deforested, which is delaying the start of the Southern Monsoon, leading to reduced rainfall. A recent study found that the deforestation may trigger a tipping point that will dry out and destroy large parts of the Amazon.[13]

If recent changes aren't bad enough, predictions for the future are downright harrowing. In his book *The Uninhabitable Earth*, David Wallace-Wells pours through the scientific literature to map out current effects and predictions for the future. Here are some scenarios, per Wallace-Wells:

- At 2°C, the ice sheets will begin their collapse, 400 million more people will suffer from water scarcity, major cities in the equatorial band of the planet will become unlivable, and even in the northern latitudes heat waves will kill thousands each summer. There would be thirty-two times as many extreme heat waves in India, and each would last five times as long, exposing ninety-three times more people. This is our best-case scenario.

- At 3°C, southern Europe would be in permanent drought, and the average drought in Central America would last nineteen months longer and in the Caribbean twenty-one months longer. In northern Africa, the figure is sixty months longer—five years. The areas burned each year by wildfires would double in the Mediterranean and sextuple, or more, in the United States.

- At 4°C, there would be eight million more cases of dengue fever each year in Latin America alone and close to annual global food crises. There could be 9 percent more heat-related deaths. Damages from river flooding would grow thirtyfold in Bangladesh, twentyfold in India, and as much as sixtyfold in the United Kingdom. In certain places, six climate-driven natural disasters could strike simultaneously, and, globally, damages could pass $600 trillion—more than twice the wealth as exists in the world today. Conflict and warfare could double.[14]

On the present trajectory, the world is heading toward 2.5°C (4.5°F) to 2.9°C (5.2°F) of global warming by 2100. Sixty percent of the leading climate scientists believe we will reach 3°C or more. Even if all emission reduction pledges were honored—which is not currently being done—we would expect to reach just below 2°C, which would almost certainly trigger a series of tipping points.[15]

Critics of environmentalists will tell you that pointing these things out is "alarmist" or "pessimistic." But it's reality. And yes, it is *ultra* alarming. It's precisely why all of us need to take the environment seriously. The time to act is now.

Degrowth and global warming

Needless to say, we *really, really* don't want to overheat the planet. And it is here that the case for degrowth makes its first scientific argument. Following the precautionary principle—i.e., that we shouldn't risk irreversible, catastrophic damage to our one and only habitat—we don't have time to avoid catastrophic warming if we keep growing the global economy.[16] We need to reduce and cap aggregate growth in an effort to halt climate change.

This finding is contentious to some, who maintain that GDP growth can be "decoupled" from material resource use.[17] Decoupling takes two forms: *relative* decoupling, where resource use increases slower than GDP growth, and *absolute* decoupling, where GDP grows while resource use declines. Obviously, absolute decoupling is preferable to relative decoupling: in this scenario, the economy grows while also using less materials than before. It's an essential concept to understand, because most "green growth" solutions assume we can keep growing by decoupling economic growth from resource use and GHG emissions.

Let's start our consideration of decoupling with climate change. As of 2024, we're on track to hit the 1.5°C threshold within a decade.[18] At present, countries across the world are installing renewable energy technologies like solar panels and wind turbines to replace fossil fuels. Yet we cannot switch off fossil fuels overnight and keep the economy going—we have to *phase them out*. And while we are trying to switch from fossil fuels to renewable energy, we're still using dirty energy sources for production and consumption. If we're consuming more material resources every year in general—which requires energy for production, transportation, and so on—then we're adding more fuel to the fire. As degrowth scholar Jason Hickel puts it, growing your economy while trying to stop polluting the atmosphere is like trying to run down an up escalator or pouring sand into a hole that keeps getting bigger.

In 2020, a team of scientists published a two-part systemic review of 835 studies on decoupling growth from resource use.[19] The researchers conclude that "large rapid absolute reductions of resource use and GHG emissions cannot be achieved through observed decoupling rates, hence decoupling needs to be complemented by sufficiency-oriented strategies and strict enforcement of absolute reduction targets."[20] A 2023 study evaluating the absolute decoupling of eleven high-income countries deepened this conclusion, finding that emissions reductions fell short of Paris-compliant rates. "To meet their 1.5°C fair-shares alongside continued economic growth, decoupling rates would on average need to increase by a factor of ten by 2025 and by a factor of 12 by 2030," the authors found.[21] Decoupling is simply too slow and limited an approach.

Jason Hickel and Giorgos Kallis provide valuable insight into why "green growth" is not feasible.[22] At a global level, material resources use has not been decoupled from GDP growth (see Figure 2.2). Moreover, significant decoupling has only occurred in a handful of individual countries. Some argue that technological factors could enable efficiency gains that result in drastic decoupling—as much as 70% less material intensity. Yet this claim is not only unproven, it would also only be *temporary*, because resource efficiency has physical limits. There will always be minimum requirements for water use in agriculture, land use for food production, and so on. Efficiency gains yielding absolute decoupling would reduce material resource use for a period of time, but once those gains have been exhausted, material resource use would increase again. This point cannot be emphasized enough: those who argue that growth can continue forever are denying the nature of exponential growth and cannot respond to these points. But they cannot be cast aside. There's no way around this problem.[23]

Climate models produced by the world's dominant body on climate change, the International Panel on Climate Change (IPCC), assume continuous GDP growth.[24] To stay within the Paris limits, the IPCC builds "negative emissions" geo-engineering fixes into its models, such as bioenergy with carbon capture and storage (BECCS). The bioenergy element involves planting fast-growing vegetation such as trees or energy crops to absorb carbon from the atmosphere. The vegetation would then be burned in power plants and the carbon emissions captured and stored under-ground. The technology hasn't proven it can work at scale, and it and would require an industrial-scale mobilization: bioenergy crops would require a landmass up to three times the size of India—in addition to "enormous capacities for transporting and storing the carbon dioxide extracted from the atmosphere."[25]

The time frame to produce BECCS is also daunting. As Wallace-Wells puts it, "One estimate suggests that, to have hopes of two degrees, we need to open new full-scale carbon capture plants at the pace of one and a half per day every day for the next seventy years. In 2018, the world had eighteen of them, total."[26] In addition to its steep cost, the BECCS "solution" would harm biodiversity, requiring "more than a doubling of the amount of water used currently for irrigation" and substantial deforestation.[27] Moreover, land in the Global South would be appropriated for the energy privilege of the Global North.[28] Not surprisingly, activists are opposing carbon capture projects as a smokescreen for business-as-usual politics.

The IPCC acknowledges, "Implementation of [carbon capture and storage] currently faces technological, economic, institutional, ecologi-cal-environmental and socio-cultural barriers. Currently, global rates of CCS deployment are far below those in modelled pathways limiting global warming to $1.5\,°C$ to $2\,°C$."[29] Casting aside serious problems and a deep pool of scientific skepticism, it states with "high confidence" that "Enabling con-ditions such as policy instruments, greater public support and technological innovation could reduce these barriers."[30]

A conservative organization, the IPCC carries more weight than any other scientific body on climate change. That it would build an unproven technology into its climate mitigation models is truly alarming. Diplomats from 193 governments appoint the lead authors, which sets political bound-aries on the agenda, framing, and findings. The latest report included 721 authors from 90 countries, drawn from academia, industry, government, and non-governmental organizations. Leading experts in their field are selected and the chapters go through a rigorous peer-review process. Yet this process has been insufficient to date: its recent report finally mentioned degrowth a handful of times, but failed to build degrowth into its mitigation scenar-ios. That's a long way from acknowledging an existential crisis we have little time to prevent.[31]

BIODIVERSITY LOSS AND HABITAT DESTRUCTION

Biodiversity loss and habitat destruction presents a second crisis caused by economic growth, but it receives much less attention than climate change. Our ecosystems are essential to humans because they supply us with food, water, and air. Healthy and stable ecosystems are required for fertile soil, pollination, fresh water, nutrient-rich food, and medicine. At least 40% of the world's economy and 80% of the needs of the poor are derived from biological resources. If we degrade or collapse our ecosystems, people will suffer severe consequences.[32] Needless to say, biodiversity is also important because *other species have value*—and we're tragically killing them off at an alarming rate.

According to scientists, humans are initiating a Sixth Mass Extinction. A mass extinction event occurs when species vanish at a much faster rate than their rate of replacement. Such events could entail a loss of as many as 75% of all living species in a short geological time (less than 2.8 million years). Several studies show that during the "Anthropocene"—the era of humans— the rate of species extinction is 100–1,000 times more than the normal "background" extinction rate, and it's getting worse.

In a massive 2019 report spanning 1,800 pages, the Intergovernmental Science-Policy Platform on Biodiversity and Ecosystem Services (IPBES) found around 1 million animal and plant species are threatened with extinction, many within decades, as "a direct result of human activity." To name just one example, the South African penguin went from 1 million breeding pairs in the early 1900s to 10,000 today, thanks to overfishing and climate change.[33] As the United Nations (UN) notes, the "culprits are, in descending order: (1) changes in land and sea use; (2) direct exploitation of organisms; (3) climate change; (4) pollution and (5) invasive alien species."[34]

In its 2022 report, the World Wide Fund for Nature (WWF) found there has been an eye-watering "69% decline in the relative abundance of monitored [wildlife] populations between 1970 and 2018."[35] Among their findings:

- Latin America showed the greatest regional decline in average population abundance (94%), followed by Africa (66%), Asia-Pacific (55%), North America (20%), and Europe and Central Asia (18%).

- Freshwater species populations have seen the greatest overall global decline (83%).
- More than 1 million plant and animal species are on the brink of extinction.[36]

The study is measuring loss in *populations* of animals in specific areas, *not total species loss.* Nevertheless, scientists universally regard these steep declines as alarming.[37] The causes of biodiversity loss are human activities. In the WWF report, key drivers include fossil fuels, land and sea use, overexploitation, pollution, and invasive species created by human displacement.[38]

Added to this, the first global scientific review of insect biodiversity found "dramatic rates of decline that may lead to the extinction of 40% of the world's insect species over the next few decades," mostly due to the use of pesticides for industrial agriculture.[39] Insects are deeply woven into the web of life, providing sources of nutrition to birds, reptiles, amphibians, and fish, among their other roles. One of the study's authors, Francisco Sánchez-Bayo, told the *Guardian*, "The 2.5% rate of annual loss over the last 25–30 years is 'shocking' … It is very rapid. In ten years you will have a quarter less, in 50 years only half left and in 100 years you will have none." The collapse of insect populations threatens the "catastrophic collapse of nature's ecosystems."[40]

In other words, humans are not only overheating the planet, they are rapidly eradicating the intricate balance of life they and other species rely on. We're committing ecocide.

Material flows scientists have reviewed the literature on resource use to get a sense of environmental and ecological destruction at the present rate of growth. In 2012, Monika Dittrich et al. published the first report to systematically assess worldwide trends and dynamics of material extraction, trade, consumption, and productivity, covering the years 1980 to 2008. The authors evaluated the primary resources forming the material basis for all human activities: biomass (from agriculture, forestry, fishery, and hunting), minerals (industrial and construction), fossil energy carriers (coal, oil, gas, peat), and metal ores (ferrous and non-ferrous).[41]

Of these categories, minerals made up 40% of global material consumption in 2008. Within this category, construction minerals have high degrees of carbon emissions (especially in the production of cement) and increase the loss of fertile land areas, while metals degrade ecosystems and pollute water and soil. Fossil fuels are the primary driver of climate change, first and foremost due to exceptionally high CO_2 emissions. The increasing harvest of biomass is putting pressure on water resources (e.g., from agriculture and energy) while intensifying the use of fertilizers, pesticides, and herbicides.

The authors conclude that the level of global resource use at the time measured (2008) is not sustainable, and "we need to reduce our resource use in absolute terms." They assert, "biodiversity loss, desertification, and soil erosion are clearly linked to our use of natural resources." A truly green economy therefore requires "a radical reduction in the scale, volume and rate of human resource use" in a way that will also "satisfy the material needs of the [global] population." Because billions of people are living in poverty, they conclude, "A strategy of reducing global resource use therefore needs to fully address *distributional* aspects, both between different countries and regions and—to a growing extent—also within countries" (emphasis added).[42]

Several subsequent studies corroborate this position. A 2014 study evaluated a series of footprints, finding overshoot in material resource use and carbon, as well as aspects of land and water footprints. The authors conclude, "The various components of the environmental footprint of humanity must be reduced to remain within planetary boundaries. Improved technologies (eco-efficiency) alone will not be sufficient to reach this goal."[43] Two UN reports studying the sustainability of material footprints recommended the consumption of 6–8 tons per capita globally by 2050.[44] Several other studies have come to similar conclusions.[45]

The toll on the environment is already devastating, and getting worse. The 2014 UN Environment Programme report notes:

About a quarter of the earth's land area is highly degraded (up from 15% in 1991) and 5.2 million hectares of forests are lost every year. Rivers and lakes are drying up, groundwater aquifers are getting depleted, oceans are becoming acidified, and more than 30% of global fisheries that are harvested are overfished. 27% of the world's 845 species of reef-building corals have been listed as threatened and an additional 20% are considered near threatened.[46]

This is directly connected to resource use:

> During the 20th century, extraction of construction minerals grew by a factor of 34, industrial ores and minerals by a factor of 27, fossil fuels by a factor of 12 and biomass by a factor of 3.6. The total material extraction increased by a factor of about 8 to support a 23-fold GDP growth.[47]

It should come as no surprise that material resource use is causing biodiversity loss and habitat destruction. One study found that resource footprints are good proxies for environmental damage. The authors assessed nearly 1,000 products to evaluate the connection between material footprints and environmental damage, finding that land and energy use in particular are driving biodiversity loss.[48] Other studies confirm that economic growth is causing biodiversity loss.[49]

The double-emergency of climate change and biodiversity loss are two sides of the same coin. Yet at this point in history, habitat destruction and overexploitation—rather than climate change—is the primary driver of biodiversity loss. However, as global temperatures rise, climate change will become the lead destroyer. In the meantime, we need to understand that overheating the planet is *not* our only concern. Even *without* global warming, we would need to halt economic growth to preserve biodiversity and keep our ecosystems healthy. Economic growth has breached environmental limits, and further growth is a wrecking ball on the planet.

DEGROWTH AND DISTRIBUTION: IS THERE ENOUGH TO GO AROUND?

The scientists and political ecologists studying the relationship between our ecological footprint, economic growth, and environmental resilience—sampled above—speak of the need for the "contraction and convergence" of material resource use.[50] The "contraction" part means humans *as a whole* need to consume fewer resources. We cannot continue to overtill the soil, overexploit the land, and fill the sky with planet-warming gases. In other words, our total planetary footprint must not exceed Mother Nature's limits.

However, reducing the amount of *aggregate* (total) resource use leaves us with a moral dilemma: there are billions of poor people living in squalor. This is the "convergence" part. Let's consider the two in turn.

Contraction

Ecological economics uses a doughnut model for sustainable economy developed by economist Kate Raworth. Those in the center circle fall short of basic social needs, but those outside the doughnut push the planet beyond its boundaries. We want everyone to fit inside the doughnut, the safe and just space for humanity.[51]

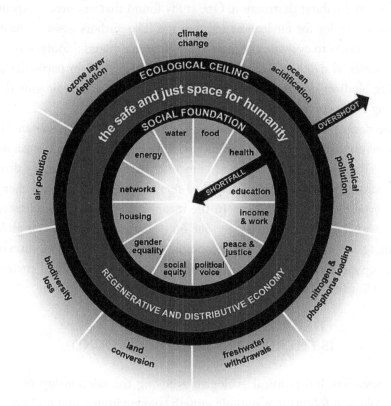

Figure 2.3 The doughnut for justice and sustainability

Source for Image: Wikipedia.[52]

The catch is that safe and just space leaves hardly any room for inequality. The UN projects the global population will reach 9.7 billion people by 2050 and 10.4 billion by 2100, but with gains in equality and education that generally correlate with lower reproduction rates, global population could instead peak at about 8.5 billion by 2050 and decline to 7 billion by 2100.

At present, there are 8 billion people. Of those 8 billion, just over half are in poverty, living under a meager $7.40 per day—the minimum necessary for basic nutrition and normal life expectancy. Humanity is currently consuming about 100 billion tons of material resources per year. That 100 billion tons forms the basis for the global economy, which has a GDP of a little over $100 trillion.[53]

According to the World Bank, the global per capita income in 2022 was just over $20,000.[54] That income per person includes *all* people on planet Earth, from babies to the elderly and unemployed. Distributed evenly, a family of four would have almost $80,000 per year of income. But the situation is actually tighter than that. Materials flow scientists sampled earlier have found that we need to *reduce* aggregate material resource use from 100 billion tons to as low as 50 billion tons or less. At 50 billion tons, global GDP would halve, and 8 billion people would be left with $10,000 per head.

It's important not to misread those numbers, as it's not exactly clear exactly what they would allow each one of us to consume for two reasons. First, they don't adjust of cost of living by location. If you're reading this and live in New York City, the available income may appear low. If you're in Johannesburg or Istanbul, it would be much better.

Second, and more importantly, an income calculated in today's economy is not easy to compare to an income in a degrowth economy.[55] Here's why. In a degrowth economy, we would be forced to make our economies *much* more efficient and less wasteful, which would free up resources for a green transition *and* non-excessive consumption. Things like luxury consumption, fast fashion, advertising, planned obsolescence, military spending, private jets, individual-oriented transportation (cars instead of buses and trains), and industrial meat production would be radically scaled down or eliminated. We would also cut waste (especially in our food systems), localize more of our production, improve recycling, and so on.

Wherever the fine details lie, degrowth economists contend that everyone can be provided with a decent standard of living.

Convergence

However, there is a catch: degrowth would require those consuming more than their fair share to consume less, as *there would be no room for class.* The rich economies would reduce their size and eliminate excess consumption, while the poor economies would *grow* more quickly and efficiently. They would have to liberate themselves from the yoke of Western colonizers, who would be made to *support*, rather than *exploit*, those in the South.

Mass redistribution of wealth also just makes sense. It's not just the disgusting fact that billions of people are living in squalor while a numerical minority appropriates the fruits of their labor. It's also the case that a small amount of resources does more for the poor more than it does for the wealthy. "Using food as an example," Kohei Saito notes, "increasing the overall caloric intake by just 1% would save 800,060,000 people from starvation."[56] The fact that we're not trying to balance wealth in the world is even more criminal when you look at it from that perspective.

As we'll see in future chapters, you can imagine why the growth conversation is so threatening to elites and professional intellectuals, who mostly ignore it. If we can't keep growing sustainably, wealth and income distribution becomes a fixed, zero-sum game: if someone consumes more, then someone else consumes less. So we really only have two choices. One, we can lock the global poor into poverty so that the rich and Westernized middle classes can maintain their levels of consumption. Or two, we can massively redistribute wealth and income within and between countries, so that everyone can enjoy a decent standard of living. This would leave everyone on the planet with a comfortable lifestyle, possibly at the lower-middle-class standard of Western countries. But it would also require us to *redesign the economy* so it creates and sustains equality and ecological harmony. Capitalism does the opposite, so we need *system change*, as we'll see in Chapters 8-9.

* * *

Before we discuss digital degrowth solutions, we need to bring back digital colonialism and capitalism which, we'll see, is fundamentally unsustainable and driving ecocide.

3
Digital Degrowth

We've now established two things: that the digital economy is dominated by the United States through the processes of digital colonialism, and that the capitalist growth machine is destroying our one and only planet. Given that we are already over-consuming the planet's finite resources, we need to reduce and cap economic growth. But this leaves us with a moral problem: most of the world's people are poor, and they need to obtain a decent standard of living. Without growing the global economy, we can only redistribute wealth and income. The only just and sustainable way forward is to abolish class everywhere: there are not enough material resources to give 8 billion people a quality standard of living if the wealthy minority continue to hold the world's income and wealth.

In this chapter, we're going to begin connecting the dots by merging the digital economy with degrowth. Given that inequality isn't compatible with a fair and sustainable global economy, and given that the Americans dominate the lucrative digital economy, then fixing the colonial North–South divide under the current arrangement is impossible. We can't have tech corporations worth more than most countries' annual production, with rich executives, shareholders, and white-collar engineers eating more than their fair share of the planet's finite wealth.

As we will see, the process of digital colonialism produces a fundamentally unsustainable and unjust *ecologically unequal exchange* and *division of labor*. This is made all the worse when we consider that the rich countries in the North—led by the United States—owe both *climate* and *ecological debts* to the South. These concepts form the basis for *digital degrowth*.

Let's dig in.

ECOLOGICALLY UNEQUAL EXCHANGE

As noted in the previous chapter, when we account for all human activity added up across all societies, humans are consuming 100 billion tons of material resources per year. That said, people—and societies—don't all consume equally. For starters, there's a North–South divide whereby those in the rich countries (the Global North) consume way more than the people in poor countries (the Global South). The 2019 United Nations Sustainable Development Goal (SDG) report broke this down under SDG #12, Responsible Consumption and Production, as can be seen in Figure 3.1:

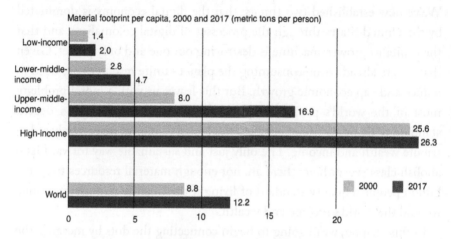

Figure 3.1   Material footprint by country income brackets
(courtesy of United Nations Publications)

Source: United Nations, "Ensure Sustainable Consumption and Production Patterns." 2019.[1]

As you can see, by 2017, people in the high-income countries used 26.3 tons per person per year, compared to 2.0 in the low-income countries. The sustainable limit is thought to be somewhere around 6–8 tons.[2]

The UN also notes that there is a *net transfer* of material resources from poorer countries to rich: "On a per-capita basis, high-income countries rely on 9.8 metric tons of primary materials extracted elsewhere in the world."[3] The UNEP's 2014 report elaborates on this:

Average use of resources in some developed countries is as high as 30–40 tonnes/person/year, compared to 2 tonnes/person/year for some of the developing countries. Overall, an average citizen in a developed country uses each year nearly 24 times as much of material resources and 12 times as much energy as one in a developing country.[4]

In academic literature, this asymmetry is called *ecologically unequal exchange*. Under ecologically unequal exchange, the rich countries possess more power than poor countries, which they use to bargain down the poor and gain access to the resources needed for economic growth. Through this process, wealthier cities, nations, and regions accumulate technological infrastructure critical to development.[5]

In 2021, a collection of scholars, Dorninger et al., published an empirical assessment of ecologically unequal exchange at the global level.[6] They found that in addition to a net transfer of resources (materials, energy, land, and labor) from poor countries to rich ones, "high-income countries obtain significantly higher revenues for the resources they export than poorer nations, which is mostly due to the positions occupied in global supply chains and their respective roles in the world economy"—i.e., capitalist globalization. As a result, "Unequal trade patterns arise from and reproduce global socio-economic inequalities and hamper socio-economic sustainability through environmental burden-shifting to poorer nations."[7]

The study, which covers 170 countries and encompasses 99.2% of the world population as of 2015, also found that "[high-income] countries net appropriate a disproportionately large share of materials, energy, land, and labor through international trade." Moreover, high-income countries are "the only significant net appropriators" of resources. For its part, "China acted as a net provider of embodied materials, energy, and labor," while "all income groups but the [high-income] countries were net providers of labor." The high-income countries were the largest net appropriators of land, while the low-income countries were major providers of land.[8] We can add to this that ecologically unequal exchange shifts pollution to the South and depletes its nonrenewable resources (including minerals).[9]

There are no surprises here. Most of the people of working age are employed—the global unemployment rate is 5.1%—yet there are billions of working people living in squalor.[10] As the documentary film *Black Gold* illustrates, Ethiopian farmers picking coffee beans sold to Starbucks "toil in their bare feet."[11] They were fighting for a higher sale price so they could meet basic needs—proper nutrition, clean water, clothing—and send their children to school, in hopes they can one day escape poverty. The farmers were making less than a dollar a day for an eight-hour shift. Meanwhile, a Starbucks barista in the US gets about $15 an hour to pour the coffee, while the rich executives and shareholders capture the majority of the money and wealth produced along the supply chain. Unequal exchange is a core feature of the global economy.

DIGITAL SUPPLY CHAINS AND
LABOR IN THE GLOBAL SOUTH

As we saw in Chapter 1, under classic colonialism, the colonial powers relied on ownership and control of territory and infrastructure, the exploitation of labor, and the appropriation of raw materials for manufacturing in the imperial core. Today, manufacturing has moved down the hierarchy of global value, displaced by an advanced high-tech economy in which American transnational corporations are firmly in charge. It is here that we can start bringing digital colonialism back into the conversation.

Big Tech giants exploit their ownership of digital infrastructure, knowledge, and the means of computation to keep the South in a situation of permanent dependency. The North dominates the higher-level "thinking" while the South is exploited for menial tasks along the supply chain, such as digging in the dirt for metal, assembling iPhones in sweatshops, and performing repetitive "point-and-click" data labeling for artificial intelligence.

The degree of exploitation is intense. In 2022, *TIME* ran an article exposing Sama, a San Francisco-based contractor to Facebook operating out of Kenya that paid its employees $1.46 to $2.20 per hour (after taxes) for a 45-hour workweek. The workers were tasked to scrub psychologically disturbing content—e.g., videos of murder, rape, suicide, child sexual abuse, dismemberment, and torture—from Facebook, so that users don't have to see them. "The work that we do is a kind of mental torture," one of the workers told *TIME*. "Whatever I am living on is hand-to-mouth. I can't save a cent. Sometimes I feel I want to resign. But then I ask myself: what will my baby eat?" At least two employees were diagnosed with mental illnesses, including post-traumatic stress disorder (PTSD), anxiety, and depression, while others said they were traumatized, but couldn't afford access to quality health care. Sama also stood accused of suppressing attempts to unionize. The workers are suing Sama, Facebook parent Meta, and another outsourcing company in the mix, Majorel, for $1.6 billion in compensation.[12]

American tech giants are able to exploit the Global South in such a brutal fashion in part because they monopolize the core knowledge critical to the end products and are able to subjugate people who are already poor, thanks to centuries of colonization. Apple, for example, extracts rents from its intellectual property and branding for its smartphones, and it coordinates production along the commodity chain. The company doesn't actually manufacture the iPhone, it produces the designs and outsources the production process to the South. As such, it accumulates the majority of the profits, taking advantage of the cheap labor provided by the global poor. Lower-level producers, such as the phone assemblers at manufacturing plants hosted by Taiwan-owned Foxconn and the chipmakers supplying processors, make much less profit by comparison. Those along the supply chain are subordinate to the demands and whims of Apple, which commands the production process.

Some of the so-called "intellectual property" produced by Big Tech transnationals is appropriated, rather than produced in-house. Sometimes they acquire promising startups to ingest their intellectual property, whereas other times they co-author with universities.[13] A 2020 study by scholars Cecilia Rikap and Bengt-Åke Lundvall found that workers at companies like Amazon, Microsoft, and Google co-author with university researchers, but rarely share patents with them. Many of those researchers are from the Global South (e.g., China and India), suggesting a predatory process of "knowledge and rent extraction from emerging and developing countries."[14] This is worth keeping in mind when marveling at the latest-and-greatest innovations of the tech giants—some of that innovation is usurped from less powerful workers.

Global South worker exploitation is most grotesque in the mines. The best-known example takes place in the Democratic Republic of Congo, where (predominantly Chinese-based) corporations dominate cobalt mining. An essential component of lithium-ion batteries, cobalt prevents cathodes (components that absorb electrodes inside the battery) from overheating, thereby extending the life of the batteries. The DRC is home to over half the world's cobalt reserves and about 70% of global cobalt production.

Over the past few years, a University of Nottingham professor, Siddharth Kara, visited the DRC mines for his book, *Cobalt Red: How the Blood of the Congo Powers our Lives.*[15] Kara detailed how inside the cobalt mines and throughout the countryside, there are hundreds of thousands of people, including tens of thousands of children, who dig with small tools or bare hands for cobalt. While reports of exploitation in the cobalt mines have been public for more than a decade, Kara's book finally struck a chord with global audiences.[16]

The exploitation is so extreme it's hard to fathom. Wages are often a dollar or two a day, with a ceiling of around $15 dollars. Total salaries paid out to workers of a Swiss-owned mine, Glencore, comprised just 0.1% of the company's profits in 2022.[17]

While the availability of data about mining wages across the world varies, it is clear that the Global South is grossly exploited. In Chile, workers employed by the mines earn somewhere between $1,430 and $3,000 per month, whereas monthly wages in Argentina can be as low as between $300 and $1,800. In 2016, the monthly minimum wage of miners in Bolivia was *increased* to $250. By contrast, Australian miners earn around $9,000 per month; their salaries can reach $200,000 per year.[18]

In addition to worker exploitation, mining also stresses planetary resources, pollutes the environment, and destroys biodiversity. The global mining industry, encompassing mining for metals and fossil fuels, accounts for 10% of the world's energy consumption corresponding to 80% of the world's electricity use. Mining areas impact as much as 37% of the Earth's terrestrial land area (assuming impacts extend 50 km for mine sites and excluding Antarctica). And this is just the beginning. The transition to metals-based energy may require twice the copper and 40 times the lithium we use today by 2040. The metals industry presently accounts for 4–7% of global GHG emissions. Yet for every gigawatt of clean energy installed, millions of tons of CO_2 emissions can be avoided.[19]

In many instances, mining is highly destructive to biodiversity and local habitats. According to environmental scientist Simon Meißner, "construction and operation of mining facilities may lead to long-term impacts such as loss of vegetation and faunal habitats, modification of landforms, changes in soil profiles or modifications to surface and subsurface drainage."[20] Another study of 62,381 mining properties found that "an expansion in mining areas globally will threaten PAs [protected areas] and Key Biodiversity Areas" and that mining for renewables "may also disproportion[ally] increase the threats to biodiversity within currently protected areas." Without strategic planning, the study found, "new threats to biodiversity" from industry growth "may surpass those averted by climate change mitigation."[21]

Mining can also drain local water resources, depending on the mining site. According to Meißner, metal mining and refining usually consumes insignificant amounts of local freshwater. However, in some cases the mines over-consume at regional or local scales, depending on the level of fresh-water available in combination with water consumption of the mining operations. Places of over-drainage include basins in Chile, Australia, and Southern Africa, among others.[22]

Over half the world's lithium resources "lie beneath the salt flats of the Andean regions in Argentina, Bolivia, and Chile"—one of the world's driest regions.[23] In Chile's Salar de Atacama, for instance, lithium mining is consuming 65% of the region's water. Drainage is heavily impacting the local farmers, who grow quinoa and herd llamas, while nearby inhabitants are forced to fetch water from other areas.[24]

Even where sites do not over-drain local freshwater, mining operations often pollute water supplies. At mining sites, "acid rock drainage, leaks from tailings, waste rock dumps or direct disposal of tailings into waterways may contaminate surface and groundwater bodies."[25] At US mine sites, over 50 million gallons of water with arsenic, lead, and other toxic materials pours into local streams and ponds every day. As noted earlier, consequences for biodiversity may reach as far as 50 km from the mines.[26]

The mining industry also poses severe risks to tropical forests worldwide. A 2017 study of Brazilian mining found "significantly increased Amazon forest loss up to 70 km beyond mining lease boundaries, causing 11,670 km² of deforestation between 2005 and 2015. This extent represents 9% of all Amazon forest loss during this time and 12 times more deforestation than occurred within mining leases alone."[27]

In the Congo, millions of trees have been slashed for mining operations, which contaminate the local areas with toxins. Large swaths of land, reaching the size of London, have been razed, with military forces forcibly displacing the natives from their homes to clear the way for new mines. The water is contaminated with toxic effluents.

The toll on human health is extreme.[28] Cobalt, Siddharth Kara remarks, is:

> toxic to touch. It's toxic to breathe ... I have seen thousands of women with babies strapped to their backs inhaling toxic cobalt dust day in and day out, 10-year-old children caked in toxic filth, exposing themselves

to toxic cobalt. And the ore that these children are digging that has cobalt in it often has traces of radioactive uranium. So, the public health catastrophe on top of the human rights violence on top of the environmental destruction is unlike anything we've ever seen in the modern context.[29]

Women at the mining sites have "metal concentrations that are among the highest ever reported for pregnant women," while occupational mining is associated with fetal abnormalities.[30] Sexual violence is prevalent: women are raped and often turn to prostitution to survive.[31] Pit walls and tunnels often collapse, causing brutal injuries—crushed legs, arms, and spines—or death.

Simply put, mining in the Congo is among the most brutal forms of modern-day slavery. Chinese corporations are primarily responsible for the exploitation, as they own and operate the overwhelming majority of the mines. On a global scale, China also holds 90% of the mineral *processing* capacity for cobalt, lithium, and nickel, as well as the lion's share of rare earth metals.[32] While the Americans and Europeans are trying to decouple from Chinese supply chains, at present, they are reliant upon China.

Electric vehicle batteries are a large part of this story. They have to move cars around, which typically weigh 1–2 tons. EV batteries are thus enormous, requiring 1,000 times the amount of cobalt than a smartphone battery. The World Bank reports that cobalt production will have to increase 500% by 2050 in order to meet global demand.[33]

The digital sector intensifies electric vehicle battery consumption through e-hailing services like Uber and Lyft. The US dominates at the global level, with Uber, Lyft, and inDriver taking 38% of the worldwide market share as of 2022, compared to Estonia's Bolt (5%), Malaysia's Grab (4%), and China's DiDi Rider (3%).[34] Uber takes 25% of the global market itself; it operates in 72 countries (compared to DiDi's 17).

China produces over half (59%) of the world's electric vehicles and half the world's EV batteries. Its sales outside the mainland are growing, but not yet sizable—in Europe, it only accounts for 8.2% of sales. The US places a whopping 100% tariff on cars made in China (compared to Europe's 9%) to price them off the market. Yet most countries aren't buying electric vehicles.

EV sales are most prevalent in China (29% of sales), compared with Europe (21%), the United States (8%), and the rest of the world (2%).[35]

While EVs soak up 40% of the cobalt used, portable electronics take up an additional 30%.[36] In 2019, families of children killed or injured while mining in the DRC sued Tesla, Microsoft, Apple, Alphabet, Dell, Glencore, Umicore (Belgium), and Huayou Cobalt Co. (China), alleging they were "knowingly benefiting from and aiding and abetting the cruel and brutal use of young children" and therefore violated the Trafficking Victims Protection Reauthorization Act (TVPRA) and several common law based causes of action.[37] In response, the Big Tech companies issued gushing statements affirming their commitments to "human rights" and "respect for workers." They denied knowingly sourcing any cobalt connected to child labor or misconduct.

In November 2021, the US District Court for the District of Columbia dismissed the suit, claiming the plaintiffs didn't have adequate standing (grounds to launch a case). The court argued that the defendants (mining companies) did not employ any of the plaintiffs (people filing the lawsuit), and therefore did not cause the injuries suffered. "… it takes many analytical leaps to say that the end-purchasers of a fungible metal are responsible for the conditions in which that metal might or might not have been mined," the judge reasoned, "especially when that mining took place thousands of miles away and flowed through many independent companies" before reaching the defendants. The judge also denied the defendants "knowingly" benefited from "participation in a venture" which violated TVPRA, reasoning that a supply chain itself is not a "venture." The court stated that "the plaintiffs' allegations showed that their decision to start a "career" in cobalt mining was due to economic necessity and not coercion on the part of defendants," and argued that "Section 1595 of the TVPRA would not apply because there is no clear indication from its language that it has extra-territorial reach."[38]

The episode illustrates that the colonial-capitalist-white supremacist ethos is deep in the bones of the US legal system. As scholars Steve Tombs and David Whyte put it in their book, *Corporate Criminal: Why Corporations Must Be Abolished*:

the supply chain is—among other things—a technique for contracting out crime ... Tying down suppliers via contracts in order to maximize profitability at the top end of the supply chain ... builds in conditions of plausible deniability: if something goes wrong, both the explanation of the cause and the blame can be passed down the supply chain.[39]

The idea that the poorest of the poor Africans would willingly start a "career" putting their safety and health at risk to dig in the dirt for toxic minerals—all for a few bucks a day—says all you need to know about the United States.

Big Tech companies are among the richest and most powerful companies in human history, with surveillance capacities rivaling powerful nation-states, yet they are supposedly powerless to figure out what is going on in the mines. That a researcher like Siddharth Kara, whose investigation informed the lawsuit, was able to walk right into the Congo and document the whole process—replete with photographs, video footage, and interviews—makes a mockery of the alibi. What matters to Big Tech is putting rosy statements about human rights in glossy PR materials before Western audiences, just in case they hear about these matters from the press.

Table 3.1 Top 50 Mining Corporations (Global)

Country	Market Cap	%	Corporations	%
Australia	334.3	27.2	8	16
Canada	176.3	14.3	9	18
China	165.6	13.5	10	20
US	117.2	9.5	5	10
Other	435.7	35.4	18	36
TOTAL	**1,229.1**	**100**	**50**	**100**
Global North	806.9	65.6	30	60
Global South	422.2	34.5	20	40

Author's table and calculations. Source for data: Mining.com, 2023.[40]

While Chinese corporations savagely exploit the Congo, it is critical to note that China's footprint in the global mining sector still lags behind the West, as demonstrated in Table 3.1.

Other supply chains feature different shades of hyper-exploitation.[41] As Tombs and Whyte observe, "sub-contracting relationships … impose ever tighter margins down [the] supply chain, so that for some organizations, at some points in the chain, the only way of meeting contractual obligations whilst still making a profit is to break the law."[42]

The main manufacturer of iPhones and other consumer electronics, (Taiwan-owned) Foxconn, works Chinese laborers to the bone in sweatshops. Workers are forced to produce output at breakneck speeds, measured down to seconds. The single largest private employer in mainland China, Foxconn received bad press in 2010 when the media reported on a wave of worker suicides. In response, the company infamously put up suicide nets at worker dormitories. Working conditions are grotesque: as many as seven workers share a room, and they are paid as little as $324 per month. The wage is "barely enough to cover rent and food costs," one Foxconn worker told the media outlet, *Rest of World*.[43] In some locations, worker salaries can reach about $5.50/hour—if they're willing to work 60-hour weeks.

As Cecilia Rikap notes, Foxconn is a "complier" company—a subordinate of the master corporation commanding the rest of the companies from the top of the supply chain. In this case, Apple plans the production process—for example, it changed the screen of its iPhones weeks before a launch, forcing Foxconn to react and produce it—and it monitors on-site production and processes and delivery times. To be sure, Foxconn innovates production processes, but only in response to the designs defined by the Big Tech monopolies. In "accordance with complier firms," Rikap observes, "Foxconn enjoys a positive—but lower than Apple's—profit rate … precisely, in part, by reducing labour expenditures both in terms of wages and benefits."[44]

To squeeze those profits, employees endure unsafe working conditions. The company has stripped worker benefits, forced employees to put in 100 hours of overtime during peak production season (in violation of China's legal limits), and violently suppressed worker protests over low pay, safety hazards, and unpaid bonuses.

The mass exploitation of Global South workers along the supply chain is a major feature of digital colonialism. While the Western media huffs and puffs about the alleged threat of China's growing economic and technological power, Chinese workers toil their lives away in sweatshops to assemble iPhones, mostly for latte-sipping yuppies in the Global North. This power dynamic of course goes in one direction. There are no Americans or Europeans in extreme poverty breaking their backs for 60+ hours a week so that Chinese people can snap high-resolution selfies halfway across the world.

When all is said and done, American corporations benefit the most. Since the outset of iPhone production years ago, profits have accumulated in the US. "The total manufacturing cost of each iPhone was $178.96 and sold for $500" around 2010, researcher John Smith notes, "yielding a gross profit of 64 percent to be shared between Apple, its North American suppliers and distributors, and the U.S. government." Chinese assembly cost just $6.50 (3.6% of total manufacturing cost).[45]

While there is a great deal of consternation about offshoring US manufacturing jobs to China, as well as how China "steals" American intellectual property, it's also the case that cheap Chinese goods benefit American consumers.[46] Ecological destruction is also offshored to China, where production for companies like Apple saddles workers and communities with air pollution, water degradation, chemical emissions, heavy metal discharges, hazardous waste, and exposure to substances that cause life-threatening illnesses and cancer—an issue we'll return to in the next two chapters.[47]

* * *

The ecologically unequal exchange and division of labor created by digital colonialism marks the evolution of American Empire. To be sure, China has a substantial role as a South-South exploiter. But it is also a victim of the United States, the apex predator.

Yet the problem with Big Tech is *much worse* than its Global South labor exploitation. Environmental economics and justice *compounds* the culpability of the American Empire when considering that the United States owes the Global South climate and ecological debts. We turn to this topic next.

ENVIRONMENTAL DEBTS

If you live in a wealthy country, chances are you have a decent place to live, a car or affordable public transport, a workplace with modern facilities, electricity and clean water, air conditioning and heat, a nice smartphone with internet, and a job that provides you with a large enough wage or salary to entertain yourself. This setup required energy and material resources to build. By contrast, Global South societies have been exploited so badly that they haven't been able to build a "modern" standard of living for more than a small percentage of their population. The poor majority live in shacks and shanty-towns, receive pennies for their labor, and experience food insecurity. Basic amenities and infrastructure are lacking, such as quality buildings, machines for production, access to facilities for transportation, electricity, water, health care, and high-speed internet. To fix this issue, billions of people populating hundreds of thousands of cities and towns need new infrastructure and ser-vices. This too requires energy and material resources to build.

The rich countries have used most of the resources extracted throughout history to develop their economies, and now they have modern facilities to enjoy and power their production. However the global poor cannot enjoy this kind of setup without burning more energy and consuming more mate-rial resources to build it. Because our "carbon budget" is limited—meaning we have a limited amount of carbon left to burn before we trigger tipping points—and because there are limitations on how much material resources we can sustainably consume, we now have to decide who gets to use what. From an ethical standpoint, this means accounting for more than just the present distribution of wealth and income. The rich countries spent centu-ries polluting the atmosphere and eating up nature's finite resources to build their societies. We need to account for the past.

This leaves humanity with two forms of debt that need to be honored if we're to have a just transition to a sustainable global economy. The first is a *climate debt* tasking rich countries to account for their historical coloniza-tion of the atmospheric commons—the skies all humans share—via carbon emissions and subsequent damage caused by climate change. The second is an *ecological debt* requiring rich countries to account for their disproportion-ate share of historic material resource use and damage caused by ecological destruction. Let's consider each in turn.

CLIMATE DEBT

Since around 1850, at the onset of the Industrial Revolution, humans have emitted about 2,500 gigatons ($GtCO_2$) of carbon. We can emit less than

500 $GtCO_2$ to stay under the 1.5°C Paris target—our total *carbon budget*. And even then, we should be doing everything humanly possible to keep CO_2 emissions as far under that threshold as possible, given that every bit of heating makes the planet a more hostile place.

In 2019, the United Nations estimated that global GHG emissions need to be slashed by 7.6% every year for the next decade to meet the 1.5°C Paris target. Five years later, we're off to a bad start. A record 36.8 billion tons of carbon dioxide was emitted globally in 2021, and in 2023 we smashed previous temperature records.[48] In 2023, the US extracted more oil than ever before, and likely more gas. The UN Emissions Gap Report 2023 found that "The world is witnessing a disturbing acceleration in the number, speed and scale of broken climate records." Even if we meet the National Determined Contributions pledges made under the Paris Agreement, we are on track to hit between 2.5°C and 2.9°C this century. The report calls for countries to accelerate "economy-wide, low-carbon development transformations."[49]

In an important journal article published in *Lancet Planetary Health*, Jason Hickel quantified national responsibility for climate breakdown using a *per capita* (per person) definition for fair shares of CO_2 emissions.[50] At present, China's *total* emissions are double that of the US (though lower on a *per capita* basis), while India's emissions fall just under the European Union (also much lower per person). Africa accounts for the smallest share of GHG emissions, at just 3.8%.[51] Those in the West who point a finger at China and India not only ignore the fact that those countries have way more people (1.4 billion each) than the US (340 million) and Europe (740 million), they also erase *historic* emissions used for economic development.

Incorporating "fair shares" into climate mitigation responsibilities is critical to environmental justice. Climate change started over a century ago, not yesterday, so we need to look at who has done the most damage over time in order to determine national responsibilities going forward. "When it comes to climate change," Hickel observes, "what matters is stocks of CO_2 in the atmosphere, not annual flows; so responsibility must be measured in terms of each country's contribution to cumulative historical emissions."[52]

As we can see, despite only housing 340 million people—4% of the world's population—the US has contributed 40% of the national overshoot emissions. The Global South, which accounts for 85% of the world's population, has contributed just 8%.[53] China is approaching its fair share limit, while poor countries like India aren't even close. Even then, if India used up its remaining budget, it would push the world past its climate goals. We can thank the rapacious resource consumption of the colonial powers for putting humanity into this situation.[54]

Table 3.2   National Overshoot for Climate Breakdown

Location	Overshoot (%)
United States	40
EU-28	29
Rest of Europe	13
Rest of Global North	10
Global South	8
TOTAL	**100**
Global North	*92*
Global South	*8*
TOTAL	*100*

Source: *Jason Hickel, 2020.*[55]

Even though digital technology seems intangible, it also contributes to global carbon emissions. According to research by the Shift Project, digital technologies—defined as telecommunications networks, data centers, terminals (personal devices), and IoT (Internet of Things) sensors—consumed 5% of the world's energy and emitted 3.5% of global greenhouse gas in 2019 (up from 2.9% in 2013). The authors found ICT emissions are growing by about 6% per year, which is incompatible with the Paris Agreement goals.[56] The lower bound estimate for the digital sector is 1.4%—a finding that should be viewed with caution, as it comes from ICT industry researchers working for Swedish telecommunications giants Ericsson and Telia Company AB.[57] Other models put emissions somewhere in between.[58]

We can approximate national contributions to carbon emissions within the tech sector by drawing upon data published by *ElectronicsHub*.[59] The outlet used publicly available environmental, social, and governance (ESG) and corporate social responsibility (CSR) reports to tabulate emissions figures for 100 of the largest technology companies. *ElectronicsHub* didn't provide their entire dataset (which I requested via email but received no response), and the emissions *do not include "Scope 3" (supply chain) emissions*, which account for even greater shares of emissions (explained below). Here's the breakdown of the subset of the 100 leading emitters:

Table 3.3   Carbon Emissions of Big Tech

Location	Carbon Emissions	%	Companies	%
United States	58,818,872	46.1	24	48
South Korea	27,808,465	21.8	2	4
Taiwan	17,902,939	14.0	3	6
China	12,166,582	9.5	6	12
Japan	5,735,738	4.5	4	8
Switzerland	1,315,338	1.0	2	4
Germany	1,201,678	0.9	2	4
Netherlands	1,065,634	0.8	2	4
France	554,619	0.4	1	2
Finland	501,600	0.4	1	2
Argentina	355,064	0.3	1	2
Singapore	148,347	0.1	1	2
Sweden	117,000	0.1	1	2
TOTAL	127,691,876	100	50	100
Global North	*115,170,230*	*90.2*	*43*	*86*
Global South	*12,521,646*	*9.8*	*7*	*14*

Author's table and calculations. Source for data: ElectronicsHub, 2023.[60]

Taken as a percentage of global carbon emissions, which is currently 32.7 billion metric tons per year, the top 50 corporations sampled comprise about 0.34% of the global total. *ElectronicsHub* compiled data from ESG and CSR reports "to find the total of direct *and indirect* carbon emissions" for the 100 companies in the database. Here the devil is in the details. The standard framework for company emissions reports is called "emissions scopes." The terms Scope 1, 2, and 3 cover sources of emissions. *Scope 1* emissions come from sources that are directly controlled by the company, such as factory fumes. *Scope 2* accounts for indirect emissions from energy, e.g., if a company buys electricity from the local supplier. *Scope 3* accounts for indirect emissions from sources not owned or directly controlled by the company, but related to their activity (e.g., along the supply chain). The United Nations Global Compact finds that Scope 3 emissions constitute more than 70% of most companies' emissions, while the nonprofit CDP put it at 75%.[61]

A 2022 report found that Big Tech giants are not committed to reducing their full value-chain emissions. Moreover, corporations are not adequately disclosing the carbon footprints of their supply chains.[62] A study sampling 56 major tech companies found more than half excluded emissions along the supply chain, amounting to a carbon footprint about the same as Australia's. Moreover, companies like Apple and Microsoft claim they will be "carbon-neutral" across their entire supply chain by 2030, but they will substantially depend upon negative emissions offsets that we've seen are unreliable.[63]

As we can see, the United States emits almost half the total carbon of the top 50 tech corporations culled from company reports. The North emits about 90%, and the South about 10%.[64]

There is only so much more carbon humans can emit before triggering catastrophic tipping points. We've already spent four fifths of the *carbon budget* that would keep us under the 1.5°C limit. From this perspective, we're still "overspending," although the "we" here doesn't refer to the victims in the South, but the neocolonial perpetrators in the North.

The Paris Agreement stipulates that countries have *shared and differentiated responsibilities* to mitigate the climate crisis. This means that the duties of countries to take climate action vary by national circumstances. However, the North, led by the United States, refuse to acknowledge their historical climate debt.

In a just and sane world, the US would make deeper cuts than it pledged under the Paris Agreement. Instead, even though it's the world's leading historical glutton, the US does the opposite—it tries to maximize its own growth, consumption, and global share of the economy while falling short on its emissions reductions. A 2020 report by the US Climate Action Network argued that the US should reduce its emissions to 195% below its 2005 levels, reflecting a fair share range of 173–229%. The range calculated "reflect[s] the perspective that [it is] appropriate not to include the income and emissions of the 'relatively poor' in the assessment of their countries' Capacity and Responsibility."[65]

Moreover, the tone for the rest of the world is set at the top: if the US refuses to make drastic cuts, and instead continues to burn fossil fuels, the rest of the world will have a harder time competing in the global market. The damages wrought by climate change hit the Global South the hardest, despite the fact that the South has done almost nothing to create climate change.

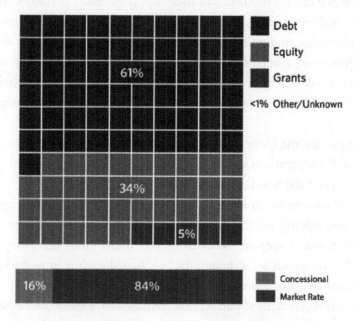

Figure 3.2 Climate financing: debt, grants, and loans (courtesy of Climate Policy Initiative, © 2022)

Source: Goswami and Rao, 2023.[66]

Instead of paying out reparations to the South for damages created by the US and Europe, they mostly offer climate *loans*, adding to the already-odious debt the South owes to the North. According to the Centre for Science and Environment, from 2011–2020, only 16% ($468.5 billion) of total climate financed is "concessional"—meaning in the form of low-interest loans or grants (free money).[67] Meanwhile, Oxfam International has stated the wealthy G7 countries (Canada, France, Germany, Italy, Japan, the UK, the US, and the EU) owe the low- and middle-income countries $13 trillion in unpaid aid and funding for climate action. "It's the rich world that owes the Global South: the aid they promised decades ago but never gave, the huge costs from climate damage caused by their reckless burning of fossil fuels, the immense wealth built on colonialism and slavery," Oxfam said.[68] At the 2023 UN COP28 summit, the US pledged just $3 billion to support climate action in developing countries, about 20% the size of its $14.5 billion aid package to support Israel's military bombardment of Gaza a month prior. Scholars estimate that on the current trajectory, the Global North would owe the Global South $192 trillion for environmental damages even if they *adhere to* "net zero" pledges to decarbonize by 2050.[69]

When Representative Brian Mast (R-FL) asked Biden's then-climate envoy, John Kerry, if the US would pay reparations to countries suffering floods, storms, and other climate-related catastrophes, Kerry said, "No, under no circumstances." America's selfish, rapacious cruelty has no boundaries.[70]

ECOLOGICAL DEBT

From a degrowth standpoint, carbon debt is a critical topic, but it's heavily complicated by broader considerations of aggregate resource use. As we've seen, degrowth is not only necessary to keep warming under the 1.5°C "safe" level, it's essential to keep us from destroying biodiversity. This means that building a sustainable, resilient global economy requires us to reduce and cap aggregate resource use.

The rich countries didn't get rich simply by building their societies using fossil fuels. They ransacked the rest of the world's material resources. A 2022 study found that between 1960 and 2018, the Global North appropriated $62 trillion from the Global South—a plunder of wicked proportions. Even worse, that amount increases to $152 trillion when considering lost growth. During the past year alone, the authors found that $2.2 trillion was appropriated—"enough to end extreme poverty 15 times over."[71] Though primarily appropriated by the Global North's rich, those resources have also been used to build the high-quality infrastructure that neighborhoods and communities enjoy.

From a moral perspective, the North owes massive reparations to the South, independent of an environmental context. But from an ecological perspective, large-scale reparations are *required*. Because we need to reduce and cap aggregate material resource use, the *only* way to fix this problem without locking the world's people into miserable poverty is to massively redistribute resources from North to South. This is where the second aspect of degrowth enters the picture. In addition to a carbon debt, there is a broader *ecological* debt owed to the Global South. And because capitalism has also concentrated resources everywhere, massive resource redistribution must occur *within* all countries, including the Global South.

Simply put, ecological debt is the debt owed to others who have consumed more of their fair share of the Earth's finite resources. As Andrew Simms notes in *Ecological Debt: Global Warming and the Wealth of Nations*, the concept was hinted at in the nineteenth century, when British imperialists realized their standard of living was predicated on draining the resources of their colonial subjects. But its contemporary origins as an explicit concept traces back to a 1992 report by South American academics called *Our Common Agenda*. Due to the plunder of finite resources which powered Northern industrialization, they argued, "the industrialised countries have incurred an ecological debt with the world."[72]

A 2022 study published in *The Lancet Planetary Health* quantified national responsibility for a related concept, *ecological breakdown*, based on a fair-shares assessment for resource use over the past half-century—the time period for which there's been a massive acceleration of global resource extraction and overshoot. Fair shares were calculated by combining the national share of resource use, 1970–2017, and the national share falling within safe planetary boundaries. National responsibility, then, is the sum of national overshoot divided by the sum of global overshoot during that period. The authors found the following:

> High-income nations are responsible for 74% of global excess material use, driven primarily by the USA (27%) and the EU-28 high-income countries (25%). China is responsible for 15% of global excess material use, and the rest of the Global South (i.e., the low-income and middle-income countries of Latin America and the Caribbean, Africa, the Middle East, and Asia) is responsible for only 8%. Overshoot in higher-income nations is driven disproportionately by the use of abiotic materials, whereas in lower-income nations it is driven disproportionately by the use of biomass ... high-income nations are the primary drivers of global ecological breakdown and they need to urgently reduce their resource use to fair and sustainable levels. Achieving sufficient reductions will likely require high-income nations to adopt transformative post-growth and degrowth approaches.[73]

82

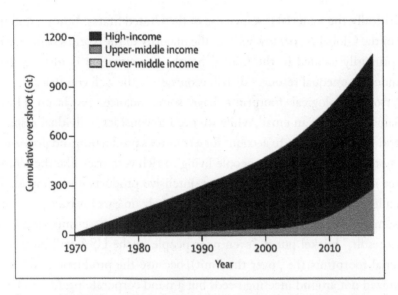

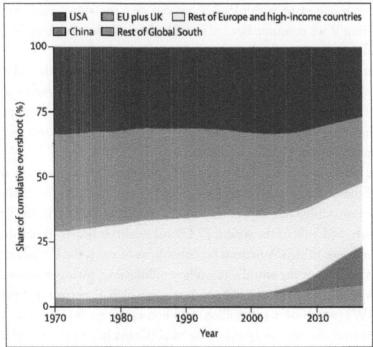

Figure 3.3   National responsibility for ecological breakdown:
a fair-shares assessment of resource use, 1970–2017
(courtesy of Jason Hickel)

Source: Hickel et al., 2022.[74]

83

Critically, the material resource use of the United States, Europe, and the rest of the Global North towers over the majority of the world's people, who are primarily located in the Global South. The situation is further compounded by unequal resource distribution *within* the rich countries.

Personal ecological footprints have some nuance. As Jason Hickel explained to me in an email, while we need to consider individual resource footprints, we also have to account for a country's production and provisioning systems. This is because people living in rich countries like the United States may have to consume resource-intensive products and services, for no fault of their own. For example, they may rely on cars for transportation, consume products with planned obsolescence, or purchase imported food. "As a result," Hickel put it, "even poor people in the USA will have high material footprints (i.e., over the limit), because the production system is organized not around meeting needs but around corporate profits."[75] Thus, when each one of us is thinking about our own individual consumption, wondering if we consume beyond our fair share, we have to keep in mind the constraints of our local economy.

That said, we still have to account for national, North–South, and class-based shares of consumption. The United States, for example, accounts for 27% of the world's ecological overshoot. Yet those resources are captured by ruling-class elites, who consume an over-the-top, "how can this be real?" portion of the world's finite resources.

The US houses just 4% of the world's population, but possesses about 45% of the world's gross financial assets and 31% of the world's wealth. (By comparison, China has 18% of the world's people, holds 14% of the financial assets, and 19% of the wealth.)[76] Global wealth is heavily concentrated into the hands of rich American households: as of 2023, the US is home to over 22 million of the world's 59 million millionaires, giving it 38% of the world's total.[77] The US also has 50.1% of ultra-high-net-worth individuals (UHNW) (worth over $50 million) and houses the most billionaires (735 of 2,630), accounting for 27.9% of the total (China has 13.5% of UHNWs and 18.8% of the billionaires).[78]

As one can imagine, elite consumption is a major driver of planetary breakdown. One study found that by 2050, direct energy consumption by the world's millionaires (measured in US dollars) will deplete 72% of the remaining carbon budget, which is, of course, unsustainable.[79] Moreover,

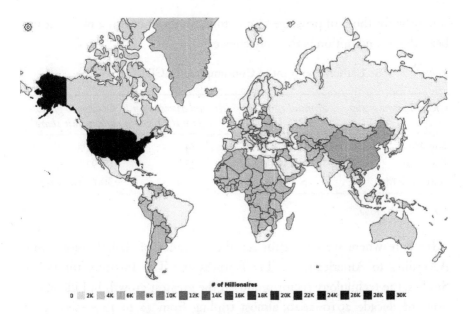

# of Millionaires

0 | 2K | 4K | 6K | 8K | 10K | 12K | 14K | 16K | 18K | 20K | 22K | 24K | 26K | 28K | 30K

Figure 3.4   Millionaires by country (courtesy of Shane Fulmer,
World Population Review https://worldpopulationreview.com)

Source: World Population Review, 2023.[80]

elite accountability goes much beyond personal consumption. As Oxfam observes, "unlike ordinary people, 50% to 70% of their emissions result from their investments." The organization's analysis of the investments of 125 of the world's richest billionaires found that "on average they are emitting 3 million tonnes a year, more than a million times the average for someone in the bottom 90% of humanity."[81] And even beyond elite consumption, in a fair share scenario, Westernized middle classes would have to slash their carbon emissions by 90% by 2030 so that the global poor can consume their fair share.

But when we go beyond carbon emissions and account for aggregate resource use, the matter is *much* worse. Let's do the math.

Because the total ecological footprint is too high, aggregate worldwide material use must be reduced and capped. Thus, living within planetary boundaries leaves us with two choices, noted earlier. One, we could keep the global poor locked into miserable conditions of poverty for eternity so that those who consume beyond their fair share can continue to enjoy their present standard of living. Or two, we could radically redistribute wealth and income, so that the global poor can enjoy a decent life. However painful it may be for those of privilege to confront, for anyone with a moral heartbeat, the second option is the only choice.

Table 3.4 The Carbon Footprint of Consumption by Class

Global income group	Annual earnings (2015 USD)	Annual average per capita tCO2e	Change to get to carbon "fair share"
Top 1%	> $109,000	74	97% cut
Top 10%	> $38,00	23	91% cut
Bottom 50%	> $6,000	0.7	300% increase

Source: Bhalla, 2021.[82]

It's here where we can again see the relevance of digital colonialism. According to Americans for Tax Fairness and The Institute for Policy Studies, the technology sector produced the greatest growth in billionaires over the decade 2010–2020, almost tripling from 42 to 124—second to financial billionaires (170), many of whom are of course heavily invested in the tech sector. In 2023, 69 members (17.3%) of the Forbes 400 wealthiest people in the US generated their fortunes from tech—the highest of any sector.[83] As of December 2023, eight of the top ten richest people in the world were American tech oligarchs, with a combined wealth of $1.126 trillion, as seen in Table 3.5.

Table 3.5 The Ten Richest Individuals in the World by Net Worth

Rank	Name	Net worth	Source	Country
1	Elon Musk	$245.3 B	Tesla, SpaceX	USA
2	Bernard Arnault & family	$189.7 B	LVMH	France
3	Jeff Bezos	$168.4 B	Amazon	USA
4	Larry Ellison	$146.5 B	Oracle	USA
5	Warren Buffet	$119.3 B	Berkshire Hathaway	USA
6	Bill Gates	$117.6 B	Microsoft	USA
7	Mark Zuckerberg	$115.9 B	Meta/Facebook	USA
8	Steve Ballmer	$112.8 B	Microsoft ·	USA
9	Larry Page	$111.7 B	Google	USA
10	Sergey Brin	$107.3 B	Google	USA
TOTAL (USA)		**$1244.8 B**	—	**USA**

Source: Author's table and calculations. Forbes, 2023.[84]

Since their scale of wealth is hard to fathom, documentary maker Joseph Pisente of *Real Life Lore* created a short film breaking down how we might think about the wealth of Jeff Bezos. At the time of the film (2021), Bezos possessed $204.6 billion. Consider the following:

- If we take Haiti, Madagascar, Mozambique, Malawi, Zambia, the Democratic Republic of the Congo, the Republic of the Congo, Burundi, Uganda, the Central African Republic, Cameroon, Djibouti, Sudan, Chad, Niger, Benin, Togo, Burkina Faso, Mali, Mauritania, Liberia, Sierra Leon, Guinea, Guinea-Bissau, The Gambia, Syria, Afghanistan, and Ukraine—nearly 270 million adults representing 3.5% of the human population—Jeff Bezos, a single man, has more wealth than every single person living in all these countries have combined.
- If you were immortal and had a job that paid you $8,000 per hour every single day that you were alive, if you first got the job at the time of the birth of Christ, and worked continuously, making $8,000 an hour every single hour that has ever happened since then, across more than 2,000 years of history, you still would not have anywhere near close to enough wealth as Jeff Bezos has.

Figure 3.5   The grotesque wealth of Jeff Bezos

In 2020, Jeff Bezos's net worth was equivalent to all the adults living in these countries. Source: Real Life Lore, 2020.[85]

- Jeff Bezos's wealth increased by $13 billion in a single day, more than the entire GDP of Madagascar, a country of over 26 million people. Bezos's $204.6 billion is more than the GDP of Indonesia, a country of 267 million people.
- The average American worker's salary is $49,764 per year. They would have to work for 4,111,405 years to earn as much as Jeff Bezos.
- When Bezos increased his net worth of $70 billion in a single year (2019–2020), he earned $9 million an hour, $146,000 per minute, and $2,489 every second.
- During that year, in just nine minutes, Bezos accumulated more than the average college-educated American woman in her entire lifetime. In 5.5 hours, he accumulated more than the entire net worth of David Solomon, the CEO of Goldman Sachs. Within eight hours, he accumulated more than the entire GDP of the island of Tuvalu. By the end of the first day, he surpassed the net wealth of Beyonce, and by the end of the week, he accumulated more than the entire annual profits of Pizza Hut, Taco Bell, KFC, and Wing Street—all combined. Within two months, he accumulated the net wealth of Zimbabwe's GDP, a country with 16 million people.[86]

The statistics are so outlandish that they almost take on a cartoonish "fun facts" tone. But it's worth reminding ourselves that this neocolonial wealth concentration is materialized through extreme forms of violence and appropriation impacting billions of people and the environment.

Of course, the tech moguls don't use their billions to purchase millions of cars, houses, or shoes. Much of their wealth takes the form of company shares and other property. Yet they do heavily over-consume at a personal level: a study of billionaires found they have carbon footprints thousands of times greater than average citizens, even in rich countries.[87]

More importantly, the rich profit from the ownership of the means of production and assets, oversee the capitalist machinery that produces these outcomes, and possesses enormous political and social power to keep the system intact. Despite the outrageous spectacle of ultra-rich executives, it's worth stressing that these are institutional problems rather than the problems of ultra-wealthy celebrities. If one rich CEO resigns, another will step in as a replacement.

As of 2018, 69 of the 100 largest entities in the world were corporations—the rest were nation-states.[88] As we saw in Chapter 1, many of the tech giants have more wealth than the GDP of entire countries. We arrived at that conclusion by comparing market cap (akin to the *total value* of corporations) with annual GDP (how much a country produces in a single year). It would take South Africa, the richest country in Africa with a GDP of $419 billion, about 28 years to produce the $11.7 trillion accumulated to date by the top seven American tech giants (Apple, Microsoft, Alphabet/Google, Amazon, Nvidia, Meta/Facebook, Tesla). By the end of 2023, those "Magnificent Seven," as the American press calls them, made up 30% of the S&P 500 (an index of the top 500 corporations listed on US stock exchanges).[89]

The concentration of resources by corporate behemoths is also reflected in the paltry size of their workforce. In 2011, the world's 44 largest corporations totaled 11% of GDP, but accounted for just 0.4% of the world's economically active population. The digital sector appears to exacerbate this trend. For instance, at the end of 2023, Apple had a market cap of $2.974 trillion and employed 164,000 people, whereas General Motors had a market cap of $44.31 billion with a workforce of 167,000. Nvidia had a $1.555 trillion market cap and employed just 26,196 people.[90]

While the upper 1% appropriates the majority of the wealth, there is also a problem with the tech industry's average worker. From an ecological standpoint, Big Tech firms pay their coders and engineers well above the global fair share. According to press reports, average compensation at Google is just shy of $300,000, while high-end managers earn $500,000 to $1 million.[91] Microsoft pays close to $200,000, while Amazon just increased its based salary cap from $160,000 to $350,000. New artificial intelligence jobs at companies like Walmart and Netflix are paying out as much as $900,000 or higher.

These salary ranges extend beyond the familiar Big Tech giants. Research group Levels.fyi conducted a survey from many leading tech firms, revealing that in 2022, tech firms pay a median salary of around $180,000 to entry-level engineers and over $300,000 to engineering managers. Pay in US cities was considerably higher than non-Western ones—twice that of China and four times that of India, the only two Global South countries sampled.[92] Another survey, conducted by Stack Overflow, which includes a broader sample, finds similar results, with median American engineering salaries clustering around $140,000–220,000 compared to $15,000–42,000 in India.[93]

American tech giants are also poaching talent, what is sometimes called the "brain drain"—a further appropriation of resources from the South. Consider, for example, Andela, a US-headquartered corporation that provides a "job placement network" for African coders. Andela received (uncritical) media attention in 2016 when the Chan–Zuckerberg Initiative—the philanthrocapitalist foundation of Facebook Mark Zuckerberg and his wife, Priscilla Chan—poured $26 million into the company.[94]

These kinds of ventures are owned and controlled by elite capitalists. Consider Andela's co-founders:

- CEO Jeremy Johnson, a Princeton dropout, also co-founded 2U, which eventually acquired South Africa's most "successful" startup, GetSmarter, for $103 million. (GetSmarter was co-founded by two white entrepreneurs with privileged backgrounds, Sam and Rob Paddock.)
- Christina Sass, Andela's first COO and Ivy League alum, subsequently founded Dive In, a venture capital firm that advises tech founders and companies.
- Nigerian entrepreneur, Iyinoluwa Aboyeji, a Canada-educated and ex-Director, now works with multiple firms. Aboyeji proudly invests in Moove, Uber's exclusive fleet provider for Nigerians. Uber pays drivers about N60,000 ($63) per week and is subject to multiple nationwide worker strikes.[95]
- Nadayar Enegesi, a former Director, subsequently founded Eden Life, a Nigerian e-commerce platform profiting from gig worker exploitation.[96]
- Brice Nkengsa, a Canadian-educated ex-Director, is now an angel investor, as well as a software engineer for San Francisco software unicorn CircleCI.
- Ian Carnevale, a University of Toronto alumnus, is now founder and CEO of Volley, a JobTech company that uses AI to personalize emails.

In other words, these are Western or Western-educated elites that are exploiting Global South labor for personal gain. This pattern of tech "entrepreneurship" pervades the South.

In a 2014 unlisted promotional YouTube video, Andela spun its exploitative agenda as one benefiting the global poor. "If you believe that brilliance is evenly distributed but opportunity is not," CEO Jeremy Johnson said, "then you have to conclude that there are places [like Africa] where there are staggering numbers of extraordinarily bright people, who just don't have a path in the formal economy."[97] Enter Andela.

The company has four stages of recruitment. In the first and second, interested Africans take a home study curriculum with ten modules, and then a psychometric and technical test based on that curriculum. In the third, if they score highly, they are invited for interviews. Finally, those who make the cut are invited for a two-week boot camp. Sass remarked, "these young [Africans] travel sometimes two hours one way, to arrive at 7:30 am, for an *unpaid* two-week boot camp to learn intro coding programming skills."[98] After those two weeks, the highest-performing participants are asked to join Andela.

Johnson and his colleagues like to brag that Andela has received over 70,000 applications, but accepted just 0.7% into its company. The fellows are "the best example of the truth that brilliance is evenly distributed around the world," he puts it, making Andela "ten times more selective than Harvard."[99]

After six months of training, Andela recruits are paired up with American and other tech giants. In 2019, internal tensions inside the company spilled into the press, when the *BBC* falsely reported Andela's in-house developers make just one third of the salary their international clients pay Andela recruits. The ratio was actually *lower*. So low, in fact, that some Andela workers called their company "The Plantation." This led one employee to ask, "Why is it the private sector that needs to come in and innovate? Why can't schools, governments, etc., do that job?"[100]

Andela emphasizes its services to US tech behemoths.[101] For example, after Apple announced its new programming language, Swift, in 2014, Sass said proudly, "[Andela] could turn around, shift our training to say, "for the next three weeks, you're going to focus on nothing but this," and then we go to the global marketplace and say, "we now have 50 Swift developers.""

Andela has also launched numerous partnerships and projects with foreign tech giants. Its clients include Amazon, Salesforce, Facebook, Google, Microsoft, IBM, Udacity, and the UK's BBC, along with other Fortune 500 firms and Silicon Valley startups. Carnevale said their goal is "to bridge the digital divide between the US and African tech sectors."[102]

In 2019, when *Forbes* asked Sass if her company offers its workers to foreign firms at a discount, Sass responded, "The cost of an Andela worker may be cheaper than a top-level developer in San Francisco. But that's not the reason to hire our people. They should look at our people through the lens of diversity."[103] Thus it's plausible that Andela workers are paid less because they live in Africa. Moreover, we don't have good data about fulltime employment, job security, and earnings disparities, so that we can evaluate earnings from an environmental and social justice perspective. I've emailed the company and called their New York offices for an interview, but have never received a response.

Over the past few years, Andela has spread its tentacles. It expanded partnerships with countries like Egypt and Rwanda to 37 other countries and now features developers sourced from Africa, Asia, Latin America, North America, and Europe. It also acquired technical skills assessment and certification platform Qualified, giving it access to 3.6 million engineering users, as well as the recruitment platform Casana.

Andela is a vulture capitalist firm, primarily backed by US investors, founded by a mix of Western white neocolonizers and African comprador capitalists to exploit African poverty. Its model is to take a bunch of money from rich Americans, set up shop in Africa, invite tens of thousands of people to train for no pay, select the elite tiny percentage of them, put them to work on projects for their colonial masters that dominate their digital economy and destroy their environment, and then publish glossy materials and promotional videos with testimony from black faces to tell the world they're saving the Africans. With no sense of shame, Sass says Andela's name is inspired by Nelson Mandela.

Andela may be the largest "education and training" firm servicing Big Tech, but there are countless others sprouting up across the Global South. Almost nobody pays attention.

* * *

If we're to resolve the environmental crisis, we have to share equally what we produce in harmony with nature. We cannot have an economy that concentrates wealth. The digital economy drives an ecologically unequal exchange and division of labor that benefits American companies, whose rich owners and overpaid white-collar workers are consuming more than their fair share of the global wealth pie.

Before moving on, it's worth noting that digital colonialism is a global phenomenon which impacts every society, including the super-poor countries that have almost no access to digital tech. I once interviewed someone from Madagascar involved in a computer-based education pilot project, and she told me that most of the country has limited or no connection to the internet. With a population of about 30 million, its per capita GDP is just $500 per person. Madagascar depends on agriculture, mining, and clothing production to produce its livelihood. Yet the country is so poor in part because its raw materials extraction cannot command high prices in the global market. Through the ownership of advanced technology and knowledge in combination with market mechanisms and government policies like those described in Chapter 1, the rich countries monopolize products and services everybody needs, but hardly anybody else can supply. As economist Ha-Joon Chang puts it, doing "the more difficult things" that others cannot easily do—such as producing a semiconductor or inventing a medicine—brings you "higher incomes."[104]

That the US happens to own and control the digital economy is not an arbitrary coincidence, as if they're like Global South countries who happen to export the world's coffee because have the climate required to grow it. The Americans have taken a hold of—and maintain hegemony over—the digital economy because it is enormously lucrative for American corporations. As we will see in later chapters, it is also a multifaceted source of power, conferring its owners political and social power in addition to unfathomable riches.

But before we address that, we need to dig deeper into the relationship between the digital economy and the environment. The next two chapters will detail the climate and ecological impact of various industries, from cloud computing and semiconductors to digital agriculture and fast fashion. After that, we'll look at broader concerns about technologies of violence and their relationship to environmental justice.

93

4
Cloud Colonialism

The digital world may seem intangible, a "virtual" universe with little relationship to material reality, as invisible to us as the carbon accumulating in the atmosphere. We've seen, however, that this is an illusion. The digital economy is actually central to the environmental crisis. It drives rapacious growth and concentrates wealth, income, and power at precisely the time we need to create genuine equality.

As is always the case, harms are the worst in the Global South, thanks to the North–South divide deepened through the process of digital colonialism. In this chapter, we'll take a look at the physical toll of the digital economy on the environment from a digital degrowth perspective. Here we'll start with a concrete example on the ground—Amazon's colonial headquarters in Cape Town, South Africa—before moving on to cloud computing, data centers, and artificial intelligence. In the following chapter, we'll expand this to other topics, such as agriculture and digital consumerism.

EAST INDIA COMPANIES

In February 1510, three Portuguese ships, led by Francisco de Almeida, stopped in Table Bay (located in present-day Cape Town) for fresh water on their journey back to Portugal. Almeida and his men traded iron for cattle with the indigenous !Urill'aekua Khoikhoi (Goringhaiqua) on friendly terms. It wouldn't last long. Crew members visited the Khoikhoi at the modern-day suburb of Observatory, but were chased out after attempting to steal cattle. One hundred and fifty armed men returned, but were defeated at what became known as the Battle of Salt River. The Khoi victory stopped the Portuguese from creating a slave colony in present-day South Africa.

Unfortunately, indigenous South Africans weren't in the clear. On April 6, 1652, the Europeans returned. This time, they landed by ship on the shores of present-day Cape Town. Their leader, Jan van Riebeeck, commanded a group of 82 men and eight women to build a refreshment station for the Dutch East India Company (VOC). The station provided fresh water, vegetables, fruit, meat, and medical assistance to the VOC's trading ships passing along the southern tip of Africa for their colonial expeditions in the "East Indies" (East Asia). Early on, there were friendly relations with the two local indigenous groups, the Khoikhoi and the San, and trading commenced.

The VOC initially instructed Van Riebeeck not to colonize the area, but within five years, permits were issued allowing nine company servants (who became known as Free Burghers) to farm along the Liesbeek River. Business opportunities arose from other ships passing by the Cape, and the Dutch settlers began seeking out more cattle and land. Just seven years into their arrival, with Dutch farmers encroaching on their land and cattle, the first Khoikhoi–Dutch war broke out.

In his diary, Van Riebeeck described the minutes of a meeting between the Dutch and the Khoikhoi leaders as follows:

They spoke for a long time about our taking every day for our own use more of the land which had belonged to them from all ages and on which they were accustomed to pasture their cattle. They also ask whether if they were to come to Holland, they would be permitted to act in a similar manner, saying, "it would not matter if you stayed at the fort, but you come into the interior, selecting the best land for yourselves and never once asking whether we like it, or whether it will put us to any inconvenience."

[The Khoikhoi] therefore insisted very strenuously that they again be allowed free access to the pasture. They objected that there was enough grass for both their cattle and ours. "Are we not right therefore to prevent you from getting any more cattle? For if you get many cattle, you come and occupy our pasture with them, and then say the land is not wide enough for us both? Who then with the greatest degree of justice should give way: the natural owner or the foreign invader?"

They insisted so much on this point that we had told them that they had now lost that land in war, and therefore could not expect to get it back. It was our intention to keep it.[1]

The Dutch were victorious, and the event marked the beginning of 180 years of violent conquest and genocide spanning 16 separate Khoi and San wars of liberation and resistance. The Cape Colony became a critical site of European colonialism at the Southern tip of South Africa.

As historian Kenneth Vickery notes, the Khoi and San were either pushed outside Dutch settlements or reduced to a servile working class. A three-tiered labor system emerged. The VOC company and its officials were at the top, the predominantly Dutch-descended settlers in the middle, and a laboring class at the bottom, itself partitioned between indigenous laborers and imported slaves. The European colonizers were not only exploitative of humans, they ravaged nature, wiping out indigenous animals like the blue buck, the quagga, and the cape lion.

Members of the Khoi and San, sometimes called Khoisan, have been violently reduced to about 1% of the South African population. Almost five centuries after European arrival, struggles continue—this time with a different foreign power: Amazon.

"SAME COLONISTS, DIFFERENT SHIPS"

Many years ago, at the start of the twentieth century, the land where the indigenous Khoisan thwarted the Portuguese and resisted colonization was appropriated by white-owned South African Railways. The area was eventually used for welfare programs benefiting poor whites clustering around the city, while blacks were pushed further to the outskirts of Cape Town. During this time period, a key actor in our story, the River Club, was born.

On May 19, 2015, the sacred land, which indigenous people call Igamirodi!khaes, was sold by the state-owned railway Transnet to private real estate owners, Liesbeek Leisure Properties (LLP). Obtained well below the market price of 12 million Rand (about $640,000), within months, it was resold to Liesbeek Leisure Property Trust (LLPT) for R100 million ($5.3 million). Something was amiss.

Until the time of sale, the land was zoned as an Open Space in recognition of its value to indigenous cultural heritage and environmental sensitivity. But the LLPT, which operates the River Club, began development in 2016, and it put in an application to rezone it for "mixed-use development" in 2018. Members of First Nations (indigenous) and environmental groups raised objections. What followed unleashed a nationwide controversy over indigenous heritage, environmental sustainability, and American tech colonization.

The River Club is part of a broader property, the Two Rivers Urban Park (TRUP)—one of Cape Town's largest "urban green lungs"—located within Observatory, now a Cape Town suburb. The land is situated at the conflu-

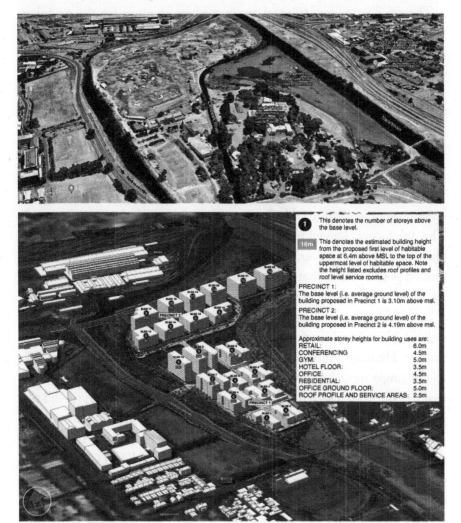

Figure 4.1   Amazon's development project on indigenous land in Cape Town

Snapshots of the River Club. Top image: Google Earth.
Bottom image: Royal Observatory Cape via Facebook.[2]

ence of the Liesbeek and Black Rivers, and serves as a vital floodplain that absorbs the heavy winter rains periodically flooding the area. Those opposing the construction discovered documents on a website of the project's consultants slating Amazon as a future tenant. According to Leslie London, a professor at the University of Cape Town investigating the proposal, the developers said in their court papers that the project would be doomed if Amazon pulled out.

The city's municipal tribunal announced its approval for the rezoning, and the next day the press announced Amazon would be establishing an African headquarters in Cape Town. The issue was now in the national spotlight.

A large network of indigenous organizations, environmentalists, and civic organizations united to oppose the construction. The City of Cape Town's own Environmental Management Department opposed the authorization of the project, on grounds that preservation of the land would mitigate flooding and preserve biodiversity (e.g., wetland habitats). The Department issued an appeal finding "13 categories of irregularities, inconsistencies and misinformation relating to heritage, environment and planning matters."[3] The developers planned to lift the area six meters so it could infill the flat plain and Liesbeek River, turning it into a stormwater swale—an underground pool of water that will well up when it rains. They would then lay 150,000 square meters of concrete on top.

In addition to environmental risks, there was the problem of erasing indigenous cultural heritage. The heritage authority for the approval process, Heritage Western Cape, said the site "could be regarded as one of the single most historically significant sites in the country."[4] It found that transforming a sacred indigenous site into a commercial center did not comport with the law. In an episode of my podcast, *Tech Empire*, Tauriq Jenkins, the High Commissioner and spokesperson for the Goringhaicona Khoi Khoin Indigenous Traditional Council (GKKITC) and Chair of the A|Xarra Restorative Justice Forum at the University of Cape Town, explained the issue. The heritage site is where the "original sin" happened, Jenkins said. "In terms of our spiritual sense of restoration, of restorative justice, this is our epicenter, this is our ground zero precinct."[5]

The area is more than a historical site recognizing genocide, resistance, and restoration for First Nations (indigenous people). Prior to being closed off by developers, indigenous ceremonies were still being performed at the site. There is a deep spiritual connection to the land, a remaining connection to the past in a region paved over by colonizers and neo-apartheid "developers." Nadine Dirks, a campaign organizer for the Liesbeek Action Campaign, explained that this is a place where unions (marriage) took place and people played under the stars. "To strip away that part of the land and look at it as just an empty lot or a place that needs development ignores all of us [indigenous persons] in this in the city and in this country who are still very much alive and have no say in what happens in this land," she said. The rivers are also considered sacred. "To redirect a sacred river, to infill a sacred river is deeply insensitive. It's a violation also to the understanding of the symbiotic relationship that the indigenous communities have with the river, the embankments, and the stars," Jenkins added.[6]

A series of legal battles ensued. The City of Cape Town, the Department of Public Works and Transportation, and the Department of Environmental Affairs and Development Planning sided with the landowners in their legal battles. For Amazon's proponents, the gloves came off.

Emails purporting to be from the indigenous A|Xarra Forum were distributed from a false email address, defaming leaders of the Khoi opposition. Labels like "descendants of colonialists," "snake oil salesmen," "hypocrite," "collaborator," and "conmen" (among others) were levied at those opposing the construction, with warnings that they will be held "accountable." The A|Xarra Forum denounced the emails, which were fake. Opponents of the developers claim the metadata—information about the senders embedded within the emails—suggests they were authored by one of the consultants working on behalf of the development project.[7]

Alongside smear campaigns, a divide-and-conquer campaign was launched when a pro-development "First Nations Collective" set to benefit from the Amazon project appeared out of nowhere. "We had never heard of this entity called a First Nations [Collective]," Jenkins remarked. If you're in places "like the United States," you hear the term and go, "wow this is the body that is representing everything, First Nation, San and Khoi ... well, that's absolutely not the case," he added.[8]

In 2022, the "Collective" assaulted Chief Aùtshumao! Francisco MacKenzie at a protest against the project and verbally attacked Jenkins, who eventually became the subject of a vicious smear campaign. That March, the Western Cape High Court issued an interdict to halt construction on grounds that "meaningful consultation" with Khoi and San First Nations People was needed, in addition to a review of environmental land use authorizations.

The developers continued building, despite the interdict. Its lawyers then launched an appeal alleging that Jenkins falsely claimed to represent the GKKITC which, along with the Observatory Civic Association (OCA), represented 22 San and Khoi groups. The Supreme Court of Appeals rescinded the interdict in November on grounds that it was obtained through "fraud." Many of the big South African media outlets ran with the story, reducing the struggle to one man (Jenkins) alongside a barrage of pro-Amazon propaganda.

Jenkins was denied an opportunity to defend himself in court and left saddled with legal fees. The OCA, drained of funds, settled in June 2023 in exchange for waiving most of their legal costs. "The city is pleased with this outcome and the clear message it conveys—that the city will always vigorously defend planning decisions taken correctly, and will act to protect Cape Town's reputation as a leading global investment destination," said Mayor Geordin Hill-Lewis.[9]

But the story wasn't over. The next month, four whistleblowers submitted affidavits—including WhatsApp screenshots—demonstrating that the allegations against Jenkins were false. According to one whistle-blower, the pro-Amazon "First Nations Collective" introduced one of the (then pro-Amazon) indigenous actors, ex-GKKITC member Ebrahim Abrahams, to the LLPT's Jody Aufrichtig (director) and Mark Fyfe. Over lunch, Abrahams and the developers came up with a plan to defame Jenkins and undermine the GKKITC. Put another way, Abrahams, a former member of Jenkins's group *resisting* the Amazon project, joined forces with a newly formed *pro-Amazon* group (called "Krotoa of the Goringhaicona"), which served as a front organization collaborating with the property owners (LLPT) striking it rich from the Amazon deal.

Joined by LLPT attorney, Tim Dunn—who falsely claimed he received a Master's degree in law and stands accused of representing Cape Town's Willow Arts Collective while holding a conflict of interest with other clients[10]—Abrahams met with the group he "founded the (Krotoa of the Goringhaicona)." Together, they drew up affidavits pretending to be leaders of Jenkins's organization, the GKKITC. In those documents, presented to the Cape Town High Court, they claimed to have held a meeting where they revoked Jenkins's authority and withdrew objections to the Amazon-River Club project. The judges bought the story and gave the green light to developers. Eight months later, in July 2023, Abrahams says he blew the whistle because he was sick of the lies. He claims the developers promised each of the financially vulnerable indigenous group members R2 million (over $100,000) and a home, but they were never paid. The documents have been published in the press.[11]

At the time of writing, lawyers acting for Jenkins, on behalf of the GKKITC, are asking the Western Cape High Court to rescind the ruling that deemed him illegitimate and institute a case against the development. Meanwhile, the Amazon construction project continues. If it is completed, the heritage site will be paved over for Amazon's new Africa headquarters building. Two other buildings will be used for its cloud computing business, Amazon Web Services (AWS), ostensibly part of its R30 billion ($1.6 billion) investment in AWS South Africa. Another building will house a call center; the company's South African call center workers are paid just R67.45 ($3.50) per hour. Those low-income workers will likely need to spend as much as 40% of their income to travel to work. Meanwhile, the LLPT is building luxury housing on the premises for those who have the money. In other words, the project reinforces apartheid residential segregation.[12]

Added to this, Amazon is now set to launch its e-commerce platform in South Africa. The company squeezes local sellers who use its marketplace services, taking a significant cut of their profits, while self-preferencing its own products. It is already eating into the revenue of South African e-commerce platforms, which will almost certainly intensify with the construction of the new headquarters. Amazon is also sucking up renewable energy, while poor communities go without electricity. The company opposes union drives, and it surveils its delivery and warehouse workers with micro-managed productivity quotas. There are other abuses it will likely be involved in.[13]

The arrangement will reproduce the three-tier labor system originally established by the Dutch settlers. At the top, the foreign executives, investors, and local landowners will rake in the lion's share of the revenues and profits. In the middle, Amazon will poach limited (probably mostly white) skilled engineers and deepen the country's dependency on its wide-reaching product lines. At the bottom, black laborers will internally migrate on a daily basis to slave away at the phones and other menial tasks in return for scraps.

Amazon's intrusion into Cape Town epitomizes how digital colonialism evolves from history, connecting to indigenous, environmental, and national concerns for autonomy, liberation, and ecological harmony. The old colonial themes of lawfare, exploitation, colonization, divide-and-conquer, white supremacy, and ecocide have been upgraded for the twenty-first century. As Jenkins warns:

> the irony of having the world's largest company and the world's richest man wanting to put a price on something that is so sacred to all of us means that it opens up a very dangerous precedent for all First Nations and indigenous groups around the world, in Africa, and indigenous communities around here, because it means that what is sacred will be commodified.[14]

Indigenous and environmental opposition groups occasionally made disparaging remarks about Amazon's exploitative business model, but they never demanded Amazon leave South Africa altogether. They simply asked the company to find another location. Even such a trivial inconvenience was too much to ask for Amazon, which, in a show of power, likely did not want to set a precedent where it capitulates to activist demands. London, Jenkins, and countless others have reached out to Amazon to voice questions and concerns. Amazon remains silent.

THE BIG DATA–AI–CLOUD NEXUS

South Africa was first colonized by the Dutch, then the English, to secure hegemony over the naval passageway to India. Over time, tensions rose within Britain, whose costly and violent venture was lacking any clear rationale. But then diamonds were discovered in present-day Kimberley (1867), followed by gold in present-day Johannesburg (1886). A bloody war between the British and the Dutch-descended "Afrikaners" for South African land soon commenced.

102

Upon discovery of diamonds and gold, "diggers" rushed in, looking to strike it rich. The minerals at the surface were easy pickings. In a short time, heavy machinery was needed to dig deeper and specialized chemicals were required to break down and refine the minerals. Economies of scale (where more units of production can be produced with fewer input costs) led to the consolidation of land and ownership. It was impossible for a digger with a pick-and-shovel to compete against those with the engineers and machines. Concentrated wealth and power took over.

Today, cloud computing centers occupy a similar place in the digital ecosystem. As user experiences moved from isolated desktop "personal computers" to internet-connected devices, new facilities were built to provide data storage, online platforms, and computation. Clouds became centralized "brains" of the digital ecosystem. Expensive cloud centers, packed with highly specialized equipment, such as semiconductors, server racks, hard disk drives, and advanced cooling systems, are now critical to the digital economy. Computer engineers with deep knowledge of software and networking services build the most sophisticated software components to service clients.

American Big Tech giants, backed by rich investors, seized on the opportunity to build and take control of the cloud. Much like the 750+ US military bases on foreign soil, the Americans are constructing cloud centers—like Amazon's facilities in Cape Town—as sites of digital colonization throughout the world. Once these centers are built, they are owned by the imperial core. Companies migrate their services to the American cloud, while software engineers spend thousands of hours honing their skills on the cloud providers' software interfaces. This leaves countries outside the United States with two options: appropriate US property (the cloud centers) and face the wrath of American backlash, or become dependent upon their foreign masters. Elsewhere, I've dubbed this "infrastructure-as-debt."[15]

Big data is at the center of cloud computing. As we saw in Chapter 1, what is (misleadingly) called "artificial intelligence" relies upon gigantic sums of data fed to the machines so they can "analyze" and "generate" things for the human programmers. Because the "statistics-based" approach to AI makes heavy use of data and computer processing, it has a substantial environmental footprint. However, while a lot of data used for AI is stored and processed in clouds, the two don't always go hand-in-hand. For instance, smartphones utilize AI within the phone itself—e.g., to make your photos look better—without transmitting your data to the cloud. (This is called "edge" computing, where the "edge" is a standalone device like a phone, laptop, or CCTV camera.) Conversely, big data is often transmitted to or stored in a server farm somewhere, whether it utilizes AI or not. According to a leading market intelligence firm, International Data Corporation (IDC), only 20% of data center capacity is dedicated to artificial intelligence, and only 100,000 of the 13 million or so annual server sales (0.8%) are specialized for AI.[16]

Thus, these three elements—big data, AI, and the cloud—are distinct, but they often overlap.

There's growing attention to the carbon and ecological footprints of data centers (which include clouds as well as server farms that host data for companies) by the US-centered tech "left." Across the board, these intellectuals ignore the more general ecologically unequal exchange that takes place in the cloud computing economy. We can't emphasize this part enough, as there can be no such thing as "green" cloud corporations, for reasons discussed in the previous chapter (and further explained below). Ecologically unequal exchange is *central*. Moreover, much of the internet is now operated on the cloud, and so whoever owns the cloud has extraordinary power—an issue of American Empire that we'll return to in subsequent chapters. For now, let's review the core elements of big data, AI, and the cloud in terms of both ecologically unequal exchange (digital colonialism) and environmental footprints.

CLOUD COMPUTING: AN AMERICAN GRAVY TRAIN

Cloud computing emerged in the 2000s with the launch of Amazon Web Services. AWS offered a storage and computing platform so that companies wouldn't have to bother with developing and maintaining their data centers in-house. Crucially, the service is *scalable*: as companies need more storage or computing power—say, during the holiday season—they can purchase it without having to buy extra hardware that will sit idly after it is no longer needed (e.g., when the holiday season is over). Microsoft soon

104

followed with its Azure cloud platform, which helped keep its business relevant beyond the era of desktop computers.

Since that time, the American tech giants have dominated the global cloud computing market. The worldwide market share of the leading cloud infrastructure providers breaks down as follows:

Table 4.1   Top Cloud Computing Companies by Country

Country	Company/Product	%
USA	Amazon AWS	31
USA	Microsoft Azure	24
USA	Google Cloud	11
China	Alibaba Cloud	4
USA	Salesforce	3
USA	IBM Cloud	2
USA	Oracle	2
China	Tencent Cloud	2
TOTAL	—	**79**
USA	(6 companies, above)	73
China	(2 companies, above)	6
Other	—	21

Author's table and calculations. Data is for Q4 2023.
Source: Synergy Research Group via Statista, 2023.[17]

Just three American tech giants dominate the market: Amazon, Microsoft, and Google, with a combined 66% of the global market. China's Alibaba Cloud and Tencent Cloud are second, with 6%.

But the business from cloud computing (and data centers more generally) isn't restricted to the cloud owners. The facilities used to store and process data aren't empty warehouses: they are packed with equipment usually manufactured by other companies, including computer processors, server racks, hard drives, computer memory, and so on. Because these are collectively dominated by the US, the cloud is a gravy train for multiple American tech giants. Let's briefly review the stuff of the cloud.

Computer processors (CPUs) are used to crunch the data and run software powered by Amazon Web Services and Microsoft Azure. Intel and AMD, two US-based chip behemoths, take 91% of the data center CPU market.[18] Just 5% of the computer processors used in the cloud are sourced from Arm Holdings, a Japanese-owned chip company based in the UK.[19]

Another kind of computer processor, the Graphical Processing Unit (GPU), is heavily used to process data for artificial intelligence. According to a 2023 analysis, US tech giant Nvidia lays waste to the competition, providing 85% of AI workloads to the top six cloud providers and 95% of the market for GPUs used for AI.[20]

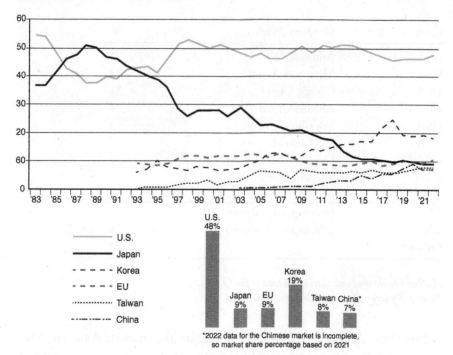

Figure 4.2   Semiconductor market share by country
(courtesy of *SIA Factbook 2023*)

Source: Semiconductor Association of America, 2023.[21]

As of 2022, America had 48% of the total semiconductor market, compared to China's 7%, primarily based on its role in assembly, packaging, and testing—the low-end part of the supply chain heavily concentrated in Asia.[22] China also produces some low-end chips.[23] The US took the reins from Japan in the 1990s, secured by the rise of the Intel-Microsoft alliance whereby Intel and Microsoft Windows—the desktop operating system that had over 90% market share—were designed to work together. (The alliance was so tight the press called them "Wintel.")

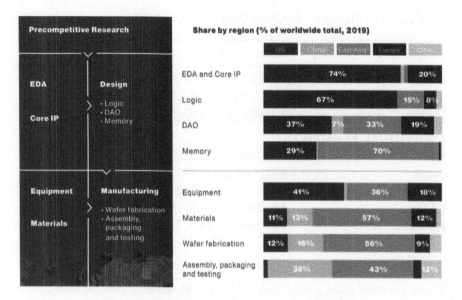

Figure 4.3   Semiconductor supply chain by country
(courtesy of "Strengthening the Global Semiconductor Supply Chain in an
Uncertain Era")

*Note: EDA = electronic design automation; DAO = discrete, analog, and other
(including optoelectronics and sensors). 1. Mainland China. 2. East Asia includes
South Korea, Japan, and Taiwan. Source: Varas et al., 2021.*[24]

Additionally, 90% of cloud storage drives—the devices used to store big data—are hard disk drives (HDD). Within the HDD market, two American companies, Seagate (43%) and Western Digital (37%), take 80% of the pie, followed by Japan's Toshiba (20%). Servers—the racks of machines inside the data centers—are also dominated by the United States. About 14 million units ship out every year, with about 40% sold to cloud providers. America's Hewlett Packard, Dell, and IBM take 36.3% of the global server market, followed by China's Inspur and Lenovo (16.4%).[25]

And finally, memory chips—the semiconductors that store very fast, short-term memory for computers, typically in the form of DRAM—are dominated by South Korea's Samsung and SK Hynix, which together take around 70% of the global DRAM market, followed by the US's Micron Group (typically over 20%).[26] (Finally, something the US doesn't dominate!)

Thus, we can summarize the industries we've been considering thus far:

Table 4.2   The Market Inside Cloud Computing Centers

Component	Revenue (2022)	Projections	Growth %
Semiconductor (all)	$592 billion	$1.884 trillion (2032)	12.3
Cloud (all)	$480 billion	$2.297 trillion (2032)	17
Hyperscale cloud	$80 billion	$935 (2032)	27.9
INDIVIDUAL ELEMENTS			
CPU	$106 billion	$185 billion (2032)	5.8
Server	$105 billion	$153 billion (2028)	3
Memory (DRAM)	$97 billion	$126 billion (2031)	3
GPU	$42 billion	$773 billion (2032)	33.8
Hard Disk Drives	$36.5 billion	$127 billion (2033)	12

Author's table.[27]

These are *total* sales, not *strictly* sales to data centers. Nevertheless, data centers (including cloud providers) are major purchasers of semiconductors and servers, and US-based corporations dominate sales in four of the five core components (CPUs, GPUs, HDDs, and servers).

Added to this, the data center market is increasingly concentrating into *hyperscale* clouds. A hyperscale cloud is a gigantic cloud center for enterprises built to scale service loads up and down, depending on the demand. It's estimated that there are over 900 hyperscale data centers in operation, with a market of $172 billion as of 2022.[28] By one estimate, Amazon takes 32% of the hyperscale market, followed by Microsoft (23%) and 10% for Google—a combined 74%. Of the remaining 26%, the companies "with the highest growth rates are Oracle, Snowflake, MongoDB, Huawei, and three Chinese telcos."[29]

Finally, we should note that major AI companies are working closely with the cloud giants. Microsoft owns 49% of OpenAI, the maker of ChatGPT, which runs on Microsoft's Azure cloud. Meanwhile, Amazon and Google have invested billions in the AI startup, Anthropic, which runs its operations on AWS and Google Cloud. This has triggered questions of anti-competitve conduct by regulators.

In sum, we can observe that the cloud and related industries are growing rapidly. The United States is *by far* the primary beneficiary of these trends. The cloud market, which was worth $109 billion in 2012,[30] has been growing by a factor of four every ten years. In addition to producing inequality and driving ecologically unequal exchange, the extent of its direct impact on the environment is a critical question.

We'll return to the latter issue below. For now, we should keep in mind that the carbon emissions of semiconductor production are skyrocketing and on track to overshoot Paris climate commitments.[31] While the production of AI *models* is not carbon-intensive, the mass production of GPUs by companies like Nvidia, as well as the resources to construct data centers, is.[32]

The rapid growth of cloud, hyperscalers, and GPUs is in part fueled by the expected AI boom from recent innovations such as conversational AI (e.g., chatbots like ChatGPT) and generative AI (e.g., software that can create images from text, like DALL-E). As noted earlier, about 20% of data center capacity is devoted to AI, and the data volumes used to power it is expected to grow exponentially. This tracks with broader trends in data production. In 2010, there were two zettabytes of data produced globally. By 2022, almost 100 zettabytes were created. (A zettabyte is a trillion gigabytes.) Of that, about 2% of data produced and consumed is saved and retained into the following year.

AI training models consume energy, an issue that has been exaggerated by high-profile members of the tech pseudo-left.[33] For example, a commonly-cited 2019 study by Strubell et al. found that a natural language processing (NLP) model emits over 78,000 pounds (35 metric tons) of carbon over the course of its development; a larger model (called a transformer) uses over 600,000 pounds (272 mt).[34] Tech "leftists" note that this is the equivalent of more than a hundred round-trip flights from the US to China, which sounds big.[35]

Saying that a transformer model emits 600,000 pounds of carbon is like saying I have 600,000 blades of grass in my backyard—the number sounds big and scary until you put it into context. In 2018, aviation accounted for 1 Gt (1 billion mt) of CO_2,[36] so 272 mt is actually 0.000027% of total aviation emissions. By my calculation, building a large AI model accounts for just ~0.000007% of the 37.4 billion[37] total metric tons of worldwide annual carbon emissions in 2023—7 *ten millionths* of 1%.

So if we're being honest, these are not substantial shares on a global scale. The CERN particle-physics lab in Geneva, Switzerland, by contrast, emits 223,800 tons of carbon equivalent greenhouse gases per year, just for physics research.[38] That's over 800 *times* more than a large AI model and almost 6,000 times a small model. To the best of my knowledge, there are no studies on the total number of the large models in use—a friend of mine working in the industry suspects hundreds. It's not like there's a ChatGPT being built in every town.

There doesn't seem to be good data on how much training AI models contribute to overall ICT emissions. The big business-affiliated International Energy Association[39] points to two studies (one by Google, the other by Facebook) suggesting the training phase accounts for 20–40% of total AI energy use, while up to 10% is consumed for experimentation and 60–70% from implementation (using the AI for applications).[40] But that's just Google and Facebook; other companies may approach AI differently. And remember, AI is only a fraction of the total digital ecosystem.

A 2023 study found that AI's total energy usage appears "almost negligible" at present,[41] but may become more substantial. The carbon footprint of *using* large generative AI models is higher than it is to train them.[42] OpenAI CEO Sam Altman recently said an AI-powered future needs "an energy breakthrough"—such as cheaper renewables or a hypothetical solution, nuclear fusion—due to its projected energy consumption. However, Altman and Microsoft are also pushing nuclear fusion as investors in the fusion startup, Helion Energy.

Nobody is quite sure how this will turn out. As Joshua Dávila notes in his book, *Blockchain Radicals*, moral panics about the electricity consumption of tech goes back over two decades. As early as 1999, *Forbes* claimed the internet was using 8% of US electricity but could take up nearly 50% by 2020.[43] Similar projections about data centers have not materialized.[44] Hardware efficiency gains and improvements to AI algorithms might mitigate growing energy use. The question is how much these kinds of innovations will counteract broader growth in the industry.

As we'll see in the next section, the cloud has *not* become the environmental monster some feared over a decade ago—at least so far. Nevertheless, analysts plausibly believe cloud computing's modest environmental footprint will continue to grow. And of course, it is imperative to make all aspects of computing, including AI, as eco-friendly as possible.

Before we dig deeper into data centers, including footprints, let's take a look at two widely discussed technologies hosted on the cloud—

cryptocurrency and internet data traffic—as they've piqued the interest of environmentalists.

Cryptocurrency is primarily mined in data centers. According to The Shift Project, Bitcoin, which accounts for about half of all cryptocurrency, contributes as much as 10% of data center energy consumption.[45] For a while, China was mining two thirds of all Bitcoin. But in 2021, China banned cryptocurrency. The US filled the vacuum and now leads the world with 35.4% of all Bitcoin mining.[46]

The Shift Project has also reviewed data traffic. In their assessment, data traffic comprises as much as 55% of total digital energy consumption. Video data flows account for about 80% of global traffic, and the infrastructure to power online video constitutes about 1% of global carbon emissions, comparable to the carbon emissions of Spain.[47]

As we might expect, online video services are dominated by the United States. Like most studies on tech, the Shift Project does not tabulate responsibility by country. Instead, the authors assess the data by type. They break video into two primary segments, 20% "other" (covering video surveillance, Skype, Zoom, etc.) and 60% "online video." The latter is divided into video on demand (34% of all video traffic), pornography (27%), "tubes" (21%), and others, such as social media and websites (18%). US platforms dominate the streaming video-on-demand market.

Table 4.3 shows that US VOD providers have many times the *paid* subscribers and revenue as China. The disparity is even worse when considering two things. One, the YouTube platform *including* unpaid visitors soaks up the lion's share of visitors and unpaid revenues—it has about 2.7 billion monthly active users (MAU) (and generated $31.5 billion in ad revenue for Google in 2023), which brings US VOD platforms to almost 4 billion MAUs. By comparison, China's top ten VOD platforms pulled about 1.7 billion MAUs in 2023, with a fraction of the revenue. Two, as is usually the case with Chinese tech, the country's VOD providers are heavily concentrated inside of mainland China (whereas the US has global reach).[48]

Pornography also features the unsustainable mix of traffic intensity and wealth concentration. The total value of the porn industry is difficult to determine given that most companies are privately held and withhold financial details. We at least know that Canada-based company MindGeek, renamed Aylo in 2023, is the major player in the industry, with a sprawling

111

Table 4.3   Streaming Video-on-Demand Platforms: US vs China

Company	Subscribers	Revenue (B)*
Netflix	261 million	33.7 billion
Amazon Prime	208	>35.2†
Disney+	150	8.4
YouTube Premium	100	>15†
Max	98	12.9
Paramount+	63	7.13
Hulu	49	9.6
Peacock	31	2.8
ESPN+	26	n/a
Apple TV+	25†	n/a
Starz	16	n/a
TOTAL (US)	**1.027B**	**125B‡**
Tencent Video	119	>40.5†
IQIYI (Baidu)	102	4.3
Youku-Tudou (Alibaba)	60†	n/a
TOTAL (CHINA)	**281B**	**45B‡**

Author's table and calculations.[49]
* *Subscriber numbers in millions, rounded; revenue in billions, rounded.*
† *Amazon Prime Video is mixed in with Amazon Prime in some countries. Amazon's total subscription fees totaled $35.22 billion in 2022. YouTube and Google One together pulled $15 billion in revenue in 2023. Apple doesn't release its TV+ subscriber count, its numbers are an estimate. Tencent "value-added subscription" services amounted to $40.5 billion, including Tencent Music, WeChat, and other services. Youku-Tudou reportedly had 30 million paid subscribers at the end of 2016, "the last date such a figure was released."*[50]
‡ *Rough estimates that include some missing data and some inflated numbers based on company reports that mix VOD with other services, as noted.*

empire of popular video platforms and revenues of $455 million in 2022. MindGeek was acquired by Ethical Capital Partners for an undisclosed sum in 2023. Its Pornhub website receives about 1.5 billion unique visitors per month and was the twelfth most visited website in the world in June 2023. The other major pornography platform is the London-based OnlyFans, which generated over $1 billion in revenue and paid out over $5 billion to content creators in 2022. OnlyFans drew 67% of its revenue from the US, 15% from Europe, and 18% from the rest of the world. The company is targeting "major growth regions" in Latin America, Europe, and Australia.[51]

The OnlyFans company itself is said to employ just 61 people as formal employees—netting a lot of wealth for a small number of people—while its set of over 3 million content creators net unequal earnings. The best study to date found the top 10% of OnlyFans accounts makes 73% of the money; the top 1% takes 33%—"less equal than an apartheid state," in the words of its author, Tom Hollands. Top earners capture tens of millions of dollars, while the median income is just $180 per month, less than minimum wage.[52]

"Tube" sites—general-purpose online video-sharing platforms—are dominated by YouTube.[53] Data on video for the Shift Project's "other" category includes many variables, including social media, but we can safely assume that America's Instagram and Facebook as well as China's TikTok are central contributors.

Lastly, 5G networks have also garnered attention as energy-intensive infrastructures. In 2020, the French High Council for Climate found that 5G rollouts could increase its digital sector's carbon footprint by 18–44% by 2030. China's Huawei captured the highest mobile base station market share in 2021 with 30%, followed by Sweden's Ericsson (23.5%) and Finland's Nokia (20.0%). Once again, China's 5G companies are limited on foreign soil, thanks in part to US sanctions and pressure on its allies. That same year, Huawei held just 20% of the market *outside* its borders, compared to Ericsson's 35% and Nokia's 25%. And it should be noted their 5G market share only appears to account for the central component, *base stations*. Other components, such as 5G chipsets and networking infrastructure are typically provided by the likes of US corporations such as Qualcomm, Intel, Broadcom, Cisco, and so on.[54]

* * *

In short, cloud computing boosts other tech companies integrated into the cloud. This interlocking structure helps to explain the dominance of US tech corporations, which forms an American cartel.

THE PHYSICAL CLOUD: ENVIRONMENTAL FOOTPRINTS

As we've seen, the cloud is a crown jewel of the American Empire. It produces an ecologically unequal exchange and division of labor that undermines the possibility of a just and sustainable future. For that reason alone, isolated considerations about the impact of environmental footprints, such as carbon emissions and water usage, are missing the centerpiece of the story.

That said, let's dig into those latter issues. Over the past several years, there's been growing attention to the environmental footprint of the cloud, primarily through carbon emissions and water usage. Assessing this with clarity and precision is unfortunately hampered by a lack of precision, consistent definitions, and politicized contestations. As far as definitions go, we should note up front that the line between "cloud" and "data center" is blurred, with the former typically reserved for large data centers owned by the tech giants and the latter for smaller centers owned by a long tail of companies most people have never heard of.

When we read studies on the climate or ecological footprint of the "cloud" or "data centers," we can't be sure what people have in mind unless the authors make it explicit—which is rarely the case. In fact, in many instances people circulate factoids online without appearing to have read up on them. This, in turn, can lead to disparities in study results and widely circulated and misleading figures.[55]

With that caveat in mind, a comprehensive review of the literature on the *carbon footprints* of data centers reveals that a mix of (often poor) disparate data points and methods has yielded a variety of results, with no firm consensus on the numbers. Our best studies find that data centers consume between 1–2% of global electricity demand and contribute at minimum 0.6% of global greenhouse gas emissions. That said, usage isn't evenly spread, and it is putting stress on national electricity grids in several countries. In Ireland, data centers are said to consume 17% of the country's electricity (a figure the industry disputes), prompting protests and ongoing legal battles.[56]

Nevertheless, data center carbon emissions have *relatively* decoupled from growth over the past decade—meaning, data workloads have grown many times faster than CO_2 emissions, due to technological efficiency gains.[57] But these gains may be short-lived. Some were achieved when smaller companies migrated their data to more energy-efficient hyperscalers. At the same time, data center operators also began introducing measures to reduce energy use, such as improving cooling techniques and increasing the temperature of operations. The creation of smaller, more energy-efficient computer processors by the semiconductor industry has also helped, but those gains may slow down as transistors approach the width of a single atom. Moreover, the shift to artificial intelligence makes heavy use of GPU processors, which are energy gluttons. Recalling our rice-on-the-chessboard story in Chapter 2, exponential growth simply cannot continue.

Within this context, the major players, including Amazon, Google, and Microsoft, are on a "massive spending spree for renewable energy."[58] In the US, data centers now consume two thirds of the renewable energy contracts available to corporations. The tech giants make grand claims about being "carbon-free" and "100% renewable," but they don't advertise that they are relying on "renewable energy credits" to "offset" their carbon emissions. In other words, they are still burning fossil fuels. Using this greenwashing method, Meta calls its data centers "100% renewable," Amazon says AWS is "85% renewable," and Google says it is "64%" carbon-free.[59] All three cloud giants aim to operate "100% carbon-free" data centers between 2025 and 2030, but again, they will still burn fossil fuels. In addition to generating their own carbon emissions, the lion's share of emissions take place along the supply chain. Moreover, the data centers will be using a large share of the finite renewable energy grid which, as we've seen, entails heavy Global South labor exploitation.

In addition to carbon emissions, environmentalists are also drawing attention to the *ecological* footprints of data centers, especially with respect to water use. According to the United Nations, there may be a 40% shortfall in the supply of fresh water by 2030 (largely due to mismanagement and industrial agriculture), and it's imperative that we consider the water footprints of all industries.[60] "Crucial for industry and agriculture," data center researcher David Mytton notes, "the availability and quality of water is a growing global concern. Projections suggest that water demand will increase by 55% between 2000 and 2050 due to growth from manufacturing (+400%), thermal power generation (+140%) and domestic use (+130%). ICT is another sector contributing to that demand."[61]

Data centers use water indirectly for electricity generation (via thermoelectric power) and directly (to cool their infrastructure). In the US, their total water usage is still just a small proportion of the total national share. Like many mining operations, however, water withdrawals are often problematic to people at the local level, especially in water-constrained areas. While the tech giants are starting to disclose more data on water usage, about two thirds of data centers are *not* tracking their water or carbon usage.[62]

In general, the water use of data centers is very small. Crop production accounts for an estimated 95.4% of the total water footprint among all US industries.[63] In the US, which houses somewhere between a quarter and a third of the world's data centers, Mytton found, "data centre water consumption (1.7 billion litres/day) is small compared to total water consumption (1,218 billion litres/day)" (or about one tenth of 1%).[64] A study trending among the tech pseudo-left predicts an enormous expansion of water use based on maximum, upper-bound projections extending into the future. But they never contextualize the findings to the bigger picture, and high-end predictions have turned out much smaller than feared over the past couple of decades. Because these are complex systems, we cannot predict environmental footprints with high confidence far into the future.[65]

Due to the sometimes negative impacts on surrounding environments, local communities have been protesting the opening of new data centers over the past few years. Beginning in 2019, cloud giants Google and Microsoft have faced resistance to the expansion of new data centers in Chile (against Google and Microsoft) and Uruguay. The protesters maintain that potable water should go to the people, not water-guzzling data centers for extractive imperialists. Similar protests are sprouting up in the Global North.

In addition to water usage, data centers churn out waste. A server typically lasts about 4–6 years before it is replaced. One study found 28% of data centers re-use or repurpose the hardware for a while, but a good percentage will eventually become e-waste—a topic we'll address in the next chapter.[66]

In our final assessment, we can see that the cloud has not wrought the devastation of other sectors, such as energy and agriculture, but the situation cannot be assumed unproblematic or stable. Cheap tricks, like improving cooling systems, shifting to hyperscalers, or tweaking algorithms to draw less energy cannot continue forever.

Moreover, technological innovations may make production more materially efficient while leading to *even higher material resource use*. This outcome was observed by economist William Jevons during the Industrial Revolution, who noticed that the use of coal spiked following the invention of the steam engine, even though the steam engine *reduced* the amount of coal needed to power applications. Steam engines made coal more affordable, so its total use exceeded prior levels—what political ecologists call the *rebound effect*—a phenomenon that has since been widely observed, especially in the digital sector.[67] The more computers become efficient and abundant, the more we manufacture and use them. This is why we see the use of materials like silicon—a semiconductor used widely to manufacture ICTs like computer processors and memory—has increased over time, even though processors have become more computationally and energy-efficient. The big question is how long we can keep expanding infrastructure like data centers, and to what effect.

The most recent assessment by IDC—a capitalist "market intelligence" firm—estimates that data center energy consumption will more than double by 2027. While the IDC doesn't call for degrowth, it notes that past efficiency gains "can inadvertently give the impression that the data center industry is rapidly becoming more sustainable," which it claims may not last given its "continuous and rapid expansion." This assessment is shared by a variety of researchers, who expect increases in data center material resource use despite future efficiency gains.[68]

Wherever the truth lies, we should remember that climate and ecological footprints of the cloud are only a small part of the story. While we shouldn't ignore them, they have absorbed the attention of activists, scholars, policy-makers, and the tech giants themselves. This is a narrow, imperialist way of looking at the issue that benefits the corporations, and it is growing among the American School of intellectuals, thanks in large part to Big Tech itself.

For example, the co-author of the AI training model article referenced above, Emma Strubell, previously worked for Meta, Google, and Amazon, and is now an Assistant Professor at Carnegie Mellon University, which has a cozy relationship with Microsoft. A recent paper by Strubell, co-authored with several Microsoft researchers and Microsoft-affiliated institutions, evaluates the carbon intensity of AI in cloud instances. However, the authors endorse certification systems for "Green AI," based in part on "initiatives like the Green Software Foundation" that "are making important progress towards measuring and mitigating the carbon footprint of software in general." The Green Software Foundation's "team" includes representatives from Google, Intel, Microsoft, Accenture, Shell Oil, Mastercard, Mercedes-Benz, and other corporate giants. The project is a liberal-progressive imperialist exercise in greenwashing. These corporations, including Big Tech, *cannot* be green.

Researchers like Microsoft's Kate Crawford are also pushing the liberal-progressive view, arguing that "pragmatic actions to limit AI's ecological impacts" are possible through "a multifaceted approach including the AI industry, researchers and legislators."[69] This is the imperialist corporate greenwashing of the American tech "left," a topic we will return to in Chapter 9.

The central harm is hidden in plain sight: the cloud is a gravy train for the American Empire that destroys the planet and produces ecologically unequal exchange. The technologies filling the warehouses are American, as are the software and services running on them. Every US cloud center opened is another act of racist-imperialist class war waged by Americans against the planet.

5
Digital Ecocide

In the last chapter we interrogated the relationship between cloud computing and the environment. We saw that its energy and water footprints are mostly problematic at a more local level—though this may change in the coming years. In truth, the deeper environmental harm is ecologically unequal exchange benefiting Americans.

But there are other specific aspects of the digital economy that deserve special attention. In particular, tech corporations are digitalizing agriculture, a sector that contributes mightily to greenhouse gas emissions, deforestation, and desertification. Moreover, we'll see that the digital economy is intimately tied to new forms of consumerism, from online advertising and e-retail to fast fashion and e-waste. These, too, are quite alarming, as they contribute mightily to a *digital ecocide* killing the planet.

ALL YOUR FARMS BELONG TO US

If you are reading this book and from a rich country, chances are you are not one of the 1.23 billion people employed in the world's agrifood systems. Yet millions of farmers around the world are toiling away to put food on our tables. Agriculture is the second-largest contributor to global warming, and it is the top contributor to deforestation. Big Tech has already made moves to dominate that sector, too. Microsoft and Amazon are rapidly moving into the agriculture space, while agribusiness giants like Bayer-Monsanto and John Deere are upgrading and investing heavily in their own digital solutions.

So, if we want to get a picture of how to solve our environmental problems while ensuring the survival and thriving of our global population, we can't get around farming. In fact, if digital justice activists are concerned with water, they should be centering their attention on digital agriculture, which they're mostly silent on. But before we get to AgTech, we need to understand the agricultural landscape.

119

During the Industrial Revolution, Western ruling classes enclosed the land, forcing agrarian workers off the farms and into the factories. They've never gone back. In 2022, just 1.2% of the US labor force worked on farms. Agriculture is scarcely discussed in America, partially because most people don't farm. However, in the Global South, farming remains dominant. In 2019, 3% of people from high-income countries worked in agriculture, compared to 59% of people from low-income and 38% from lower-middle-income countries.[1]

Small-scale farming supports about 500 million households worldwide. According to the OECD, "small farms with less than two hectares of land represent 84% of farms globally, but produce only one-third of global crop production." Yet megafarms dominate food production, and increasingly so. According to the US Department of Agriculture, in 2023, large-scale farms (at least $1 million of gross cash farm income) accounted for about 3% of farms, but 52% of the value of production. The median household income of large farm operators was over $500,000 in 2022.[2]

Towering over the farms—large and small—is the agribusiness sector. US farm revenues were about $550 billion in 2022, while the top 30 US agribusiness corporations netted close to $1 trillion.[3] "Agribusinesses mostly don't farm," author Timothy A. Wise notes, "but they make a great deal of money off agriculture. They produce inputs like fertilizer, seeds, pesticides, and tractors," and on the output side, they trade, ship, and process food.[4] Much like Big Tech, at a global scale, many of the top companies' revenues exceed the GDP of the countries where they operate. As we'll see in a moment, the industry is going digital.

At the global level, US agribusiness corporations once again take the top slot. By my calculations, of the top 15 global agricultural corporations listed in a *Yahoo! Finance* article, the United States takes 55.6% of the revenue, followed by five countries from Europe (25.3%) and four from the Global South (19.1%). China has one company totaling 2.9%.[5]

This comports with data from nonprofit ETC Group's 2022 report, "Food Barons 2022," which tracks the top corporations in every major subsector of agriculture. Of the 88 companies holding revenues, 41.9% are American, followed by Europe (31.4%) and China (7.2%). India, home of the so-called Green Revolution (discussed below) with 1.4 billion people (18% of the world's population), has just 0.3%, and the Global South, with about 85% of the world's population, has 11.3% (owing mostly to China and Brazil).

Table 5.1   Revenues of Top 88 Agribusiness Corporations Worldwide

Location	Revenue (mil)	%	# Co's	%
USA	995,855	41.9	30	34.1
Europe	745,573	31.4	38	43.2
China	169,872	7.2	7	7.9
India	7,380	0.3	2	2.3
Other	456,145	19.2	11	12.5
TOTAL	2,374,825.8	100	88	100
Global North	2,107,245.8	88.7	75	85.2
Global South	267,580	11.3	13	14.8

Author's table and calculations. Source for data: ETC Group, 2022.[6]

America also leads the world in agricultural *exports*, despite falling behind both China and India in total *production*. In 2020, the US ranked third in global agricultural output ($307.4 billion)—encompassing both domestic and international sales—far behind China ($1.56 trillion) and India ($403.5 billion). Yet despite employing a small fraction of China and India's agricultural sector, it led the world with $147.9 billion of all exports. China ($67.29) was fifth and India ($32.1) was 16th.[7]

In 2022, the CEO of food giant Archer Daniels Midland, Juan Luciano, made about $25 million in compensation. The average farmer in one of its client countries, Malawi, earns about $400 per year. A Malawian *smallholder* farmer, representing 80% of the country's farmers, makes just $100 per year.[8]

American dominance on foreign shores is connected to the so-called Green Revolution. As the OECD puts it, "Innovations in animal and crop genetics, chemicals, equipment, and farm organization" unleashed a wave of productivity outpacing land use and population growth.[9] Transnational corporations locked up the technologies and consolidated power.

On the surface, the Green Revolution might seem like a good thing. More food was produced per person on less land. But in many respects, it has been a total disaster, especially for the Global South. As presented by academic

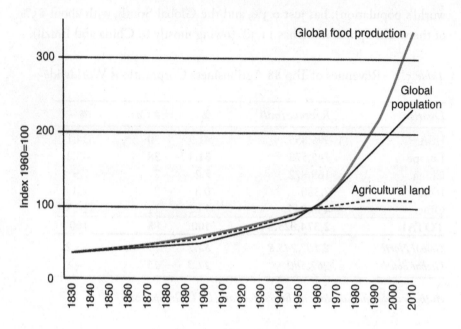

Figure 5.1 The "Green" Revolution and agricultural output (courtesy of OECD)

Source: OECD, 2019.[10]

and popular food critic Raj Patel, the short version of it goes like this: in the 1940s, at the behest of the Rockefeller Foundation, the Mexican Agriculture Plan was launched to develop techniques for higher-yielding crops which could be transferred to other regions and climates. US plant biologist Norman Borlaug joined the project and by 1954 developed "miracle wheat," which was then "spread by the Rockefeller and Ford Foundations through the world, in the 1950s and 1960s, with other crops—notably rice—added to the menu, with the help of the US government toward the end of that period."[11] The period is said to have ended in 1970. Total food production more than doubled in the developing world.

Yet there's more to the story. As Patel points out, despite a dramatic expansion of caloric output, when removing China from the equation, hunger increased by more than 11% by 2000. By 2021, almost one in ten people were affected by hunger and around 2.3 billion people (29.3% of the world) were moderately or severely food insecure. By 2020 almost 3.1 billion people could not afford a healthy diet, and the situation has been getting *worse* since 2015. This includes India, the poster child of the Green Revolution's alleged success. A 2023 systematic review found that the Green Revolution has done little to impact food insecurity and malnutrition, which is on the rise despite the increased availability of food. The country ranks a ghastly 107th on the Global Hunger Index. A minimum of 200 million Indians are malnourished and almost three quarters struggle to afford healthy food.[12]

Research has challenged the extent of so-called "miracle" yields. From the outset, implementation of the Green Revolution required a transition to large-scale, chemical-intensive farming, which was dependent upon imports from—surprise, surprise—American corporations.[13] This played out across the world, as Washington pushed an input-intensive model that required heavy use of fertilizers, pesticides, farming equipment, and freshwater irrigation, giving rise to corporate concentration based on industrial monocropping (planting the same crop on the same plot of land, over and over) and simple crop rotation (e.g., rotating between corn and soybeans).

While it's ignored outside of left circles, the Green Revolution's neocolonial model connects to America's Cold War imperialism and white supremacy. Its chief architects—from Norman Borlaug to the Big Foundations, State Department, and Central Intelligence Agency (CIA)—were obsessed with preventing an allegedly looming Malthusian population boom that would leave billions in the South starving. (Malthusianism is the theory that population growth will outstrip food production and cause poverty, famine, and unrest, first published in 1798 by British political economist Thomas Malthus.) Desperate for food, they believed poor people in the Global South would foment communist revolution and threaten the capitalist West. For the Green Revolution's engineers and supporters, Third World farmers were also backward peasants who needed their cutting-edge science and technology to save them from their "primitive" ways.

This *raison d'etre* provided the ideological foundation for state intervention, in the form of subsidies and trade policies that would tilt the market toward widespread adoption. The American government doled out $3 billion *per year* in the mid-1960s (around $30 billion in 2023 dollars), while the Agency for International Development (USAID) tied aid to the adoption of its Green Revolution agricultural model.[14] This put pressure on countries to shift from small-scale farming to industrial monoculture—to the benefit of American corporations locking up the inputs and supply chain, as well as large-scale farm owners in the Global South collaborating on their agenda.

As scholar Max Ajl explains, industrial crop overproduction drove down margins, forcing farmers to keep production high just to fight off debt. The US also dumped its own surplus production in the South, undermining smallholders and forcing them to focus on export-oriented crops. Green Revolution production prioritized crops like wheat to feed urban populations, while rural communities and their lands were stripped bare—water tables were drained and the soil was tilled lifeless. Many farmers, in turn, fled for the cities, marking a new era of land enclosure.

The integration of GMO (genetically modified organism) seeds into the Green Revolution took flight in the 1990s, when, at the behest of agribusiness corporations, the World Trade Organization blessed the patenting of genetically modified crops. Giants like Monsanto (purchased by Bayer in 2019) became household villains, cornering the market with proprietary seeds tethered to its own agrochemical inputs (e.g., Roundup herbicide) and crop monoculture (soybean, corn, wheat, cotton). At present, just six corporations own 77.6% of the agrochemical/seed market.[15]

Today, we're left with the perverse outcome that caloric production is at an all-time high, but billions are hungry. Here, we're back to our recurring theme of the book: a predominantly US-driven neocolonial system that produces an unequal ecological exchange and division of labor. Masses of farmers remain poor in the presence of abundance, often unable to adequately feed themselves and their families. Their hardship is directly connected to the loss of sovereignty among indigenous and other small-scale farmers through corporate plunder. "On a world scale," Ajl notes, "84 percent of farms are smaller than two hectares, but they only operate around 12 percent of farmland. The largest 1 percent of global farms operate over 70 percent of global farmland."[16] Smallholder farmers and peasants likely feed the majority of the global population (outside the industrial North),[17] but prices are pushed down by an input-intensive, heavily subsidized industrial monopolies that leave them poor and hungry. Small agriculture feeds the world, industrial agriculture feeds the capitalists. Corporate concentration is wrecking the North as well, where factory farms in states like Iowa—the birthplace of Borlaug—are burying smallholder families.[18]

In addition to undermining farmers, industrial agriculture damages our health. In the US and other places with lax regulations, crops are doused with chemicals and seeds are genetically modified despite the potential for serious health repercussions for farmers and consumers. The poor are stuck with unhealthy, processed foods while quality "organic" foods—what should just be "normal" food—are priced at a premium.

Worst of all, industrial agriculture is environmentally destructive. The food system accounts for 80% of the planet's deforestation, consumes 70% of its freshwater, and is the greatest driver of terrestrial biodiversity loss. Around 37% of the land used for the major crops—accounting for over 80% of all calories harvested—goes to applications other than directly feeding people, e.g., animal feed and industrial products using plant-based ingredients, such as biofuels, bioplastics, and pharmaceuticals. (About 51% of land was used to feed people in the 1960s.) Livestock grazing, in turn, requires inordinate amounts of land, often cleared through deforestation; it is responsible for around 11–17% of global GHG emissions (with cattle farming emitting 62%).[19]

The most recent and comprehensive study found that a third of all greenhouse gas emissions come from food production, with the US and EU the only two of the six major economies emitting more than their share of the population. Beef production supplies less than 5% of protein and 2% of the world's calories, but uses 60% of the world's agricultural land.[20]

Industrial agriculture is also ruining the Earth's soils. Soil is loaded with living organisms like bacteria, fungi, and earthworms, and it stores 80% of the carbon in terrestrial ecosystems. Healthy soil is essential to our well-being. Yet monocropping, agrochemicals, and heavy tillage erodes the soil, reduces fertility, and hinders its ability to absorb water and sequester carbon.[21] (Soil carbon sequestration refers to the storage of carbon inside soils.)

Due to the combination of global heating and industrial agriculture, we're rapidly degrading the land and converting it into desert. Over the past 40 years, "nearly 33% of the world's arable land has been lost to erosion and pollution," one study found.[22] In 2022, a five-year UN investigation found that on the current trajectory, an additional area the size of South America will be degraded by 2050. Drylands—areas with a scarcity of water—cover about 41% of the Earth's surface and are home to one of every three people. Under moderate and high-end climate change scenarios, dryland may increase by an additional 11% to 23% by the end of the twenty-first century. Between 1985 and 2015, 6% of the world's drylands were desertified "by unsustainable land use practices compounded by anthropogenic climate change."[23]

To sum up, industrial agriculture devastates the farmer, the consumer, and nature.

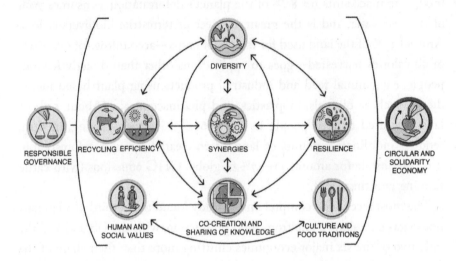

Figure 5.2 Agroecological modeling (Source: Food and Agriculture Organization of the United Nations. Reproduced with permission)

Source: FAO, 2018.[24]

Environmentalists typically favor *agroecology* as an alternative to industrial agriculture. The UN's Food and Agriculture Organization's "The 10 elements of agroecology" provides a good starting point for understanding the phenomenon.[25] At a technical level, agroecology privileges biodiversity through crop, natural habitat, and animal synergies; the co-creation of traditional/trader and scientific knowledge; and greater resource-use efficiency, waste recycling, and resiliency against extreme weather events and pest outbreaks. To accomplish this, agroecological systems create complex ecosystems that mix and match a wide variety of life forms. There is no cookie-cutter model, but they typically integrate a multitude of methods appropriate to their environments based on agroecological principles. For instance, they might "selectively combine annual and perennial crops, livestock and aquatic animals, trees, soils, water and other components on farms and agricultural landscapes."[26]

126

At the social level, agroecology relies upon local autonomy and adaptive capacities to empower people and provide jobs; secures healthy, diversified, and culturally appropriate diets; calls for equitable access to land and natural resources, as well as transparent governance; and promotes fair and short distribution networks that build solidarity and circularity by re-connecting consumers to producers. Agroecology is generally participatory, bottom-up, and decentralized; enhances soil health; and ensures animal health and welfare. Agroecological principles can also help green our cities to the greatest extent possible.[27]

As Max Ajl points out, a variety of studies demonstrate that agroecological principles enhance soil health and reduce carbon emissions, possibly to the point of negative emissions. Moreover, Ajl notes:

> In the entire peripheral world, smallholder agriculture is the basis for resistance to capitalism: by de-commodifying access to food, by closing off market opportunities for corporate sellers of agro-industrial inputs, by reclaiming land from export-oriented commodity crop production and giving it to poor people for accumulation from below, by increasing the embeddedness of national agricultural systems, and by creating larger internal markets that can form the basis of a sovereign industrialization.[28]

Around 30% of the world's farms have redesigned their production systems around elements of agroecology. Yet much like socialist tech projects (such as those detailed in Chapter 8), agroecological systems receive very little financial support.[29] With added research and development and pro-farmer policies, we can bolster productivity while making life more pleasant and rewarding for farmers. For these reasons, agroecology is gaining serious traction, from civil society and social movements to financial institutes and development agencies.

AGRIBUSINESS GOES DIGITAL

In 2006, the Alliance for a Green Revolution in Africa was launched. Largely the brainchild of the Rockefeller Foundation, AGRA was originally funded by donors at the Rockefeller Foundation and the Bill & Melinda Gates Foundation (BMGF), who pumped a combined $150 million into the project.[30] Rockefeller had "already spent more than $600 million (in current dollars) on Green Revolution work around the world, including nearly $150 million during the last seven years in Africa," the Gates Foundation boasted of its ally.[31] By 2023, AGRA had raised over $1 billion, with two thirds from BMGF, as well as additional funds from Rockefeller and USAID.[32]

Smallholders make up 80% of all farms in Africa, and produce the overwhelming majority of the food. Yet the yields are much lower than many other parts of the world—around 17–20 kg per hectare (15 times lower than the Netherlands). Using Green Revolution farming methods, AGRA promised to double the yields of 30 million small farmer households in 13 African countries, which they claimed would cut hunger in half and reduce poverty.[33]

The real-world results have been a disaster. In 2020, a landmark study, "False Promises: The Alliance for a Green Revolution in Africa (AGRA)," published by African and German organizations, found that under AGRA, annual yield increases did *not* improve over the pre-AGRA period, while the number of hungry people *increased* by 30% in the 13 focus countries. There was also strong evidence of negative environmental impacts (such as damages to soil and land use expansion). This was the result despite the fact that Green Revolution solutions were heavily subsidized, and therefore *costly*.[34]

The following year, the Alliance for Food Sovereignty in Africa (AFSA), representing 200 million small-scale food producers, alongside 160 international organizations from 40 countries, penned an open letter demanding donors cease funding the Alliance for a Green Revolution in Africa (AGRA). AFSA and other critics charge that AGRA locks smallholder farmers "into a vicious cycle of expensive inputs, low crop prices, and increasing debt"—to the benefit of American and other foreign corporations at the expense of poor Africans. The alliance also says "agroecology is what our continent needs," Million Belay and Bridget Mugambe explain in *Scientific American*.[35]

If the Green Revolution was "a mix of government policy, subsidy, fertilizers, pesticides, hybrid seeds, birth control and philanthropy to ensure that more cheap food would postpone the inevitable communist dawn," as Raj Patel puts it, then its newest addition is digital technology, this time alleging it will save the environment.[36] The merging of the two streams is deepening every day, but it's largely ignored by the US-Eurocentric tech "left," who spend their days thinking about their own societies, where most people don't farm. We can see this on full display in Africa, a new laboratory of the Green Revolution's evolving colonial experiment.

Microsoft—with Bill Gates still Chairman of the Board (he stepped down as CEO in 2000 and as Chairman in 2020)—signed a partnership with AGRA in September 2019. The company announced it would be delivering technological solutions (what the industry calls "AgTech") that tie into the AGRA agenda. Kenya and South Africa became early testing sites. In time, Microsoft and AGRA expanded their work with governments (Nigeria, Rwanda, Ghana, Tanzania, Uganda, Malawi, and Ethiopia) and agribusiness giants, where they developed partnerships with the likes of Bayer, Yara, Syngenta, Nestle, Rabobank, and OLAM.

Gates made headlines in 2021 when it was reported he is the largest landholder in the United States (holding 270,000 acres, about 0.03% of the total). Bill and his wife, Melinda, have harmed the Global South through the support of hyper-capitalist development projects that often benefit themselves. The largest philanthropic venture in the world, "Almost 90% of this funding goes to groups in North American and Europe whilst just 5% is directly channelled to African NGOs," the nonprofit, GRAIN, observes.[37] Eighty-five percent of BMGF funds for agriculture support *industrial* agriculture, and the organization puts no money into agroecological development. At present, the BMGF, Microsoft, and AGRA are working in close connection to develop industrial-oriented AgTech products, all in the name of helping smallholder farms.[38]

Microsoft offers a variety of solutions, which began with a project called FarmBeats. Launched in 2015, FarmBeats is a platform designed to collect data from a variety of sources and store them on the Microsoft Azure cloud. FarmBeats does not offer an app or AgTech products for consumers. As was explained to me in an interview with Microsoft, FarmBeats is not farmer-facing—meaning, a grower might not even know that the software they are utilizing makes use of FarmBeats. Rather, it's a business-to-business platform created for third-party AgTech vendors that provides data tools for them to build their solutions on top of the FarmBeats back-end (behind the scenes) solution.

FarmBeats (now called Azure Data Management for Agriculture, or DMAg) was designed to collect data in the field from a variety of instruments:

- *Sensors* collect information about things like soil moisture, light, humidity, and temperature.
- *Drones* collect visual images for things like thermal and multi-spectral imagining, crop counting, evaluating drainage, monitoring livestock, and so on.
- *Machines* like tractors collect data about their behavior (e.g., their position in the field, speed, etc.) and information about the environment (cameras to evaluate crop quality, sensors to detect wind speed and direction, etc.).

Data from instruments located at the farm itself is transmitted to the Azure cloud. Additionally, an *external* stream of data is pulled from *satellites* (which provide images from the skies) and *weather stations* (which provide data about local weather conditions and predictions). Data from the farm and external streams are pooled into the Azure cloud. Over a farmer's career, a crop is tilled about 40–50 times (once per year), which doesn't provide enough information for analysis. So the data is pulled in from many thousands of fields to get a sense of how farming works across many fields. The companies then build models of each specific farm (its terrain) and run simulations (to predict what will happen on the farm, e.g., in terms of yields). In addition to aggregating and contextualizing the info, data is also "normalized"—meaning, it's put into standardized forms so that information from, say, a John Deere tractor can work with data from, say, AgCore.

Microsoft says it doesn't get access to the data. Instead, the company offering the solution creates a contract with the farmer about how the data will be shared. The models Microsoft works on are created through collaborations with their partners and academics, and the partners train their models on the Azure cloud. Microsoft makes its money by charging clients for its cloud solution. To make sure it profits from the technology, it locks up some of the source code and registers patents. The Microsoft engineer and CTO of agri-food who started FarmBeats, Ranveer Chandra, has registered over 150 patents to date (up from 85 a few years ago), including for Microsoft AgTech solutions.

Microsoft told me products like Azure Data Management for Agriculture (DMAg)[39] are well-suited to large and medium-sized farms—not smallholders. Poor farmers in the Global South can't afford the on-the-farm infrastructure like sensors, drones, and "smart" machines like John Deere tractors. Moreover, sometimes they don't have broadband infrastructure available to transmit the data (and even then, they almost certainly wouldn't be able to afford the bandwidth).

If they cannot afford on-the-farm tech deployments, then they can only utilize the *external* stream of data—images from satellites and weather stations—which is piped directly to the Azure cloud by the external providers (without charging farmers). But this provides farmers with much less data. For example, satellite images transmit "ten meter by ten meter" per pixel image. At that low resolution, the images can't infer which crop is where, so they can't do things like multi-cropping. And of course, without the sensors, the amount of "intelligence" about their farm is reduced to almost nothing.

The price of Azure DMAg isn't available online. Azure charges for usage on the cloud, so a very data-intensive setup would cost more than a lighter setup. Before it was retired, one FarmBeats user said that it cost around $250–300 per month. That's about 10 *times* the annual farmer salary in Malawi, even putting aside the up-front cost of the initial infrastructure.

"Smart" AgTech solutions like Azure DMAg are ideal for farms at least tens of hectares in size, Microsoft told me. But as we've seen, about 75% of the world's 570 million farms are two hectares or less. Given that so many of the world's smallholder farmers are so poor, a solution like DMag is out of reach for the vast majority of farms in the Global South.

Added to this, it appears that solutions like DMag *by its nature* will work best with more simplified scenarios, e.g., monocropping, because that reduces the number of variables involved, making outcomes easier to predict. If farms run complex multi-cropping systems (which provide 20% of the world's food supply)[40] and mix various forms of vegetation, animals, and farming methods, then it would be harder to generate accurate predictions about successful farming techniques and crop yields. Agroecological systems utilize *principles*, not specific recipes, and they have a much wider variety of inputs and methods. Big data systems talk a good game, but it's worth remembering that machines are not actually intelligent, and that the promises of AI are frequently empty hype.

AgTech platforms also typically integrate with other Big Agribusiness companies and facilitate greenwashing scams. Bayer's Climate Fieldview platform, which runs on Azure DMAg, recommends Bayer products such as agrochemicals to farmers. If farmers agree to use Fieldview, they can also enroll in Bayer's Carbon Programme, which may pay them to perform low- or no-till farming and plant cover crops,[41] which then allows Bayer to claim carbon credits for alleged carbon sequestration. The company launched the program just after a 2020 agreement to pay out over $10 billion in settlements, covering about 160,000 federal lawsuits alleging its Roundup weed killer gave the plaintiffs cancer. (The lawsuits are ongoing.) Critics allege the low- or no-tillage farming promoted by Bayer for its Carbon Programme requires the use of even more Roundup. They also point out that carbon credits—the purchase of negative (i.e., "offsetting") measures that allow a company to claim less carbon emissions than it actually produces—have a miserable record in reducing actual carbon emissions, and are really a veiled greenwashing exercise to keep emissions-producing profits flowing. Bayer also purchased majority shares in cover crop supplier, CoverCress.[42]

Most AgTech products for low-income smallholders simply use mobile phones to provide market-based services and advice. For example, Digi-Farm, developed by UK-based Vodafone's subsidiary, Safaricom, provides a chatbot called Arifu that sells inputs and insurance, buys and sells their produce, and offers them loans via the FinTech giant, M-Pesa. The Digi-Farm eMarketplace was launched in partnership with Amazon, which supplies its AWS cloud computing backbone for the solution. Supposedly Digifarms helps Africans by banking the "unbanked" (providing them with financial services), but this is hardly a humanitarian service. As GRAIN notes of services like DigiFarm:

> To become bankable, farmers must conform to the system—they must buy the inputs that are promoted and sold on credit (at high interest rates), follow the "advice" of the chatbot to qualify for crop insurance (which they must pay for), sell their crops to the company (at a non-negotiable price), and receive payments on a digital money app (for which there is a fee). Any missteps can affect a farmer's credit worthiness and access to finance and markets. It's contract farming on a mass scale.[43]

Two years after its 2017 launch, over 500,000 farmers have used its services in 30 countries to date. Yet a peer-reviewed study from 2018 found fewer than 1% of Kenyan farmers used mobile money for agricultural loans, and less than 15% used mobile financial services for agriculture.[44] That data was supplied about six years ago, and uptake may have grown considerably since then.

In fact, info on usage is mixed and somewhat dated for a rapidly expanding industry. In 2021, about $18.2 billion was invested in agrifood technologies globally, and an industry survey found that 87% of agricultural businesses are currently using AI technology, up from 74% a year prior.[45] Yet a 2019 study surveying the literature found variable rate technologies—AgTech that automates activities like the application of fertilizers, seeds, and irrigation water at different rates in different locations (an indicator of "precision" agriculture)—rarely exceeds 20% of farms. The authors also found, "The biggest gap in PA adoption is for medium and small farms in the developing world that do not use motorized mechanization."[46]

For small farms in the Global South, then, AgTech seems as though it is most commonly used to connect smallholders to local markets, as well as to push agribusiness products on farmers via SMS or chat apps like WhatsApp, Facebook, or Telegram.

Critics accuse AgTech platforms of de-skilling indigenous and other smallholder farmers by pressuring them to adopt industrial monocropping connected to agribusiness products. If tech platforms dictate instructions to small farmers with the carrot (cost savings and subsidies) and the stick (loss of savings and higher prices), they will eventually lose their traditional knowledge of agroecological techniques. This is a serious threat.

Moreover, the Big Tech platforms collect farmer data using dubious "terms of service" where they are forced to "agree" to have data about their farms and practices collected by the app providers. From there, farmers are often *not* told that their data has value, how it is monetized, or who it is shared with.

Unfortunately, there is no easy way to break down the digital farming industry by size, as many companies don't disclose revenues or profits specific to AgTech. Nevertheless, we know there are plenty of other platforms operating in the AgTech space. John Deere, for example, has a Digital Agriculture Hub, and now hires more software engineers than mechanical engineers. Other companies involved include Google, Meta, Syngenta, Alibaba, Walmart, Yara, and Corveta.

It remains to be seen how far AgTech extends into the South. For now, the prime beneficiaries are the tech and agribusiness giants who are pushing their tech products onto farms for industrial agriculture. Farmers in poor countries like Malawi earn $100 of disposable income per year, whereas the rich executives and shareholders in the industry are swimming in cash—thanks to ecologically unequal exchange—while perpetuating a model that is destroying the planet. As with everything else, this dynamic is not only radically unjust, it is perpetuating ecocide.

DIGITAL CONSUMERISM

We have seen that to save the planet we need to reduce and cap the aggregate material resource use of humanity. For that scenario to be fair and just, we need to eliminate inequality within and between countries—universal class abolition. Neocolonial extraction continues in order to grow profits for the rich, fueling ever-higher degrees of mass production for consumption secured primarily by the wealthy, led by the US and its European cousins. If the Global South were to obtain Global North standards of living, we would need at least three planet Earths to provide for everyone. The consumerist model created by the West over the past two centuries has to end. And fast.

It's alarming, then, that little attention has been devoted to the *consumerist model* of the digital economy. Mainstream "left" critics tend to focus on monopoly power and surveillance-based advertising, without criticizing the fact that the digital economy encourages and stimulates mass production and consumption. This includes advertising, e-commerce platforms, fast fashion, pollution, and waste—including a rapidly expanding e-waste. Let's consider each in turn.

Advertising

Online platforms typically generate revenue from advertising, which pushes people to "buy, buy, buy" all day long. The idea of funding social communications on the condition that each person gets bombarded with ads urging them to purchase more goods and services is not only exploitative—it harms our planet.

There is no consensus on how many ads people see and digest per day, whether digital or not. But surveys demonstrate it's a lot. Estimates range from the thousands to hundreds. According to market research firm Yankelovich, as of 2007, the average person living in a city encountered about 5,000 ads per day—which includes brand logos on physical products—up from 2,000 30 years prior. Another study, conducted by Media Dynamics, Inc., found adults spend almost ten hours per day consuming media, seeing and processing up to 360 ads. Of those 360, they "note" 150 ads, and "engage" with 12.[47]

Most advertisements are deceptive forms of commercial propaganda. Markets, Noam Chomsky remarks, "are supposed to be based on informed consumers making rational choices, but if you turn on the TV set, you see ads are designed to create irrational, uninformed consumers making irrational choices."[48] Indeed, an advertisement for a fast food chain produces videos of food that scarcely resemble a real-life product, and the producers have no incentive to emphasize the downsides of consuming their offering. A car commercial might feature sexy women admiring a cowboy in a truck, who scales mountains and the roughest terrains. Rational, non-deceptive commercials would look very different. They might restrict information to hard facts, such as the number of calories in a McMeal and recommended frequency of consumption, fuel efficiency for cars, impact on the environment for beef consumption, and the like.

A lot of ink has been spilled on the manipulative nature of advertisements, from the content of the ads themselves to attempts at behavior modification from "targeted" advertising. For our purposes—environmental sustainability—the question remains, "do advertisements actually stimulate consumerism, or do they just switch people's preferences for this or that product?"

In their book, *Badvertising*, Andrew Simms and Leo Murray attempted to answer this question. They reviewed a wide range of studies available on the impact of advertising and consumerism, including those that controlled for variables (to separate out correlation and causation). They found that "exposure to advertising did lead to more desire for advertised products, which, in turn, led to higher materialism. There was a self-reinforcing dynamic between exposure to advertising, holding materialistic values and the desire to acquire."[49]

Across cultures, three things stood out. First, "young people who are more materialist are not as happy" as their non-materialistic counterparts.[50]

Second, the "link between materialism and television consumption, which is saturated with advertising, is clear."[51] Although TV is mentioned, the digital economy is implicated, given that "social modeling" in the studies they reviewed was found to inculcate consumerism. Social modeling occurs when "people see parents, siblings and peers act in materialistic ways, they are themselves likely to imitate those social models." With social media, the matter is acute: not only are people inundated with advertisements from the platforms themselves—e.g., in the form of ads spliced in between Instagram posts, at the beginning of YouTube videos, or while swiping through dating apps—but they are also receiving ads via "influencers" who push products as paid "brand ambassadors" for major companies. Influencers, in turn, pose as "hip" peers and contemporaries that people aspire to emulate.

In South Africa, the harmful connection between social media and consumerism is on full display. The country is ranked the most unequal in the world, having been racked by a transition from apartheid to neoliberal capitalism. The result is not a "post-apartheid" society, as it's usually described, but a *neo-apartheid* society suffering from deep inequalities. Instagram feeds are packed with displays of conspicuous consumption and excessive valorization of wealth, while dating apps are filled with overtures for money in exchange for sex. This, too, likely provokes a degree of unhappiness and dysfunction, as capitalism has a hierarchical pyramid structure. The mass majority can never "win." These kinds of dynamics appear neglected by social media researchers, who are typically from the North.

Top-down concentration plays out in the global advertising industry as well. Once again, the US reigns supreme. At the top of the pyramid, Google (39%), Facebook (18%), and Amazon (7%) soak up 64% of the online ad market. China's closest competitor, TikTok, takes just 3%.[52]

And third, Simms and Murray found a "link between materialism—and therefore advertising—and unsustainable consumption behaviour."[53] Advertisements also likely push people to work more hours, Simms and Murray discovered. Tyler Durden summed up the industry in the movie,

Fight Club: "Advertising has us chasing cars and clothes, working jobs we hate so we can buy shit we don't need."

E-commerce

In addition to advertisements, online platforms have been engineered to speedily deliver the wishes of our every consumerist desires. Amazon—the so-called "everything store"—has developed an ultra-sophisticated two-day delivery system via its Prime service so that anything, even a set of toothpicks, can be at your door within a day or two. Fast delivery, in turn, increases total CO_2 emissions via more frequent (and less full) truck dispatches. Moreover, e-commerce has increased the scale of overseas shipping, which of course uses more resources than local shipping.[54]

E-commerce is quite visible because it is new and growing in popularity. However, physical stores are still overwhelmingly dominant. In the US, e-commerce still only accounts for 13% of total retail sales (compared to 87% in physical stores) whereas in China, online retail takes just over a quarter.[55]

Nevertheless, China accounts for 111 billion parcel shipments per year, or 73.5% of the global shipping total. The United States is second at 21.2 billion (13.2%), followed by Japan (9.1 billion parcels amounting to 5.7%).[56] The US spends the most on parcel shipments at $188 billion of $491 billion globally.[57]

As a whole, e-commerce traverses borders less fluidly than more software-intensive products like streaming entertainment or search engines. For example, Amazon Marketplace ships physical goods, which requires extensive logistics infrastructure and adaptation to local cultures and businesses. If you're a company in the US, it's easier to offer a product like YouTube to a Brazilian than it is to ship them a physical item or set up an e-commerce business that interacts with local businesses and consumers.

For this reason, many tech giants outside the US succeed in the e-commerce sector, as they are able to copy Silicon Valley before the Americans get there. For example, Argentinian e-tailer MercadoLibre (meaning "free market") has become Latin America's largest corporation with a market cap of $82 billion at the time of writing. Dubbed the "South American Amazon," it was founded in 1999 by (now-billionaire) Marcos Galperin, who saw an opportunity to replicate eBay while pursuing his Master's degree in Business Administration at Stanford University. A quarter century later, the behemoth has its own online marketplace, logistics infrastructure (including a cargo airline, Meli Air), payment platform, streaming entertainment, and cryptocurrency. With operations in 18 of 33 Latin American countries, it is the largest e-commerce provider in the region with about 20% of e-retail sales in 2021.[58]

Whereas Amazon faces some competition in Latin America, it has successfully colonized European e-commerce. After establishing a presence in Germany in 1998, it expanded rapidly and took 53% of the market as of 2020—more than the next nine e-commerce brands *combined*.[59] The Americans have also colonized some other regions. For example, Walmart (through its 2018 purchase of Indian e-tailer, Flipkart) and Amazon have taken over Indian e-commerce with 48% and 26% of the market, respectively.[60]

In China, US e-retailers gave it a shot, but failed. Walmart has a substantial presence as the fourth-largest *brick-and-mortar* retailer in China (with over 5% of the market),[61] and physical stores still account for almost three quarters of total retail sales in the country. Yet both Walmart and Amazon have failed to crack into the online space. The latter tried its luck in China, but failed and exited the market in 2019.

American companies dominate global e-commerce in terms of *market cap*, with Amazon leading the way.[62] But the wider picture has some important nuances. On a global scale, China possesses the largest e-commerce *marketplace*, and Chinese consumers shop online at a greater rate than any other country. Alibaba, which operates the online shopping platforms Taobao and Tmall, accounts for 23% of worldwide merchandise volume, followed by Amazon (12%) and China's JD.com (9%), Pinduoduo (8%), and Duoyin (4%).[63] Yet Alibaba's e-commerce sales are primarily located *inside* China (71% of its total revenues) rather than internationally (7%).[64] Amazon, by contrast, does not provide data separating e-commerce from other products at the international level. If we extrapolate from *total* e-commerce sales across countries and regions, we can estimate that 44% of the company's *total* revenue (including other segments, like cloud computing) comes from e-commerce inside the US and 19.6% from international e-commerce—higher than China's. The others on China's list primarily derive their income from domestic sales. Thus, we can conclude that China pushes more e-commerce than any other country in the world, albeit mostly inside mainland China.

Fast fashion

That said, there is one *global* e-commerce sector that China now clearly dominates: fast fashion, an industry that brings together many of the threads we've discussed. Over the past several years, the Chinese app Shein (pronounced SHE-in) has taken the world by storm with its cheap clothes and quick-churning product lines. The company—which sells in almost every country *except* China—offers up to 10,000 new products *each day*. For those who haven't used the app, clothing items like dresses or swimsuits can retail for just a few dollars. By the end of 2022, Shein held about half of all US fast fashion sales.[65]

A similar platform, Temu (owned by Chinese tech giant, PDD Holdings), has also exploded onto the scene over the past three years. Unlike Shein, Temu is not a fast fashion producer (it does not produce or manufacture its own products). Rather, it offers an online marketplace of third-party sellers offering a wide variety of cheap products (over 200 categories). Products at Temu are as much as 70% cheaper than similar items listed at Amazon, while women's fashion products at Shein are 39% to 60% lower than those of H&M. The two corporations are expected to generate revenues of $33 billion and $16 billion, respectively, by the end of 2023. (The former is netting a small profit of $800 million, while the latter is operating at a loss.)[66]

Because they have direct access to foreign markets, Chinese e-commerce platforms like Shein and Temu might initiate a race-to-the-bottom war with Western (and other wealthier) businesses to cut prices and lower labor and environmental standards. Decades ago, US clothing companies were notorious for outsourcing manufacturing to Asian sweatshops. Today, the Chinese are cutting out the Americans to fatten the pockets of their own business elites.[67]

Like so many other Chinese tech companies, Shein essentially copied the West. It didn't invent "fast fashion"—that "innovation" goes to Spain's Zara. It also learned from Amazon's partnership with Chinese manufacturers and businesses, who now comprise 28% of the company's gross merchandise value (sale of goods).[68] It's no surprise, then, that Shein ramped up the industry to an "ultra" fast level, given China's toxic mix of cheap labor, mass manufacturing capacity, penchant for intensifying Western tech, and twenty-first-century capitalist instincts. Favorable economic policies—especially a lack of export taxes in China and import taxes in the US (for orders under $800)—combined with social media marketing campaigns peddled by influencers on TikTok helped them secure Western markets.

This would seem an amazing success story, except it's not. In no time flat, Shein attracted the attention of Western critics for its shady and brutal business practices, rekindling China's reputation as the land of sweatshops. While the company refuses to disclose its source of apparel and muzzles its subcontractors, we at least know that it outsources production to networks of sweatshops along a "flexible" chain of 8,000 suppliers centered in the garment hub of Panyu, Guanzhou.[69] With 400,000 clothing factories in China, Shein can place steep demands on manufacturers and their labor forces—or move on without skipping a beat. Meanwhile, Vietnamese factories, which often pay less than half of Chinese wages, are a stone's throw away.[70]

Shein's apparel is produced by (disproportionately female) human laborers in China—not machines—who sew anywhere from several hundred to several thousand items per day, depending on a product's complexity. Its workers, many of whom migrate from other provinces, can slave away as long as 12–17 hours, for less than $2 per hour, with one day off per month, no contracts, and no overtime or benefits, often under hazardous conditions (such as fire risks)—all in violation of local and foreign laws. As Elizabeth Cline, policy director of fashion accountability watchdog Remake, put it: "[Chinese workers] have to be flexible and work all night so the rest of us can press a button and have a dress delivered to our door for $10."[71]

Swiss foundation Public Eye revealed rampant labor exploitation across the supply chain, followed by investigative journalists who snuck in cameras to provide first-hand evidence. Competitors like H&M, (Zara parent) Inditex, ASOS, and Boohoo are by no means paragons of equality—they, too, exploit cheap labor in the Global South—but they at least publish detailed information on their supply chain such as factory lists (with contact info) and codes of conduct. Shein, by contrast, only provides lofty PR. It even lied about compliance with international labor standards bodies.[72]

Some of the cotton for Shein's (and Temu's) garments is sourced in Xinjiang, where the Chinese Communist Party (CCP) oversees the extreme repression and exploitation of Uyghur Muslims.[73] Shein also scrapes the internet to copy designs from small labels (undermining their sales), fails to screen out offensive products (such as a Muslim prayer mat sold as a Greek rug), offers unsafe children's clothing (such as flammable or poisonous materials), and is allegedly exploiting loopholes to reduce import duties in countries like South Africa (which undermines their local businesses).

Average Shein shoppers in the US have middle-class incomes, and are not poor, as we might have guessed—they are simply looking for good deals.[74] We can conclude, then, that poor people in one part of the world are virtually enslaved to mass-produce goods people don't need in another part of the world. In this case, even when Chinese companies "win"—meaning their rich benefactors like Shein's founder and Washington University alum, Chris Xu, obtain substantial market share—China is still losing, if by "China" we mean its everyday laborers who remain trapped within the colonial order engineered by the global capitalism. The whole thing is insane.

But the problems don't end there. Fast fashion corporations not only exploit workers, they also ravage the environment. The fashion industry accounts for 8–10% of global CO_2 emissions (4–5 billion tons annually). In the EU, it has the fourth-highest negative impact on climate change and the third-highest on land and water use.[75] On top of this, the industry is growing at an exponential rate—thanks in large part to the creation of fast fashion by the West in the 1990s:

- Clothing production has doubled since 2000 (from 100 billion to 200 billion units a year) while garment usage (measured in days worn per item) has decreased by 36%.
- Total global consumption (62 million tons per year) is projected to almost double by 2030 (to 102 million).
- The average person today buys 60% more clothing than in 2000. As of 2018, the average American purchased 68 items of clothing per year (or one item every 5.4 days).
- The fashion industry's global carbon emissions are on pace to double by 2030.[76]

141

Kirsi Niinimäki and her colleagues explain how the industry operates. The supply chain starts with raw materials (synthetic chemicals like polyester, cotton, and wood) and is then shipped to manufacturers who spin them into yarn. The yarn is then shipped to textile manufacturers, who knit or weave them into fabrics. Textiles are then used by garment and trims manufacturers to produce clothes, who ship their product to retail distribution centers, then on to retailers, end consumers, and finally, the trash bin at the end of a product's life. Online sales are increasingly shipped by the more carbon-intensive air cargo (instead of less carbon-intensive boats), and garments may be shipped across the world several times over during the production process.[77]

The levels of waste and pollution are staggering:

- Less than 1% of used clothing is recycled into new garments.
- Every year some $500 billion in value is lost due to clothing that is barely worn, not donated, recycled, or ends up in a landfill.
- Ninety-two million tons of garments end up in landfills each year, equivalent to a full dump truck every second. This will reach 134 million tons per year by 2030.
- US consumers throw away 81.5 pounds of clothes every year.
- A study of 20 countries revealed people do not wear at least half the clothes they own.
- About 30% of the clothes produced are never sold.
- The volume of textiles in US landfills doubled over the past two decades.
- Just 12% of the material used for clothing is recycled.
- Synthetic chemicals like polyester can take two centuries to decompose.
- Textile treatment and dyeing are responsible for 20% of global water pollution.
- Synthetic textiles release around 35% of all microplastics into the ocean.
- It takes 20,000 liters of water to produce 1 kg of conventional (non-organic) cotton.
- Every year 150 million trees are razed for cellulosic fabrics.
- The US dumps about 500,000 tons of secondhand clothing per year in low- and middle-income countries like Southeast Asia, Latin

America, and Africa. These "imports" undermine their local industries, including traditional styles.[78]

Environmental hazards are typically endured by workers and communities in the Global South producing products for the Global North (a form
of *environmental racism*). For instance, cotton—which accounts for 25% of
textile materials (second only to polyester's 51%)—is extremely water-in-
tensive and often grown for export. Almost half of local water use impacts
are caused by cotton cultivation for foreign demand. Textiles are responsible
for 7% of local groundwater and drinking water losses globally, especially in
water-stressed areas such as China and India.[79]

The fashion industry also pollutes local water supplies. "In Cambodia,"
Niinimäki et al. observe, "the fashion industry [is] responsible for 88% of all
industrial manufacturing (as of 2008), [and] has caused an estimated 60%
of water pollution and 34% of chemical pollution."[80] A small percentage
(~0.5%) of the 15,000 chemicals used for textiles are identified as dangerous
(e.g., ecotoxic or cancerous) to workers, consumers, biodiversity, local ecosystems, and the environment. The impact is especially bad in the South,
which tends to be an "anything goes" land of extremes where rich people
dump on the poor and regulations are non-existent or neglected.

Dumping on the South: the rise of e-waste

Clothing is not the only Western item dumped on poor countries in connection with the digital economy. Faster, newer devices like smartphones
become available on the market every year, and we happily chuck them
away for something better, even if they still work. Many of those devices
have toxic chemicals, and they are being illegally shipped by the tons to the
Global South.

Electronic waste, or "e-waste," is usually defined as electronic equipment that has been thrown out by the owner with no intention of re-use.
This includes things like computers, televisions, monitors, microwaves, and
mobile phones. E-waste typically contains toxic materials such as metals
(e.g., arsenic, copper, lead, mercury, nickel), plastics (e.g., PVC), and hazardous chemicals (e.g., brominated flame retardants). These elements seep into

143

soil, air, water, and living things and they poison humans, plants, microbes, and animals.

The hazards of e-waste are well-documented. According to a *Lancet Planetary Health* review of 70 unique studies, "Elevated toxic chemicals negatively impact on neonatal growth indices and hormone level alterations in e-waste exposed populations." There are "possible connections between chronic exposure to e-waste and DNA lesions, telomere attrition, inhibited vaccine responsiveness, elevated oxidative stress, and altered immune function"—things nobody would want to experience.[81] Another study found children and pregnant women exposed to e-waste were found "especially susceptible during the critical periods of exposure that detrimentally affect diverse biological systems and organs ... Exposure to contaminants associated with e-waste during gestation, infancy, or childhood can lead to obesity, asthma, or neurodevelopmental disorders," impaired fetal development, decreased child growth and development, lower semen quality, and poor cardiovascular health.[82]

Toxic exposure is primarily derived from the informal recycling sector—where poor workers use chemicals, fire, and their own hands to pick apart other people's e-waste to sell any remaining materials of value—as well as through inhalation, ingestion, and dermal absorption of contaminated soil, dust, air, water, or food sources. Par for the course, e-waste disproportionately impacts the Global South—especially millions of women and children living and working near digital dumpsites.[83]

Measured on a per-person basis, the Global North creates the lion's share of the world's garbage. The United States leads the pack: it produces far more waste and recycles far less than other developed countries. But rich countries don't like contaminating their own living spaces, so they ship a lot of their waste to poor countries. To keep their consumerist lifestyles going, they are advocating recycling as a means to decouple material resource use from economic growth. Under this scenario, a *linear* (cradle-to-grave) consumption model would give way to a *circular* (cradle-to-cradle) one.[84]

As the nonprofit Resilience points out, the so-called "circular economy" has three severe limitations. First, modern products (such as computers and LED lights) are too complex to recycle. The elements which can be re-used are of inferior quality (called "downcycling"). Second, recycling requires processing materials, and that requires energy and materials for the processing itself. Even if we use 100% renewables such as solar panels, wind turbines, and lithium-ion batteries, those will eventually run out of energy, and they are difficult to recycle (so they are landfilled or incinerated). Third, even if we could magically recycle *all* material resources, most materials are accumulated in buildings, infrastructure, and consumer goods. The key word here is "accumulate"—we don't throw away buildings, lamps, sidewalks, and the like on an annual basis. Rather, we keep making new things, and then we retain most of what we created.[85]

By Resilience's calculations, 71% of resources cannot be recycled or re-used (44% of which are energy sources and 27% of which are added to existing stocks). It follows we can only reduce our ecological footprint "by reducing total [resource] use."[86] Those who espouse a circular economy as a grand fix to the environment—such as the Ellen MacArthur Foundation—are only focused on the small percentage of re-usable resources available to economies. Building a more "circular economy" won't counteract the limits to growth.

Of course, waste exports to the South are nothing new. Researchers have documented the practice for decades. In 2017, the United States exported about a third of its recycling. Seventy-eight percent percent of that landed in Global South countries with poor waste management (e.g., China, India, Malaysia, and Indonesia). According to the World Health Organization, the overwhelming majority of e-waste is illegally traded or dumped in low- or middle-income countries.[87]

In 2016, a GPS tracking project by the Basel Action Network found that 40% of US e-waste was illegally exported, with 93% moved to developing countries (mostly China). China decided to "shut its doors to foreign trash" the following year, so the US diverted its exports to poor African and Asian countries—including when it was banned by international law.[88]

As part of the "waste trade," goods and scrap materials are shipped to the South, which processes them for parts or repairs them for shipment back to the North as part of the "circular economy." Studies show that the social and environmental burdens of this model are unequally distributed between the North and South.

Electronic waste fits squarely within this dynamic. Americans trash over 150 million phones per year (over 400,000 per day). They only recycle around 15% of their e-waste, and so they ship a large amount to poor coun-

(a)

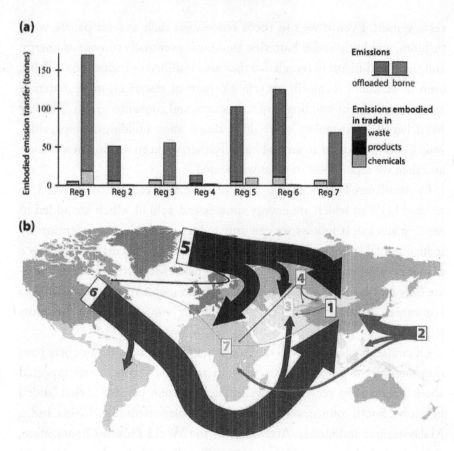

(b)

Figure 5.3   The flow of PBDE emissions (Creative Commons CC-BY 4.0)

The global flow of the toxic flame retardant, PBDE, largely from e-waste.
Source: Tong et al., 2020.[89]

tries. Let them suffer the environmental hazards. Tracing a toxic flame retardant, polybrominated diphenyl ether (PBDE), Tong et al. found that "core regions have off-loaded PBDE emissions, mostly associated with the disposal of electrical and electronic waste (e-waste), to semi-core and peripheral regions in mainland China and the Global South." PBDEs are now restricted for new products because they damage human and animal health, but existing products will be used and recycled over decades. Half of China's PBDE emissions are linked to imported e-waste.[90]

Thus, rich countries in the North disproportionately consume electronic goods and then ship their e-waste to poor countries in the South. And the problem is escalating. Electronic waste is one of the fastest-growing

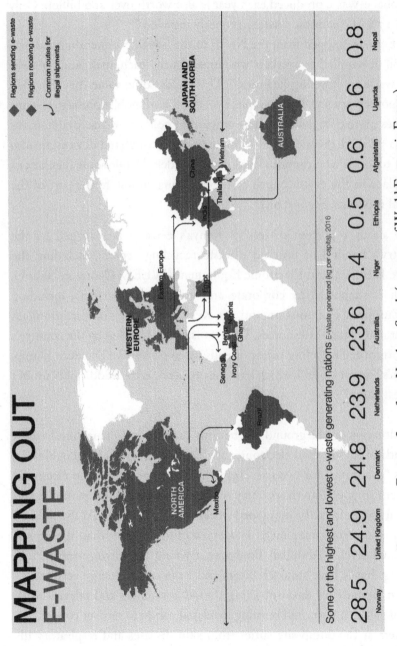

Figure 5.4 E-waste flows from North to South (courtesy of World Economic Forum)

Source: PACE & WEF, 2018.[91]

waste streams: 53.6 million tons (Mt) of e-waste was produced in 2019—about 5% of all global waste—and it is projected to reach 74.7 Mt by 2030. The global e-waste produced each year is also worth over $60 billion. Only around 17% of electronic waste is properly recycled.[92]

The e-waste shipped from the North to the South is either dumped into a landfill or handled by workers who break, burn, leach, melt, and dismantle the waste in recycling facilities.[93] This yields some value they can cash out (at poverty wages). For example, a metric ton of mobile phones contains 100 times more gold than the same amount of gold ore; e-waste contains as much as 7% of the world's gold.[94] Some of the secondhand devices are also sold off to locals who cannot afford newer models. While some regulations are in place in the South, much of the recycling simply forms part of the informal economy. For instance:

> Only about 1 percent or less of Kenya's e-waste is managed by the country's handful of licensed e-waste recycling centers, including the Waste Electrical and Electronic Equipment (WEEE) Centre in Nairobi, which is supported by corporate and government partners, including the European Commission and the Kenyan Ministry of Environment, Water and Natural Resources. The rest is either handled by the country's large, informal recycling sector or ends up in places like Dandora Dump, Kenya's biggest landfill, which stretches 30 acres in the middle of Nairobi's poorest slum.[95]

The situation on the ground can be truly horrific. In Ghana, hundreds of thousands of tons of used electronics are illegally dumped at Agbogbloshie, Ghana's "graveyard" for e-waste. Approximately 30–40% of the electronic equipment shipped into the country is not in working condition (junk), and most of it comes from the developed world (mainly Europe). At the site, soil contamination from toxic metal is over 100 times higher than the typical background level.[96] Abdullah Boubacar, a young man living nearby, told *Bloomberg* that "I have stomach ulcers and I run out of energy very easily." Boubacar "spends his days smashing up old computers and televisions in search of valuable parts and burning insulated cables to recover copper."[97]

Workers at the dump site suffer from skin diseases and respiratory illnesses due to e-waste contamination. "The workers can't do anything about it because they have to earn a living, so it's a trade-off. They earn money but their health suffers," said Professor Julius Fobil at the University of Ghana's School of Public Health. "In total, about 80,000 men, women, and children subsist from the Agbogbloshie dump, living either on-site or in the adjacent slum."[98]

* * *

Figure 5.5   E-Waste at the Agbogbloshie dump in Ghana

E-waste at the Agbogbloshie dump in Accra, Ghana.
Top image: Yeung, 2019. Bottom image: Steele, 2021.[99]

149

We've now seen that digital colonialism is driving a worldwide ecologically unequal exchange and division of labor. This phenomenon runs straight through the digital economy, from the more invisible elements like streaming entertainment and cloud computing to the more visible elements like agriculture and e-commerce.

This is a central problem for the environment. It's not simply that the digital economy has unsustainable climate and ecological footprints. It's that digital colonialism and capitalism drive growth and concentrate wealth, reinforcing the US and Global North's material resource use and power despite the environmental debts owed to the Global South. This radically undermines the prospect of a just and sustainable economy. It cannot continue.

The only solution to the environmental crisis is to abolish class and inequality in every society. With respect to digital tech, this means eradicating digital colonialism and capitalism through a revolution based on digital degrowth. We'll discuss ideas about how to do that in Chapters 8–9.

Before we address solutions, if we're going to actually make all forms of ecosocialist degrowth a reality, we need to recognize that there will be fierce resistance from power elites, especially by those who own the means of violence. It's here that we begin to see how digital technology connects to the environment in more ways than one.

6
The Big Tech Military Machine

Technological dominance provides much more than a source of economic power for the American Empire. Unlike oil or steel, US tech products are multifaceted, performing a wide array of functions, from providing new ways to communicate with friends and family to the administration of surveillance, repression, and violence. This latter function—the integration of advanced technology into the military, police, courts, prisons, and border patrol—is a stupendous source of twenty-first-century geopolitical power and social control, the topic of this and the following chapter.

Before we turn to technology, it's worth our while to consider a few facts about American history. From the moment Europeans arrived on American shores, they have been at war. First, they exterminated the Native Americans through a genocidal process of colonial conquest. At the end of the nineteenth century, they began expanding in earnest across the ocean with murderous military incursions into Cuba, the Philippines, Hawaii, and China, with expansion continuing during the Progressive Era. During the New Deal era, Franklin D. Roosevelt extended the global presence of US military bases—which now exceed 750 overseas bases in over 80 countries—and built up the war economy, setting the stage for post-World War II American military dominance.[1]

On his way out of office, Dwight D. Eisenhower famously warned Americans that the "military-industrial complex" is a major source of power that needs to be reined in. Instead, the American military empire established global hegemony, waging wars and staging military coups across the Third World during the Cold War era. With the fall of the Soviet Union, the pretext for US military interventions collapsed. Nonetheless, American militarism didn't skip a beat. It ravaged Iraq during the first Gulf War and put up sanctions that killed around half a million children. After the 9/11 attacks, the US reinvigorated its "war on terror" with the invasions of Afghanistan and Iraq. For years, the US accounted for about half the world's military spending. Today, it spends 38% of the world's total (compared to 14% by China and 3% by Russia).[2]

Throughout all these periods, the US also supported tyrannical regimes—from apartheid South Africa to apartheid Israel—increasingly waged covert wars, and dominated the global arms industry with around half the world's arms production and sales. Washington's New Cold War nemesis, China, doesn't have a tiny fraction of the US's military footprint and history of interventions.

The "greatest purveyor of violence in the world," Martin Luther King, Jr. once put it, the US continuously wages violent wars against the poor people of color in the Global South, overthrows democracy, and provides military assistance to the majority of the world's dictatorships—all in service to corporate America and the US government.[3]

Esteemed US diplomat George Kennan explained modern US foreign policy goals in National Security Memorandum No. 68 of 1948:

> We [the United States] have about 50% of the world's wealth but only 6.3% of its population ... In this situation, we cannot fail to be the object of envy and resentment. Our real task in the coming period is to devise a pattern of relationships which will permit us to maintain this position of disparity without positive detriment to our national security. To do so, we will have to dispense with all sentimentality and day-dreaming; and our attention will have to be concentrated everywhere on our immediate national objectives. We need not deceive ourselves that we can afford today the luxury of altruism and world-benefaction.[4]

The Global South was to "fulfill its major function as a source of raw materials and a market" for the developed capitalist countries, to be "exploited," in Kennan's words, for the reconstruction of Europe and Japan.[5] Kennan advocated "local police repression" in the face of any "Communist" political representation. Here, the term "Communist" generally referred to indigenous people resisting Western grand designs to "exploit" them as "a source of raw materials and markets." "It is better to have a strong [authoritarian] regime in power than a liberal government if it is indulgent and relaxed and penetrated by Communists," Kennan said.[6] Where needed, "harsh government repression" was to be used to suppress indigenous resistance.

The human toll was ghastly. Along the way, victims were massacred and tortured. Villages were razed to the ground and people were rounded into concentration camps. In Indochina, to pick one example, then national-security adviser Henry Kissinger transmitted Nixon's orders for "A massive bombing campaign in Cambodia. Anything that flies on anything that moves"—a blanket order for genocide that was executed through a carpet bombing campaign that dropped 2.7 million tons on a poor and defenseless people.[7] Families were destroyed. Millions of lives have been ruined. From its inception, the United States and its allies have opened up the jaws of hell on the world's people, continuing into the present. America is the most brutal, warmongering tyrant on the planet.

This presents a serious problem for us. We saw in the previous chapters that to have a just transition to a sustainable economy, we need to radically redistribute our economic resources from North to South, rich to poor.

The problem is that the general structure of American imperialism and global capitalism remains intact. If any movement to accomplish this goal becomes an actual threat—i.e., more than just people talking about this—the American ruling classes and its allies in the North and the South will unleash the tools of violence on the people of the world. Anyone pushing back will be tarred and feathered as "communists," "ecoterrorists," or whatever other label needs to be conjured up to demonize environmental defenders and eradicate attempts to save our planet. And if the world's people try to defend themselves, they will continue to suffer on the front-lines of repression.

From a global perspective, then, the US military, powered by Big Tech, is the most dangerous organization on the planet. As part of a worldwide demilitarization effort, it must be dismantled, along with other tools of policing repression, so that people can liberate themselves and protect life on Earth.

SURVEILLANCE FOR THE AMERICAN EMPIRE

The gathering of intelligence is critical to US military campaigns. When the US invaded the Philippines in 1898, it knew next to nothing about the population. Surveillance technologies became an indispensable tool to help the American invaders understand and subjugate the natives.

As historian Alfred McCoy demonstrates, the emergence of the modern US surveillance state—made possible by "America's first information revolution"—traces back to this imperialist venture. Drawing upon the latest-and-greatest inventions of the late nineteenth century, the US military exploited new *information and communications* technologies (Thomas Edison's telegraph, Philo Remington's typewriter, Alexander Graham Bell's telephone, John Gamewell's police telegraph/telephone call-box system), *storage* technologies (Melvil Dewey's Dewey Decimal System, Herman Hollerith's punched card system), *biometric* analytics (such as fingerprinting and Alphonse Bertillon's photographic identification), *statistical* methods (such as statistical regression), and thousands of human operatives to pacify and subjugate the Philippines. The US Army carried out massacres, burned villages, rounded up hundreds of thousands of Filipinos into concentration camps, and destroyed the resistance.[8]

The surveillance outfit was headed up by General Ralph Van Deman in 1901, later known as the "father of US military intelligence." Lessons learned were soon repatriated to the United States. During World War I, Van Deman collaborated with the Federal Bureau of Investigation (FBI) to design the US internal security apparatus based on Philippine experience. The new technologies were used to surveil and repress communists, anarchists, radical labor leaders, and worker revolts during the first Red Scare.[9]

A century later, during the first decade of the 2000s, a succession of National Security Agency (NSA) whistleblowers began revealing some details about how the spy agency is working with Big Tech corporations like AT&T to suck up information about the world's people from the internet. Wikileaks also appeared on the world stage with a system to publish leaked documents about government secrets, including mass surveillance. On June 1, 2013, Wikileaks founder Julian Assange penned an op-ed for *The New York Times*, "The Banality of Don't Be Evil," detesting the privacy-eroding practices of Google and other Big Tech giants as a form of authoritarianism unto itself. The "erosion of individual privacy in the West and the attendant centralization of power make abuses inevitable, moving the so-called "good" societies closer to the "bad" [authoritarian] ones," Assange wrote.[10]

Four days later, on June 5, 2013, journalists began leaking Edward Snowden's cache of documents detailing the breathtaking scope of the NSA's mass surveillance programs. The first program revealed, PRISM, demonstrates that by way of secret agreements, the NSA accesses and collects data from the emails, documents, photos, and data hosted by top Big Tech firms, including Microsoft, Yahoo, Google, Facebook, PalTalk, YouTube, Skype, AOL, and Apple. Other major programs illustrate the unchecked power of public–private surveillance in the digital age. Here's a partial list:

- Through Tempora, the UK's equivalent to the NSA, the Government Communications Headquarters (GCHQ) taps major fiber-optic cables—the main arteries of the internet—and shares the data captured with the NSA.
- The XKEYSCORE software allows US spies to search through the NSA's massive data troves in a Google Search-like fashion.
- The Muscular program planted backdoors into critical infrastructure like Cisco routers headed overseas.
- The NSA hacked Chinese mobile phones, collecting over 900 billion SMS messages, and it infiltrated the servers of Chinese companies like Huawei.[11]
- Through the Optic Nerve program, the GCHQ collected the webcam images of 1.8 million Yahoo users even if they were not suspected of doing anything wrong, including sexual content.
- The NSA is collecting the data of encrypted communications in hopes that it can one day decrypt the content.

While the US government justifies all of this on grounds of "national security"—a euphemism for American imperialism—leaked documents showed the opposite. The NSA and its allies targeted human rights organizations like the Egyptian Initiative for Personal Rights and the Legal Resources Centre in South Africa; hacked the communications of world leaders like Germany's then-Vice-Chancellor Angela Merkel and Mexico's then-President Felipe Calderon; and spied on Brazilian oil giant Petrobras.

Another trove of classified information called Vault 7 was leaked by Wikileaks in 2017. Though it received less attention than the Snowden leaks, Vault 7 exposed the Central Intelligence Agency's (CIA) surveillance and cyberwar capabilities. This included the ability to compromise smart devices (e.g., TVs), car software, operating systems, and web browsers. The CIA has a rich record of foreign intervention on every continent, including the torture, assassination, surveillance, infiltration, and overthrow of political actors deemed threatening to US state-corporate interests.

There are more revelations from recent leaks, too long to list here. Despite the fact that the world's people are the ones most harmed by the United States, when the conversation turned to the ethics of NSA surveillance, the US intelligentsia focused on the unlawful surveillance of *American* citizens given that the NSA is only supposed to intercept *foreign* communications. As US Congressman Trey Gowdy (R-SC) asserted, approvingly, "non-citizens who are not in the United States [are] not afforded any protections under the 4th Amendment."[12] That is to say, if you're a foreigner, the Americans have the right to spy on everything you do.

THE BIG TECH MILITARY MACHINE

Technology has always been critical to US military power. As noted in Chapter 1, Washington subsidized the development of many of the foundational digital technologies to build up its military supremacy. By 1969, the Commander-in-Chief of US forces in Vietnam remarked:

> On the battlefield of the future, enemy forces will be located, tracked, and targeted almost instantaneously through the use of data links, computer assisted intelligence evaluation, and automated fire control. With first round kill probabilities approaching certainty, and with surveillance devices that can continually track the enemy, the need for large forces to fix the opposition physically will be less important … With cooperative effort, no more than 10 years should separate us from the automated battlefield.[13]

Ten years was an overstatement, but we are much closer to that reality than ever before.

Contemporary military innovations heavily rely on the private sector—another new development characteristic of today's digital militaries.[14] This is especially the case with digital technology, where the US depends on Big Tech to secure military supremacy.

The integration of Big Tech with the US military first gained considerable public attention with Google's Project Maven. Established in 2017, the project uses artificial intelligence to turn reams of data—e.g., visual data obtained from surveillance drones and satellite imagery—into "actionable intelligence" that will "improve warfighting speed and lethality" for the military.[15] Because humans cannot possibly review the many hours of video footage collected by surveillance devices, AI can be used to identify things of interest to them. Examples include *objects* (e.g., vehicles, persons, etc.), *characteristics* (e.g., the "red car"), *actions* (e.g., a bicycle in motion, a person running), and *analytics* (e.g., heat maps documenting how often people walk on a sidewalk, patterns of ship positions).

When Google workers discovered their company was contracted to supply the Department of Defense (DoD) with drone analytics capabilities, some of them launched a petition and forced their company to cancel the contract. However, new contracts were then awarded to Microsoft ($30 million), Amazon ($20 million), and IBM ($1.7 million) to fill the void. It's since been revealed that Maven ingests data obtained from captured enemy material, social media monitoring, maritime, and publicly available information, and that the system is being used against the Russians in Ukraine.[16]

Following the lead of Big Tech workers—themselves a problem we will return to in Chapter 9—three other projects came to public attention at the time. The first was a $10 billion cloud computing contract for the Pentagon's Joint Enterprise Defense Infrastructure (JEDI).

The JEDI project aimed to bring legacy systems into "one big cloud," which would pool data together into one pot. As Jamie Wylly, Vertical Lead for Defense and Intelligence at Microsoft, put it:

> The US Army has almost 1,200 data centers, which they're trying to consolidate down to a couple of hundred, because those separate data centers … create silos of information. But of course, this is why the entire US Department of Defense wants to move to the cloud—to be able to transform the way that they look at information and make it available securely to as many people as possible.[17]

After a contentious fight for the contract by Amazon, Microsoft, and Oracle, JEDI was eventually scrapped for a "multi-cloud" replacement called the Joint Warfighting Cloud Capability (JWCC). (A multi-cloud option uses cloud computing services from at least two cloud providers to run their applications.) In late 2022, JWCC contracts were awarded to Microsoft, Amazon, Google, and Oracle totaling $9 billion.

A third project, Google and Amazon's Project Nimbus cloud computing contract to service the Israeli government and defense establishment, has also received attention from the mainstream media. For this project, Google and Amazon were awarded a $1.2 billion cloud computing contract to service the Israeli government, including the Israeli Defense Forces (more accurately deemed the Israeli Occupation Forces, or the IPO).[18]

Microsoft's HoloLens mixed reality military tech was the fourth Big Tech military project to make headlines. The headsets can collect data from sensors and overlay imagery in the user's field of vision. Microsoft first developed HoloLens for business and consumer applications and later adapted it for military applications. According to the company, the headsets "allow soldiers to see through smoke and around corners, use holographic imagery for training and have 3D terrain maps projected onto their field of vision at the click of a button."[19] They also provide thermal vision, night vision, tactical "heads-up," and passive targeting (allowing soldiers to identify targets without being seen).

Microsoft is now slated to deploy 120,000 headsets to the US Army, to the tune of $21.88 billion. It seems unlikely that the headsets have ever been used on the battlefield, but Microsoft delivered them to the Israeli and Ukrainian militaries around the time it signed its contract with the US military. They have likely delivered headsets to other countries as well.[20]

The partnership of Big Tech with the US military and its allies has a long history extending far beyond these four examples. And it is baffling that the mass media and tech "left" has done little to expose it. For example, as early as 1999, Microsoft licensed software to the Israeli Occupation Forces. As anti-imperialist scholar Yarden Katz documents in an article ignored by the mainstream, shortly after Israel's murderous incursion into Jenin (2002), Microsoft posted a billboard on the main Israeli highway stating, "To the security forces and emergency services, the heart thanks you." This was followed by a three-year, $35 million Microsoft contract with the Israeli government to "provide unlimited products to the Israeli Army and defense ministry, and broadly exchange 'knowledge' with the Army."[21]

Other examples abound. Consider a few from the last decade or so:

- In 1998, Microsoft published a pilot's manual, *Microsoft Combat Flight Simulator*, a software application designed to train combat pilots.
- In 2012, Microsoft scored a $700 million contract to service the US Navy.
- In 2012, Google's then-CEO Eric Schmidt co-authored *The New Digital Age*, which praised war criminal Henry Kissinger throughout.
- In 2013, Amazon beat out IBM for a $600 million CIA cloud computing contract—years before the JEDI project was announced.
- In 2014, the National Geospatial-Intelligence Agency (NGA) became the first US intelligence agency to host an operational capability on AWS Cloud Commercial Services, with participation from Lockheed Martin for world mapping.
- In a 2014, Microsoft said it was "at the heart of NATO's Connected Forces Initiative," based on its commitment to "support [NATO's] peacekeeping missions throughout the world."
- In 2015, Eric Schmidt hosted Kissinger for a fireside chat at Google. The following year, he chaired the DoD's new Innovation Advisory Board. Schmidt subsequently co-authored a book, *The Age of AI*, with Henry Kissinger in 2021.
- As early as 2016, Microsoft was helping the Ukrainian Army integrate HoloLens into its LimpidArmor tank system.[22]

Microsoft's military empire

The extent of Big Tech's current integration into modern militaries is scarcely documented by the intellectual classes, and is poorly understood.[23] The narrow focus on just four projects has come at the expense of a broader outlook connecting Big Tech to the American Empire and the environment. When press articles and critics focus on individual pieces of technology, they miss the forest for the trees.[24] An unlisted YouTube video from Microsoft and its military partner, Thales—a leading military contractor from France—provides a good starting point for how Big Tech integrates into modern militaries. It's worth quoting in full:

Modern warfare is collaborative by nature. But in the past, information was exchanged manually from one unit to another. Today, operations are conducted with coalition forces, and are joint by design—across land, sea, air, space, and cyber. So, information needs to reach the entire battlespace simultaneously. It must be networked, interoperable, and accessible from anywhere. This is the Connected Digital Battlespace, enabled by Thales and Microsoft. It enhances situational awareness between coalition forces and improves decisiveness, giving your forces a tactical advantage.

Thales Digital Connected Battlespace connects vehicles, weapons, specialist equipment, and soldiers, through cameras, sensors, satellite, and [software] applications, on a secure and robust cloud. And it delivers up-to-date awareness for the entire theater and [headquarters], in the forward-deployed operations center, and to tactical units. Sensor data automatically triangulates from multiple sources, including body-worn devices, for more complete situational awareness, giving you a common operating picture, with options analyzed and recommended by artificial intelligence, and systems to support people with augmented reality. Forces receive near-instantaneous awareness to respond to threats. When you can gather intelligence from battlefield action, manage data according to mission criticality, analyze it using AI, and store it securely in the cloud, you have strategic choice, faster responses, and decision superiority across the connected digital battlespace.[25]

Figure 6.1 Microsoft's military ecosystem

A schematic representation of Microsoft's military ecosystem.
Source: Microsoft, 2022.[26]

In other words, modern militaries are using digital technology as if a complex, integrated machine, with a collection of complementary parts working together to plan, understand, and carry out military operations. Microsoft's involvement is as deep as it gets. As Agnus MacGregor, a former British Army officer who now serves as Microsoft's General Manager of Worldwide Defense & Intelligence, stated in an interview with military news outlet *Defense24*, "whether it's NATO or European Union countries, whether it's in the Indo-Pacific region, whether it's Latin America, [Microsoft] is operating around the world ... it might sound a little arrogant but there's not an area of the military spectrum that I don't think we're operating in."[27] Other actors mentioned by MacGregor include Africa, the Middle East, and the Five Eyes intelligence alliance (Australia, Canada, New Zealand, the United Kingdom, and the United States), who were heavily featured in the Snowden leaks.

MacGregor said that whereas state sector institutions like the US Defense Advanced Research Projects Agency used to develop cutting-edge military technologies, now the private sector is at the helm of innovation. "Over the 40 years that Microsoft has been operating we've learned how to operate in this space," he boasted.[28]

Additional insights about Microsoft's military enterprise were disclosed in a set of interviews featured on the Microsoft *GovPod* podcast. The interview subjects said that today's vehicles—be they tanks or the new F-35 joint strike fighter planes—are equipped with sensors that collect massive amounts of data. It doesn't make a lot of sense to push "refined intelligence,' from the air back to a command center," said AT Ball, a retired colonel who spent 30 years serving in the US Army and is now Managing Director of Public Safety and Security for Microsoft in Asia. Ball said it makes more sense to store and process the data in the vehicles themselves—also called analytics "at the edge," where the "edge" is the devices in use (e.g., a smartphone or fighter plane). Intelligence that is sometimes collected off-site in a cloud server farm "can live in a small box with the computing power of the cloud, like, for instance, inside that drone, then we can obtain those same insights," the podcast host, Mia Reyes, added.[29]

No one company can develop all of this alone, so the vendors and governments work together. MacGregor said Microsoft works with other "local companies," from manufacturers to integrators. Microsoft partner Thales, offering the Digital Connected Battlespace platform mentioned earlier, is the 14th largest military corporation in the world, with $9.6 billion in revenues in 2022. And it's not the only military partner in the Microsoft military ecosystem. In 2007, Microsoft began providing its ESP visual simulation platform to Northrop Grumman, the world's second-largest military corporation. The platform is used "to develop enhanced capabilities for joint military command, control, communications, computers, intelligence, surveillance, reconnaissance (C4ISR) and route and mission planning."[30]

In 2022, Microsoft partnered with Lockheed Martin, the world's largest military contractor (with $63.3 billion revenue), to collaborate on the delivery of 5G technology across terrestrial and space-based networks for "joint-all domain military operations" at the tactical edge. Clients include the US military and NATO.[31] Lockheed Martin was also the first non-government entity to move its own mission workloads inside the Microsoft Azure Government Secret cloud for "classified cloud innovations," and the two companies are working together on AI-based modeling and simulation capabilities for the DoD.[32]

Other Big Tech military contractors

It would be a mistake to single out Microsoft, however. The company may be the largest Big Tech player in the military space, but it's possible that it discloses more of its projects and partnerships with violent authorities than other Big Tech companies—giving us the clearest insight into how Big Tech operates in this space. And even that information is likely a small slice of its total military footprint. In 2021, under pressure from investors,* Microsoft hired the law firm, Foley Hoag, to investigate its human rights impact with respect to US police, immigration enforcement, and "other government contracts." Foley Hoag contacted me and attached a document disclosing that per Microsoft's request, the investigation "will *not cover* (1) Microsoft's business relationships with the U.S. Military; (2) specific aspects of Microsoft's contracts with government entities." It appears Microsoft doesn't want critical attention to this aspect of its business.

---

* This was largely prompted by my 2020 feature pieces, "The Microsoft Police State" and "Microsoft's Iron Cage", which we'll return to later.

Even though public disclosures are limited for all companies involved, there is a wealth of information on other tech companies. For the sake of brevity, I'll provide a brief sample.

Amazon services the DoD's JWCC cloud computing project and Israel's Project Nimbus. But it, too, does much more than this. Like Microsoft, Amazon works with Lockheed Martin, Northrop Grumman, and Raytheon. It has its own set of resources devoted to "National Security and Defense," with staff, products, and services operating across the world.

Like Microsoft, Amazon offers its services to militaries. The DoD is working with AWS and its satellite initiative (Project Kuiper) to integrate cloud and satellite connectivity into its space communications; the Air Force initiated its Cloud One platform in 2017 to "[provide] access to apps and information and broader connectivity using virtual assets from big-name players including Amazon and Microsoft" (as well as Google and Oracle); and the Marines Corps are testing AWS data analytics for its warfighting modernization effort in the Indo-Pacific.[33]

Other Big Tech corporations work on a dizzying array of military projects, each supplying their own component parts. Intel is first in line to build special facilities that produce chips for the US military and intelligence community as part of the CHIPS Act—with a contract worth $3.5 billion in the works—and it provides services for aerospace and war technology. AMD is collaborating with Cisco to modernize the war industry's tech infrastructure, while Nvidia is working with the Department of Defense on holistic AI solutions.[34] Other companies, such as AT&T, Verizon, Adobe, Cisco, Dell, Palantir, and Elon Musk's SpaceX—in addition to countless smaller tech companies operating quietly in the background—all have their hands in the military-industrial complex.[35]

Perhaps the most detailed knowledge we have about the deployment of the Big Tech military machine took place in the Middle East. In Afghanistan, the US flew giant surveillance balloons equipped with surveillance sensors to suck up data about what was happening on the ground. Meanwhile, the DoD created biometric profiles on millions of Afghans. Palantir Technologies developed software to provide US forces with a "god's-eye" view of the population. The company pooled the data and ran analytics to detect "patterns of life," identify "terrorists," and predict their physical movements as targets for killing. The project followed on the heels of experiments in Iraq, where Palantir and US forces hoovered up data about over 3 million Iraqis, including iris scans, fingerprints, and DNA.[36] According to Brown University, the post-9/11 wars took the lives of 4.5–4.7 million people—including 940,000 due to direct violence (encompassing 432,000 civilians)—created 38 million refugees, and cost the US federal government $8 trillion.[37]

Yet data on the tech industry's military services—which projects they participate in, how much they make as a whole, and what is being used in the real world—remains difficult to obtain. Some of these projects are only revealed through Freedom of Information requests from governments by journalists.[38] Nevertheless, we can safely conclude that in the twenty-first century context, the US military and its allies couldn't function—let alone maintain technological supremacy—without the assistance of Big Tech.

The US military and ecocide

Concerns about the integration of Big Tech into the US military and its allies goes beyond enhancing the sophistication of military power at the core of global empire. Modern militaries are environmentally destructive in and of themselves. They emit greenhouse gases into the atmosphere, damage local habitats, and destroy infrastructure that needs to be replaced through new construction projects.

The US military leads the way as the largest single polluter of any single agency or organization on the planet. In his 2009 book, *The Green Zone: The Environmental Costs of Militarism*, scholar Barry Sanders was the first to tabulate the estimated climate impact of the US military. After digging through a maze of government documents, whether hidden or obscured, Sanders found that "The military—that voracious vampire—produces enough greenhouse gases, by itself, to place the entire globe, with all its inhabitants large and small, in the most immanent danger of extinction."[39] With some 30 million acres of property overseas (including about 750 military bases) and 23 million acres at home (including about 900 military bases), the Pentagon is "the world's largest landlord."[40] On these properties, the military constructs buildings and operates heavy machinery that guzzles inordinate amounts of fossil fuels.

During military combat, machines like aerial surveillance drones and fighter jets soar through the skies to watch over enemies and drop bombs down below. An F-16 fighter plane uses 1,680 gallons of fuel *per hour*. In the second Iraq War, the US Air Force stated that from March 19 to April 9, 2003, it dropped over 30,000 sorties. During the first 24 hours, it was expected the US would deliver 800 Tomahawk cruise missiles—one every four minutes—totaling 2.4 million pounds of explosives. All of this requires massive amounts of energy. Of course, there's much more: the military operates a wide range of other vehicles, like M-1 Abrams tanks, Apache helicopters, and Humvees. It invests in research and development, produces and manages waste, flies its top brass around in luxury planes—the list goes on and on.[41]

With vehicles consuming over 2 million gallons of oil per day, the Pentagon uses enough oil in one year to power all the country's transit systems for 14–22 years. The official numbers of the entire military are obscured. The Defense Energy Support Center (DESC) reports 395,000 barrels of oil are used per day, enough to power Greece. But the numbers are much higher, as Sanders demonstrates.[42]

By 2022, the average American soldier consumed 22 times the gallons of fuel during the Iraq invasion than they did in World War II.[43] Research by scholar Neta Crawford, published a decade after Sanders, presents evidence that the Department of Defense emitted 55 million tons of *carbon dioxide equivalent* (which converts non-carbon gases to carbon measurements) in 2019. When accounting for the wider military *industry*, emissions rise to 153 million tons per year, equal to the combined emissions of the world's 45-smallest emitting countries, or that of Sweden, Denmark, and Norway combined.[44] Dr. Stuart Parkinson expanded the tally even further by calculating the US military's total "carbon boot-print," which accounts for military equipment, bases, vehicle use, as well as other, related emissions, upping the number to 340 million tons per year, or about 6% of the national total. On a worldwide scale, Dr. Parkinson estimated the carbon footprint of all militaries to be 5–6% of all global emissions.[45] (Civil aviation, by comparison, accounts for about 2% of global GHGs.)

According to Crawford, the US military consumes about three quarters of the world's jet fuels. Yet the prospect of electrifying heavy-duty machinery like tanks and fighter jets is not even close to reality. The idea of "greening" the military by reducing its emissions—an objective of progressive Democrats like Elizabeth Warren[46] (as well as the US military itself)—is not only grotesque, it is hopeless, as it focuses on non-tactical, light-duty vehicles.[47] It also fails to account for the fact that militaries are capital-intensive and compete for technological supremacy. This means militaries are in a constant race to build new equipment and infrastructures that can beat real or imagined enemies. As resource-hungry growth industries, their GHG emissions are mighty contributors to the climate crisis.[48]

Most importantly, the US military functions as guns for American capitalism, immediately disqualifying it from being "green." The idea of a "green" military is an oxymoron used by apologists for the American Empire. Progressive researchers like Neta Crawford argue that the US military is an "imperfect agent" that can do better in the world.[49] Unlike Barry Sanders, who connects US *militarism* to environmental destruction, Crawford, who omits Sanders's work in her book, disconnects the Pentagon from its capitalist foundations. Applying carbon tunnel vision, she then wonders why her government won't gently reduce its military size—she recommends cutting military bases by a paltry 20%—to reduce its climate impact.[50]

The idea of "greening the military" also ignores its *ecological* footprint, directly through warfare and production along the supply chain. Although it's not often discussed, war is a biodiversity killer. Between 1950 and 2000, over 80% of conflicts took place directly within biodiversity hotspots—areas where species are largely contained to the local habitat and generally sensitive to human disturbance.[51]

The word "ecocide" was coined in 1970 by biologist Arthur W. Galston, in reference to the mass destruction of the environment through the use of "defoliation" herbicide by the United States in Vietnam. Eventually known as Agent Orange, the chemicals were produced by American agribusiness corporations, including Dow Chemical and Monsanto, and deployed by the US military to destroy enemy forests and crops. At least 21 million gallons were sprayed. In South Vietnam, 43% of the farmland and 44% of the forests were sprayed at least once by US defoliation missions.[52] After defoliation campaigns, Jon Mitchell wrote in his harrowing book, *Poisoning the Pacific: The US Military's Secret Dumping of Plutonium, Chemical Weapons, and Agent Orange*, the "Jungles fell quiet as the chemicals killed first the insects, then small birds and frogs; sometimes monkeys fell stunned from the trees. In village farms, flocks of chickens and ducks died, and fish floated dead to the surface of ponds."[53]

The Vietnamese Association of Victims of Agent Orange (VAVA) contend that 4.8 million people have suffered illnesses or have been left with disabilities due to exposure. Corporations like Monsanto have been fighting the lawsuits in court, denying responsibility. To this day, babies in Vietnam and the babies of war veterans are likely born with birth defects due to US biological warfare.[54]

Other areas in the region were badly affected by US—and, in a few instances, Japanese—military campaigns. For decades, the US military dumped, burned, and buried toxic waste and hazardous chemicals in the waters of the Asian Pacific. Nuclear bombs were exploded at the islands, sometimes underwater. The natives living nearby were contaminated by the fallout, which US authorities officially deny. Local marine life and habitats were ruined. The US often lies or refuses to fully account for its contamination from active bases and operations overseas, which costs billions of dollars in addition to the wicked toll on life.

A 2023 study on the environmental impacts of Russia's invasion of Ukraine estimated that the war emitted over 120 million tons of greenhouse gases over 12 months, equivalent to the annual emissions of Belgium. Military vehicles, the construction of new arms, the re-building of civilian infrastructure, mass migration, gas pipeline leaks, and even an increase in the number and area of forest fires all contribute to GHG emissions. Ukraine is suffering from high degrees of air pollution, as well as water and soil contamination. The Russian military has conducted operations in over one third of the country's protected areas. In addition to its human toll, the war is devastating the Ukrainian environment.[55]

Channeling the savage conduct of the US in Indochina, Israel's genocidal bombardment of Gaza is also a campaign of ecocide. "Toxic chemicals and explosives rain down on the strip; sanitation and water treatment systems are destroyed ... dust and debris from destroyed buildings pollute the air and ground ... leaving a new layer of toxic chemicals in its soil," *Al Jazeera* reported shortly after the October 2023 invasion.[56] Israel has repeatedly assaulted the environment in Palestine over the years. Even in times of peace, it has flattened land for the so-called "buffer zone" between the wall and Gaza and sprayed herbicidal chemicals that have damaged its crops.[57]

Many scholars argue that climate change increases the risk of violent conflicts within and between countries.[58] Of course, it's impossible to predict the future. But if we cross tipping points and create a drastically more hostile environment, triggering more numerous and intense droughts, heatwaves, wildfires, storms, floods, population die-offs, not to mention events like pandemics, cascades of collapse, and mass migration, it's quite likely that conflict over scarce resources will occur, with the wealthier countries poised to impose their will through military power. What do we think will happen when people can no longer live in the Middle East, or when the West Bank's crops are scorched by droughts?

The US was born out of slavery and genocide, Jim Crow apartheid, and global empire. Now it is spearheading the ultimate horror, worldwide ecocide. The American military, powered by Big Tech, will do everything it can to maintain US hegemony. Predicated on North–South wealth disparities, the American Empire will bury all of humanity underground—and much of other life with it—before it gives up its wealth and power. It is the greatest threat to life on Earth in human history.

7
Surveil and Punish

If national liberation struggles and the environment are threatened by US military intervention, it's also the case that activist struggles are increasingly endangered by high-tech surveillance. As the planet heats up, the forces of repression are expanding their powers through sophisticated new tech. Smart camera networks, facial recognition, license plate readers, biometrics, and vast, centralized databases are now in the hands of carceral authorities, extending their eyes and ears throughout public and private spaces—both physical and cyber—as well as their (alleged) ability to predict patterns of behavior.

While the West developed the core technologies, they are being taken up throughout the world—from China and India to Brazil and South Africa. Many Global South countries lack the resources to build or effectively deploy these systems,[1] but they can do real damage, and there is little transparency about how they are used.

As we'll see, police, prisons, legal systems, and border patrol are partnering with tech companies to build out carceral solutions covering the entire correctional pipeline, from juvenile delinquency through probation and parole.

Let's start in South Africa, where university student uprisings took the country by storm.

CARCERAL DYSTOPIAS

Almost a decade ago, a national student uprising broke out in South Africa called #FeesMustFall. University protests in the country had come and gone in the years prior, but these were on a whole new level.[2] On March 9, 2015, a University of Cape Town (UCT) student, Chumani Maxwele, hurled a bucket of feces at a statue of Cecil John Rhodes, the nineteenth-century British colonizer who brutalized the southern African population after diamonds and gold were discovered under South African soil. Perched on the Rugby Road campus at UCT, the statue overlooked the whole of Cape Town, a painful symbol of white supremacy in the world's most unequal country. Rhodes Must Fall was born.

Figure 7.1   Student protests in South Africa

Students triumphantly secure the removal of a Cecil John Rhodes statue at UCT.
Source: NPR, 2017.[3]

The movement soon spread throughout the country. At Rhodes University, where I was a PhD student, we demanded our university change its name, and protesters started calling it UCKAR (the University Currently Known as Rhodes). Meanwhile, students across campuses began to agitate for greater forms of social justice, including financial inclusion.

When South Africa transitioned from apartheid to "democracy," there were no reparations or redistribution of wealth and income. A few paltry social welfare programs were implemented, such as cheap Reconstruction and Development Programme (RDP) houses and social welfare pensions for child support and the elderly. At present, as many as two thirds of the population live on less than $3 per day. Given this situation, many of the students found themselves unable to continue their studies simply because their parents were the victims of colonialism and apartheid.

In October of that year, students forcibly shut down all 26 universities in unison—as well as some colleges (what the US calls "community colleges")—with a demand to cancel the annual tuition hike. The universities capitulated, but the battle wasn't over. The following year, the resistance movement continued, this time intensifying its set of demands. These included insourced labor on campus (to improve the working conditions of service workers), improved handling of sexual violence on campus, decolonization of the university, and free, decommodified education for all. To force their demands, students barricaded campus perimeters, shut down classes, and even burned some campus buildings to the ground. Things heated up, and the universities responded with high-tech securitized violence.

I participated in the protests at Rhodes, first as someone who attended protests in 2015, and then full-time in 2016. I joined the core group on campus, and it was there that I learned about the anxieties felt by protesters in the digital era. Students (myself included) were worried that their phones were tapped and some became scared to communicate freely and openly over electronic devices. We began to notice older males with backpacks, who nobody knew, showing up on campus. And it was during this time period that I began to notice new CCTV cameras were sprouting up like mushrooms. I asked one student leader if he was worried, he said, "no, we don't care about that." This turned out to be highly mistaken.

During a protest march to the local police station, one of our student leaders banged on the hood of a beat-up car following us around as we gathered comrades from the student residences. Once we began the march through town to the police station, the same car joined the police vehicles that tailed us to station. He was there to intimidate us. During that same march, myself and others were receiving phone calls from strange numbers with country codes from nearby countries.

There were days of complete mayhem. One time, during a peaceful press conference before the national press, fighting broke out between students and private security. Before long, security forces were firing teargas and rubber bullets indiscriminately at anyone who appeared to be involved in the protests. Shells from rubber bullets littered the campus. One student's arm was broken, others had giant bruises. During a protest at the University of the Witwatersrand, student protester Shaeera Kalla was shot nine times in the back and had to be taken to the hospital. In another incident, an office cleaner was hit by a stray bullet and lost the use of his eye.

Some of the students resorted to vandalism, often low-level incidents such as throwing rocks at campus buildings. Thanks to a proliferating network of CCTV cameras, the authorities were watching. A list of over 30 "wanted" students was created on my campus, and some students went into hiding. Eventually, leaders were brought into court. Some of them were expelled. One way to clamp down on protests is to target leaders and make examples of them.

Securitization escalated the situation toward violence. The people left standing were those who were desperate enough to keep fighting and their ardent supporters. The authorities labeled us militant minorities—after they had brought in the guns and scared most of the other protesters away.

In an interview with campus security forces, I was told that campus authorities were using facial recognition to identify persons of interest. Protesters across the universities began wearing masks to conceal their identities. But for many, it was too late. When we arrived at the police station in Grahamstown during that protest mentioned above, one of the student leaders said, "those cameras have got to go."

Beating back environmental defenders

Today, we are staring down our steepest challenge in history. We need to change our way of life. This means "system change, not climate change," as environmentalists put it. And that system change must be ecosocialist—we are simply out of time to risk letting capitalism permanently destroy our planet.

As we've seen, in order to have a just and sustainable transition, we need to abolish class. That's a daunting challenge. In the modern era, no movement has successfully created a genuinely egalitarian society—one which evenly distributes political, economic, and social power. Even so-called "socialist" countries like the Soviet Union, Mao's China, and Castro's Cuba retained a relative degree of class inequality, and the state ruled over the people with an iron fist, depriving the people of liberty and self-determination.[4]

To make degrowth a lived reality—rather than a mere theoretical vision for society—will require unprecedented levels of popular resistance. And that resistance will have to be forceful. "If we could've sorted this over a cup of tea, it would've been done by now," one protester remarked at a #FeesMustFall protest. The protesters had no choice but to *force* the issue, as authorities would not offer them help just because their demands were fair and just. Holding signs in the air and picketing for change doesn't work. The #FeesMustFall movement did eventually win some concessions, including insourced labor for service workers and a student aid program (mostly loans) to drastically reduce university exclusion among the poor African population. Yet even these minor and partial victories—hardly a mass redistribution of wealth and power—were only obtained through direct action in the face of violence.

Needless to say, the degrowth movement is not going to abolish inequality between and within countries over a cup of tea.

Environmentalists are highly vulnerable to high-tech surveillance and repression. This is especially true for those demanding radical change. If degrowth movements pick up steam, they will face the most severe repression of any movement in history, as they are calling for the speedy abolition of concentrated wealth and power.[5]

There's already a heavy dose of state repression against environmentalists. In 2022, *VICE News* published documents of FBI investigations into environmental movements as cases of "ecoterrorism," which it defines as "the use or threatened use of violence of a criminal nature against innocent victims or property by an environmentally-oriented, subnational group for environmental-political reasons."[6] Acts investigated included cutting fences to release animals from fur farms and stealing equipment from slaughterhouses. Groups investigated include Greenpeace, Earth First, and Earth Liberation Front.

While the investigations took place in the 1980s, 1990s, and early 2000s, they are relevant to today's movements. In response to the article, Greenpeace rejected the eco-terrorist label, stating, "Greenpeace USA has a 50-year tradition and track record of peaceful, non-violent civil disobedience." Rolf Skar, a Greenpeace organizer, said direct action is a "last resort." But as things heat up, both literally and figuratively, direct action will become increasingly necessary to enact radical transformations, which will in turn provoke state surveillance and repression. New laws categorizing environmental defenders as "terrorists" will almost certainly proliferate.[7]

In 2022, Privacy International surveyed climate activists to ascertain their experiences and views on technology. They found the following:

- Ninety-three percent use a computer/laptop and 83% use a mobile phone for their work.
- Ninety percent use social media for their activism.
- Fifty-nine percent felt they had been subject to tech-based surveillance.[8]

Recent episodes provide cases in point. Documents obtained by *The Intercept* revealed that law enforcement and private security officers surveiled non-violent opponents of the Dakota Access Pipeline in 2016. A "counterinsurgency" security firm, TigerSwan, conducted surveillance through "aerial technology, social media monitoring, and direct infiltration, as well as attempts to shift public opinion through a counterinformation campaign."[9] Person of Interest profiles were created and the company profiled Palestinians and Muslims.

In one instance, Oglala Lakota Sioux activist Red Fawn Fallis was tackled by three law enforcement officers and pinned to the ground, facedown. She then allegedly fired three shots from underneath her stomach (while resisting arrest) using a gun she was given by her romantic partner—unbeknownst to her, a paid FBI informant who infiltrated the group. She served four years in a federal prison. "Red Fawn was singled out by law enforcement at Standing Rock—and, sadly, she wound up bearing the brunt of police and state anger over our resistance," Chase Iron Eyes from the Lakota Law Project told the press. "Of course, we know the real criminals are the oil companies and those in government and law enforcement who aid and abet their destruction of Mother Earth."[10] As activism expands, these kinds of events will occur more frequently.

Environmentalists in the Global South are especially vulnerable to carceral authorities and digital surveillance. A 2022 report put out by Global Witness documented that 1,733 land and environmental defenders had been murdered over the past decade. At least one environmentalist is killed every two days. The deadliest countries were Brazil, Colombia, the Philippines, and Mexico. Commenting on the report, Indian activist Vandana Shiva said that environmental defenders are not only putting themselves at risk, they are:

> confronting a whole [Western] viewpoint—a way of seeing nature as something not to be cherished and protected, but to be conquered and subdued ... nearly all of the murdered environmental and land defenders are from the Global South, and yet it is not the Global South that reaps the supposed economic "rewards" of all this violence. The final, saddest truth is that this viewpoint has brought us to the brink of collapse. We are not just in a climate emergency. We are in the foothills of the sixth mass extinction, and these defenders are some of the few people standing in the way. They don't just deserve protection for basic moral reasons. The future of our species, and our planet, depends on it.[11]

In 2018, a survey conducted for a study by the Swedish Society for Nature Conservation found the following:

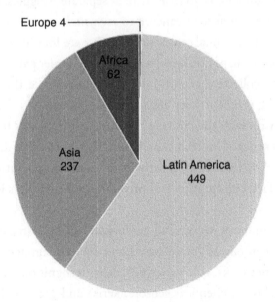

Figure 7.2 Number of environmental defenders murdered per continent, 2015–18 (courtesy of *Naturskyddsföreningen*)

Source: SSNP, 2018.[12]

175

- 17 of 25 (68%) respondent environmental organizations, all located in the Global South, are being subjected to physical or digital surveillance.
- Eighty percent said they have difficulty implementing their activities as planned.
- Almost half (44%) claim they were exposed to smear campaigns and 40% have received death threats to their employees.
- Twenty-five percent said employees or the organization's target groups have been murdered as a result of their environmental work.

Other obstacles include arrests, travel bans, fabricated charges, and frozen funding.

The growing threat of surveillance is not strictly limited to environmentalists. In fact, as we have seen throughout this book, the fight for social justice and equality goes hand-in-hand with the fight for environmental justice. Given that major causes like class abolition, anti-colonialism, social equality, and democratic self-determination are highly intersectional, generally speaking, it's impossible to treat them as separate struggles. The dangers of surveillance are therefore of concern to *everyone*.

In addition to the national security state, there are four major institutions of digitized repression: police, prisons, courts, and border patrol. Along with the military, they collectively control the means of violence, the gun pointed at the head of the people to keep the status quo intact.

Much as they do with the military, the tech "left" typically treats carceral technology as a series of individual parts, as if they are a set of disparate new toys for cops.[13] As a result, they mostly focus on the most controversial elements, such as facial recognition and predictive policing. This is the wrong approach.

As with the military, we should understand carceral technology as a machine with a centralized "brain" based on a set of integrated parts. Smart CCTV camera networks, video analytics, facial recognition and other biometrics, microphones, chemical sensors, aerial and ground drones, body cameras, police smartphones and tablets, edge analytics, internet surveillance, big data systems, and cloud computing together form a symphony orchestra of repression conducted by authorities from centralized command-and-control centers. They supercharge the means of violence.

Moreover, we should further contextualize the systems to other institutions. Centralized systems for police, prisons, courts, and border patrol—as well as intelligence agencies like those reviewed earlier—often work together, and they pull data from the open market (via data brokers) or obtain it from tech corporations, while many employees move between organizations through a revolving door. These institutions will likely develop increasing degrees of integration over time, especially as the planetary crisis heats up. Universities also develop technologies for the private sector, and they often provide support for them through publications.

Let's review the major institutions of digital repression in turn.

Digital policing

As noted earlier, I first encountered "smart" surveillance through personal experience. As I witnessed cameras going up at Rhodes University to surveil Fees Must Fall protesters, I began to inquire into the state-of-the-art developments in CCTV camera networks. I learned from a *VPRO* documentary on YouTube that the first fiber-to-the-home networks in South Africa were being rolled out in the Parkhurst suburb of Johannesburg. The primary purpose, the Parkhurst Residents and Business Owners Association (PRABOA) explained, was *not* to get high-speed internet for day-to-day use, as we might expect. Rather, they were rolled out to supercharge high-tech surveillance for private security firms. High-speed home internet was a secondary benefit.[14]

What I soon discovered was mind-blowing. Decades ago, CCTV cameras were analog devices that captured fuzzy footage recorded to VHS tapes. They were one-off units—say, at a gas station or retail store—that didn't network together across wide areas. When a crime occurred, police would have to visit the location, review the footage, and if the perpetrators fled the scene, they could either find other cameras nearby and repeat the process, or they were stuck with what they had. The capacity to surveil was therefore severely limited. This is no longer the case.

In the 1996, the first digital surveillance cameras were invented by the Swedish firm, Axis Communications. With footage now digitized and affordable internet-connected computers spreading throughout society, corporations next developed *video management software* (VMS) that would

177

bring several camera feeds together for management in a single software interface. Meanwhile, software developers began creating *video analytics* that could recognize objects (such as a "red shirt" or "car"), identify persons and objects of interest (such as faces or license plates), perform analytics (such as heat maps of people walking in a specific area), and detect behaviors (such as "running" or "riding a bicycle").

The Parkhurst rollout—a pilot project that gave rise to a company called "Vumacam"—utilized some of these "smart" features. It used the (Denmark-based) Milestone VMS, video analytics created by Israeli firm BriefCam, and a feature called iSentry for "unusual behavior detection" first developed for other uses by the Australian military. Vumacam's CEO, Ricky Croock, integrated iSentry into his private security empire.

PRABOA's chair, Cheryl Labuschagne, said Parkhurst will use "GPS technology and so on to map where incidents occur" and determine "what movement is considered abnormal rather than typical movements in a neighborhood of people walking their dogs and so on." Labuschagne didn't explain what constitutes "unusual behavior," but an iSentry promotional video filled in the gaps. Titled "Unusual Behavior Detection," the segment shows a young, black "beggar" flagged by iSentry's artificial intelligence-based video analytics. Within moments, he and an accomplice are brought to the ground by a gang of officers armed with semi-automatic guns. Labuschagne proclaims she is "really really hopeful that what we've started is a revolution" in South Africa.[15]

In early 2017, I published the first expose, "Apartheid in the Shadows," at a US-based media outlet, *Counterpunch*.[16] A couple of years later, the initiative came out of the shadows as Vumacam. The company revealed its plans to roll out 13,000 cameras, first in Johannesburg and then in other cities. (Since then, Croock said they plan to roll out over 100,000 cameras; they reached 8,000 by the end of 2023.)[17] Later that year, I published the first in-depth expose detailing Vumacam's business model and its connection to apartheid racism at *VICE News Motherboard*. This included a real-life "shift" report put out by Croock's Fibrehoods, which lists 14 incidents flagging 28 "suspicious" people in the Johannesburg suburbs. All 28 people flagged for "unusual behavior" are black, even though the majority of the suburb's population is white.[18]

The project is coupled with well-documented racist policing by South Africa's private surveillance industry.[19] As I noted in the article:

> During a November 2014 briefing on fiber-driven surveillance for Parkhurst, James Bowling, then security portfolio manager of the suburb, told the audience that security systems would be used "to start profiling people." He said a security company could take pictures and digital fingerprints with a mobile touch machine, and utilize the South African Police Service and private companies to build up profiles about people who frequent the suburb. "If they become a problem," Bowling remarked, "you've got a profile on them and you know who it is, and that's how you start to bring down the crime."

> Those walking the streets are not legally obliged to show papers or respond to inquiries from private citizens or security. "But when you have people in an intimidating vehicle with bullet-proof vests and big guns, it can ... serve to disrupt crime," another SafeParks speaker said. "If they choose not to answer and not give a valid reason for being there, then there's a reason behind it. You raise a flag."

> Six months earlier, Bowling told suburbanites that private security will stop and search people who "look out of place" and call the South African Police Service if they deem necessary ... In 2016, Parkhurst updated its SafeParks website with a message instructing its residents, "Don't feed beggars and vagrants or give them money, it encourages them to stay in the area and some of them contribute to crime."[20]

Vumacam channels the spirit of South Africa's surveillance passbooks issued to Africans under apartheid. Labeled "dompas" (dumb passes) by Africans, the passes were used to enforce residential segregation by documenting and restricting African movements. While the pass system was a *de jure* (legal) system of segregation, today's high-tech policing exacerbates a *de facto* (non-legal) form designed to restrict the presence of "outside" Africans from wealthier neighborhoods. It also undermines civil liberties such as freedom of assembly and the right to protest. Vumacam is currently expanding its footprint to other African countries.

In late 2019, the press reported that Microsoft provides Vumacam with cloud services. Vumacam has since developed a PSIM (physical security

Figure 7.3   Residential inequality in Johannesburg

Parkhurst houses are on the top, Alexandra township shacks are on the bottom.
Source for images: Google Earth.

information management) called Proof, hosted on Microsoft Azure. The app is listed in Microsoft's online AppSource repository, where it even advertises "CCTV Assistance During Civil Unrest."[21]

Public–private partnerships help police authorities extend their network far and wide. Smart camera networks are expensive, so it is not surprising that Vumacam is now partnering with South African police to give them access to its private surveillance network. Added to this, Vumacam or the police may eventually allow private citizens to plug their own private cameras into the network as a way to further privatize costs. Many (often racist) suburbanites and businesses disregard civil rights and liberties to police the African "threat."

But the buck doesn't stop there. In a set of interviews, South African city authorities told me they have used surveillance cameras to monitor activists, from Fees Must Fall protesters to labor unions marching in the city. Additionally, university security authorities told me they are intensifying surveillance technologies on campus by installing equipment with facial recognition, microphones, chemical sensors, video analytics, and fingerprinting—in large part due to fears of student protesters.

In 2022, Panyaza Lesufi, the Premier (head) of the Gauteng province (which houses Johannesburg and Pretoria, two of South Africa's four major cities), announced plans to install facial recognition cameras "on every street" in Gauteng alongside a fleet of aerial police drones and other high-tech policing technologies. A soccer stadium-sized facility would be constructed to house the surveillance footage and staff humans to spy on the province, while extending lethal arms to authorities (e.g., crime wardens). The announcement reeks of political grandstanding,[22] but the provincial government will be spending a substantial share of its upcoming (almost $100 million) budget on its authoritarian "e-policing" project.

* * *

The ideas and technologies foundational to Vumacam are not native to South Africa. American police and tech corporations are leading pioneers of the dystopian PoliceTech solutions spreading rapidly throughout the world. In the mid-2000s, the NYPD created a Domain Awareness System (DAS) in partnership with Microsoft.[23] Formally revealed to the public in 2012, the system, also called Microsoft Aware, pooled the latest-and-greatest technologies with various records databases into a master intelligence-based command-and-control center. The NYPD claims it "utilizes the largest networks of cameras, license plate readers, and radiological sensors in the world."[24]

Microsoft Aware features over 9,000 NYPD and privately owned CCTV cameras. Aware also ingests data from environmental sensors (to detect radiation and dangerous chemicals), microphones (via ShotSpotter's gunshot detection system), GPS (to locate police vehicles), police body cameras, and automatic license plate readers pipe data back to headquarters. In addition to this, over 33 billion records from disparate "data silos" were consolidated into its server farms.

The system has featured video analytics (which the NYPD now claims it doesn't perform, and the ACLU contests)[25] and runs facial recognition scans on footage for investigations after an incident occurs. It also deploys a predictive policing investigative product, Patternizr, which attempts to identify those responsible for committing crimes (post-incident), and it works in conjunction with its analytics engine, "CompStat 2.0" (which features data visualizations).[26] The NYPD uses other technologies, such as drones, x-ray vans, and Stingrays (devices that spy on cell phones nearby and can be used to track locations), which may be integrated into Aware.

In short, the NYPD centralizes an array of sensors and data to perform sophisticated analytics. As part of the Microsoft Aware deal, the City of New York takes 30% of the profits from additional sales to other cities. Since 2012, Microsoft Aware has been deployed in Atlanta, Washington DC, Bulgaria, Singapore, and Brazil. Singapore is an authoritarian state, while Brazil's police are even more violent than that of the US. Most details are not publicly available, but *The Intercept* reported that the system has been used to target Black Lives Matter activists in Washington, DC. IBM has also deployed a pilot "skin tone" detection video analytics for the system in NYC (which it eventually terminated).[27]

Microsoft has also been involved in other major policing initiatives via its Public Safety and Justice division. The majority of its policing projects are developed by Microsoft partners who host their PoliceTech on the Microsoft Azure cloud. In 2014, Microsoft lavished praise on a predictive policing project developed by its partner PredPol (since renamed Geolitica) for the Los Angeles Police Department (LAPD).[28]

PredPol came under fierce criticism for producing racist outcomes through a vicious feedback loop. Cops arrest people of color at disproportionately high rates (irrespective of actual criminality). The software sends police to communities of color. With more cops on the prowl, they are more likely to find crime or enter into altercations with the locals. Each new arrest is recorded in the software database, which flags communities of color as crime-ridden hotspots. The algorithm directs cops back to those communities, where they make more arrests. Rinse and repeat.[29]

One Microsoft partner, Kaseware, provides a surveillance platform resembling Aware to Michigan State Police, upon which a social media surveillance company, ShadowDragon, operates. Kaseware's Chief Business Operator, Mark Dodge, is a former naval intelligence and CIA officer who previously helped develop Microsoft Aware for the NYPD.[30]

In Cape Town, South Africa, Microsoft piloted its Microsoft Advanced Patrol Platform (MAPP), which it said it was extending to Durban. Tasked to protect private property in the world's most unequal country, it's no surprise that South African police are more violent than American police. MAPP draws upon an extensive array of third-party surveillance vendors to equip police vehicles with a variety of gadgets: facial recognition cameras, a 360-degree high-res camera, an automatic license plate reader that can scan 5,000 license plates per minute, and a proximity camera that alerts officers when the vehicle is being approached. Aerial surveillance drones can follow the vehicle from the skies, while remote-controlled ground robots like the "Jack Russell" and "Bloodhound" can climb stairs and obstacles. Officers are provided with real-time information, including about criminal suspects. The vehicles being used don't sport Microsoft insignia, so the public can't identify MAPP-powered cars in the real world. Details about deployment are unavailable, and there's no accountability.[31]

Additional Microsoft police solutions are too numerous to list.

Other US-based Big Tech companies are also working with police departments, most notably Amazon and Palantir. The former's flagship offering is Amazon Ring, a camera installed at the doors of private citizens which allows them to view footage outside their home. Unlike CCTV networks, Ring cameras aren't stitched together in a centralized platform to view all the feeds at once. Nevertheless, Ring owners can post videos to an app called Neighbors, which can be made available to the public or local authorities. At the time of writing, Amazon rolled out its Ring civilian cameras in at least 29 countries.[32]

Other Big Tech companies, including Palantir, IBM, Dell, Cisco, Google, and X (formerly Twitter) provide or have provided solutions for police and security forces across the world. And while the tech giants capture most of the media attention, a shadow industry of surveillance companies supplies

183

a great deal of the technology. Most people have never heard of the three major VMS providers—Milestone (owned by Canon), Avigilon (owned by Motorola), and Genetec—even though they are central to smart camera networks. The media and academics are interested in getting clicks (drawing attention to their publications). If Amazon or Google are involved, it's sensational, and intellectuals gain prestige for reporting it. If Avigilon signs a new contract with a major city, it doesn't reach mainstream news.

China is also a major player in the global police surveillance space. Its industry cropped up almost overnight thanks to Chinese Communist Party subsidies to state-owned entities like Hikvision and Dahua. During the 2010s, the two quickly flooded the market with cheap cameras. Surveillance is a "grudge purchase" (meaning, nobody wants to spring for it), and despite the low quality of their products, the low prices gave them an advantage against higher-priced Western products. The US and other countries have since put sanctions on them and other Chinese surveillance providers, in the name of "national security."

China's use of technology to police its own population is not unique, but it is more repressive than in many Western countries given the authoritarian governance of the CCP. China's power elites crack the whip hard on dissent, as evinced by their extensive censorship of the internet and repression of activists. In just one example, left-wing students at a top Chinese academy, Peking University, went missing in 2018 after protesting in support of workers.[33]

The situation in Xinjiang also speaks volumes to the character of the CCP. Western journalists and refugees have documented the severe economic exploitation and repression of Uyghur Muslims in the cotton-growing northwestern Xinjiang region.[34] Some of the findings have been politicized or lack solid rigor for precise claims, but the evidence of systemic repression is thoroughly documented. For example, journalists have sneaked out footage of areas plastered in facial recognition and other biometric tools. On multiple occasions, surveillance media outlet IPVM obtained documents demonstrating that Hikvision cameras, often powered by semiconductors from the US firm, Nvidia, is deploying video analytics built to identify Uyghurs.[35]

Over the past decade, Huawei became another major player in the Global South policing space via its *safe city* projects, which it claims to have deployed in over 160 cities spanning over 100 countries and regions. Safe cities are generally a precursor to *smart cities*, which extend surveillance to administrative tasks such as traffic management and waste refusal. Some of these safe/smart city projects hook into broader ICT infrastructure rollouts.

A now-deleted page on Huawei's website advertised safe cities projects in Lahore, Pakistan; Abidjan, Côte d'Ivoire; Mauritius; Manilla, Philippines; and Ghana. In a 2018 video I managed to capture before deletion, the Minister of National Security for Ghana, Albert Kan-Dapaah, said Huawei trained about 15,000 security officers. The project had 2,000 cameras at the time and planned to add another 8,000 in its second phase.

According to a 2023 study, China is the world's leading exporter of facial recognition technology with 201 trade deals, closely followed by the United States with 128. Cost could be a decisive influence on the choice to go with China over the West. The authors note that "autocracies and weak democracies" are more likely to import facial recognition AI from China, but they weren't able to determine possible cost differentials.[36] When faced with scrutiny for purchasing surveillance tech from China, Zimbabwe President Emmerson Mnangagwa said, "If ... China puts the best bid, which has the most value for money, and flexible terms, then we'll go for China rather than America."[37]

Israel is a final surveillance provider worth mentioning. In addition to its apartheid surveillance apparatus, the country has come under intense scrutiny for exporting spyware like the NSO Group's Pegasus to government agencies and police in a wide range of countries, including autocracies. Pegasus is expensive software that can spy on smartphone applications like WhatsApp without the user even knowing it. The software is used to target activists, journalists, and political leaders across the world. It was initially reported that clients were clustered in 11 countries: Azerbaijan, Bahrain, Hungary, India, Kazakhstan, Mexico, Morocco, Rwanda, Saudi Arabia, Togo, and the United Arab Emirates (UAE). Since then, we've learned that the FBI secretly purchased Pegasus, as have 14 EU governments.[38]

The tech-to-prison pipeline

We have seen that police tech advanced fast, thanks in large part to a shadow industry scarcely discussed. Big Tech—led by Microsoft—helped accelerate and amplify its reach through the development of the Microsoft Aware DAS and cloud-based centralization.

Yet the story doesn't stop with the police. Prisons and courts are increasingly making heavy use of digital tech, which now forms a corridor of tech-driven incarceration. This *tech-to-prison pipeline* covers the entire carceral pipeline, from "juvenile delinquency" to pretrial and probation, into prison, and after inmates are released on parole.[39]

Before we discuss the technologies, it's worth noting up front that what goes on inside prison walls is a complete nightmare. In the United States, prison correctional officers have near-absolute authority. If they accuse you of something, or abuse you, who is going to advocate on your behalf? In the eyes of society, you're a murderer, a rapist, a thief, and in all likelihood, a person of color. In many other countries, conditions are even worse.

That said, our story begins with Microsoft once again.[40] In 2011, the Illinois Department of Corrections (IDOC), embarked on a $30 million overhaul of its antiquated computer systems. IDOC covers the second-most populous county in the US—Cook County—which includes the city of Chicago, so it was imperative they get the system right. The problem—familiar by now—was that the IDOC had 28 facilities utilizing more than 40 separate computer applications. It wanted to pool information from "separate silos" into a centralized pot, just as the US military and major police forces do for their systems.

Microsoft stepped into the picture with a new high-tech solution. In conjunction with a small, Florida-based firm called Tribridge, it developed a suite of prison software applications that would eventually integrate with the courts. The first solution, called Offender 360, centralized databases in the cloud and upgraded the IDOC's prison management capabilities. Then-Governor Patrick Quinn said at the time, that Microsoft's "cutting-edge technology will give Illinois one of the most advanced criminal justice information systems in the country."

An early brochure listed a variety of features that would integrate, index, and expand every bit of data available about inmates for computer-based functionality and analytics. Capabilities include tracking an inmate's physical location and identification by attributes (height, weight, scars and tattoos, religion, etc.), categorization and classification (such as security characteristics like "aggression level" and "offender grade"), and search features for ad-hoc queries and real-time data analysis. For example, prison authorities can search for "inmates under the age of 50 with a projected parole date within five years" or inmates "classified as highly aggressive, high escape risk, with known affiliations to one or many security threat groups."[41]

As part of the system, the IDOC integrated its "Master File" about each prisoner. One of the IDOC's former inmates, Monica Cosby, explained to me the Master File includes behavioral history, staff assaults (which, Cosby said, could include false accusations), medical records, and inmate property—they monitor basically everything you own and do while in prison, she said. Information collected can then be brought up at a parole hearing and big data analytics can deem inmates as prone to violence or recidivism.

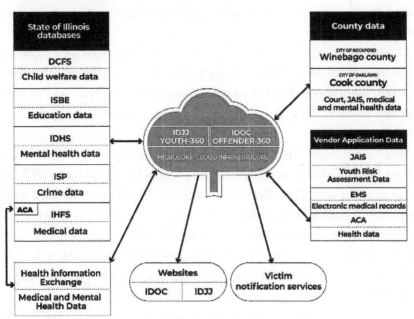

Figure 7.4   Microsoft and Youth 360 for child prisons
(courtesy of Al Jazeera Media Network)

Image: Kwet, 2020.[42]

From there, Microsoft and Tribridge developed a second solution, Youth 360, for the Illinois Department of Juvenile Justice, which manages the state's five juvenile correctional facilities. Youth 360 is similar to Offender 360 in that ingests a wide range of data about its subjects. Its information can be linked to other data systems, such as school and public health systems, and it hosts Youth Assessment and Screening Instrument (YASI) data to profile "criminogenic risks, needs, and strengths."[43] YASI is used for every youth put on probation.

A third Microsoft system, called Pretrial360, offers case management and predictive analytics software for the courts. This was rolled out to Mesa County in 2015 to assess the risk that defendants will skip trial or re-offend. While the fine details about Pretrial360 are not publicly available, some of its metrics include "criminal history tracking, mental illness, pending charges, past FTAs [failure to appear in court], and ability to track a monitoring device."[44] Several studies have shown that pretrial algorithmic assessments discriminate against black defendants, while another study found that judges across the country guided by algorithms exhibit a class bias against the poor.[45]

Other counties that have inked contracts for Offender 360's correctional software include Miami-Dade, Santa Clara, Placer, San Diego, Maricopa (the fourth-most populous US county), and possibly, San Francisco. Microsoft also provides digitization services for courts to store and perform data analytics.[46]

In addition to its "360" suite of applications, Microsoft refashioned its Aware DAS as its very own Digital Prison Management Solution (DPMS) solution for prisons. A product that combines "Microsoft technology with corrections operational knowledge," the solution "empowers agencies and prison authorities to ingest and collaborate on data to respond to real-time threats and hazards whilst streamlining operations," providing "a feature rich situational awareness platform" for authorities.[47] For prisons, Microsoft's DPMS appears unprecedented in scope and sophistication.

Microsoft has also expanded its prison footprint into the Global South. A Microsoft "Partner of the Year," Morrocco-based Netopia Solutions, offers its own "Prison Management Solution" to oversee the incarcerated. Software features include, among others, "electronic agenda planning of internal and external movements," inmate activities, as well as dashboard features, reports and statistics. Other prison solutions include the acquisition and verification of biometric data, "automatic sentence calculation" and "escape management."[48] Deployment appears to include Morocco as well as countries in North and Central Africa. Morocco has been condemned for abusing and torturing prisoners, while many other countries in Africa have brutal prison conditions.

Microsoft also has a host of "e-carceration" solutions designed for "community supervision" of inmates released on parole. Offender360 offers e-carceration capabilities, while another app called PUMA offers smartphone software for probation and parole. In the UK, Microsoft advertised its own Azure-based solution for "next generation offender tracking" that alerts police and probation officers in real-time to parole violations.[49]

People under community supervision are essentially incarcerated outside of prison walls. They are usually given GPS-enabled ankle bracelets that track their movements to ensure they keep to areas designated by the courts. For example, they may only be allowed outside of their homes from 10 am to 4 pm, and they may be subjected to drug and alcohol tests by corrections officers who can show up unannounced at any time. This extends the reach of police into private community spaces and often makes it impossible for parolees to get jobs or live a normal life.

Finally, Microsoft trains inmates across the world, from juveniles through adults, in digital literacy so that when they get out of prison, they can get jobs. Of course, they train them to use *Microsoft* software to secure a prison-to-jobs pipeline for Microsoft.[50]

* * *

Many parts of the world are moving into a high-tech surveillance state that forms a tech-to-prison pipeline which starts from youth and covers the entire carceral system. While many other companies are involved in digitizaling prisons, Microsoft stands far above the other tech giants. Details are scarce, but we could reasonably expect that other cloud providers are offering services to schools and surveillance vendors.

Digitalization projects are expensive, which limits uptake in the Global South. However, we shouldn't underestimate the spread of these technologies. Dystopian police tech like Real-Time Crime Centers and smart camera networks are being replicated throughout the world, and it's likely a matter of time before poorer countries begin "modernizing" their entire correctional pipelines.

Digital border patrol

Finally, we turn to the issue of border patrol. It's a well-known fact that climate change is pushing people to migrate in droves due to the effects of extreme weather events like flooding, droughts, wildfires, hurricanes, and cyclones. Approximately 283.4 million people were *internally* displaced— meaning people relocated *inside* their country—between 2008 and 2020, due to climate disasters.[51] At present, the majority of environmental migrants move back home and *don't* relocate to other countries, but this may change as some areas become uninhabitable or unstable due to climate change.

In many cases, violent conflict dovetails with climate change. For example, in the African country of Burkina Faso, "some of the worst violence and displacement has occurred in the poorest, most drought-affected areas where armed groups have exploited tensions over access to dwindling water sources and shrinking arable land," the United Nations High Commissioner for Refugees (UNHCR) notes.[52] The UNHCR adds that crisis situations are playing out in the African Sahel across:

> a vast region spanning several West African countries where the UN estimates that close to 80 per cent of farmland is degraded and temperatures are rising 1.5 times faster than the global average. Disputes between pastoralists and farmers over diminishing natural resources have increased over the past decade.

> The region is now home to one of the world's fastest growing displacement crises with over 850,000 people having fled violence across borders—often escaping one conflict only to find themselves caught up in another, and more than two million people displaced within their own countries, including over one million in Burkina Faso alone.

Most people leave their countries to get better-paying labor, not because they desire to leave their homelands. In Central America, for example, the combination of climate change, corporate-dominated "free trade" agreements, agribusiness-induced land enclosures, economic sanctions, and US-supported government repression has provoked waves of northward migration to the US, where migrants face a ruling class that exploits their labor (including children), as well as a xenophobic culture intent on deporting them back down south.[53]

As with police, prisons, and the courts, tech corporations—big and small—have become major contributors to twenty-first-century border patrol. A complementary set of technologies brings together yet another orchestra of repression, each with its own section playing its part. The following are tools at the disposal of border authorities:

- Biometric technologies to identify individuals include fingerprints, facial recognition, iris scans, voice recognition, and DNA samples.
- Sensors like CCTV cameras, body cameras, thermal imaging, robotic dogs, surveillance blimps, helicopters, airplanes, and drones to extend the all-seeing eye of customs authorities.
- Tracking devices like ankle monitors, smartphone apps with facial recognition, and smartwatches affixed to migrants facing deportation.
- Cloud computing, software platforms, and AI to centralize databases and function as computerized "brains" for monitoring and analytics from command-and-control centers.

These technologies integrate with human personnel and, in countries like the US and Israel, physical border walls.

In the United States, immigration enforcement is carried out by Immigration and Customs Enforcement (ICE) and by the Customs and Border Protection (CBP), both of which are housed in the Department of Homeland Security (DHS). In March 2021, the Biden administration apprehended 170,000 migrants along the southwest border—the most in any month for at least 15 years. Migrant families in federal custody, including children, have been detained and herded into chain-link cages. At least seven children died in custody or after being detained in 2019, sparking a national uproar that has been simmering ever since.

The tech company Palantir has received the most attention for its role as a supplier of border patrol tech, due to its early lead as the major platform provider to ICE. Palantir received over $150 million to run platforms for ICE's Integrated Case Management (ICM) system and its FALCON platform, which, the nonprofit group Mijente notes, forms "the backbone of ICE's tech toolkit to track down, persecute, and detain families and individuals." The ICM system was "used to track down and arrest 443 family members of migrant children in a 2017 precursor to the current family separation policy," while FALCON was used for mass raids that separated "hundreds of family members across the country."[54]

These kinds of platforms often connect to other authorities. Palantir's software is used by California fusion surveillance centers to facilitate information-sharing with police. As of 2019, the company had at least 29 active contracts worth $1.5 billion with the US federal government, which included the DHS and Department of Defense agencies such as the Army, Special Operations Command, and the US Navy. While Mijente was able to obtain public records, other Big Tech companies' contracts have not been tabulated—though we know that companies like Microsoft and Amazon lead the way.

For its part, Amazon's AWS provides the cloud backbone for Palantir, while Microsoft was awarded a $19.4 million contract with ICE. Microsoft's Aware platform also provides information, such as license plate recognition data, to ICE.[55] So too does its prison software created by Tribridge, which can identify persons of interest for customs authorities.[56] Other companies have contracts with immigration authorities, including Google, Dell, Motorola, HP Enterprise Services, and Thompson Reuters, as well as those with smaller names, such as BI and LexisNexis.

In addition to policing migrant victims, border wall systems are often environmentally destructive. The Biden administration will be waiving 26 laws to extend the US-Mexico border in the Rio Grande Valley. This includes bypassing the Safe Drinking Water Act, Clean Air Act, and Endangered Species Act. As the Center for Biological Diversity puts it:

> Hundreds of miles of wall have been built across protected public lands, communities, and sovereign Tribal nations. These barriers cut through sensitive ecosystems, destroy thousands of acres of habitat, impede the cross-border migration of dozens of animal species, cause catastrophic flooding, and separate families.[57]

Taking the connection of border walls to climate change further, a *Transnational Institute* report notes:

> Countries—which are historically the most responsible for the climate crisis—spend more on arming their borders to keep migrants out than on tackling the crisis that forces people from their homes in the first place. This is a global trend, but seven countries in particular—responsible for 48% of the world's historic greenhouse gas (GHG) emissions—collectively spent at least twice as much on border and immigration enforcement (more than $33.1 billion) as on climate finance ($14.4 billion) between 2013 and 2018.[58]

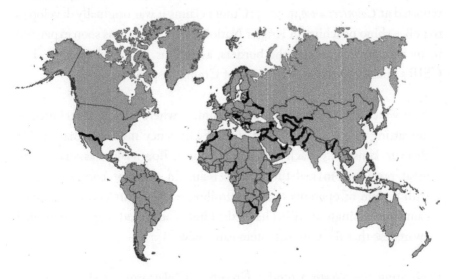

Figure 7.5   Border walls built between 1968 and 2015
(courtesy of the Transnational Institute)

Source: Benedicto, Akkerman and Brunet, 2020.[59]

These countries have been building "climate walls" that prioritize militarization in response to crises that are increasingly provoked by climate change. Of the top ten emitters, it's Global North countries (e.g., US, Germany, Japan, UK, Canada, France, Australia) that are building the walls, not the South (e.g., China, Russia, Brazil). The United States is the top spender by far, with $19.6 billion (59%) spent of the $33.1 billion total. For its part, Europe is not only building multiple border walls, the EU "has created a shadow immigration system that captures [African migrants] before they reach its shores, and sends them to brutal Libyan detention centers run by militias."[60]

As in all things digital, ruling-class elites in the South aspire to Northern models, but often lack the resources to purchase and effectively implement them. Nevertheless, they are trying.

Africa's largest research and development center, the Council of Scientific & Industrial Research (CSIR), a sprawling campus of over 30 buildings located in Pretoria, South Africa, has developed the Cmore physical security information system (PSIM)—a comprehensive surveillance platform akin to Microsoft Aware—that may be used at the northern borderlands. As I reported at *Counterpunch* in 2017, Cmore claims it was originally developed to police rhino poaching in Kruger National Park, but it was soon expanded to include applications at the borders, as well as for policing cities. The CSIR's promotional materials boast of Cmore's aspirations:

> Ever watched a crime drama or spy film ... where a team of technicians are sitting in a darkened room full of big, fancy monitors that enable them to constantly track and follow a Jason Bourne-like assailant with great precision, in real-time, while being in constant communication with a team of operatives and controlling traffic lights and surveillance cameras seemingly at will? That is the kind of advanced shared situational awareness that the Cmore system can enable.[61]

Replicating the Western model, Cmore is a "platform for shared awareness" integrating internal and external data sources to conduct surveillance, defense and policing operations. *External* sources like public webcams, CCTV networks, and aerial surveillance drones feed data to Cmore servers. *Internal* "forces in the field," such as patrol officers, use the Cmore Mobile app on mobile devices to coordinate movement and obtain real-time feedback and communications within the surveillance network.[62]

The City of Johannesburg authorities confirmed to me in a 2021 interview that they are piloting Cmore as a PSIM for police.[63] Yet we don't know much about deployment at its northern borderlands, which are porous at the moment. Migrants from countries like Mozambique and Zimbabwe are facing growing restrictions from the South African government, as well as rising xenophobia from an increasingly hostile domestic population, including black South Africans. In recent years, campaigns like Operation Dudula (meaning "push out") have been targeting African and Asian migrants and refugees with vigilante violence, arson, and murder, at times culminating in wholesale pogroms. In a 2008 xenophobic outburst, 60 people were murdered and 100,000 displaced. Other violent outbursts have since occurred.

The IPCC has classified Southern Africa as a climate change hotspot vulnerable to regional tipping points.[64] While South Africa's policing technology is expanding, it is far from mature. If you visit the central business district in Johannesburg, you won't see cameras everywhere—at least for now. But we can gain a glimpse of the future by observing the settler colonial state of Israel, which operates the most technologically advanced border patrol system in human history. In recent years, several human rights organizations have deemed Israel an "apartheid state," including two Israeli groups (Yesh Din and B'Tselem), followed by Human Rights Watch and Amnesty International. Israel uses advanced technologies that monitor and control the movements of Palestinians to keep them subjugated and segregated. These include drones, smart camera networks, electronic passports, centralized database systems, and biometric systems like facial recognition, iris scanning, and fingerprinting.[65]

A variety of corporations supply the technology required to administer the system. American attention to Israel's high-tech apartheid began in 2021 when Amazon and Google were awarded a $1.2 billion contract to supply cloud services to the Israeli government, including the Israeli Defense Forces. Documents published in the press revealed that "the new cloud would give Israel capabilities for facial detection, automated image categorization, object tracking and even sentiment analysis that claims to assess the emotional content of pictures, speech and writing."[66] Google's technologies may be used to predict future data, identify emotions from pictures, detect lies and recognize objects. Amazon's facial recognition software, Rekognition, is being used by Israeli authorities in general. Unfortunately, there is no transparency about how these cloud services are ultimately used by the Israeli cops, Border Police, and the military.

While Amazon and Google have soaked up the media attention, other Big Tech giants service Israel in the background. Microsoft plays a huge role, with services extending back decades, as scholar Yarden Katz recently documented at *Mondoweiss*. Israeli Prime Minister Benjamin Netanyahu has said that Israel and Microsoft are "a match made in heaven, but recognized here on earth."[67] The company supplies Xboxes to control military tanks; HoloLens mixed reality goggles; cloud services to support a system of ID permits; and company-designed courses are used to train officers in cybersecurity and artificial intelligence.

The NGO, Who Profits, has reported that "IBM designed and operates the Eitan System of the Israeli Population, Immigration and Border Authority (PIBA), where personal information on the occupied Palestinian and Syrian people collected by Israel, is stored and managed."[68] Eitan is used to document and control the movement of Palestinians at the main checkpoints. Other US tech companies that provide Israel with tech, investments, and education include Intel, Cisco, HP, Dell, Facebook, Apple, Nokia, Oracle, and Nvidia. The Microsoft-backed creator of ChatGPT, OpenAI, is considering investment opportunities in Israel, while China's Hikvision supplies CCTV cameras.

As mentioned earlier, Israel has its own homegrown industry of surveillance corporations. For example, in addition to NSO Group, its BriefCam video analytics software is used at home and abroad (e.g., in the US and South Africa) to enhance the power of smart camera networks. Its Elbit Systems is another major supplier of high-tech systems for border patrol. In 2014, the Obama administration contracted Israel's high-tech military to build 50 fixed surveillance towers at the US-Mexican border, which "fit into a surveillance web that operates in a much thicker border zone patrolled by other towers, cameras, motion sensors, helicopters, fixed-wing aircraft, and drones," journalist Todd Miller observes.[69]

Together, Israel and the United States are among the major exporters of border surveillance technologies across the world.[70] Yet Israel is completely dependent upon the United States to sustain its military, technological, and economic power. Above all else, it's the United States that presides over an apartheid-like international order to maintain disparities of wealth and power that benefit its state-corporate ruling class. The United States is the supreme evil—a basic observation its mainstream "left" intellectuals cannot bring themselves to state publicly.

* * *

It's within the context of US imperialism that we should view American policy. According to the United States, China poses a global military threat, violates human rights, and uses its technology for government surveillance. Yet the US war machine is the most militaristic, violent, and human rights-abusing force on the planet, backed by the most thorough and sophisticated surveillance apparatus in human history. America owns and controls the global digital economy, it manipulates trade policy to protect its corporate interests, and it dominates the technologies of violence, which it uses in the most grotesque ways at the greatest scale, both directly and through its allies. American politicians and the majority of its intellectuals are actively waging a New Cold War against China.

It's true that the CCP is a wicked, authoritarian government, and its ruling class exploits people at home and abroad. But as we've seen, on the global stage, the United States is many times worse. If you don't like the power elites in China, then you should really hate the ones ruling America.

The New York Times columnist Farhah Manjoo expresses the vulgar, racist supremacy of the typical American intellectual. As he puts it, the US is "strangling large segments of the Chinese technology industry—strangling with an intent to kill ... Considering the ways China might use the advanced chips—including in expanding its dystopian, A.I.-powered surveillance and repression regime—the strangulation is justified."[71]

That the US and its allies do this all over the world at an even greater scale—all in service of a tiny American ruling class extracting wealth and destroying life everywhere—has no relevance to Manjoo and his like-minded colleagues. The United States rules the world, and what we say goes. The hypocrisy is truly breathtaking. If you want to know how Europeans could "civilize the savages" while committing genocide and enslaving Africans, look at what Americans are saying to this day.

In his 1967 speech, "Beyond Vietnam: A Time to Break the Silence," delivered a year before his assassination, Martin Luther King, Jr. famously called the American government "the greatest purveyor of violence in the world today." What he had to say about tech in that same speech is almost never quoted: "We must rapidly begin the shift from a thing-oriented society to a person-oriented society. When machines and computers, profit motives and property rights, are considered more important than people, the giant triplets of racism, extreme materialism, and militarism are incapable of being conquered."[72] How apropos.

Today, we can add a fourth element, ecocide. We need to end the system where machines and computers, profit motives, and property rights supersede the well-being of *all life* on the planet. If we don't, the world is going to get much, much worse for the mass majority of humans—especially people in the Global South—and the other species on the planet that did nothing to deserve this.

The final two chapters of this book will present some ideas on what we can do with the limited time we have left.

8
People's Tech and a Digital Tech Deal

In previous chapters, I outlined how the digital society connects to the environment. There are limits to growth, and because capitalism is a wealth-concentrating growth system, it cannot continue for much longer without triggering an unprecedented catastrophe. Since a sustainable economy requires reducing and capping material resource use, we have to drastically redistribute wealth and income between and within countries. In order to accomplish this, we need to build an ecosocialist society—one based on harmony between people and nature.

As we'll see in the next chapter, the mild capitalist reforms widely championed by the US-centered tech "left" are not only historically ineffective, they are ecocidal, colonial, and racist. We don't have time to waste on these unethical dead ends. But that doesn't mean we can simply launch a revolution and enter into a sustainable, egalitarian digital society overnight. Time is not on our side, but it's still going to take time to make radical changes. We have to move as fast as possible while keeping a close eye on the time frames we have left before we trigger irreversible catastrophes.

In this chapter, I propose two core solutions. First, we can build an ecosocialist movement for digital degrowth in connection with activist projects already in place. I suggest the slogan People's Tech for People's Power—or *People's Tech* for short—as a modern twist on South Africa's 1980s anti-apartheid slogan, "People's Education for People's Power."[1] I like this because it embodies a *positive* vision for society (People's Tech) based on what we *want*, not simply what we *oppose*. Others might create or use whichever catchphrases they prefer.

People's Tech is a set of short- and medium-term solutions geared toward seizing the means of computation, production, and knowledge. Some of them, such as replacing your operating system or office productivity software with Free and Open Source Software (FOSS) can be implemented immediately. These are low-hanging fruit. Others, such as policies to mandate the use of FOSS in schools—which has been done with success in Kerala, India (discussed in the next chapter)—require some collective resistance, and are thus more medium-term solutions that might take 3–5 years to implement.

Still others, such as phasing out intellectual property, are more radical because they address the root causes of problems and require fundamental changes to society. These long-term solutions—here I have in mind a decade or so at most—intersect and require a re-engineering of society. For this, I propose a second solution, an ecosocialist Digital Tech Deal (DTD) inspired by indigenous and other radical "deals" proposed by the environmental movement. The DTD would be part and parcel of broader societal transformations, such as how the economy functions.

Before we get to the DTD, let's start with People's Tech.

PEOPLE'S TECH FOR PEOPLE'S POWER

In conversations about the ills of digital society—digital colonialism, surveillance capitalism, and so on—people inevitably ask, "but what can you do?" It's a fair question. Fortunately, a lot of things can be done immediately, even if they don't yet create the world we ultimately want.

To start, we need to think about property. Degrowth requires an egalitarian, ecosocialist transformation of society. In the digital domain, this requires the masses to seize the means of computation (software, hardware, and network connectivity) and knowledge (intellectual property, digital intelligence, and data) so that the means of production and knowledge can be distributed evenly to communities across the world. We the people need to take ownership of digital technologies and through them, we own and control one of the core elements of society.

The Free and Open Source Software movement—also called *Free Software* for short—was the first to formalize this kind of idea and bring it into practice. In 2016, NSA whistle-blower Edward Snowden called Free Software "the last lighthouse of freedom." It's with FOSS that we find the proximate origins of People's Tech, so we need to understand a little about Free Software and its evolution over time.

The Free Software Movement emerged in the 1980s when an MIT software developer, Richard Stallman, was famously told by Xerox he could not be given access to the computer code needed to repair their printer in the computer lab. At the time, most software developers freely shared computer code, and computer companies made their money through hardware sales. Software was typically "free" in both senses of the term: you were free to use, copy, and exchange it (it wasn't private property) and "free" as in the source code was made available for anyone to read.

The source code is key to our discussion. Computer code is the set of instructions that tells your computer what it can and cannot do. A social network can use computer code to set "algorithms" that determine which posts are most commonly seen in a news feed, or even which ones are banned, thereby shaping which information people see (and therefore think about). For this reason, the one who controls the software controls the user through the software.

Stallman and subsequent Free Software advocates understood that if companies increasingly made software "proprietary" (privately owned property), then individuals and communities would be deprived of the ability to use, understand, and control their own computer experiences. Proprietary software, then, is akin to a secret recipe, a *black box* that only the owner alone can understand and use to control the computer users. Stallman used a clever hack of copyright law to create the first "Free Software" license, called the GNU General Public License (GPL).

The GPL inverted software copyrights. Instead of obscuring its inner workings (by closing off the human-readable source code to the public) and restricting the public's freedoms to use and modify the software, the GPL granted four freedoms to the end users:

- **Freedom 0.** The freedom to run the app as you wish, for any purpose.
- **Freedom 1.** The freedom to study how the app works, and change it so it does what you want. Access to the source code is a precondition for this.
- **Freedom 2.** The freedom to redistribute copies so you can help others.
- **Freedom 3.** The freedom to distribute copies of your modified versions to others. This gives the whole community a chance to benefit from your changes. Access to the source code is a precondition for this.[2]

Freedoms 0 and 1 give you the freedom to use, study, and modify software. Freedoms 2 and 3 allow you to share and collectively modify the software; this enables community control over the software.

Any software that incorporates all four freedoms is considered Free Software (or FOSS for short). Because FOSS allows people to make and share copies for free, people can use it without paying for it. It is therefore accessible to people who don't have much money, such as those in the Global South. This book uses the terms "Free Software" and "FOSS" interchangeably.

Free Software recognizes that *property isn't neutral*—ownership relations structure freedom, equality, and power. FOSS licenses created *communal* software that anyone can *access*, so long as they have a computer device, and *control*, so long as they or others in their community have the resources and knowledge to do computer coding. The strongest versions of FOSS, called *copyleft* licenses, require continuous disclosure of the source code, effectively ensuring that all future versions of the software remain Free Software.

The Free Software Movement was born, and it spread quickly. The Linux operating system was eventually licensed under the GPL, which created an alternative to the Microsoft Windows monopoly. Today, Linux powers the majority of the world's computer servers, as well as the Android operating system. (Google makes money by adding its own proprietary apps to Android.)

As time marched on, the landscape became more complex. The internet spread, cloud computing was invented, and statistical AI took off. Big Tech companies began to use and develop their own versions of Free Software for their cloud-based platforms. They were able to make modified versions of Free Software while keeping the modifications from the public, all because many FOSS licenses didn't *require* disclosure of modifications. The Free Software community tried to plug this loophole with a new license, the GNU Affero General Public License (AGPL), but it never spread very far. The corporations were able to exploit much of the FOSS available in the service of private ownership, profit, and growth.

In a nutshell, software activists tried to give communities autonomy and built technology for equality through a clever hack of the legal system— Free Software licenses—but this was too feeble a weapon to counter the deep-seated power of corporations and the capitalist system. Unfortunately, there are no silver bullets.

While Free Software alone cannot secure digital equality, many FOSS projects provide the public with software to use free from corporate control. This is critical for four reasons. First, these projects demonstrate that we don't need corporations or a capitalist model to build cutting-edge technology. Second, because the source code is open source, we can secure our privacy better with FOSS tools, as the public can control the product and verify that it is not spying on us. Third, we can use Free Software to cut out *some*—but not *all*—of the Big Tech products in use today. As we'll see, poor communities in the state of Kerala, India have done this for over 20 years with astounding success. And fourth, as activists, we can push to scale up FOSS projects.

I've written about People's Tech solutions in great detail in my booklet, *People's Tech for People's Power: A Guide to Digital Self-Defense and Empowerment*, which is free online. Here I will present some of the key FOSS projects that you and your friends and family can download and use immediately to begin cutting out Big Tech.

Text messaging

Signal is typically the go-to Free Software app for non-corporate, privacy-respecting text messaging. It's a decent FOSS solution with solid privacy standards, but it also has some problems that make it less than ideal. Signal employees have criticized the company for prioritizing the expansion of its user base instead of working out policies that will mitigate the potential harms of new features before releasing them.[3] Its servers are centralized and it pays Microsoft, Google, and Amazon millions of dollars per year to host its services.[4]

Moreover, Signal's multimillionaire founder and CEO, Moxie Marlinspike, has taken in enough money to purchase a $4.9 million luxury home. Its top brass are paid well beyond social and planetary boundaries, with salaries of $200,000–700,000 a year.[5]

Perhaps most importantly, as the Free Software Foundation India notes, Signal pursues a vendor lock-in strategy.[6] Marlinspike threatened to sue a FOSS-based group for using the name LibreSignal as a trademark violation, and he claimed that chat app interoperability would stifle innovation.[7]

As such, Signal opposes interoperability. Even though it's a nonprofit, these choices are designed to maximize Signal's power and market share.

Other FOSS messenger services, such as Element, Quicksy, and Dino allow people to set up their own chat servers, and the apps interoperate so that users of one chat service can talk to users of another. The messenger apps Tox, Jami, and Briar use peer-to-peer models for hosting and transmitting chat apps, meaning the software has each of the user's host and transmit data across the app networks. All of them use top-notch encryption to protect your privacy.[8] These apps have a smaller user base than Signal but may be charting the best path forward for People's Tech alternatives to corporate power.

Operating systems and app stores

Operating systems and app stores are critical to our computing experiences. If your operating system is insecure, you will be vulnerable to hacking and malware like viruses and spyware. If your OS doesn't function well, your device won't work well—it might crash, run slowly, or poorly secure your system. Operating systems and app stores can also constrain choices. For instance, on Apple smartphones, you can only install apps the company allows in its official app store.

On desktops and laptops, you can replace Windows or MacOS with the GNU/Linux operating system. The Ubuntu operating system is the most popular and easiest to install and use. On smartphones and tablets, you can replace Google Android with Lineage OS or the /e/ operating system. You can also install the F-Droid app store, which only hosts FOSS apps.

Note that the Linux Foundation (which develops the Linux OS) and Canonical (which develops the Ubuntu OS) are by no means social justice-oriented or ecosocialist. The former pays out exorbitant salaries of over $500,000 while the latter is owned by South African multimillionaire, founder, and CEO Mark Shuttleworth.

Web browsers

Instead of Google Chrome, Apple Safari, and Microsoft Edge, you can use Mozilla Firefox or the Tor browser. It's important to note, however, that

Firefox derives 85% of its revenue from Google, making it a *de facto* subsidiary of Google, and it pays its CEO obscene amounts of money—outgoing CEO Mitchell Baker took a $7 million salary in 2022 before leaving the company.[9] The browser is FOSS, but the organization is steeped in class inequality and dependent upon Google for income. Mozilla is the lesser of browser evils, but it is not compatible with social and environmental justice.

If you want to browse the web with protection against surveillance, you should use the FOSS-based Tor browser. Tor bounces your requests for information from websites through a network of computers using an architecture, "onion routing," that wraps the requests in several layers of encryption. There are no known examples where Tor has been compromised. Using Tor consumes more data and is a little slower than other browsers, and a small share of websites do not work properly with Tor. If you live in a very authoritarian country, using Tor might be flagged by your Internet Service Provider and draw attention to you, so make sure to ask trusted experts for advice and use Tor with caution.

Social media and internet decentralization

As we saw in Chapter 1, Big Social Media networks are not interoperable. As Big Social networks began to take control of the social media space, Free Software hacktivists began developing alternatives that *do* interoperate via the "Fediverse," so that communities could own and control them. The FOSS-based Mastodon—a social media network that closely resembles X—became the first truly popular Fediverse network after its launch in 2016.[10]

Fediverse social media networks are typically built with FOSS software licensed under the AGPL. This allows communities to change how the platform works. Communities also create their own networks which they control. For example, if you open a Mastodon account, you can create your own Mastodon network where you and others who are part of that network decide on the rules. If you want to make it so that you only talk about cats and dogs, then you only talk about cats and dogs. There is even an easy-to-use service called masto.host which allows anyone to build their own network at a low cost (about $0.10 per user per month).

But there's more. Fediverse networks are built to interact across networks. With your Mastodon account, you can follow users in other networks, "like" their posts, or post your own comments without having to open a new account. It's as if you can create a TikTok account but interact with Facebook users, Instagram users, Reddit users, and YouTube users all from that one account. Only through interoperability could tens, hundreds, or thousands of networks be created, as people would never want to open up thousands of separate accounts.

At present, Fediverse networks still centralize authority into the hands of the network administrator. Like Big Social Media networks, they can spy on users by seeing when they log into the network, send posts, and so on. However, there are social media projects in development to fix this problem, such as LibreSocial and Panquake. These kinds of networks are built for direct democracy—they allow people to own and control their own social media space, and they are built to resist corporate and government owner-ship and control.

Open hardware, data, and AI

Some people have tried to port the idea behind FOSS licenses to hardware and data. While this is well-intentioned, there are limitations. Open hard-ware makes hardware designs open source, but it's very difficult to widely replicate some of the hardware products critical to tech, such as semiconduc-tors, because they are too complex. For instance, one kind of semiconductor, a computer processor, requires complex chemicals, machinery, testing pro-cedures, and facilities, in addition to ultra-complex hardware design. Many companies hyper-specialize in their part of the supply chain, and they have very advanced scientists and engineers developing and implementing state-of-the-art designs. This simply cannot be replicated easily across the world. The general public cannot develop its own replacements as easily as it can office software, so we need to figure out how to socialize the multifaceted supply chain across borders.

Open data and AI also face challenges. For starters, too much data is being collected about people and need to drastically curtail which data is collected about us. There is some low-hanging fruit—for example, we should abolish forced advertising and with it, data collected about us by third-party marketers. But that's only a start. For instance, it's less clear if and which medical data should be digitized and stored to advance the state of medicine. We need more popular education about data collection and use so that society can collectively determine what it wants.

For other kinds of information that we *should* collect—e.g., about the environment, or how many cars crash at a traffic intersection—we could share the data by giving the public access to databases so they can perform analytics. If some databases are too large, we could force those doing analytics to share the "digital intelligence" derived from the data.

Some AI developers are using open source models that can run on devices as cheap as a laptop. Yet some of these models are presently derived from larger-scale models developed by corporations, such as Facebook's LLaMA, which requires millions of dollars to create and connect to their software tools.[11] As a temporary measure, grassroots activists can pressure governments for funds to develop AI models that are fully free and open source while pushing to socialize the broader ecosystem and abolish corporations (e.g., via a Digital Tech Deal).

Other FOSS apps

The FOSS community has a wide variety of other solutions. Instead of Microsoft Office, you could use LibreOffice. Instead of Adobe Photoshop, you could use GIMP. There are tools like Audacity for sound editing and Kdenlive to edit videos. I provide a fuller list in my People's Tech booklet, and there are other FOSS listings online.

* * *

Just like agroecological farming, FOSS is heavily underfunded. Many of these projects survive on a shoestring budget, and we need to support them. Their existence demonstrates that another world is possible. Even so, the world we truly want requires fundamental changes to society. Just like co-ops cannot out-compete corporations, FOSS projects cannot overthrow digital colonialism and capitalism. They help us point to a better world, and they can be used to replace some of the major corporate software in the here and now. But to get where we truly want to go, we need a more organized initiative based on plans for a radical transition to an ecosocialist digital society, i.e., digital degrowth. For that, I've proposed a Digital Tech Deal.

DIGITAL TECH DEAL

Before outlining the DTD, a few preliminary points are in order.

First, no one person has all the answers, myself included. The world is a big and complex place. I can only suggest some things that can be done to point us in the right direction. It's up to everyone else to decide if they like them and to experiment.

Second, we need to understand where to draw the line for sustainable aggregate material resource use. Is it 50 billion tons for all humans per year? More? Less? For this, we need better studies so that we can make decisions about what we have the capacity to develop and how to transition to a fair and sustainable global society.

Third, we need scientists to create post-growth climate mitigation pathways.[12] Degrowth advocates have been demanding the IPCC incorporate degrowth scenarios into its models, with no success to date. This illustrates a *structural* problem with the IPCC, whose scientists are appointed by governments, which are hell-bent on growth at all costs. We need to either restructure the IPCC to make it more interdisciplinary and democratically accountable, or create a new alternative—one that follows principles of scientific objectivity without the constraints of state-corporate power.[13]

* * *

For the last several years, I've spent a great deal of time thinking about solutions that go beyond the Free Software Movement and People's Tech projects. By themselves, People's Tech solutions cannot create the ecosocialist world we need—universal class abolition, socio-economic justice, a new way of planning the economy in harmony with nature, demilitarization, and more. Capitalism is too nimble and powerful to be outmaneuvered by clever hacks or silver bullets.

The dominant approach to digital justice by the US-centered tech "left" addresses *symptoms*, such as carbon emissions, low wages, excessive wealth, high-tech surveillance, military technology, or industry concentration in a piecemeal fashion on the basis of mild capitalist reforms like antitrust, progressive taxation, business unionism, and the like. It's a racist, imperialist, ecocidal framework and agenda that we will unpack in the next chapter. But first we need to explore a digital degrowth platform.

To build digital degrowth, we need to fix multiple root cause problems simultaneously, which includes connecting our struggle to broader movements for ecosocialist transformation. To this effect, I've proposed a Digital Tech Deal—which could also be called a Digital Justice Deal—that dovetails with radical environmental "deals" such as the Cochabamba People's Agreement, the Red Nation's Red Deal, and Max Ajl's People's Green New Deal.[14] These proposals acknowledge the limits to growth and incorporate the egalitarian principles needed for a transition to digital degrowth.

Let's dig in.

SETTING THE STAGE: RADICAL ENVIRONMENTAL DEALS

In April 2010, representatives from 140 different countries gathered at the World People's Conference in Bolivia to outline an explicitly decolonial, anti-capitalist agenda to save the environment. Previous climate agreements, such as the Rio Agreement (1992), Kyoto Protocol (1997), and the Copenhagen Accord (2009) all failed to address the underlying structural causes of the climate crisis. Attendees drafted a defining document of the environmental movement, called the Cochabamba People's Agreement (CPA). The CPA declares:

> The corporations and governments of the so-called "developed" countries, in complicity with a segment of the scientific community, have led us to discuss climate change as a problem limited to the rise in temperature without questioning the cause, which is the capitalist system ... The capitalist system has imposed on us a logic of competition, progress and limitless growth. This regime of production and consumption seeks profit without limits, separating human beings from nature and imposing a logic of domination upon nature, transforming everything into commodities ... Capitalism requires a powerful military industry for its processes of accumulation and imposition of control over territories and natural resources, suppressing the resistance of the peoples. It is an imperialist system of colonization of the planet.[15]

The burdens are overwhelmingly endured by the Global South, even though the North created the crisis through the development and implementation of the colonial-capitalist system. To save our planet, then, a new *system* is needed. For the CPA, this first entails "equity among human beings," including equality, harmony, and balance with nature, and the "elimination of all forms of colonialism, imperialism and interventionism." Moreover, we need to reduce our ecological footprint (degrowth) and apply rights to Mother Earth.

Endorsing the principle of common but differentiated responsibilities, the CPA demands developed countries decolonize the atmosphere (by reducing and absorbing their GHG emissions), assume the costs of technology transfers to the South, assume responsibility for the hundreds of millions of people that will be forced to migrate due to the climate change they caused, and pay for the adaptation debt related to the impacts of climate change via an Adaptation Fund. Responsibilities extend beyond financial compensation to restorative justice, "understood as the restitution of integrity to our Mother Earth and all its beings."

Indigenous and other models of agriculture should contribute to agricultural and food sovereignty, "understood as the right of peoples to control their own seeds, lands, water, and food production." Failed capitalist projects, including industrial agriculture and carbon markets, are explicitly rejected as false solutions.

In addition to these measures, states should grant legal recognition to indigenous claims over territories, land, and natural resources (called "Land Back"). With respect to intellectual property, the CPA declares:

> Knowledge is universal, and should for no reason be the object of private property or private use, nor should its application in the form of technology. Developed countries have a responsibility to share their technology with developing countries, to build research centers in developing countries for the creation of technologies and innovations, and defend and promote their development and application for "living well."

To enforce this agenda, the CPA recommends creating "an International Climate and Environmental Justice Tribunal that has the legal capacity to prevent, judge and penalize States, industries and people that by commission or omission contaminate and provoke climate change." Global referendums and popular consultations should be created for "a broad and democratic space for coordination and joint worldwide actions."[16]

The Cochabamba People's Agreement has not been enacted, but it establishes a powerful vision from the South that can help avert an existential crisis.

Other radical environmental "deals" provide their own ideas. The most detailed are Max Ajl's People's Green New Deal (GND), the Red Nation's Red Deal, and the South African Climate Justice Charter.[17] These proposals identify capitalism and colonialism as foundational causes that must be uprooted through ecosocialist programs of profound systemic change. They acknowledge the limits to growth and incorporate the egalitarian principles needed for a just transition to a truly sustainable economy. Climate justice and social justice are understood to be inseparable, and only internationalist solutions can bring a just transition out of the environmental crisis.

Max Ajl's People's GND is the most comprehensive of the proposals. For Ajl, national liberation is central, as it's impossible for Global South countries to manage and mitigate climate change without national control over their resources. This means demilitarization, starting with the immediate removal of the US military as the world's imperialist police force. Concomitantly, the North must honor demands for ecological and climate debt, a position shared by the Climate Justice Charter.[18]

A DIGITAL TECH DEAL

None of the aforementioned deals incorporate plans for the digital ecosystem, despite its central relevance to the modern economy and environmental sustainability. Conversely, the digital justice movement has almost entirely ignored degrowth and the need to integrate the digital society into a degrowth-based ecosocialist framework. Environmental justice and digital justice go hand-in-hand, and the two movements must link up to achieve their goals.

The formulation of green "deals" to save the environment emerged because the crisis is so deeply rooted that piecemeal reforms will not get the job done. The same is true of the digital economy. Drawing upon the Green New Deal, some intellectuals have proposed racist, imperialist "Digital New

Deals," a throwback to FDR-style capitalism in digital form. But as we have seen, we can't save digital capitalism. We need plans for profound systemic change.

To fill this gap, I've proposed an ecosocialist Digital Tech Deal which embodies the intersection of degrowth, sustainability, environmental resilience, anti-imperialism, social equality, democratic self-management, class abolition, and internationalism. Like other ecosocialist deals, the DTD isn't intended to cover everything. Rather, it's a starting point that covers many of the core principles and objectives essential to averting tech-driven ecocide. What follows is a ten-point plan to guide the program.

1. Ensure the digital economy falls within social and planetary boundaries

It's a truism that the digital economy cannot exceed social (fair) and planetary (sustainable) boundaries. This means that its climate and ecological footprints need to be monitored and kept to safe levels at local, regional, and global scales informed by environmental science.

With degrowth, planning for a fair and sustainable digital economy is complex because economic planning cannot be done in isolation. Making decisions to mass-produce a new smartphone model has to be weighed against all other considerations, such as building proper homes for people who do not have them.

Sustainable democratic planning for the *digital economy* requires studies of the climate and ecological footprints of its major sectors and products, from infrastructure like laptops and data centers to products and services like operating systems and chatbots. We should be studying their impacts on socio-economic inequality under capitalism as well, so that we can evaluate their social impacts during the transition to ecosocialism. Some of this work has been done in this book and elsewhere, but we need much more clarity on these questions.

We also need to study the social and ecological impacts of *digitalization*. If Microsoft and Amazon are to offer agribusiness products that lock in an industrial model, then they are now harming the environment *even if* the digital tech itself—such as aerial drones to monitor crops—doesn't emit greenhouse gases (or even reduces them). This is important because tech giants may argue they are *reducing* harm to the environment, when in fact they are powering an environmentally destructive *model* (industrial agriculture) and concentrating wealth (via capitalist agricultural production), which is *incompatible* with a just and sustainable society.

Finally, we need to formulate timelines for just transitions in accordance with degrowth-based climate mitigation pathways. This would provide a solid foundation for a sustainable digital economy and time frames to plan just transitions as we transform various aspects of the digital economy.

2. Use digital democratic planning to create and administer ecosocialism

With a scientific basis for what can be sustainably produced in place, we can build an ecosocialist economy. Ideally, society would be engineered so that by its very nature, it's impossible to accumulate wealth and power and re-create class. The best socialists want to design society so that individuals and groups cannot concentrate on political, economic, or social power.

Several socialist systems designed to produce genuine equality have been proposed over time. Michael Albert and Robin Hahnel's "participatory economics," or *ParEcon* for short, is perhaps the most detailed, bottom-up, and democratic.[19] Let's briefly review the ParEcon system before discussing the digital element.

ParEcon begins with the egalitarian human values we want to see replace the savage brutality of capitalism. If people shouldn't be paid for their genetic talents, ownership of tools, financial wealth, or sheer market power, then how should they be paid? Albert and Hahnel propose that workers should be rewarded on the basis of effort, sacrifice, and need. If a worker puts in more *effort* by putting in more hours, then they should be compensated more than someone who does less. If a worker puts in greater *sacrifice*, say, by performing labor that is more intense or onerous to their health (such as working in a mine) than less intense or onerous labor, then they should be rewarded for it. And finally, all people have *basic needs*, such as food, housing, transportation, utilities, and health care, while some people have *special needs* which builds in allowances for people who cannot work, such as some disabled people. So in short, ParEcon rewards the duration, intensity, and onerousness of socially valued work.

With ParEcon, there is no class, private ownership of the means of production, or markets. Some people still have a *little* more than others, but only due to greater effort or sacrifice. People have personal belongings, but everything needed to produce our way of life is held in common through social ownership. People coordinate production and consumption democratically without a marketplace where buyers and sellers compete to advance their own separate interests.

ParEcon's major institutions are neighborhood consumer councils and worker councils, which are organized into federations that coordinate their interrelated activities through a participatory planning procedure. Neighborhood consumer councils are organized at the household level to request the things they would like to consume. At the local level, people participate in discussions over which neighborhood public goods are to be requested. All members vote for recallable delegates to higher-level federations of consumer councils at the ward, city, county, state, regional, and national levels.

Worker councils are internally democratic with no hierarchies of authority. Each worker has a voice and votes on the governing body. Each person has a few (not just one) jobs that are balanced so that each person performs a combination of menial and empowering labor—no more "some people take out the trash all day long" while others do desirable work in pleasant settings. Worker councils are advised to create job-balancing committees to distribute and combine tasks that power the workplace.

Economic production and distribution is coordinated through a decentralized process of iterative planning. Federations of worker councils and consumer councils coordinate their needs and desires through consumer requests and worker willingness and capacity to produce.

The finer details of ParEcon, as well as responses to questions and critiques, have been laid out by Albert and Hahnel in numerous books over three decades. Needless to say, ParEcon would require a great deal of popular education, coordination, and experimentation in order to efficiently coordinate economic production and consumption. This is where digital technology can play a critical role.

The drafting process of the widely used copyleft license, the GNU General Public License version 3 (GPLv3), provides a glimpse of how technology could facilitate widespread consultation. When creating the GPLv3 in 2006, a custom FOSS tool called Stet was created for collaborative commenting.[20] Comments were made through email and web interfaces, and the software made it easy to see which sections of the license most interested commentators. Public events were also held in person in Global North

214

and South countries, and discussion committees were formed for individual users and developers, commercial entities, and nonprofits.

Other software tools used to coordinate decentralized participation in democratic processes could be utilized to incorporate grassroots input. Taiwan offers an interesting case example. According to Free Software programmer and activist Audrey Tang, who is now the country's first-ever Minister of Digital Affairs, Taiwan is:

> ... now using distributed ledgers, quadratic voting and various online open-source platforms to enable greater participatory democracy ... Roughly half the country now participates in digital governance via an online platform that allows the public to weigh in on everything from labour law (should Uber be allowed to operate in Taiwan? Yes. Can it undercut traditional taxi fares? No) to proposing their own legislation, including a ban on plastic straws in takeaway drinks.[21]

In 2023, Tang collaborated with the Collective Intelligence Policy organization to introduce Alignment Assemblies that use tech to solicit citizen opinions about the government's new AI policies. While Taiwan is not a socialist economy, these tools can be adapted for more egalitarian systems like ParEcon.

Of course, implementing a system like ParEcon is far from simple. There would need to be a planned transition, and it would evolve through experience. The topic of implementation will be taken up in the next chapter. For now, it's sufficient to note that ParEcon offers a great starting point for a resilient, egalitarian vision of society opposed to both capitalism and state "socialism" which dovetails with a DTD.

With the limits to growth and a broad vision for society covered, the remaining sections of the DTD build out some of the core essentials of an ecosocialist digital degrowth.

3. Phase out intellectual property

Intellectual property, especially in the form of copyrights, patents, and trade secrets, gives corporations control over knowledge, culture, and the code that determines how apps and services work, allowing them to maximize user engagement, privatize innovation, and extract data and rents. Economist

Dean Baker estimates that intellectual property rents cost US consumers an additional $1 trillion per year compared to what could be obtained on a "free market" without patent or copyright monopolies.[22]

Intellectuals and information rights activists have long noted that inventions of the mind are different from tangible goods in that they can be copied and consumed at effectively zero cost. Economists call knowledge "non-rivalrous." As Eben Moglen puts it, "If you could make lamb chops in endless numbers by the mere pressing of a button, there would be no moral argument for hunger."[23] But in the digital world, copyright does just this— it creates artificial scarcity in the presence of infinite abundance. If I have an apple and you eat it, then I no longer have that apple to eat. But if I have a digital book or song and you make a digital copy, then I can still enjoy my copies.

Of course, if we abolish copyright paywalls and make knowledge "free," we would have to find other ways to pay knowledge producers. This could be done in the near term. For instance, each country could give everyone a tax rebate, paid for by the rich, that allows them to pay creator associations. The associations could be decentralized by capping contributions to prevent institutional monocultures from developing. These would require legal autonomy from the state, ensuring people's freedom of speech, while conditionalities on just pay and union membership could be put in place. A portion of the revenue could also be redistributed to people in the Global South as reparations for colonialism and much-needed aid.

Instead of patents, we could also fully subsidize research and development that requires the sharing of all knowledge produced. This, researcher Dan Hind suggests, could be tied to production by co-operatives and democratic workplaces instead of private, for-profit firms.[24]

4. Socialize physical infrastructure

Physical infrastructure like data and cloud computing centers, cell phone towers, fiber-optic internet cables, satellite internet constellations, computer hardware, e-commerce logistics, research and development centers, and transoceanic submarine cables are generally privately owned—to the benefit of the ruling classes. These should instead be socially owned, produced, and operated at cost for the public good.

216

Activists have been building community-run broadband initiatives that deliver high-speed internet at lower costs than their corporate rivals. Wireless mesh networks can also help place internet services into the hands of communities. Corporate cloud centers could be transformed into publicly owned server farms that run FOSS-based solutions like OpenStack and operate for the public interest rather than profit. Infrastructure already built by the tech giants in the Global South could be given away as reparations.

Infrastructure that cannot be produced locally in a decentralized fashion—such as semiconductors—might be maintained by an international consortium that builds and maintains it at cost for the public good rather than profit.

5. Decentralize the internet

We also need to consider decentralizing internet services to be hosted directly by the people. This approach contrasts against the "client–server" model that most of the internet uses, whereby you (the client) send and request data from a server (e.g., Facebook) that acts as a middle-man between the people.

One project, called FreedomBox, offers software that can turn our laptops or any other computer into a server that allows us to run our own internet services collectively as a community. With FreedomBox, email can be self-hosted, as can online calendars and things like file storage. This would likely use more energy than hyperscale clouds. Yet the centralization of power that accompanies hyperscalers is also problematic. We can only make choices about the ecology of decentralization if we know the costs so that we can weigh the benefits of communal self-hosting against environmental impacts.

Blockchain is another tool that could help us decentralize the internet. It uses a peer-to-peer network of computers to store a shared database of transactions. Quite recently, it became a tech "left" fad to criticize internet decentralization as a right-wing libertarian idea, on grounds that many "Web 3.0" blockchain projects are capitalist. (Right-wing libertarians misappropriate the words "libertarian" and "decentralization.") But socialists of many stripes, from anarchists to democratic Marxists, have long emphasized the necessity of decentralization to a free and equal society.

Internet decentralization is about democratizing the means of production, computation, and knowledge by placing our data, online platforms, and communications into the hands of the people. For ecosocialists, it's hard to imagine what else could be desired if you want a planet of equals.

6. Socialize the platforms

Many online platforms centralize services into the hands of private owners who act as intermediaries between users. Companies like Uber and Amazon extract rent from workers and sellers, while companies like Meta and TikTok shove ads down everyone's throats.

But as we just saw, internet decentralization technologies can replace centralized platforms. We could tear down Big Social Media through projects like the Fediverse, LibreSocial, Panquake, and FreedomBox. We can replace e-commerce platforms like Amazon by making e-retail a public service.

To fully replace private platform owners, popular movements need to formulate and enact new laws to develop the alternatives, scale them up, and secure them against re-privatization.

7. Socialize digital intelligence and data

Data solutions require strong privacy protections, collective ownership, and democratic planning based on a combination of new technological and ecosocialist legal solutions. The Open Data movement pushes for a combination of privacy, security, transparency, and democratic decision-making over how data is collected, stored, and used. There are no one-size-fits-all solutions to "data privacy," but we can apply these principles to projects in all domains of life, from education and health care to city administration and transportation.

In Barcelona and Amsterdam, Project DECODE (DEcentralised Citizen-owned Data Ecosystems) was developed as a technology architecture for decentralized data governance. Utilizing a data commons model, DECODE enables local inhabitants to do things like share sensor data about noise and pollution in their area and sign petitions on digital democracy platforms (e.g., Decidim.org) without security or privacy risks. Projects like DECODE provide important models to build upon.

Some people argue that small collectives and nations require keeping non-personal data private to prevent use by tech giants. But this will likely concentrate wealth into the hands of local elites with the resources to exploit the data in the name of broad-based empowerment. The solution isn't to close off knowledge to the public. "The Master's Tools will never dismantle the Master's House," as Audrey Lorde famously quipped. Rather, we need to *extend* social and collective ownership across the digital ecosystem so that the means to appropriate workers' culture and labor are sealed off.

8. End digital consumerism

As we have seen, advertising induces consumption and pushes people toward anti-social, environmentally harmful mindsets and behaviors. Seven in ten people say digital ads are annoying, and almost four in ten (37%) of internet users worldwide install ad blockers. The global advertising industry was set to top $1 trillion in 2023. The top three ad companies—Alphabet/ Google, Meta, and Amazon took by far the largest share worldwide with about 43% of the *total* ad spend and 64% of the online market.[25]

Many cities and states have now banned outdoor billboards, from Brazil and India to France and the US. This could be expanded to include all forced advertising. Ad-dependent industries could instead receive money through tax rebates connected to decentralized associations, as recommended in Point #3 above.

Of course, producers need to communicate their products to the public. Companies could list their products in voluntarily consulted outlets like *Consumer Reports*. If forced ads are banned, some companies may try to coerce people into visiting ad outlets, where they offer coupons and rebates. Laws could therefore be passed to plug loopholes by eliminating manipulation (e.g., celebrity endorsements, paid product placement), restricting ads to product information (e.g., gas mileage and environmental impact), and regulating coupons and rebates (so people aren't forced to dig through ad databases).

In addition to banning ads, we need to end planned obsolescence. In the digital economy, devices can be designed for long-term use. This includes the "right to repair"—e.g., requiring affordable options to repair or replace parts like broken screens, batteries, and computer storage. But this has some real limitations.

The "Fairphone" smartphone, for example, sources as many materials as possible from recycled material, and it commits to "fair trade" sourced gold, silver, and cobalt. However, this doesn't imply truly *fair* wages—it simply attempts to verify that there are no *extreme* labor practices like child labor. Moreover, the company is not committed to union production, and it sources cheap labor from anti-union Chinese factories. Retailing at about $900, the Fairphone is way off-limits to most of the world's people. Moreover, under ideal conditions, only 45.1% of Fairphone materials can be recycled.[26]

To be sure, we do need the right to repair, less wasteful electronics, and more labor-friendly business practices. But there are serious limitations to recycling and "ethical consumption" that shouldn't dampen our activist demands for system change.[27]

In addition to these measures, we need better waste policies and infrastructure. The North needs to stop dumping its e-waste and other junk in the South, placing the burdens of waste disposal and recycling on the global poor. We also need to create better infrastructure for waste disposal and recycling. Several international agreements are designed to control the transboundary movement of hazardous waste. Most notably, the 2019 Ban Amendment to the Basel Convention bans the movement of hazardous wastes, including e-waste, from countries of the Organization for Cooperation and Development (OECD), European Commission, and Liechtenstein to other party countries. The United States is the only industrialized and OECD country that has *not* ratified the Basel Convention. It should be pressured to sign it, and all countries need to implement it.

Many places in the South do not have the infrastructure in place to handle hazardous materials. The North can help out by donating funds needed to build better waste and recycling infrastructure as a more general part of its reparations.

Some tech environmentalists have drawn attention to eco-friendly *biodegradable* computing. While it may be possible to replace low-level computing architecture with biodegradable parts (e.g., a circuit board for a computer mouse), this only works for "low-tech" computing.[28] There are no known prospects that biodegradable computing can power anything beyond a minuscule share of the digital ecosystem.

9. Replace military, police, prisons, and national-security apparatuses with community-driven safety and security services

There is nothing natural or inevitable about war, militarism, police, prisons, borders, or high-tech surveillance. Our goal should be to abolish these horrors. Of course, we cannot eradicate all social problems and violence. But we can build alternative ways to protect communities, prevent harms from occurring by making communities whole and healthy, and fairly adjudicate injustice.

There are some abolitionist projects and experiments in the digital space. In the US, the Carceral Tech Resistance Network (CTRN) "are campaigning against the design and experimentation of technologies by police, prisons, border enforcement, and commercial partnerships." This project connects to broader abolitionist projects in the US.

The EU's AI Act will include a partial ban on biometric surveillance and predictive policing, thanks in large part to pressure from activist organizations. Activists could build off this to extend such regulations to full-scale abolition. Closing Real-Time Crime Centers and fusion surveillance centers should also be high on the list, as should banning smart camera networks.

In South Africa, the activist group Right2Know tried to throw sand in the gears of Vumacam by challenging their wayleaves (akin to licenses) to use poles on public land, but failed in the courts. In China, activists have had some success challenging the use of facial recognition cameras by the private sector for things like real estate. Projects like these can connect to abolitionist struggles against military and carceral institutions as well as broader social justice campaigns.

10. End the digital divide

In the 1980s and 1990s, personal computers and the internet began spreading to middle and upper-class households and businesses in the Global North. Poor households and people in the Global South had minimal or no access to computers and the internet. Unequal access to tech was viewed as a form of inequality. Scholars called the situation the "digital divide."

Access to computers and affordable internet is often considered a human right. Yet extending digital technologies like smartphones, laptops, and affordable broadband internet to poor populations and countries creates a dynamic of *assimilation* into an unequal status quo that can make many things worse. After all, the present digital society is characterized by digital colonialism, concentrated markets, mass commercial and government surveillance, and planetary destruction.

Any attempt to bridge the digital divide risks increasing inequality *generally* even as it reduces a *single form* of inequality (access to tech). We should support access to tech as a human right. But the best way to bridge the digital divide is through a digital degrowth scenario that extends accessibility to the poor while also abolishing broader forms of inequality in harmony with nature.

* * *

Taken together, People's Tech and a Digital Tech Deal provide a set of concrete solutions and principles to build take action now and build toward a just and sustainable future. However, it's one thing to envision the society we want, it's another to make it a reality. That is the subject of our next and final chapter.

9
Taking Action

Throughout this book, we have seen that the American tech sector is the primary force of the capitalist suicide machine. The process of digital colonialism produces an ecologically unequal exchange and division of labor across the world, strengthens the American Empire, and radically violates planetary boundaries. The central driver of limitless growth on a finite planet, the present digital economy concentrates wealth and income at a time when the existence of class prevents a just transition to a sustainable society.

We need to reframe tech politics around a new paradigm, *digital degrowth*. That means placing the fundamentals at the center of our analysis. Digital colonialism and capitalism, American Empire, the North–South divide, climate and ecological debt, ecologically unequal exchange, and ecosocialist solutions based on full economic, political, and social equality have to take center stage.

This needs to happen fast, as we're in a serious time crunch. A fundamental transformation must be built starting *now*, not decades from now. There's no time for reformist agendas. If we're actually going to save the environment and make a harmonious society a real, lived experience—not just a dream to talk about—we likely need a revolution. We'll return to that in the last section.

* * *

This final chapter presents a few strategies and tactics to implement digital degrowth. I argue that we need to abolish the elite, US-centered knowledge institutions and their rich funders, as they are designed to manufacture consent for the American Empire. Most people do not know the basic facts and analysis outlined in this book because those with power over the conversation do not want to address them. If we're going to build degrowth, we need most people to be aware of the basics, to embrace them, and to participate in building the transition. We cannot collectively oppose something we do not collectively understand. Education is critical.

So *first*, we need to break down propaganda produced by elites by democratizing, socializing, decolonizing, and redistributing wealth and power within and between knowledge institutions.

Second, we need to take direct action against the American Empire. To this effect, I've suggested a #BigTechBDS campaign that uses boycotts, divestment, and sanctions against Big Tech and the United States.

Third, we need to build revolutionary movements intent on changing our way of life by seizing the means of production, wealth, and power from ruling-class elites. These have to be internally democratic. This is no easy task, but we cannot pretend that we can afford to ignore it, given the time frame we have to save the environment.

Let's start with education.

MANUFACTURING CONSENT: FRAMING THE DEBATE

While various intellectuals have opened up debates around surveillance, Big Tech monopolies, and so on, they also ignore the underlying fact that the US is an empire using technology to exploit the rest of the world. We have to address the dominant narrative about tech head-on because it is so poorly conceptualized, so corrupt, so anti-intellectual, and so American supremacist, it's hard to imagine it can be this bad.

The majority of this section will focus on this US-centered tech "left," which dominates the global conversation. This American School of tech politics has made no attempt to conduct simple social scientific approaches to quantifying national power and its connection to tech and the environment—which should be the starting point for a *basic* understanding of digital politics. You can't be an expert in your topic if your snapshot picture of the world is wrong. Shockingly, this is the general state of the field. Nobody has put digital colonialism and degrowth together, as if they aren't both *central* and *inseparable*.[1]

For years, I've been asking myself the question: why is the dominant narrative in tech this disconnected from reality? Why are certain things discussed or taken *seriously*, but not others? For example, why do tech "leftists" constantly talk about "surveillance capitalism" or algorithmic bias, but not digital colonialism or degrowth? Would rich Ivy League alumni and billionaire foundations pour money into research projects studying and taking action to abolish class and the American Empire?

As we'll see, the dominant narrative about tech is disconnected from reality precisely because it is connected to rich American knowledge institutions servicing the American Empire. Working within these institutions, the US-centered "digital justice" narratives are organized around two, loosely connected branches.

The first branch is political economy, centered on antitrust—a legal apparatus of so-called "fair" and "competitive" capitalism that will supposedly curb the concentrated wealth and power of Big Tech. The second branch centers on human rights, with concerns about "ethical AI," algorithmic bias, surveillance, and liberal/progressive identity politics.

The two branches sometimes complement each other. Together, they form a network of intellectuals employed by and connected to the richest and most powerful universities, corporate media, NGOs, think tanks, Big Tech corporations, billionaire philanthropists, Big Foundations, and government institutions, including the US government itself.

If the pseudo-left heralded as "thought leaders" were to deviate from the narrative desired by their paymasters, they would be punished—they would lose their fame and the funding for their research centers and extravagant lifestyles. New people would step in to replace them, and those new faces would happily reap the benefits of fame, money, and power. The dominant narrative is then ultimately a symptom of our knowledge *systems*.

It is beyond the scope of this book to provide a comprehensive account of the US-centered pseudo-left. Instead, I will provide some emblematic case examples of how they manufacture consent for American Empire. This will help explain why digital degrowth has been missing from the conversation.

For global audiences, some of the figures named in the following pages may not be familiar and seem like insider US politics. But they are among the elite influencers in tech politics that shape global conversations and impact digital justice agendas, as well as government policy.

Before we get to the tech "left," however, I want to briefly also discuss the erasure and greenwashing of degrowth in general.

Degrowth denialism

Solutions based on degrowth are very different from "ecomodernist" solutions of "green growth." Degrowth requires rapid, unprecedented, and fundamental changes based on ecosocialism and equality, whereas "green growth" reforms envision business as usual.

As we saw in the introduction, about three quarters of climate experts think we cannot continue to sustainably grow the global economy *as a whole*. Yet despite growing concern among scientists, degrowth is scarcely discussed in the mass media.[2] If you search popular news websites for degrowth (e.g., "degrowth" site:nytimes.com), you'll see almost nothing on the topic. For instance, *The New York Times* has mentioned degrowth in 29 pieces of content. Of those, 15 make passing mention (no engagement) in, say, a single sentence, often portraying it negatively. Of the 14 remaining, four argue degrowth is a scheme by "doomsayers" and generally not "plausible."[3] A mere four articles portray degrowth even somewhat positively: two of those are devoted to Herman Daly, who believed a "steady state economy" is compatible with capitalism (thus not critical of the prevailing order),[4] one to the Marxist Kohei Saito (positive), and one article gives "both sides."

The New York Times publishes about 230 pieces of content—stories, graphics, interactives, and blog posts—each day, up from 170 in 2010.[5] The above-mentioned 15 substantive articles go back to 2014 (the next closest was 1976).[6] We can therefore calculate that the *NYT* has published about 730,000 pieces over the past decade; 15 substantive articles on degrowth equates to a rate of 2 per 100,000 pieces (0.00002%) spanning the last decade. Most of the articles are negative, none engage with the core science. This is arguably the most important issue in human history.

The Washington Post, which publishes 500 pieces of content per day, has never published an original article on degrowth. *CNN* has mentioned degrowth twice—one positive, one in passing. The right-wing *Wall Street Journal*, which publishes 240 pieces per day, has mentioned degrowth twice (both negative), while *Fox News* has mentioned it eight times (all negative). Of the mass media, the *Guardian* has given degrowth the most amount of attention, with about 40 articles mentioning it in the past 15 years (35 positive). More broadly, South Africa's *Daily Maverick* has run eleven pieces (ten positive) and *Al Jazeera* eight (all positive).

What about "independent" left media? *Jacobin* magazine is explicitly anti-degrowth, regularly runs hit pieces on the topic, and rejects article submissions by leading degrowth authors. Small socialist outlets seem to give the most favorable coverage. For example, *Counterpunch.org* and *Naked Capitalism* have mentioned degrowth tens of times each (almost all positive).

No matter where you look, the topic is drowned out by a mountain of never-ending content about the Kardashians, the Ukraine war, sensational events, and the like. This needs to change.

Green colonialism

While burying degrowth, most liberal and progressive American media instead endorse the Green New Deal (GND) made popular by Alexandra Ocasio-Cortez (AOC) and Bernie Sanders. Usurping a more left-oriented GND proposed by the Green Party (which would slash the US military budget in half),[7] AOC and Senator Ed Markey's 2019 GND aims to stay under the 1.5°C threshold by achieving "net zero" emissions through a mass transition to renewables, investment in negative emissions technologies and resilient infrastructure, pollution removal, habitat restoration, greater support for small and sustainable agriculture, as well as (unspecified) assistance to other countries. The plan focuses heavily on creating millions of high-wage union jobs for American frontline communities. Bernie Sanders proposed his own GND in August 2019 based on very similar provisions. (Unlike AOC-Markey, Sanders at least acknowledged a carbon debt to less industrialized nations.)

The American GNDs are fake environmental proposals based on fake social justice. Both proposals fail to recognize the growth crisis, *ecological* debt, and the urgent need to phase out capitalism. They won't prevent the planet from overheating and are built for Americans to enjoy the spoils of empire. The "benefits" to workers under the GND only apply to marginalized *Americans*. Workers of color in the Global South are tacitly viewed as subhumans who will be treated like slaves to supply the raw materials needed to power America's "green" consumption.[8] GND authors often call themselves democratic "socialists," but they really envision FDR-style neocolonial capitalism—what is more accurately labeled *social democratic capitalism*.

227

Nevertheless, the GND has widespread support from progressives in the United States. Canadian-born intellectual Naomi Klein is perhaps its greatest proponent, having even published a video short with AOC at one of the most popular American progressive news outlets, *The Intercept*, which endorses and almost never criticizes progressive Democrats. As Max Ajl notes, Klein talks out of both sides of her mouth. In her book, *On Fire: The (Burning) Case for a Green New Deal*, she rails against "climate barbarism" and the need for an "all-out war on pollution and poverty and racism and colonialism" and the "power players" responsible.[9] Yet Klein herself never goes head-to-head with the American Empire and its progressive wing. Instead, she *praises* progressive imperialists throughout the book. For Klein, "racial capitalism, settler-colonialism, anti-capitalism, and anti-colonialism are omnipresent. But they are aesthetic, not diagnostic," Ajl remarks.[10]

If we are okay with this, we should then be okay with a book on Israeli politics that relegates Palestinians to a few lines, poverty in South Sudan that barely mentions colonialism, or a book on South African history that only mentions apartheid in passing.

Klein also gets degrowth wrong. She admits that "a growing body" of scholarship (which she doesn't engage) delineates limits to growth, a problem she says can only be fixed by reducing the consumption of the world's wealthiest 20%. But degrowth is not simply concerned with personal consumption, it's concerned with reducing the total growth of material throughput via *systemic production* as a project that must begin *immediately* (not decades from now). Despite her performative box-checking, Klein's laundry list of how to fund a GND includes a mere 25% tax cut on the top ten military corporations and a 1% tax cut on billionaires.[11]

This green colonialism perspective is tied to money. As upper-class members of the "left" intellectual class, Klein and her colleagues at *The Intercept* likely way over-consume their fair and sustainable share of the planet's finite resources. The top staff listed in their 990 tax forms collect salaries averaging about $300,000 per year, peaking out at around $500,000 (e.g., for producer/writer Jeremy Scahill).[12]

The Intercept cries poor to its audience. It forces website visitors to join its email list to keep reading its news articles for free, and then bombards subscribers with requests for donations. The outlet has hardly written a single negative word about progressive Democrats. If they did, they'd probably lose hundreds of thousands of dollars (or more) from American readers faithful to the likes of Bernie Sanders and AOC.

The Intercept has long taken millions from eBay founder Pierre Omidyar, a billionaire whose foundation, Omidyar Network, explicitly endorses "good" capitalism and has supported a wide range of neocolonial tech projects in the Global South.[13]

In April 2024, the media reported that *The Intercept* lost backing from Omidyar and is running out of money. In its newsletter, it states: "The Intercept's independent journalism depends on reader donations, not advertising dollars or big corporations." But the Annual Reports buried on their website illustrate that about 70% of their money was sourced from institutional donors, not individual members. And those institutional funds are derived from the big corporations.[14] The outlet provides a quintessential example of how Big Foundation and other donor money exercises control over the left.

Klein is a "contributing editor" at *The Intercept*, but her pay is not listed in its public financial forms (neither was its founder, Glenn Greenwald, when he was working for them), so it's not clear how much (or if) they pay her. Yet we also know she asks for tens of thousands of dollars for some of her public speeches through the Lavin Agency. Klein was called out for this years ago. In response, she said "like most people, I don't like discussing my income," and that she uses the money to pay her own staff.[15] But there's no transparency. We don't know how much she actually paid them, or how much she makes or owns in general—apparently enough to pay her own staff. Klein currently has a job as a professor, a columnist at the *Guardian US*, and sells popular books. Celebrity professors often net several hundred-thousand-dollar salaries.

Here we need to stop and be clear: equality means equality. Chris Hani, a prominent South African anti-apartheid leader assassinated just before apartheid fell, famously warned: "What I fear is that the liberators emerge as elitists who drive around in Mercedes Benzes and use the resources of this country to live in palaces and to gather riches." You don't go into social justice to get rich. And if you can't get money to do research from proper sources, too bad. Social justice is a struggle.

"Leftist" elites are unlikely to embrace and exert forceful action for a radical ecosocialist transformation because it would require them to end their upper-class standard of living. How can you preach ecosocialist degrowth when you're making $200,000–500,000 (or more) per year, unless you keep it hidden? Instead, the left-most end of the mainstream spectrum pays lip service to the genuinely egalitarian left while pushing the mild capitalist agendas of their paymasters, who reward them with lavish salaries.

It is no surprise, then, that the mainstream "left" erases or trivializes class abolition, the green colonialism baked into the GND and other racist-imperialist politics of progressive Democrats, and the Big Foundations funding them. It's here where we get our first taste of the two-faced, racist-imperialist gaslighting that permeates the mainstream, US-centered pseudo-left.

Hiding the American Empire

While much of the mass media ignores degrowth, there is considerable uptake within the scientific community and a substantive anti-colonial, ecosocialist faction growing within the environmental movement. The same cannot be said of the tech "left." Here, we have a framework problem: there is hardly any attention to digital colonialism and virtually nothing on degrowth. The conversation is completely dominated by moneyed American knowledge institutions staffed by a network of wealthy scholars feeding from the trough.

I've been studying digital colonialism for over a decade, mostly from South Africa. I've also been an unpaid Visiting Fellow at the Yale Information Society Project—which has weekly seminars, writer's workshops, and conferences—for eight years. Since I've joined Yale, I can't remember hearing a single presenter utter the words "American Empire."

Imagine trying to explain the motion of the planets without accounting for the sun. Imagine trying to discuss global politics in the nineteenth century without mentioning the British Empire, or discussing Israeli politics without ever mentioning the occupation, as if these things don't exist. We would correctly say that these accounts are racist, colonial, disconnected from reality, nonsense, and so on.

But this is the narrative expressed by the overwhelming majority of US-centered tech "leftists" today. There is no American Empire (let alone degrowth), and digital colonialism is either erased, whitewashed, trivialized, or manipulated. Long story short: the tech pseudo-left is analytically and morally bankrupt.

Of course, not everyone within this mainstream American School of intellectuals group thinks exactly the same. They take somewhat different positions that frequently overlap. Here I'll consider three themes related to this book: the New Cold War, the political economy, and human rights. Let's briefly review each in turn.

The myth of US–China parity

According to most tech narratives, there is an epic battle between the US and China for global tech supremacy, as if there is close parity between the two. As data colonialism scholars Nick Couldry and Ulises Mejias *wrongly* frame it, the global digital economy is dominated by "two poles," the US and China.[16] But as we've seen, the digital economy is *unipolar*. One country *alone* dominates at the global level: the United States of America.

The "two poles" propaganda allows Western intellectuals to avoid the uncomfortable fact that the US has just 4% of the world's population, but has supremacy over the most lucrative and powerful part of the global economy and society, the digital ecosystem. To accomplish this, they typically cherry-pick a few examples where China has a visible global market share: 5G base stations (Huawei), social media (TikTok), e-retail (Shein, Temu), and scientific publications in the field of artificial intelligence—which they place alongside the anachronistic use of GDP to measure national economic power.

The West's US–China "close parity" claim is akin to saying, "black Americans are doing well, just look at Lebron James, Beyonce, and Michael Jordan!" But if you keep adding up *all* 340 million Americans, from rich to poor, you find that blacks own just 16% of the median wealth of whites and earn 32% less income. There is no parity.

If we applied the same *basic* standards of social science to tech, we would tabulate the broad digital economy. I did this in Chapter 1 and subsequent chapters, where we saw that the US towers above everyone else. We also need to account for other factors, such as climate debt, ecological debt, and ecologically unequal exchange. But the tech pseudo-left has not done this.[17] It is a monumental failure.

231

That these issues have been erased, whitewashed, trivialized, or manipulated is not arbitrary. It is a reflection of American supremacy. Digital colonialism is more than a system of political and economic domination. It is also about psychological and ideological domination.[18]

Noam Chomsky and Edward Herman famously demonstrated how the mass media manufactures consent on behalf of the American Empire. Journalists may courageously report the facts, but they also internalize the interests of state-corporate power, and the picture of the world they present reflects the interests of the ruling class. Through the omission of key facts, "selection of topics, distribution of concerns, emphasis and framing of issues, filtering of information, and bounding of debate within certain limits," the mass media set "a general agenda that others more or less adhere to."[19] This is how it works with the tech "left" across the media and other knowledge institutions.

Antitrust's racist imperialism

The US-centered tech "left" promotes a "good" (progressive) capitalism while imposing sharp limits on permissible thought—including the themes, core facts, and framework established in this book. Many of the so-called tech "critics" either work for (or take money from) Big Tech, Big Foundations, or other elite institutions. At the left-most end of the spectrum, they might make a few abstract comments paying lip service to anti-colonialism and anti-capitalism accompanied by staunch, uncritical support for mild capitalist reforms and progressive politicians. In South Africa, we call this duplicity, "talk left, walk right."

Over the past few years, this pseudo-left began taking umbrage at the concentrated wealth of Big Tech. To address the political economy issue, the law-heads turned to antitrust—antimonopoly laws to make capitalism "fair" and "competitive." In the US, "neo-Brandeisian" antitrust scholars and intellectuals such as Lina Khan, Tim Wu, Matt Stoller, Barry Lynn, David Dayen, Zephyr Teachout, Fiona Scott Morton, Eleanor Fox, Cory Doctorow, Sanjukta Paul, and Sandeep Vaheesan took to the history books to revive an older, "progressive" approach to antitrust.[20]

Neo-Brandeisians argue that Big Tech giants use their monopoly power to eliminate competition. They slash prices to undercut smaller businesses, use their deep pockets to buy up competitors, and leverage their infrastructure to self-preference their own products and services. This undermines democracy and harms workers, small businesses, and consumers. Progressive antitrust aims to rein in these practices and make twenty-first-century capitalism more "fair" and "competitive." If you're uncomfortable with the economic fortunes and political power of Big Tech, you'll probably find yourself reading about antitrust.

I concur with neo-Brandeisians that we should trace the history of antitrust to better understand its nature. But that's where our agreement ends.

The first federal antitrust law, the Sherman Antitrust Act, was passed in 1890. This was an era of Jim Crow racism, intense patriarchy, anti-socialist class war, indigenous genocide, and budding American imperialism. Were the founders really concerned with "democratic and egalitarian relations," as a leading neo-Brandeisian scholar, Sanjukta Paul, argues? What did they actually think?

Let's start with John Sherman, the first drafter from whom the Sherman Antitrust Act derives its name. In a frequently cited passage, Sherman told Congress, "If we will not endure a King as a political power we should not endure a king over the production, transportation, and sale of any of the necessities of life."[21] Yet Sherman's *general* praise of corporations seven paragraphs prior is omitted by neo-Brandeisians. "Experience has shown," Sherman stated:

> that [corporations] are the most useful agencies of modern civilization. They have enabled individuals to unite and to undertake great enterprises only attempted in former times by powerful governments. The good results of corporate power are shown in the vast development of our railroads and in the enormous increase of business and production of all kinds.[22]

The reference to railroads is astounding. During this time period, railroads were the engines of corporate industrialization, making possible regional specialization by speeding up communications and the transport of goods for trade. As historian Gabriel Kolko notes, "The 'Robber Barons,' for the most part, consisted of railroad speculators."[23]

Across the world, the railroads were vessels of robbery by foreign empires, the "open veins" of the Global South. In the US, railroad construction not only required violent labor exploitation, mostly carried out by Chinese immigrants, they were tied to Westward colonization. John Sherman would know. His brother, William Tecumseh Sherman, was a leading US military general on the Western frontier, where he carried out genocide against the Plains "Indians." William once said, "We must act with vindictive earnestness against the Sioux, even to their extermination, men, women and children ... during an assault, the soldiers cannot pause to distinguish between male and female, or even to discriminate as to age."[24] Using scorched earth tactics, Sherman massacred their sacred buffalo, rounded indigenous people into concentration camps, and helped secure railroad expansion from the "thieving, ragged Indians."[25] These were the "good results of corporate power" lauded by William's brother, John, who made similar remarks about Native Americans in his *Recollections*.

The other founding fathers of antitrust fared little better. The Southern Democrats (e.g., James K. Jones, James Z. George, John H. Reagan, and George Vest) were a collection of former slave owners, Confederate military officers, administrators of indigenous land theft and genocide, secessionists, and vulgar anti-black racists and sexists. On the Northern Republican side, Orville Platt introduced the racist-imperialist Platt Amendment, contributed to indigenous land theft and cultural assimilation of Native Americans, and explicitly opposed populism and socialism in support of inequality. Two other Northern Republicans, George Edmunds and George Hoar, were considered the leading authors of the final bill. But they also scorned socialism, communism, anarchism, and direct elections of the Senate, on grounds that more direct forms of popular control would destroy the constitution.[26]

As Gabriel Kolko and similar critics demonstrate, antitrust was not about equality. Rather, it was part of a broader effort to rationalize industry through business regulation. Big business of the time wanted the government to set guardrails against the "destructive competition" that made it too risky to invest in large-scale industrial projects like railroads.

As time marched on, industry concentration continued to rise in the US, irrespective of which administration or political party held power. This inconvenient fact was documented in the first comprehensive empirical study of US industry concentration, "100 Years of Rising Corporate Concentration," published in 2022. Reviewing the data beginning in 1917—the earliest period from which they could find quality data—the authors found market concentration increased across industries at a steady pace for the following century, thanks to increased economies of scale and technological intensification. Crucially, concentration rose during *all* antitrust regimes, from progressive to neoliberal. The authors "do not find evidence that antitrust shapes the economy-wide business size distribution."[27] Imagine there were a 100-year-old policy to stop carbon emissions, but emissions never stopped going up. At what point would we say it's a failed policy?

Instead of endorsing socialist solutions, antitrust advocates endorse capitalist "competition" as the medicine for corporate concentration. But competition is only good for those who can compete. In South Africa, as many as two thirds of the population lives on $3 or less per day. Who will compete with the rich countries once new antitrust regulations are put in place—the global poor living in shantytowns, or the middle- and upper-class people living in the North? There is no discussion of—let alone plan to end—digital colonialism, as if it doesn't exist. The message to the Global South is clear: we owe you nothing.

The Europeans fare no better. Just as they criticize the power of the American Big Tech giants, European politicians in the EU, France, Germany, the UK, and the Netherlands are seeking to build their own tech "unicorns"—startups worth a billion dollars or more—as fast as possible. For Europe, antitrust is merely a tool to cut down the US supergiants to make space for the rise of European giants.

Added to this, antitrust is ecocidal. Even if Meta, Alphabet, and Amazon were broken up into smaller companies and prevented from blocking competition, more numerous landlords on smaller plots of land would all collectively grow the economy at the same rate as their bigger predecessors. The environment is almost never discussed by anyone in the antitrust community, as if it has no relationship to tech. Its "good capitalism" agenda is not only racist and imperialist, it is divorced from reality. For the left, antitrust should be opposed as a false solution at odds with the environmental crisis.

Human rights and billionaire funding

In addition to political economy, the other major branch of the tech "left" aims to explicitly address issues of *social* inequality, with a focus on anti-racism. If you're reading about how tech impacts people's lives, you'll likely be

235

reading about issues like "algorithmic bias" and "AI ethics." This strain was created in the 2010s by the corporations themselves, especially via Microsoft-funded research.[28]

In 2012, New York University (NYU) took $1.625 million from Intel—a close Microsoft partner—to conduct research on "Social Computing" under the direction of privacy researcher and professor Helen Nissenbaum. The next year, NYU's Information Law Institute received $1 million from Microsoft to study law, policy, and tech. Then in 2017, Nissenbaum left NYU to create the Digital Life Initiative at Cornell Tech, which is also in NY City and takes money from Microsoft.

In 2013, Microsoft Researcher danah boyd founded a think tank called Data & Society with money exclusively provided by Microsoft. At the time, boyd was working closely with another Microsoft Researcher, Kate Crawford, who co-authored research with boyd and worked at her think tank during its early days. Crawford is one of the leading voices in the US tech "left" circuit who propagandizes on behalf of Microsoft. Whereas previous digital justice conversations about tech focused on property (e.g., FOSS), "data ethics" narrowed the focus to the politics of data, with no criticism of private ownership and profit as such.

In 2017, Crawford left Data & Society and became the co-founder of a new think tank, AI Now, with then-Google employee Meredith Whittaker, based on funds from Microsoft, Google, and a handful of Big Foundation capitalists (including Omidyar, MacArthur, and Ford). Housed at NYU, AI Now became another propaganda center for "ethics" research in the US. Microsoft was also operating its own Microsoft Research Lab, which included Crawford, in NYC.

Needless to say, if you get your money from Microsoft, you can't take certain positions, like "all schools should replace Microsoft software with Free Software," or "Big Tech giants are modern-day East India companies," or "corporations should be abolished," or "Big Tech is an American Empire project." From day one, these NGOs were serving corporate interests. In his book, *Artificial Whiteness*, Yarden Katz lays the agenda bare:

> Funding structures facilitate this convergence between corporate patrons and their supposed academic critics. The "non-profit industrial complex," as the INCITE! collective called it, works to "manage and control dissent

in order to make the world safe for capitalism." So when nonprofits, often backed by the likes of Google and Microsoft, began offering multi-million-dollar grants to study how AI will transform society—and how partnerships with corporations can make that transformation "ethical"—academics were induced to accept the premise. And while research that challenges the basic premise is unlikely to win support, the institutes poised to receive these large grants are already aligned with the program of managing dissent to protect capitalism.[29]

So here five influential "digital justice" research organizations—NYU, Cornell Tech, Data & Society, AI Now, and Microsoft Research Lab—were all operating in NYC as a loosely knit network of researchers taking money from Microsoft.

As we saw in previous chapters, Microsoft is deeply rooted in racist, imperialist exploitation all across the world. From industrial agriculture and the cloud to police, prisons, and the military, Microsoft cannot be missed, and it is one of the most racist corporations on the planet. But strangely, almost none of this made it into the work of the leading intellectuals at these projects. Publications allegedly critical of police tech were published at Data & Society, AI Now, and by various Microsoft researchers, including Kate Crawford, danah boyd, and Sarah Brayne, all of whom branded themselves as anti-racists. Microsoft is *the* central Big Tech player in the police tech space, yet it isn't critiqued in their publications about police tech. There are plenty of other issues these scholars systematically ignore.

Eventually, outsiders began to take notice. In late 2019, MIT student Rodrigo Ochigame published an article at *The Intercept* titled, "The Invention of 'Ethical AI': How Big Tech Manipulates Academia to Avoid Regulation," where he called out Data & Society and AI Now (among others) for peddling an "AI ethics" narrative that serves their corporate masters.[30] Then in June 2020, I published "The Microsoft Police State" at *The Intercept* mapping out the expansive scope of Microsoft's relationship to police and police surveillance vendors, while also calling out AI Now. Later that year, Yarden Katz published *Artificial Whiteness*, which devoted several chapters to exposing Data & Society, AI Now, and some of the other elite academic and corporate-funded researchers.

The following year, Microsoft launched a "Race and Technology" lecture series in conjunction with NYU. The speaker lineup featured 14 prominent researchers, including Sareeta Amrute (Data & Society), Ruha Benjamin (Princeton, author of *The New Jim Code*), and Simone Browne (Princeton, author of *Dark Matters*). All speakers were people of color. A lecture host confirmed to me that the speakers were paid, though Charelton McIlwain (NYU, author of *Black Software*), who co-organized the event with Microsoft, went silent after I asked him how much.

The only two speakers to even mention *anything* about Microsoft's connections to race were McIlwain and Benjamin, both of whom said almost nothing. McIlwain only mentioned it after I asked him to address my article at *The Intercept* during the Q&A. He responded that his primary concern is "thinking about a different future" rather than focusing on the companies "that have been implicated in building the infrastructure that has done so much damage in terms of race that we see today."[31] Apparently it doesn't matter if you airbrush the worst culprit from the picture, and that it is paying people of color to portray itself as hip to anti-racism.

It's possible the speakers know nothing about what Microsoft does as a worldwide oppressor of people of color, and are therefore highly ignorant about tech politics. Alternatively, they're aware of Microsoft's racist-imperialist empire and choose to stay silent, and are paid sell-outs. One might imagine a set of speakers taking money from warplane manufacturer Boeing to promote "world peace" or a seminar series sponsored by Bayer-Monsanto to address food justice.

The issue of corporate-funded tech reached a head in late 2020 when Google terminated "AI ethics" researcher Timnit Gebru. Gebru was previously a Microsoft postdoc who made inroads with the NYC crowd while working on the gender and racial bias of facial recognition products. Microsoft showcased her work as evidence of the company's supposed commitment to social justice and anti-racism. Gebru apparently didn't bother to look into anything the company does—meaning her digital justice literacy was effectively nil—and her next stop was Google, which she also apparently didn't look into (or chose to ignore). Like Microsoft, Google hired her to make it look like it, too, is hip to social justice.

We don't know how much Gebru was taking, but I was told by a former Google employee that they were netting $300,000 per year as an ethics researcher. While at Microsoft, Gebru also co-founded the nonprofit, Black in AI, which took money from Big Tech (Google, Microsoft, Facebook, Airbnb) and Big Foundations. Black in AI then helped set up a Google research lab in Accra, Ghana, thereby expanding the colonial frontier into Africa. It's not clear how much (or if) Gebru was also receiving for her work at Black in AI.

Then, in 2020, Gebru co-authored a paper, "The Dangers of Stochastic Parrots," which claimed large language models that companies like Google use pose environmental and social (algorithmic bias) dangers to society. The authors referenced Strubell et al.'s claim that training AI models is carbon-intensive, but as we saw in Chapter 4, the finding was sensational, amounting to less than one millionth of 1% of global emissions for a large model like ChatGPT. Google refused to give the publication a green light (explaining that it doesn't account for energy efficiency gains), and Gebru stated she would leave the company if it wouldn't disclose who objected to the paper. At the end of the month, Google terminated her employment. The American intelligentsia erupted, claiming she was wrongly fired.

Whatever one thinks of Google's behavior is irrelevant. There was no reason to champion a Google "ethics" propagandist. If Gebru had adhered to minimal standards of honesty, she would've never been hired by Microsoft or Google in the first place. She could never say these modern-day East India companies have colonialism hardwired into their DNA, that they're fundamentally exploitative, that they must be abolished, that expanding into the Global South is an act of neocolonial conquest, and so on. Even the environmental section of the "Stochastic Parrots" article was nonsense, because it wasn't contextualized to degrowth, ecologically unequal exchange, and environmental debts. Companies like Google *can't* be green, as they are a leading force of the capitalist suicide machine—the central and indispensable point Gebru erased. The idea that Gebru was "courageous" is absurd—she was selling out social justice for years alongside her elite colleagues in return for a (likely enormous) Big Tech paycheck.

From there, Meredith Whittaker and AI Now stepped in to rebrand themselves by pointing out what leftist critics were saying about *them* publicly: that you can't take money from Big Tech and do honest research. This, too, was pure manipulation, as Whittaker didn't name the people and organizations most responsible in her subsequent statements to the press and publications. This includes her AI Now co-founder Kate Crawford, danah boyd's Data & Society, Helen Nissenbaum's Digital Life Initiative at Cornell Tech, NYU, Ryan Calo and colleagues' Tech Policy Lab at the University of Washington, Big Tech/Foundation-backed Black in AI—the list goes on. If Whittaker truly cared about the impartiality of research, she would've named names and said *all* research on Big Tech's dime, herself included, should be re-examined for bias, and all current researchers taking the money are problematic. As just one example, Whittaker, Crawford, and Sarah Myers West co-authored an article that quoted Melinda Gates on the mistreatment of women in the tech sector, as if Gates champions the well-being of women, rather than mass oppressing them. Skip to the last page, and it says, "Pivotal Ventures, founded by Melinda Gates, provided support for this project."[32]

Around this time, Crawford left AI Now, which pivoted to full Big Foundation funding, as did Gebru, who founded her own NGO, DAIR, with Big Foundation money (Ford, Rockefeller, MacArthur, Open Society, and Kapor). But Big Foundations are pro-capitalist agenda-setters with billion-dollar endowments tied up in Wall Street (and thus American imperialism and class war). There is a long history of dirty deeds from the Big Foundations, and what they bankroll today is just an evolution of their American imperialist class war. They will never fund researchers who strongly oppose the American Empire, class society, and the foundation system. Thus, taking money from Big Foundations is arguably *worse* than corporate money, because the agenda is hidden.

(There is growing left opposition to the Big Foundations and NGOization of movements that sell out anti-capitalist and anti-colonial struggles, but it's still at the margins.)[33]

A few examples are exemplary. We have seen that the Rockefeller and Ford Foundations funded the imperialist Green Revolution. Rockefeller was instrumental in its most recent iteration, AGRA, now opposed by millions of African farmers. Rockefeller president, Rajiv Shah, was a former Director of Agriculture (among other roles) at the Bill & Melinda Gates Foundation and an administrator at the United States Agency of International Development (USAID), an agency that also pushed the Green Revolution and has long been instrumental to US imperialism.[34] While working for USAID, Shah penned an essay, "Embracing Enlightened

Capitalism." "In the late 1980s and early 1990s," Shah remarks, "foreign aid focused on stabilizing economies suffering from debt, most typically through structural adjustment advocated by the West."[35] For students of economic history, those structural adjustment programs wrecked the Global South, forcing them to cut social welfare programs while opening them up to foreign economic penetration—i.e., US imperialism. Today, Shah says, the Global South needs to embrace American corporations such as Walmart, Alcoa, PepsiCo, and Coca-Cola as the leaders of development. For Shah, the South's future is "Profit. Wealth. Development ... the future of our field [of aid for development]." That's Rockefeller.

A former banker, Ford Foundation CEO Darren Walker argues that "there is no better mechanism to organize an economy than capitalism." There are "shortcomings," he admits, but we need "a new form of stakeholder capitalism" inclusive of "employees, the communities, and suppliers." Walker says corporate boardrooms "need to change" to have more diversity, otherwise "you are not likely to see the material, sustainable change at the C-suite and within the company more broadly."[36] And there needs to be more sharing of wealth so that people replicate his life story: moving from the bottom 1% to the top 1%. That's Ford.

Other foundations, such as Open Society, Omidyar Network (including Luminate), MacArthur, Mozilla, as well as Melinda Gates's private investment company, Pivotal Ventures, are pumping money into the tech "left" all over the place. Australia-based Minderoo Foundation is funded by a right-wing mining tyrant Andrew Twiggy Forrest, the country's second richest person, who has been sued by multiple indigenous groups over land disputes. Minderoo funds Safiya Noble and Sarah Robert's Center for Critical Internet Inquiry at UCLA, as well as projects at Cambridge, Oxford, NYU (previously Meredith Whittaker), and others.

The foundations in the tech "left" space have similar ideologies and agendas. As of 2018, the US accounted for $890 billion (almost 60%) of the global $1.5 trillion in foundation assets. (By contrast, China accounted for $14.2 billion, or 1%.) The American foundations push racist-imperialist reforms like antitrust and narrow causes like algorithmic bias. Moreover, CEOs of the Big Foundations like Shah and Walker earn over $1 million in salary, while other high-level staff earn as much as several hundred thousand dollars per year.

241

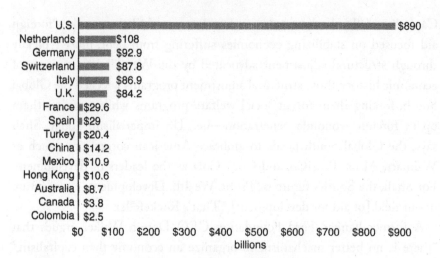

Figure 9.1 Global endowment assets

Source: P&I, 2018.[37]

Foundation grant recipients typically include elite academia, where universities like Yale and Harvard already have endowment funds exceeding $40 billion. As noted, elite professors are making several hundred thousand dollars per year. Claudine Gay, who was unjustly harassed out of her president job at Harvard by supporters of Israeli apartheid, will be returning to Harvard political science with a salary of around $900,000, the press reported in early 2024. The social justice "left" is silent on this.

Almost every influential figure in the tech "left" intellectual class gets money from a rich American institution. A *de facto* vanguard, the "thought leaders" of the tech pseudo-left form a cartel across elite academia, social media, corporate media, and NGOs. Most people have no clue that there's a class system behind the scenes within the intellectual world, with lavish rewards for a tiny minority who "gather riches" as skilled propagandists for the powerful.

PEOPLE'S EDUCATION FOR PEOPLE'S POWER

Speaking of the American academy, Joy James, a prominent black feminist in the US, points out:

Elite academics are *not* a revolutionary cadre; they rarely personally know revolutionaries (unless [former] political prisoners). On-the-ground activists work with considerable risk and no wealth. Elites offer more peer-recognition to progressive (or conservative) associates than to working class militants. The political economy of social justice produces employment, honoraria, royalties, and stellar salaries, generating personal wealth or portfolio management with low risk of surveillance and repression. Progressive academics performed for Obama the labor that [elite media pundit] Van Jones provided to Trump: Airbrush to transform revolutionary demands for power and community-defense into "non-reformist reforms" or "revolutionary reforms" (oxymorons). Before abolitionism, there was revolutionary struggle.[38]

James decries elite black "left" faculty salaries reaching hundreds of thousands of dollars, and states that there needs to be a limit on accumulation. Of course, this applies to *all* identities, as elite white/male/etc. "leftist" faculty also receive grotesque salaries, almost certainly exceeding those of blacks/females/etc. on average. The point is these elite academics are sellouts who now accumulate "hundreds of thousands or millions of dollars" through social movements, and they need to "stand down" in the face of genuine leftist demands for socialism, as James puts it.[39]

Obviously, this won't work as a *voluntary* measure. As a first step, then, the degrowth left can demand that we institutionalize a *fair and sustainable* standard of living for intellectuals based on maximum incomes and wealth, calculated in accordance with social and planetary boundaries,[40] as a means to abolish class within and between knowledge institutions. Student activists have objected to the exorbitant salaries of university presidents (e.g., in the US and South Africa), and this could be extended to other faculty and administration.

Pay based on maximum standards of living would end the perverse incentives to sell out to both wealthy institutions and crowd-sourced funding (e.g., small individual donations). Individual income is already publicly disclosed in some sectors, and this could be extended to household income and assets, making cost-of-living adjustments for location and special considerations (such as odious debt, retirement funds, or dependencies). Loopholes—such as fancy trips and dinners listed as "work expenses"—would need to be identified and closed, but this would be a start. Paid speeches would be canceled or reduced to reasonable compensation at fair hourly rates and made public, perhaps with exceptions for those unable to make ends meet.

To complement these measures and prevent "brain drain" to other organizations, sectors, or locations, we would have to push for the extension of maximum standards of living to the rest of society.

Socializing knowledge institutions is much more than just addressing individual pay inequities, however. Knowledge institutions are unequally resourced both within and between countries. Big corporate news media organizations sit in skyscrapers that look down on the ants they influence, while small media scrounges for crumbs down below. Elite universities hoover up dirty money and grants from American billionaires, while poor academies in the South languish in poverty. This must end as well.

For the lower-hanging fruit in universities, we should immediately end digital metrics, such as bibliometrics (e.g., citation counts), patent counts, and university ranking systems. These "metrics of inequality" systematically favor elite influencers, universities, and countries in the North, who are then able to attract more funding and amplify their voices.[41] Scholars, departments, and universities are quantified and financially rewarded for bibliometrics. This reinforces academic inequality, unleashes a vicious competition among scholars, and creates perverse incentives to chase citations and selfish accolades, degrading the quality of research and "science," all in the name of "merit" and "accountability." Recognizing its unethical and unscientific absurdities, places like Rhodes University in South Africa and Utrecht University in the Netherlands have recently withdrawn from the international ranking system. Others should immediately follow suit and further oppose the quantification of intellectual output.

This is just a start. At a deeper level, we should push hard to end copyright paywalls and democratically fund news media, NGOs, print publishers, and academia. As an immediate alternative, we could make use of "People's Taxation" rebates. A People's Taxes movement would go beyond social welfare measures by appropriating the wealth of the rich for the explicit socialization of *institutions themselves*. Rebates would be used to fund knowledge institutions in ways that give the people the power to decide what gets funded. A portion of funds could be channeled to Global South populations as a form of reparations, who can decide on how that money is used themselves. Multibillion-dollar university endowment fund money would be channeled to local communities, as well as other academic institutions in the North and South. Big Foundation money would be forced to do the same. This would help democratize access to knowledge and the knowledge production process. Before implementation, participants across industries and countries would be consulted and a plan drawn up to ensure small organizations can thrive in a post-paywall era.

The size of organizations would ideally be limited to prevent institutional monocultures from arising. Budgets would account for the type of media: those covering local politics for a printed medium may require less money than those covering international events with video production, while scientific investigations requiring expensive laboratories likely need more funds than literature departments. All knowledge centers would be socialized/de-privatized with no bosses; fair, sustainable, and equitable salaries; horizontal decision-making structures; balanced responsibilities for empowering and menial labor; and institutional autonomy from the state (e.g., the state would be prevented from intervening in cases of legally protected speech). Through these measures, we'd be transitioning toward an ecosocialist world of participatory economics.

Funds could be channeled to the South to help bridge the digital divide and provide it with the means to produce, moderate, and exchange on social networks and other digital products and services. This, of course, only makes sense in direct consultation with affected populations. People in the South, for example, would need to evaluate and exercise autonomy over where that money is spent, with firm accountability measures put in place to prevent local elites from appropriating the funds. Bridging the digital divide would almost certainly be of lower priority than other use cases—people might rather spend money on building homes instead of tech, for instance. But if the other industries (e.g., construction, agriculture, etc.) make complementary efforts, this strategy could be coordinated to cover *all* the essentials of society.

Education and technology would also be democratized. The education sector itself is a critical battleground. As I detailed in my PhD dissertation, *Digital Colonialism: South Africa's Education Transformation in the Shadow of Silicon Valley*, schools are a key site for American tech colonization. Children become tech users at an early age, and the poor in the South often have limited or no access to digital devices and the internet. Schools then become primary sites of digital access and education for low-income youth.

Here, too, there are avenues for opposition to Big Tech. Perhaps the best example of successful resistance to digital colonialism has taken place in Kerala, India, where Free Software has been made mandatory in schools through a project called Kerala Infrastructure and Technology for Education (KITE).[42] Originally named IT@School, the initiative began in the early 2000s when Microsoft was the lead colonizer of the Global South's digital economy. In an effort to fend off Microsoft, a combination of Free Software activists, unions, government officials, and education sector workers successfully pushed the Kerala government to give the boot to Microsoft and switch all their software to FOSS.

The movement succeeded and Free Software has powered public schools for over 20 years in Kerala, the state with India's highest-performing educational outcomes. To this day, all of the operating systems, office software, education software, online services, and school devices are using FOSS. In addition to this, KITE has an impressive array of other projects. It has extended broadband to schools and customized its own version of the GNU/Linux operating system. For its "Little KITEs" program, student experts train mothers and community members to use computers—a project that is being replicated in Finland based on consultation with KITE project leaders.

Unfortunately, intellectuals have almost entirely missed this historical site of resistance, despite it being the longest and most successful defiance of digital colonialism and Big Tech in the internet era.[43] On the world stage, Kerala is quite poor, with a per capita GDP of about $4,400. If Kerala can pull this off, most countries in the world can, too.

In addition to FOSS in schools, we need a new curriculum at all levels of the education system. A colleague of mine, Murray Hunter, wrote a fun book, *Boris the Baby Bot: A Little Book About Big Data*, for young children (and free to download). We should be creating books like these to cover all ages, from early childhood, primary, and secondary schools through adult education centers, community colleges, and universities. Students and educators alike need to keep up with the times and become lifelong learners.

We should also be paying closer attention to radio, mastering video editing, and engaging with adult education. In the Global South, many people still get their news from radio first and don't know how to read well. People of all ages and locations enjoy listening to people speak and watching videos, which are widely accessible.

Last but not least, the workplace is an absolutely critical site of education. A democratic society requires collectively managed education and understanding at all ages, from children to adults. The majority of the world's adults work a job, and it is exhausting to come home, do housework, and then read a book about the miserable state of the world. Workers could be building self-managed unions that demand time for worker self-education and group discussions. Unions have historically been a site of worker education, and workers could get paid to spend time learning and discussing politics at the local, regional, national, and global scale, in addition to formal classes and vocational training at external institutions. Educational activity would be horizontally self-managed within the workplace so that workers control the conversations.

#BIGTECHBDS

In a 2003 speech, Nelson Mandela stated:

> If there is a country that has committed unspeakable atrocities in the world, it is the United States of America. They don't care for human beings.

Speaking during the lead-up to the 2003 US invasion of Iraq, Mandela referenced the long, murderous record of American violence against the world's people. Indeed, for Mandela, Africans, and the people of the world more generally, the Americans have been the leading global force of tyranny and oppression. Overtly and covertly, the US supported South African colonialism and apartheid right up to the end. Washington placed Nelson Mandela and his party, the African National Congress (ANC), on the US "terrorist list" as part of its Cold War interventions to suppress liberation struggles in Southern Africa.

Starting in 1958, South Africans waged a boycott, divestment, and sanctions (BDS) campaign against companies profiting from sales in South Africa in order to strangle the apartheid system. Their campaign, joined by anti-apartheid activists across the world, targeted South African organizations (such as universities, grocery stores, and banks) and foreign companies doing business with the South African government and the private sector. Foreign tech providers were a major target. American "Big Tech" giants of the day were the top suppliers of computer technology to apartheid South Africa, which completely relied on foreign imports for computer technology. Leading US suppliers included corporations like IBM, Apple, HP, and Honeywell. By 1986, US corporations accounted for over half the computer market in South Africa.[44]

Mainframe computers—refrigerator-sized devices used to manage databases of information (similar to the cloud)—were widely used to guide the operations of modern business, government surveillance, and the administration of racial oppression. The apartheid government used these computers "for everything from collecting statistics on racial classification to guiding shells during attacks in Angola," anti-apartheid activist Richard Knight wrote.[45] One major recipient, the Council of Scientific and Industrial Research (CSIR), which developed the Cmore surveillance PSIM detailed in Chapter 7, was developing technologies of violence like armored vehicles for the apartheid military and police forces to patrol black people living in the townships.

BDS sanctions targeted both South African apartheid and its military aggression in nearby Southern African countries. The tactics produced a tangible cost to the apartheid system. First and foremost, BDS helped raise awareness about apartheid and brand South Africa as a pariah in the eyes of the international community. It also created a modest degree of economic costs for the South African ruling class. That said, it was ultimately the popular resistance movement inside the country that threw off the yoke of (formal, white-ruled) apartheid.

Not surprisingly, US corporations attempted to weasel their way out of withdrawing business from South Africa. As the anti-apartheid movement heated up, Reverend Leon Sullivan, a black minister on the Board of General Motors, introduced the infamous Sullivan Principles (based on previous experiments at Polaroid). These were a set of corporate social responsibility (CSR) principles that asked US corporations operating in South Africa to administer racial equality measures like equal pay for equal work, non-discrimination in hiring, and workplace desegregation. The proposals were widely rejected by anti-apartheid activists as corporate PR for apartheid profiteers.

Today, Big Tech workers have pushed their companies to stop funding certain projects like Google's Project Maven and Google and Amazon's Project Nimbus in Israel. While these initiatives may be well-intentioned, they are more or less New Sullivan Principles. Big Tech corporations are the apartheid equivalents of the global community. They cannot be made ethical, and even if we try to stop their worst excesses, they are predicated on colonialism and ecocide. The average workers are also heavily overpaid. Like elite tech "left" intellectuals, they are a "labor aristocracy" enjoying the spoils of empire and have no material self-interest in taking an ethical stand.

It should also be added that the anti-apartheid movement failed in many critical respects that we should draw lessons from. Today, South Africa is a neo-apartheid state. Inequality was slightly reduced *between* races, but it *increased* in general. Now there is a small middle class and "black faces in high places," but residential segregation is deeply entrenched alongside mass poverty and inequality. Apartheid didn't end, it evolved.

Genuine leftists support Palestinian liberation, and most support BDS against Israel. This should be reconfigured. The United States is the apex predator sitting atop an apartheid-like world system. That the US provides the support enabling the oppression of Palestinians is just one awful thing among many it does across the world, from smashing the Middle East and supporting dictatorships to exploiting global supply chains and over-eating the planet's finite wealth. The US is the Godfather, and it's time to target the Godfather himself.

To this effect, the internationalist left should launch a BDS campaign targeting the United States. BDS against Israel could be rolled into this campaign, as Israeli supremacy is tethered to the US.

The left should launch a #BigTechBDS campaign that learns from South African and Palestinian experiences.[46] To start, we could follow in the footsteps of Kerala and make Free Software mandatory in schools and the public sector, alongside boycotts of leading Big Tech giants wherever possible.

The initiative would adopt an anti-colonial, degrowth-based ecosocialist agenda. Environmentalists would link up with digital justice advocates. I believe this makes sense given that the environmental movement has a sizable, genuinely left-wing faction.

An intellectual boycott could target American knowledge institutions—especially top-ranked universities, corporate media, think tanks, and NGOs—demanding that intellectuals provide transparency about their finances, stop taking exorbitant salaries, and pressure their universities to institute the recommendations of the previous section—including bans on Big Tech and Big Foundation funding. A cultural boycott could target American entertainers, many of whom are amassing obscene amounts of wealth. Activists and workers could push for divestment from the worst corporations—especially in tech—and demand the socialization of knowledge institutions. Sanctions would be difficult to start, as solidarity movements would have to pressure multiple countries to unite against the American Empire—no easy task.

Whether using BDS or not, activists might decide to target companies from other countries, such as China's Huawei for supplying surveillance technology to the Global South, or Estonia's Bolt (alongside Uber) for colonizing transportation in countries like South Africa. A #BigTechBDS campaign would demand a positive vision of full equality, based on things like People's Tech and a DTD, to secure a new society that is fully egalitarian.

CLASS WAR AND REVOLUTION

Finally, we need to think deeply about what kind of society can foster degrowth and how to transition to that society. Some work on transitions is in progress, but much more work needs to be done.[47] This book has offered some suggestions on the digital component, and how it can dovetail with society-wide projects like ParEcon.

Degrowth scholars typically speak of a world where people "flourish" in harmony with each other and nature, but people have never been able to create economic equality through persuasion and without conflict. Attempts to abolish class in countries like Russia, China, and Cuba have been ugly affairs that were captured by elites. The state seized the means of production and ran the societies with an iron fist. Economic inequality decreased but was not eradicated, and the "red bureaucracy" became the new bosses of the workers, much like capitalist societies.

Anarchists, by contrast, tried to create societies based on full political, economic, and social equality, without resorting to authoritarian politics.

They argued that the means shape the ends, so only through democratic means where people work together as equals could society build a truly egalitarian future.

Every major organization—from universities to retail chains—has a top brass in charge that appropriates worker labor and consumes more than their fair share. They need to be challenged everywhere. The International Workers of the World (IWW) subscribed to this philosophy. Formed in 1905, they included all workers irrespective of their skill level, race, and gender, with an aim to abolish capitalism and class while also replacing the state (government by a minority) through bottom-up reconstructions of governance, all in solidarity with workers across the world. We need these kinds of radical, internationalist, egalitarian unions seeking to take over the workplace and abolish class—rather than the *business unionism* of the tech "left" that focus on better pay and workplace conditions, even if they selectively support individual causes like Palestinian liberation.

As the IWW grew by the thousands, the US government, corporations, and armed vigilantes crushed them with force. "Criminal syndicalism" laws were passed targeting the IWW and radical unions. IWW members were murdered, lynched, tortured, prosecuted, imprisoned, harassed, surveiled, censored, deported, and fired from their jobs.[48] There are other examples like this throughout history.

Needless to say, those with the wealth and power will not give it up without a fight. There are no examples of movements trying to abolish class without violent resistance from authorities. Why would it be any different this time? Because it's rational, and science is on our side? Those who want degrowth will have to force the issue through unprecedented levels of strikes, direct action, and civil disobedience. There will almost certainly be many bloodbaths. Degrowth scholars sweep this issue aside, but we need to tell the truth. Degrowth will not become a reality without a serious fight.

In addition to this, major issues need better explanations, such as coordinating international trade, how to democratically enforce resource caps, and what to do about our legal systems. Degrowth scholars often endorse bottom-up democracy and criticize *capitalism*, but there's little engagement with the minority rule of the *state*. Constitutions are built around the sanctity of private property, and there is a deeply entrenched set of legal arrangements that have to be transformed. Do we need new constitutions?

251

If so, how do we draft them? Do some people still get to live in luxury houses? We still have "socialists" committed to liberation parties and leaders who believe in vanguard parties that should take command of the state, the economy, and exercise power over the people. Is it really enough to simply challenge capitalism? On the flip side, bottom-up collective resistance takes time for education and organization. It took anarchists decades before they launched a revolution in 1930s Spain. But we don't have generations to fundamentally transform society. While it's beyond the scope of this book, these are important questions that need better answers.

At this moment, we badly need more education and exposure to the basic issues. A minority cannot liberate society. At the same time, the majority of people have to strongly desire equality and degrowth if it's going to become a reality. We need a mass awakening of the people. Reformers believe that these kinds of changes are utopian and unrealistic, but it's these "pragmatists" who are unrealistic. Business as usual cannot hold.

No matter what we do, our way of life is going to radically change in the not-too-distant future. This generation will either change the world for the better—which will require sacrifice through resistance—or the elites will change it for the worse by triggering irreversible disasters. We need to force the conversation into public consciousness.

Today, we have no choice but to create a fundamentally egalitarian society based on harmony with each other and nature. We have to shift our mindsets and recognize that the time is now to be courageous, rock boats, get a little uncomfortable, reach out to each other, talk, form groups, join groups, and find things we can do—on the internet, at our workplaces, and in our communities. The American Empire must be dismantled along with the class system in every country. We're in a total crisis that few have been truly exposed to, but word can travel fast. Survival is our strongest instinct. We need to rebel, before it's too late. Let's get this going.

Notes

INTRODUCTION

1. Guillermo A. Lemarchand, Ernst Mayr, and Carl Sagan. "Ernst Mayr and Carl Sagan Debate about the Probability of Intelligent Life In The Universe." *arXiv preprint arXiv*:1012.2591 (2010).
2. Noam Chomsky, "Human Intelligence and the Environment." *Chomsky.info*, September 30, 2010, https://chomsky.info/20100930.
3. Lewis C. King, Ivan Savin, and Stefan Drews. "Shades of Green Growth Scepticism Among Climate Policy Researchers." *Nature Sustainability* 6(11), 1316–1320 (2023).
4. Ernst Mayr, *This is Biology: The Science of the Living World* (Universities Press, 1997), x.

1. DIGITAL COLONIALISM

1. Responsibility for this issue is a bit complex, as media relies upon advertising and should instead be socialized. See Chapter 8.
2. Liesbeek Action Campaign, "Amazon: Same Colonists, Different Ships." *Observatory Civic Association*, November 24, 2021, https://obs.org.za/cms/wp-content/uploads/2021/11/Press-Release-%E2%80%93-Amazon-Protest-%E2%80%93-Same-colonists-different-ships.pdf.
3. For what follows in this section, including references, see Michael Kwet, "Digital Colonialism: US Empire and the New Imperialism in the Global South." *Race & Class* 60(4), 3–26 (2019); Michael Kwet, "Digital Colonialism: The Evolution of US Empire." *Transnational Institute*, March 4, 2021, https://longreads.tni.org/digital-colonialism-the-evolution-of-us-empire.
4. Some intellectuals insist that today's world is not "colonial," as formal control over sovereign territories and people are mostly in the past. Others insist that colonialism has evolved and the term should still be used to emphasize the fact that colonialism isn't dead. This book uses the term "digital colonialism" in agreement with that second camp.
5. *International Monetary Fund*, "World Economic Outlook Database: October 2023."
6. Luis R. Martínez, "How Much Should We Trust the Dictator's GDP Growth Estimates?" *Journal of Political Economy* 130(10), 2731–2769 (2022); *Money & Macro*, "The Chinese Economy is Sixty Percent Smaller Than We Thought," October 27, 2022, www.moneymacro.rocks/2022-10-27-china-smaller; Clay Chandler, "Chinese corporations Now Dominate the Fortune Global 500 List

of Biggest Companies by Revenue—but they Are Far Less Profitable Than Their U.S. Rivals." *Forbes*, August 18, 2022, https://fortune.com/2022/08/18/fortune-global-500-china-companies-profitable-profitability-us-rivals.

7. Starrs has been working on this thesis for over a decade, with supervision by leading political economists, including the late Leo Panitch, Sam Gindin, and Noam Chomsky.

8. Sean Starrs, "American Economic Power Hasn't Declined—It Globalized! Summoning the Data and Taking Globalization Seriously." *International Studies Quarterly*, 57(4), 817–830 (2013). See also, Stephen G. Brooks and William C. Wohlforth, "The Myth of Multipolarity: American Power's Staying Power." *Foreign Affairs*, April 18, 2023, www.foreignaffairs.com/united-states/china-multipolarity-myth.

9. Daniel Foelber, "20 'Tech' Stocks Make Up Over 35% of the S&P 500. Here's What That Means for Your Portfolio." *The Motley Fool*, January 28, 2024, www.fool.com/investing/2024/01/28/20-tech-stocks-sp-500-buy-2024-invest.

10. Dorothy Neufeld and Bhabna Benerjee, "Ranked: The 100 Biggest Public Companies in the World." *Visual Capitalist*, December 26, 2022, www.visual-capitalist.com/biggest-public-companies-in-the-world-2022.

11. Omri Wallach, "The World's Tech Giants, Compared to the Size of Economies." *Visual Capitalist*, July 7, 2021, www.visualcapitalist.com/the-tech-giants-worth-compared-economies-countries.

12. *Companiesmarketcap.com*, "Top Tech Companies. November 9, 2023."

13. Of note, some companies aren't "publicly listed" in Table 1.2, meaning their stocks aren't traded on the public market. This includes, most notably, China's Bytedance (owner of TikTok) and Huawei as well as the US's Stripe, Databricks, and X (formerly called Twitter). This doesn't change the overall picture of American dominance, as unlisted Chinese and American tech giants have comparable market value and revenue. Also note that there's a blurry line between a "tech" company and a non-tech company, and databases also vary which companies they include under tech. No matter where you draw the line or what database you use, adding a company to the list here and subtracting one there doesn't move the needle with respect to which country is dominant in any substantive way.

14. Sean Starrs, Personal email, October 18, 2020.

15. Numbers compiled from Federica Laricchia, "Revenue of Apple by Geographical Region from the First Quarter of 2012 to 1st Quarter 2024." *Statista*, February 2, 2024, www.statista.com/statistics/382175/quarterly-revenue-of-apple-by-geograhical-region.

16. Numbers compiled from *Dazeinfo*, "Microsoft Annual Revenue by Geography: Fiscal 2002–2021," August 20, 2021, https://dazeinfo.com/2019/11/11/microsoft-revenue-by-geography-by-year-graphfarm.

17. Numbers compiled from Tiago Bianchi, "Annual revenue of Alphabet from 2011 to 2023." *Statista*, January 31, 2024, www.statista.com/statistics/507742/alphabet-annual-global-revenue; Tiago Bianchi, "Revenue Distribution of

Alphabet from 2015 to 2023, by Region." *Statista*, January 31, 2024, www.statista.com/statistics/266250/regional-distribution-of-googles-revenue.

18. In this case I use the lump sums from Amazon's "2022 Annual Report" and designate 53.3% of AWS sales to North America (which includes Canada), subtract out an estimated 18.4% for Canada (the percentage of its value added [$8.5 billion] vis-a-vis the United States [$37.69 billion]), and subtract out Amazon Canada's $11.568 billion e-commerce sales in 2022. International revenue includes Canada's estimated share. See *Amazon*, "2022 Annual Report," 66; HG Insights, "The AWS Ecosystem in 2024," 2024, https://hginsights.com/blog/aws-market-report-buyer-landscape, 7; *PublicFirst*, "The Impact of AWS in Canada," https://awscanada.publicfirst.co; *Amazon*, "AWS Economic Impact Study," 2023, https://assets.aboutamazon.com/58/65/29ea168a483997 9aa779700ba42c/aws-us-eis-2023.pdf, 4; *ECDB*, "amazon.ca," https://ecommercedb.com/store/amazon.ca.

19. Numbers compiled from Thomas Alsop, "Nvidia Revenue Worldwide from 2017 to 2023, by Region." S*tatista*, March 1, 2023, www.statista.com/statistics/988037/nvidia-revenue-by-country-region.

20. Numbers compiled from *GlobalData*, "Meta's Annual Revenue (2010–2021, $ Billion)," www.globaldata.com/data-insights/internet-services-social-media-technology-media-and-telecom/metas-annual-revenue.

21. Numbers compiled from Mathilde Carlier, "Tesla's Revenue in the United States, China, and Other Markets from FY 2018 to FY 2022." *Statista*, March 17, 2023, www.statista.com/statistics/314759/revenue-of-tesla-by-region.

22. Numbers compiled from Thomas Alsop, "Broadcom's Revenue by Country Worldwide from 2016 to 2023." *Statista*, January 4, 2024, www.statista.com/statistics/977873/broadcom-revenue-by-country.

23. Numbers compiled from Lionel Vailshery, "Oracle's Revenue from FY2015 to FY2023, by Region." *Statista*, February 9, 2024.

24. Numbers compiled from Lionel Vailshery, "Annual Revenue of Adobe Inc. from Fiscal Year 2018 to 2023, by Region," *Statista*, February 12, 2024, www.statista.com/statistics/1223429/adobe-revenue-region.

25. Numbers compiled from Salvador Rodriguez and Georgia Wells, "TikTok Parent ByteDance Turns Operating Profit, Sees Revenue Slow," *Wall Street Journal*, October 2, 2023, https://archive.is/IJf7N; Mansoor Iqbal, "TikTok Revenue and Usage Statistics (2024)." *Business of Apps*, January 8, 2024, www.businessofapps.com/data/tik-tok-statistics.

26. Numbers compiled from Matthew Johnston, "How Alibaba Makes Money." *Investopedia*, January 31, 2023, www.investopedia.com/articles/investing/121714/how-does-alibaba-make-money-simple-guide.asp; as well as MarketScreener. These numbers designate 20% of Alibaba's cloud revenue to foreign sales (which is likely an overestimate); international commerce retail and wholesale categories are also designated to foreign revenue.

27. Numbers compiled from Daniel Slotta, "Huawei's Revenue from 2012 to 2022, by Geographical Region." *Statista*, September 29, 2023, www.statista.com/statistics/368509/revenue-of-huawei-by-region.

28. This is an estimate based on assigning the $6 billion in overseas revenues expected to be generated in 2023 by its e-commerce platform, Temu, to foreign revenue, compared to its trailing 12-month revenue of $23.44 billion. See Andrew Buck, "Temu Revenue, Growth, Usage and Downloads Statistics for 2024." *MobiLoud*, www.mobiloud.com/blog/temu-statistics; Companiesmarketcap.com, "Revenue for Pinduoduo (PDD)." November 14, 2023, https://web.archive.org/web/20231114234131/https://companiesmarketcap.com/pinduoduo/revenue.

29. These numbers do not reflect Meituan's recent expansion into Hong Kong; nevertheless, the company has been reluctant to venture beyond mainland China.

30. This data is compiled from a combination of the gaming segment, which comprised 85.2% of the company's total revenue (74.57 billion yuan of a total 87.5 billion yuan), and the reported total that the overseas market accounted for about 10% of its revenues in 2022. See Lai Lin Thomala, "Revenue of NetEase Inc. from 2017 to 2022, by Segment." *Statista*, May 10, 2023, www.statista.com/statistics/1118186/netease-revenue-by-segment; Ann Cao, "NetEase Says it Does Not Expect to Launch Any New Video Games with Overseas Studios Until At Least 2025 After Blizzard Break-Up." *South China Morning Post*, February 24, 2023, https://archive.is/JzFLd.

31. Anton Harber, "How Google and Facebook are the Biggest Threat to South African News Media." *Financial Mail*, November 15, 2017, www.businesslive.co.za/fm/features/cover-story/2017-11-16-how-google-and-facebook-are-the-biggest-threat-to-south-african-news-media.

32. See Kwet, "Digital Colonialism: US Empire"; Kwet, "Digital Colonialism: The Evolution of US Empire."

33. *Startup Genome*, "The Global Startup Ecosystem Report 2023 [version 5]." August 18, 2023.

34. Sean Starrs, "American Economic Power Hasn't Declined—It Globalized! Summoning the Data and Taking Globalization Seriously." *International Studies Quarterly*, 57(4), 818 (2013).

35. Numbers compiled from Alexandra Borgeaud, "Information Technology (IT) Investments Worldwide in 2021, by Country." *Statista*, March 31, 2023, www.statista.com/statistics/1331124/global-it-investments-by-country.

36. Jessica Rawnsley, "Where's Europe's Foreign Direct Investment Coming from Right Now?" *Sifted*, November 25, 2022, https://sifted.eu/articles/foreign-direct-investment-europe-brnd. For Asia in Europe, data on foreign investment in tech sector for the region as a whole seems hard to come by, but with just 18% of FDI within Europe, it cannot be very high.

37. *The African Private Capital Association*, "Venture Capital in Africa Report: April 2023." 2023, www.avca.africa/media/m3db4yto/02175-avca-vc-report-2023_4-final-1.pdf.

38. *Briter Bridges*, "Africa's Investment Report 2021." 2021, https://briterbridges.com/africainvestmentreport2021.

39. Joanna Glasner, "Here's What's Driving Latin America's Rank as the World's Fastest-Growing Region for Venture Funding." *Crunchbase*, January 21, 2022, https://news.crunchbase.com/startups/latin-america-venture-growth-start-ups-2021-monthly-recap; Cara Lyttle and Deepti Aggarwal, "FDI in Latin America in 2021: The State of Play." *Investment Monitor*, August 29, 2022, www.investmentmonitor.ai/insights/fdi-in-latin-america-in-2021-the-state-of-play.

40. Numbers compiled from Joanna Glasner, "These Were Latin America's Most Active Investors in A Record Year." *Crunchbase News*, January 24, 2022, https://news.crunchbase.com/startups/latin-america-most-active-investors-startups-vc.

41. Adam Hayes, "Venture Capital: What Is VC and How Does It Work?" *Investopedia*, January 27, 2024, www.investopedia.com/terms/v/venturecapital.asp.

42. Douglas Rushkoff, *Throwing Rocks at the Google Bus: How Growth Became the Enemy of Prosperity* (Portfolio, 2016).

43. N. Grassano et al., *The 2022 EU Industrial R&D Investment Scoreboard* (Publications Office of the European Union, 2022).

44. Ibid.

45. *Trademarks* are a recognizable sign, design, or expression (such as a logo or the name of a company) that distinguish a product or service from others of its kind. *Trade secrets* are confidential information that can be withheld or sold under a license. With a patent, you have to disclose your technology in return for monopoly ownership. But sometimes companies just keep it confidential if they think others can't replicate it. Google, for example, keeps the algorithm of its search engine secret, much like Coca-Cola keeps the formula for its soft drink recipe under wraps. Companies must identify information, e.g., manufacturing processes and formulas, in order to ensure they are protected by trade secret law. Data on trade secrets is scarce by comparison to patents and copyright.

46. Alex He, "What Do China's High Patent Numbers Really Mean?" *Centre for International Governance Innovation*, April 20, 2021, www.cigionline.org/articles/what-do-chinas-high-patent-numbers-really-mean; *Centre for Strategic & International Studies*, "Are Patents Indicative of Chinese Innovation?" https://chinapower.csis.org/patents.

47. *OECD*, "Triadic Patent Families (indicator)." www.oecd-ilibrary.org/industry-and-services/triadic-patent-families/indicator/english_6a8d1of4-en; Arnold et al., "Can Europe's economy ever hope to rival the US again?," *Financial Times*, May 13, 2024, https://www.ft.com/content/93f88255-787b-4c06-849c-f7722c83e8b6

48. Holly Fechner and Matthew S. Shapanka, "Closing Diversity Gaps in Innovation: Gender, Race, and Income Disparities in Patenting and Commercialization of Inventions." *Technology and Innovation* 19 (2018), 727–734.

49. *World Intellectual Property Organization*, "The Global Publishing Industry in 2021" (Geneva, 2023).

50. *Statista*, "Forecast of Digital Media revenue by segment in the World from 2019 to 2027." February 9, 2024, www.statista.com/forecasts/456462/digital-media-revenue-in-the-world-forecast; J. Clement, "Estimated Annual

Gaming Revenue of Leading Gaming Companies Worldwide in 1st Quarter 2023." *Statista*, September 4, 2023, www.statista.com/statistics/421848/ game-revenues-global-companies; *Statista*, "Filmed Entertainment Revenue in Selected Countries Worldwide in 2021." January 19, 2024, www.statista. com/statistics/296431/filmed-entertainment-revenue-worldwide-by-country; *IFPI*, "Global Music Report 2023." 2023, www.ifpi.org/wp-content/ uploads/2020/03/Global_Music_Report_2023_State_of_the_Industry.pdf; *Statista*, "Global Comparison." 2024, www.statista.com/outlook/dmo/digital-media/digital-music/music-streaming/worldwide#global-comparison; Joshua P. Friedlander, "Year-End 2022 RIAA Revenue Statistics." *RIAA*, www. riaa.com/wp-content/uploads/2023/03/2022-Year-End-Music-Industry-Revenue-Report.pdf; Steven Bertoni, "Inside Davido's Global Music Empire." *Forbes*, April 22, 2023, www.forbes.com/sites/stevenbertoni/2023/04/22/ inside-davidos-global-musical-empire.

51. Nathan Reiff, "10 Biggest Software Companies." *Investopedia*, October 31, 2023, www.investopedia.com/articles/personal-finance/121714/worlds-top-10-software-companies.asp.

52. See Noam Chomsky, *Power and Prospects: Reflections on Nature and the Social Order* (South End Press, 1996); Yarden Katz, "Noam Chomsky on Where Artificial Intelligence Went Wrong." *The Atlantic*, November 1, 2012.

53. Gary Marcus, *Rebooting AI: Building Artificial Intelligence We Can Trust* (Pantheon, 2019).

54. David Reinsel, "The China Datasphere: Primed to Be the Largest Datasphere by 2025." *IDC*, January 2019, www.seagate.com/files/www-content/our-story/ trends/files/data-age-china-idc.pdf.

55. Bhaskar Chakravorti et al., "Which Countries Are Leading the Data Economy?" *Harvard Business Review*, January 24, 2019, https://archive.is/7kN8K.

56. Christopher Tozzi, *For Fun and Profit: A History of the Free and Open Source Software Revolution* (MIT Press, 2017); James Wallace and Jim Erickson, *Hard Drive: Bill Gates and the Making of the Microsoft Empire* (Wiley, 1992).

57. Nick Srnicek, *Platform Capitalism* (Polity, 2016).

58. Michael Kwet, "Fixing Social Media: Toward a Democratic Digital Commons." *Markets, Globalization & Development Review* 5(1) (2020), https:// digitalcommons.uri.edu/mgdr/vol5/iss1/4.

59. For a comprehensive overview of acquisitions by Google (Alphabet), Apple, Facebook (Meta), Amazon, and Microsoft, see Benedetti et al., "The GAFAM Empire." www.theglassroom.org.

60. Herbert Horan, "Uber's Path of Destruction." *American Affairs Journal* 3(2), 2019.

61. See, for example, Eben Moglen, "Eben Moglen Plone Speech, Annotated." 2006, http://www.geof.net/research/2006/moglen-notes.

62. Paul N. Edwards, *The Closed World: Computers and the Politics of Discourse in Cold War America* (MIT Press, 1997); Janet Abbate, *Inventing the Internet* (MIT Press, 1999); Yasha Levine, *Surveillance Valley: The Secret Military History of the Internet* (PublicAffairs, 2018); Meghan Gross, "Laying the Foun-

dation for a commercialized Internet: International Internet Governance in the 1990s," *Digital Technology, Culture and Society* 4(3), www.tandfonline.com/doi/abs/10.1080/24701475.2020.1769890.

63. Bill Clinton, "President and First Lady." *The White House*, https://clinton-whitehouse4.archives.gov/WH/EOP/html/principals.html.

64. Joe Biden, "Remarks by President Biden in Press Conference." *The White House*, March 25, 2021, www.whitehouse.gov/briefing-room/speeches-remarks/2021/03/25/remarks-by-president-biden-in-press-conference.

65. Jason Douglas and Tom Fairless, "It's U.S. vs. China in an Increasingly Divided World Economy." *Wall Street Journal*, November 2, 2023, https://archive.is/OGG8P.

66. Noam Chomsky and Vijay Prashad, *The Withdrawal: Iraq, Libya, Afghanistan, and the Fragility of U.S. Power* (The New Press, 2022).

67. Leo Panitch and Sam Gindin, *The Making of Global Capitalism: The Political Economy of American Empire* (Verso, 2012).

68. Adam Thierer, "15 Years On, President Clinton's 5 Principles for Internet Policy Remain the Perfect Paradigm." *Forbes*, February 12, 2012, www.forbes.com/sites/adamthierer/2012/02/12/15-years-on-president-clintons-5-principles-for-internet-policy-remain-the-perfect-paradigm.

69. Kai-Fu Lee, *AI Superpowers: China, Silicon Valley, and the New World Order* (Harper Business, 2018).

70. John Pilger, "John Pilger Q&A: 'US Missiles are Pointed at China.'" *Al Jazeera*, December 6, 2017, www.aljazeera.com/features/2017/12/6/john-pilger-qa-us-missiles-are-pointed-at-china.

71. China's only foreign military base is located in the small African country of Djibouti, though it may be planning to build a few additional bases in Asia and Africa.

72. James Peck, *Washington's China: The National Security World, the Cold War, and the Origins of Globalism* (University of Massachusetts Press, 2006).

73. The restrictions were imposed despite NSA spying on Huawei. See Malarie Gokey, "Obama Defends NSA Spying on Huawei—Furious China Demands Explanation." *Tech Times*, March 24, 2014, www.techtimes.com/articles/4753/20140324/obama-defends-nsa-spying-on-huawei-furious-china-demands-explanation.htm.

74. Michael Kan, "U.S. Stops Intel from Selling Xeon Chips to Chinese Supercomputer Projects." *Computerworld*, April 9, 2015, www.computerworld.com/article/2908371/us-stops-intel-from-selling-xeon-chips-to-chinese-supercomputer-projects.html.

75. Jeremy Ney, "United States Entity List: Limits on American Exports." *Belfer Center*, February 2021, www.belfercenter.org/publication/united-states-entity-list-limits-american-exports.

76. Recent trade restrictions seem to be having an impact. See Qianer Liu, Eleanor Olcott, and Ryan McMorrow, "Tightened US Rules Throttle Alibaba and Baidu's AI Chip Development." *Financial Times*, October 20, 2023, www.ft.com/content/ef157204-a204-4512-8c50-fe60e166b41e; Roula Khalaf,

"Costs of US Chip Curbs Force China's YMTC Into Major Fundraising Round." *Financial Times*, November 2, 2023, www.ft.com/content/4dcaaf91-d77f-4c70-97bf-69ba6a4e94f9; Farhad Majoo, "Biden Just Clobbered China's Chip Industry." *New York Times*, October 20, 2022, www.nytimes.com/2022/10/20/opinion/biden-china-semiconductor-chip.html.

77. *Semiconductor Industry Association (SIA)*, "2023 Factbook." 2023, 3.

78. This includes restrictions on the export of chipmaking metals (gallium and germanium, and rare earths), banning the purchase of US-based Micron's memory chips by "critical national infrastructure operators," restrictions on the export of drones, and banning the use of iPhones by government officials for work. The latter will likely cost Apple $2 billion revenue during Q2 2023. See Richard Waters, "Apple Fails to Dispel Worries Over Hardware Outlook and China Sales." *Financial Times*, November 3, 2023, www.ft.com/content/6d19ef61-8d1d-4afc-832a-b2d3524d665c. Of note, China's attempt to influence policy or impose costs against countries offending its interests have been largely ineffective. See Lingling Wei, "Chinese Pressure Tactics Against Other Countries Largely Ineffective, Study Finds." *Wall Street Journal*, March 21, 2023, www.wsj.com/amp/articles/chinese-pressure-tactics-against-other-countries-largely-ineffective-study-finds-3f49561f.

79. Katherine Tangalakis-Lippert, "RESTRICT Act Explained: Proposed TikTok Ban is 'a PATRIOT Act for the Digital Age,' Some Lawmakers Say." *Business Insider*, April 23, 2023, www.businessinsider.com/what-is-restrict-act-explained-tiktok-ban-summary-2023-4. See also, Lorraine Mallinder, "What's Really at Stake in the US Moves to Target TikTok?" *Al Jazeera*, January 2, 2024, www.aljazeera.com/features/2024/1/2/whats-really-at-stake-in-the-us-moves-to-ban-tiktok; Yuka Hayashi and John D. McKinnon, "U.S. Looks to Restrict China's Access to Cloud Computing to Protect Advanced Technology." *Wall Street Journal*, July 4, 2023, https://archive.fo/FBdXo.

80. *McKinsey & Company*, "The CHIPS and Science Act: Here's What's In It." October 4, 2022, www.mckinsey.com/industries/public-sector/our-insights/the-chips-and-science-act-heres-whats-in-it.

81. Yuka Hayashi, "Why the White House Went to Wall Street to Revive the U.S. Chips Industry." *Wall Street Journal*, August 15, 2023, www.wsj.com/amp/articles/why-the-white-house-went-to-wall-street-to-revive-the-u-s-chips-industry-feoaoaac.

82. Amanda Chu, Oliver Roeder, and Alex Irwin-Hunt, "Inside the $220bn American Cleantech Project Boom." *Financial Times*, August 16, 2023, www.ft.com/content/3b19c51d-462b-43fa-9e0e-3445640aabb5.

83. Guy Chazan, Sam Fleming, and Kana Inagaki, "A Global Subsidy War? Keeping Up with the Americans." *Financial Times*, July 13, 2023, www.ft.com/content/4bc03d4b-6984-4b24-935d-6181253ee1e0.

84. Mathieu Pollet and John Hendel, "The West is on a World Tour Against Huawei." *Politico*, November 28, 2023, www.politico.eu/article/west-world-tour-huawei-china-telecom; Michael Peel and Simeon Kerr, "UAE's Top AI Group Vows to

Phase Out Chinese Hardware to Appease US." *Financial Times*, December 7, 2023, www.ft.com/content/6710c259-0746-4e09-804f-8a48ecf50ba3.

85. Burcu Kilic and Renata Avila, "Opening Spaces for Digital Rights Activism: Multilateral Trade Negotiations." *Internet Policy Observatory*, May 31, 2018, www.citizen.org/article/51451-2; Vahini Naidu, "Knowledge Production in International Trade Negotiations is a High Stakes Game." *London School of Economics*, June 14, 2019, https://blogs.lse.ac.uk/africaatlse/2019/06/14/knowledge-production-international-trade-digital; Deborah James, "Big Tech Seeks to Cement Digital Colonialism Through the WTO." *Latin America in Movement*, April 7, 2019, www.alainet.org/en/articulo/200804.

2. WHAT IS DEGROWTH?

1. When people like Bill Gates, Steven Pinker, and Hannah Ritchie celebrate capitalism, they point to the fact that the extreme form of global poverty—those living under $1.90 per day—has been drastically reduced over the past several decades. Critics respond that those gains are not only minimal, they are unethically low given the enormous productivity gains that have occurred during those few decades. This argument should extend to China sympathizers on the "left" as well. Despite poverty alleviation in China, hundreds of millions still languish in poverty, while the 1% of Chinese elites have accumulated almost all the productivity gains. See Javier C. Hernández and Quoctrung Bui, "The American Dream Is Alive. In China." *New York Times*, November 18, 2018; Dylan Sullivan, Michail Moatsos, and Jason Hickel, "Capitalist Reforms and Extreme Poverty in China: Unprecedented Progress or Income Deflation?" *New Political Economy* 29(1), 2023.

2. John Bellamy Foster, *Capitalism in the Anthropocene: Ecological Ruin or Ecological Revolution* (Monthly Review Press, 2023); Kohei Saito, *Slow Down: The Degrowth Manifesto* (Astra House, 2024); Donella H. Meadows et al., *The Limits to Growth* (Potomac Associates, 1972).

3. Kai Heron and Lauren Eastwood, "Introduction – Degrowth: Swimming Against the Ideological Tide." In Lauren Eastwood and Kai Heron (eds.), *De Gruyter Handbook of Degrowth* (De Gruyter, 2024), 7–18.

4. In the last two decades, several studies have affirmed that the Club of Rome's 1972 projections were generally accurate. See Meadows et al., *Limits to Growth: The 30-Year Update* (Chelsea Green, 2004); Ugo Bardi, *The Limits to Growth Revisited* (Springer, 2011); Graham Turner, "Is Global Collapse Imminent? An Updated Comparison of *The Limits to Growth* with Historical Data." *Melbourne Sustainable Society Institute, The University of Melbourne*, 2014; Gaya Herrington, "Update to Limits to Growth: Comparing the World3 Model with Empirical Data." *Journal of Industrial Ecology* 25(3) (2021); Nebel et al., "Recalibration of Limits to Growth: An Update of the World3 Model." *Journal of Industrial Ecology* 28(1) (2024).

5. Georgos Kallis, "Why Malthus's Gospel of Growth Was, and Still Is, Wrong." April 14, 2021, www.cato-unbound.org/2021/04/14/giorgos-kallis/why-malthuss-gospel-growth-was-still-wrong.

6. *Food and Agriculture Organization of the United Nations*, "COP26: Agricultural Expansion Drives Almost 90 Percent of Global Deforestation." June 11, 2021, www.fao.org/newsroom/detail/cop26-agricultural-expansion-drives-almost-90-percent-of-global-deforestation/en; Joël Foramitti et al., "Why Degrowth is the Only Responsible Way Forward." *Resilience*, September 23, 2019, www.resilience.org/stories/2019-09-23/why-degrowth-is-the-only-responsible-way-forward; Xiao-Peng Song et al., "Global Land Change from 1982 to 2016." *Nature* 560 (2018); John Alroy, "Effects of Habitat Disturbance on Tropical Forest Biodiversity." *PNAS* 114(23) (2017).

7. Jason Hickel and Stéphane Hallegatte, "Can We Live Within Environmental Limits and Still Reduce Poverty? Degrowth or Decoupling?" *Development Policy Review* 40(1) (2022).

8. Damian Carrington, "World's Consumption of Materials Hits Record 100bn Tonnes a Year," *Guardian*, January 22, 2020, www.theguardian.com/environment/2020/jan/22/worlds-consumption-of-materials-hits-record-100bn-tonnes-a-year; *United Nations*, "The Sustainable Development Goals Report 2019." 2019, https://unstats.un.org/sdgs/report/2019/The-Sustainable-Development-Goals-Report-2019.pdf, 46–47.

9. *S&P Global*, "Fossil Fuels 'Stubbornly' Dominating Global Energy Despite Surge in Renewables: Energy Institute." June 26, 2023, www.spglobal.com/commodityinsights/en/market-insights/latest-news/oil/062623-fossil-fuels-stubbornly-dominating-global-energy-despite-surge-in-renewables-energy-institute.

10. Herring et al. (eds.), "Explaining Extreme Events of 2020 from a Climate Perspective." *Bull. Amer. Meteor. Soc.* 103(3) (2022); *UNDRR*, "The Human Cost of Disasters: An Overview of the Last 20 Years (2000–2019)." 2020, http://www.undrr.org/quick/50922.

11. McKay et al., "Exceeding 1.5°C Global Warming Could Trigger Multiple Climate Tipping Points." *Science* 377(6611), www.science.org/doi/10.1126/science.abn7950.

12. Georgina Rannard, Erwan Rivault, and Jana Tauschinski, "Climate Records Tumble, Leaving Earth In Uncharted Territory—Scientists." *BBC News*, July 22, 2023, www.bbc.com/news/science-environment-66229065.amp.

13. Nils Bochow and Niklas Boers, "The South American Monsoon Approaches a Critical Transition in Response to Deforestation." *Science Advances* 9(40) (2023).

14. David Wallace-Wells, *The Uninhabitable Earth: Life After Warming* (Tim Duggan, 2019).

15. *UNEP*, "Emissions Gap Report 2023: Broken Record—Temperatures Hit New Highs, Yet World Fails To Cut Emissions (Again)." Nairobi, 2023, doi: 10.59117/20.500.11822/43922; Jeff Tollefson, "Top Climate Scientists Are

Sceptical That Nations Will Rein In Global Warming." *Nature*, November 1, 2021, www.nature.com/articles/d41586-021-02990-w.

16. Kriebel et al., "The Precautionary Principle In Environmental Science." *Environ Health Perspect* 109(9) (2001).

17. This is the position of Max Roser and Hannah Ritchie, who run the Bill & Melinda Gates-funded project, Our World in Data, out of Oxford University.

18. Nicola Jones, "When Will Global Warming Actually Hit the Landmark 1.5 °C Limit?" *Nature*, May 19, 2023, www.nature.com/articles/d41586-023-01702-w.

19. Wiedenhofer et al., "A Systematic Review of the Evidence on Decoupling of GDP, Resource Use and GHG Emissions, Part I: Bibliometric and Conceptual Mapping." *Environmental Research Letters* 15(6) (2020); Haberl et al., "A Systematic Review of the Evidence on Decoupling of GDP, Resource Use and GHG Emissions, Part II: Synthesizing the Insights." *Environmental Research Letters* 15(6) (2020).

20. Haberl et al., "A Systematic Review of the Evidence," 3.

21. Jefim Vogel and Jason Hickel, "Is Green Growth Happening? An Empirical Analysis of Achieved Versus Paris-Compliant CO_2–GDP Decoupling In High-Income Countries." *The Lancet Planetary Health* 7(9) (2023), e763.

22. Jason Hickel and Giorgos Kallis, "Is Green Growth Possible?" *New Political Economy* 25(4) (2020).

23. See also Parrique et al., "Decoupling Debunked: Evidence and Arguments Against Green Growth as a Sole Strategy for Sustainability." *European Environmental Bureau* (2019); Vadén et al., "Decoupling for Ecological Sustainability: A Categorisation and Review of Research Literature." *Environmental Science & Policy* 112 (2020); Hubacek et al., "Evidence of Decoupling Consumption-Based CO_2 Emissions from Economic Growth." *Advances in Applied Energy* 4(19) (2021).

24. Lorenz T. Keyßer and Manfred Lenzen, "1.5 °C Degrowth Scenarios Suggest the Need For New Mitigation Pathways." *Nature Communications* 12(2676) (2021).

25. Oliver Geden, "The Dubious Carbon Budget." *New York Times*, December 1, 2015, www.nytimes.com/2015/12/01/opinion/the-questionable-accounting-behind-the-worlds-carbon-budget.html; see also Phil Williamson, "Emissions Reduction: Scrutinize CO_2 Removal Methods." *Nature* 530 (2016).

26. Wallace-Wells, *The Uninhabitable Earth*, 46.

27. *Fern*, "Six Problems with BECCS." 2018, www.fern.org/fileadmin/uploads/fern/Documents/2021/Six_problems_with_BECCS.pdf; see also Heck et al., "Biomass-Based Negative Emissions Difficult to Reconcile With Planetary Boundaries." *Nature Climate Change* 8 (2018).

28. Creutzig et al., "Considering Sustainability Thresholds for BECCS in IPCC and Biodiversity Assessments." *GCB Bioenergy* 13(4) (2021).

29. *Intergovernmental Panel on Climate Change (IPCC)*, "Climate Change 2023: Synthesis Report—Summary for Policymakers." 2023, www.ipcc.ch/report/ar6/syr/downloads/report/IPCC_AR6_SYR_SPM.pdf, 21.

30. IPCC, 21; see also Smith et al., "Biophysical and Economic Limits To Negative CO_2 Emissions." *Nature Climate Change* 6 (2016).

31. Adam Lucas, "Risking the Earth Part 2: Power Politics and Structural Reform of the IPCC and UNFCCC." *Climate Risk Management* 31 (2021); Timothée Parrique, "Degrowth in the IPCC AR6 WGIII." April 7, 2022, https://timotheeparrique.com/degrowth-in-the-ipcc-ar6-wgiii.

32. Tom Zeller Jr., "Failed Efforts in Protecting Biodiversity." *New York Times*, January 31, 2010, www.nytimes.com/2010/02/01/business/global/01green. html. The Biodiversity Intactness Index (BII) measures the resilience of a functioning ecosystem, from 0-100%. If the BII is 90% or greater, an ecosystem is functional and intact. If it drops below 90%, it may function less well and reliably. If it drops to 30% or less, the area's biodiversity has been depleted and is at risk of collapse. The current global average is 77%, with risk spread unevenly across different areas. See *WWF*, "Living Planet Report 2022: Building a Nature-Positive Society." https://wwflpr.awsassets.panda.org/downloads/lpr_2022_full_report.pdf, 46.

33. De Vos et al., "Estimating the Normal Background Rate of Species Extinction." *Conservation Biology* 29(2) (2015); Kiley Price, "Saving the African Penguin from Climate Change and Overfishing." *Ars Technica*, December 29, 2023, https://arstechnica.com/science/2023/12/saving-the-african-penguin-from-climate-change-and-overfishing.

34. *UN*, "UN Report: Nature's Dangerous Decline 'Unprecedented'; Species Extinction Rates 'Accelerating.'" May 6, 2019.

35. *WWF*, "Living Planet Report 2022," 32. The organization tracked 31,821 populations of 5,230 vertebrate species between 1970 and 2018.

36. Ibid.

37. Elizabeth Anne Brown, "Widely Misinterpreted Report Still Shows Catastrophic Animal Decline." *National Geographic*, November 1, 2018, https://archive.is/LCawk.

38. Species displaced by humans carry diseases and compete with native species over food and land.

39. Francisco Sánchez-Bayo and Kris A.G. Wyckhuys, "Worldwide Decline of the Entomofauna: A Review of its Drivers." *Biological Conservation* 232 (2019), 9.

40. Damian Carrington, "Plummeting Insect Numbers 'Threaten Collapse of Nature.'" *Guardian*, February 10, 2019, www.theguardian.com/environment/2019/feb/10/plummeting-insect-numbers-threaten-collapse-of-nature.

41. Dittrich et al., "Green Economies Around The World? Implications of Resource Use for Development and the Environment." Vienna, 2012, www.boell.de/sites/default/files/201207_green_economies_around_the_world.pdf.

42. Ibid., 10, 72.

43. Arjen Hoekstra and Thomas Wiedmann, "Humanity's Unsustainable Environmental Footprint," *Science* 344(6188) (2014), 1117.

44. *UNEP*, "Decoupling Natural Resource Use and Environmental Impacts from Economic Growth." 2011, https://wedocs.unep.org/handle/20.500.11822/9816,

29; *UNEP*, "Managing and Conserving the Natural Resource Base for Sustained Economic and Social Development." February 7, 2014, www.resourcepanel.org/reports/managing-and-conserving-natural-resource-base-sustained-economic-and-social-development, 9.

45. *WWF*, "Living Planet Report 2022," 6; Michael Lettenmeier, Christa Liedtke, and Holger Rohn, "Eight Tons of Material Footprint—Suggestion for a Resource Cap for Household Consumption in Finland." *Resources* 3(3), 2014; Stefan Bringezu, "Possible Target Corridor for Sustainable Use of Global Material Resources." *Resources* 4(1) (2015).

46. *UNEP*, "Managing and Conserving the Natural Resource Base," 2.

47. Ibid., 3.

48. This approach allowed the authors a degree of precision: they could get beyond simplified connections between material resource use to environmental impacts. See Steinmann et al., "Resource Footprints are Good Proxies of Environmental Damage." *Environ. Sci. Technol.* 51(11) (2017).

49. Marques et al., "Increasing Impacts of Land Use on Biodiversity and Carbon Sequestration Driven by Population and Economic Growth." *Nature Ecology & Evolution* 3 (2019); Otero et al., "Biodiversity Policy Beyond Economic Growth." *Conservation Letters* 13(4) (2020).

50. UNEP, "Decoupling Natural Resource Use," 29–32.

51. Kate Raworth, *Doughnut Economics: Seven Ways to Think Like a 21st-Century Economist* (Chelsea Green Publishing, 2017).

52. *Wikipedia*, CC BY-SA 4.0 "Doughnut (Economic Model)." https://en.wikipedia.org/wiki/Doughnut_(economic_model).

53. *United Nations*, "World Population Prospects 2019: Highlights." 2019, https://population.un.org/wpp/Publications/Files/WPP2019_10KeyFindings.pdf; B. Callegari and P.E. Stoknes, "People and Planet: 21st-Century Sustainable Population Scenarios and Possible Living Standards Within Planetary Boundaries." *Earth4All*, 2023, https://earth4all.life/wp-content/uploads/2023/04/E4A_People-and-Planet_Report.pdf; Jason Hickel, "At This Rate, It Will Take 200 Years To End Global Poverty." April 27, 2019, www.jasonhickel.org/blog/2019/4/27/200-years-to-end-poverty.

54. *The World Bank*, "GDP Per Capita, PPP (Current International $)," https://data.worldbank.org/indicator/NY.GDP.PCAP.PP.CD.

55. See Jason Hickel, "The Fallacies of GDP Reductionism: A Response to Warlenius." July 31, 2023. Max Roser picks out Denmark's poverty line—$30 per day—as a baseline standard and argues that the global economy needs to increase by over *five times* its present size, what he calls a "realistic scenario," for the 85% of the world's people who live under $30 per day to catch up. (See Max Roser, "How much Economic Growth is Necessary to Reduce Global Poverty Substantially?" *Our World in Data*, March 14, 2021, https://ourworldindata.org/poverty-minimum-growth-needed.) But the *global* per capita GDP (by PPP) of $20,000 is already equal to $55 per day, and at $10,000 it's equal to $27 per day, which is just under Demark's poverty line *before* any attempts to reconfigure the economy in a sustainable, egalitarian fashion.

In Roser's "realistic" scenario, *inequality* is also equivalent to that of Denmark, where the top 10% make ten times more (~$113,000) than the lowest 10% ($13,000) (See *Statistics Denmark*, "Income inequality." www.dst.dk/en/ Statistik/emner/arbejde-og-indkomst/indkomst-og-loen/indkomstulighed.) Roser also offers a "perfect equality" scenario, which he claims would require an economy 2.7 times larger than today's economy by the end of the century—due to population growth. But this once again disregards any consideration of reconfiguring our economies to radically prioritize need and cut waste, as well as the possibility that the global population could decline without any coercive policies due to rapid gains in education and equality.
56. Saito, *Slow Down*.

3. DIGITAL DEGROWTH

1. *UN*, "Ensure Sustainable Consumption and Production Patterns." 2019, 46–47.
2. The UN doesn't specify population sizes to the income brackets, but Dorninger et al. separate them as follows: high-income countries make up 15.5% of the world's population in 2015, upper-middle income countries 16.1%, lower-middle income 15.7%, and low-income 15.3%. It's probably the case that these numbers are similar for the UN in its chart. See Dorninger et al., "Global Patterns of Ecologically Unequal Exchange: Implications for Sustainability in the 21st Century." *Ecological Economics* 179 (2021), 3.
3. *UN*, "Ensure Sustainable Consumption," 46.
4. *UNEP*, "Managing and Conserving the Natural Resource Base for Sustained Economic and Social Development." February 7, 2014, www.resourcepanel. org/reports/managing-and-conserving-natural-resource-base-sustained-economic-and-social-development, 9.
5. Unequal exchange in general dates back to Arghiri Emmanuel's seminal work, *Unequal Exchange: A Study of the Imperialism of Trade* (Monthly Review Press, 1972).
6. Dorninger et al., "Global Patterns of Ecologically Unequal Exchange."
7. Ibid., 2.
8. Ibid., 5.
9. Patrick Bond and Rahul Basu, "'Unequal Ecological Exchange' Worsens Across Time and Space, Creating Growing Northern Environmental Liabilities." May 19, 2021, www.cadtm.org/Unequal-ecological-exchange-worsens-across-time-and-space-creating-growing.
10. *International Labour Office*, "World Employment and Social Outlook: Trends 2024." Geneva, 2024, www.ilo.org/wcmsp5/groups/public/---dgreports/---inst/documents/publication/wcms_908142.pdf.
11. *Black Gold*, directed by Marc Francis and Nick Francis, Fulcrum Productions, 2006.
12. Billy Perrigo, "Inside Facebook's African Sweatshop." *TIME*, February 14, 2022, https://time.com/6147458/facebook-africa-content-moderation-

employee-treatment. Content moderation outsourcing to the South has long been documented, and some of the work is done in the developed world, where workers are also exploited and suffer psychological trauma. See Sarah T. Roberts, *Behind the Screen: Content Moderation in the Shadows of Social Media* (Yale University Press, 2019).

13. See DensityDesign Lab and Tactical Tech, "The GAFAM Empire." https://gafam.theglassroom.org.

14. Cecilia Rikap and Bengt-Åke Lundvall, "Big Tech, Knowledge Predation and the Implications for Development." *Innovation and Development* 12(3) (2020), 14.

15. Siddharth Kara, *Cobalt Red: How the Blood of the Congo Powers Our Lives* (St. Martin's Press, 2023).

16. Frank Piasecki Poulsen, "Children of the Congo Who Risk Their Lives to Supply Our Mobile Phones." *Guardian*, December 7, 2012, www.theguardian.com/sustainable-business/blog/congo-child-labour-mobile-minerals; *Amnesty International*, "Exposed: Child Labour Behind Smart Phone and Electric Car Batteries." January 19, 2016. James H. Smith, *The Eyes of the World: Mining the Digital Age in the Eastern DR Congo* (University of Chicago Press, 2021).

17. Shoshana Kedem, "Despite Record Industry Profits, DRC's Cobalt Miners Fall Further into Poverty." *African Business*, March 30, 2023, https://african.business/2023/03/resources/drcs-cobalt-miners-fall-further-into-poverty.

18. Michael Kwet, "Digital Colonialism: The Evolution of US Empire." *Transnational Institute*, March 4, 2021, https://longreads.tni.org/digital-colonialism-the-evolution-of-us-empire.

19. *The World Counts*, "Energy Use From Mining." www.theworldcounts.com/challenges/planet-earth/mining/energy-use-in-the-mining-industry; Sonter et al., "Renewable Energy Production Will Exacerbate Mining Threats To Biodiversity." *Nature Communications* 11 (2020); Fernanda Ferreira, "How Does the Environmental Impact of Mining for Clean Energy Metals Compare to Mining for Coal, Oil and Gas?" *Climate Portal*, May 8, 2023; *GlobalData*, "Total GHG Emissions of Major Metals and Mining Companies Worldwide by Revenue in 2021." 2022, www.globaldata.com/data-insights/mining/total-ghg-emissions-of-major-metals-and-mining-companies-worldwide-by-revenue-2090961; *International Energy Agency*, "Sustainable Recovery." 2020, https://iea.blob.core.windows.net/assets/c3de5e13-26e8-4e52-8a67-b97aba17foa2/Sustainable_Recovery.pdf.

20. Simon Meißner, "The Impact of Metal Mining on Global Water Stress and Regional Carrying Capacities—A GIS-Based Water Impact Assessment." *Resources* 10(12) (2021), 1.

21. Biodiversity impacts will "depend on the mix of technologies used, their mineral needs and methods used to mine them" and "efforts to manage their environmental impacts," the authors noted. Sonter et al., "Renewable Energy Production," 5.

22. Meißner, "The Impact of Metal Mining," 25–27.

23. *UNCTAD*, "Developing Countries Pay Environmental Cost of Electric Car Batteries." July 22, 2020, https://unctad.org/news/developing-countries-pay-environmental-cost-electric-car-batteries.

24. Amit Katwala, "The Spiralling Environmental Cost of Our Lithium Battery Addiction." *Wired*, May 8, 2018, www.wired.co.uk/article/lithium-batteries-environment-impact.

25. Meißner, "The Impact of Metal Mining," 2.

26. Matthew Brown, "50M Gallons of Polluted Water Pours Daily From US Mine Sites." *Associated Press*, February 20, 2019, https://apnews.com/article/8158167fd9ab4cd8966e47a6dd6cbe96; Sonter et al., "Renewable Energy Production."

27. Sonter et al., "Mining Drives Extensive Deforestation in the Brazilian Amazon." *Nature Communications* 8 (2017), 1.

28. Nkulu et al., "Sustainability of Artisanal Mining of Cobalt in DR Congo." *Nature Sustainability* 1 (2018).

29. *Democracy Now!*, "'Cobalt Red": Smartphones & Electric Cars Rely on Toxic Mineral Mined in Congo by Children." July 13, 2023, www.democracynow.org/2023/7/13/cobalt_red_kara.

30. Brusselen et al., "Metal Mining and Birth Defects: A Case-Control Study in Lubumbashi, Democratic Republic of the Congo." *Lancet Planetary Health* 4(4), www.thelancet.com/journals/lanplh/article/PIIS2542-5196(20)30059-0, e165; Nicolas Niarchos, "The Dark Side of Congo's Cobalt Rush." *New Yorker*, May 24, 2021, www.newyorker.com/magazine/2021/05/31/the-dark-side-of-congos-cobalt-rush.

31. One fisherman named Modeste told Kara, "Ten years ago [Mupanja] was a peaceful village. Now people come from all places to dig cobalt … There is too much alcohol and prostitution in the village … There are always soldiers here … People kill each other for cobalt." Kara, *Cobalt Red*. See also, Benjamin K. Sovacool, "When subterranean Slavery Supports Sustainability Transitions? Power, Patriarchy, and Child Labor in Artisanal Congolese Cobalt Mining." *The Extractive Industries and Society* 8(1) (2021).

32. Kandy Wong, "Europe's Big Rare Earth Discovery Seen As 'Game Changer' in Bid to Address China's Dominance." *South China Morning Post*, January 29, 2023, https://archive.is/EmVpq. For a rundown of China's market share of rare earth metals, see Laura Seligman, "China Dominates the Rare Earths Market. This U.S. Mine Is Trying to Change That." *Politico*, December 14, 2022, www.politico.com/news/magazine/2022/12/14/rare-earth-mines-00071102.

33. *The World Bank*, "Climate-Smart Mining: Minerals for Climate Action." May 26, 2019, www.worldbank.org/en/topic/extractiveindustries/brief/climate-smart-mining-minerals-for-climate-action.

34. *Statista*, "Leading Ride-Hailing and Taxi Operators Worldwide as of November 2022, by Market Share." December 19, 2023, www.statista.com/statistics/1156066/leading-ride-hailing-operators-worldwide-by-market-share.

35. Sheila Chiang, "Automakers Promote Advanced Tech to Compete in China—the World's Top EV Market." *CNBC*, August, 3, 2023, www.cnbc.com/2023/08/04/ev-makers-promote-advanced-tech-to-compete-in-china.html; Akhil Ramesh, "China's Lead Over the US in EV Markets is Huge, But Not Insurmountable." *South China Morning Post*, May 11, 2023, https://archive.is/tddK9; Jasper Jolly, "China's Share of Europe's Electric Car Market Accelerates as UK Leads Sales." *Guardian*, September 4, 2023, www.theguardian.com/business/2023/sep/04/china-europe-electric-car-market-uk-sales-mg-tesla; Kyle Stock, "Why Can't Americans Buy Cheap Chinese EVs?" *Bloomberg*, September 22, 2023, www.bloomberg.com/news/articles/2023-09-22/why-can-t-americans-buy-cheap-chinese-evs.

36. *Cobalt Institute*, "Cobalt Market Report 2022." 2023, www.cobaltinstitute.org/wp-content/uploads/2023/05/Cobalt-Market-Report-2022_final-1.pdf, 13.

37. *CBC Radio*, "Tech Giants Sued Over 'Appalling' Deaths of Children Who Mine Their Cobalt." December 17, 2019, www.cbc.ca/radio/asithappens/as-it-happens-tuesday-edition-1.5399491/tech-giants-sued-over-appalling-deaths-of-children-who-mine-their-cobalt-1.5399492.

38. Maria Piontkovska and Doriane Nguenang, "US Court Dismissed Cobalt Mining Forced Labor Lawsuit Against Tech Companies." *Baker McKenzie*, November 18, 2021, https://supplychaincompliance.bakermckenzie.com/2021/11/18/us-court-dismissed-cobalt-mining-forced-labor-lawsuit-against-tech-companies.

39. Steve Tombs and David Whyte, *The Corporate Criminal: Why Corporations Must Be Abolished* (Routledge, 2015), 31.

40. *Mining.com*, "The top 50 Biggest Mining Companies in the World." October 18, 2023, https://archive.is/eU7oh.

41. Christian Fuchs, *Digital Labour and Karl Marx* (Routledge, 2014).

42. Tombs and Whyte, *The Corporate Criminal*, 31.

43. Viola Zhou, "'iPhones are Made in Hell': 3 Months Inside China's iPhone City." *Rest of World*, January 31, 2023, https://restofworld.org/2023/foxconn-iphone-factory-china.

44. Cecilia Rikap, *Capitalism, Power and Innovation: Intellectual Monopoly Capitalism Uncovered* (Routledge, 2021), 136.

45. John Smith, *Imperialism in the Twenty-First Century: Globalization, Super-Exploitation, and Capitalism's Final Crisis* (Monthly Review Press, 2016), 28.

46. Ibid., 45.

47. Donald Clelland, "The Core of the Apple: Dark Value and Degrees of Monopoly in Global Commodity Chains." *J. World-Syst. Res.* 20(1) (2014).

48. *International Energy Association (IEA)*, "CO_2 Emissions in 2022." 2023, www.iea.org/reports/co2-emissions-in-2022.

49. *UNEP*, "Emissions Gap Report 2023," xv, xxiii.

50. Jason Hickel, "Quantifying National Responsibility for Climate Breakdown: An Equality-Based Attribution Approach for Carbon Dioxide Emissions in Excess of the Planetary Boundary." *Lancet Planetary Health* 4(9) (2020). Hickel's notion of a fair share "proceeds from the principle that all countries should

have equal access to atmospheric commons in per capita terms, which is defined here as a fair share of a safe global carbon budget consistent with the planetary boundary of 350 ppm atmospheric CO_2 concentration" (p. e400).

51. *CDP*, "CDP Africa Report: Benchmarking Progress Towards Climate Safe Cities, States, and Regions." 2020, https://cdn.cdp.net/cdp-production/cms/reports/documents/000/005/023/original/CDP_Africa_Report_2020.pdf, 3.

52. Hickel, "Quantifying National …," e399. National responsibility is measured as: (cumulative emissions—fair share) ÷ total national overshoots.

53. Even this might be understated. If we account for the colonial rule of imperial powers, countries like India and Indonesia have even *less* of a carbon footprint. See Simon Evans and Verner Viisainen, "Revealed: How Colonial Rule Radically Shifts Historical Responsibility for Climate Change." *CarbonBrief*, November 26, 2023, www.carbonbrief.org/revealed-how-colonial-rule-radically-shifts-historical-responsibility-for-climate-change.

54. Emissions of the rich within countries also bear responsibility and must stop over-emitting. See Lucas Chancel, "Global Carbon Inequality Over 1990–2019." *Nature Sustainability* 5 (2022).

55. Ibid., e403.

56. Ferreboeuf et al., "Environmental Impacts of Digital Technology: 5-Year Trends and 5G Governance." *The Shift Project*, 2021, https://theshiftproject.org/wp-content/uploads/2023/04/Environmental-impacts-of-digital-technology-5-year-trends-and-5G-governance_March2021.pdf. The authors identified five trends contributing to growing digital energy consumption: 1) video streaming and associated purchases (large TVs, etc.); 2) "assisted comfort technologies" such as home security cameras; 3) "global universalization of smartphones"; 4) booming Internet of Things and Industrial Internet of Things (the connection of devices like sensors and robots); and 5) the fact that data and computational demands are growing faster than technological efficiencies.

57. Malmodin et al., "ICT Sector Electricity Consumption and Greenhouse Gas Emissions—2020 Outcome." *Telecommunications Policy* (2024).

58. Lotfi Belkhir and Ahmed Elmelig, "Assessing ICT Global Emissions Footprint: Trends to 2040 & Recommendations." *Journal of Cleaner Production* 177 (2018); Freitag et al., "The Real Climate and Transformative Impact of ICT: A Critique of Estimates, Trends, and Regulations." *Patterns* 2(9) (2021). Estimates of GHG spanning the ICT industry are of course difficult to compute. See Jonathan Koomey and Eric Masanet, "Does Not Compute: Avoiding Pitfalls Assessing the Internet's Energy and Carbon Impacts." *Joule* 5(7) (2021).

59. Rodrigo Navarro, "The Carbon Emissions of Big Tech." *ElectronicsHub*, February 13, 2023, www.electronicshub.org/the-carbon-emissions-of-big-tech.

60. Ibid.

61. *UN Global Compact*, "Scope 3 Emissions." www.unglobalcompact.org.uk/scope-3-emissions; CDP, "CDP Technical Note: Relevance of Scope 3 Categories by Sector." 2023, 6. Emissions can vary widely, depending on the sector.

62. Day et al., "Corporate Climate Responsibility Monitor 2022." 2022, https:// carbonmarketwatch.org/publications/ccrm_2022; Wu et al., "Supply Change." 2022, www.greenpeace.org/static/planet4-eastasia-stateless/2022/10/89382b33-supplychange.pdf; Shi et al., "Are Firms Voluntarily Disclosing Emissions Greener?" *SSRN*, 2023, https://papers.ssrn.com/sol3/papers.cfm?abstract_id= 4426612.

63. Technical University of Munich (TUM), "Tech Companies Underreport CO_2 Emissions." *ScienceDaily*, 2021, www.sciencedaily.com/releases/2021/11/ 211118203514.htm.

64. The two additional datasets provided by *ElectronicsHub* measure each company's carbon emissions per employee, and carbon emissions relative to revenue. The results are approximately the same: the United States emits the most. Also note that *ElectronicsHub* pulls its data from the Companiesmarketcap.com "Top Tech" database, and that list excludes a handful of India-based corporations (which it places under other categories, such as "Software"), which may slightly skew the North vs South disparity.

65. *USCAN*, "The US Climate Fair Share." https://usfairshare.org/files/US_ Climate_Fair_Share_Infographic.pdf; USCAN, "The US Fair Share," 9.

66. Avantika Goswami and Ananya Rao, "Beyond Climate Finance: Climate Ambition in the Global South Requires Financial System Reforms." *Centre for Science and Environment*, 2023, www.cseindia.org/beyond-climate-finance-climate-ambition-in-the-global-south-requires-financial-system-reforms-11753, 11.

67. Ibid., 10–12.

68. *Oxfam International*, "G7 Owes Huge $13 Trillion Debt to Global South." May 17, 2023, www.oxfam.org/en/press-releases/g7-owes-huge-13-trillion-debt-global-south.

69. Andrew Fanning and Jason Hickel, "Compensation for Atmospheric Appropriation." *Nature Sustainability* 6 (2023).

70. Oliver Slow, "US Refuses Climate Reparations for Developing Nations." *BBC*, July 13, 2023, www.bbc.com/news/world-us-canada-66197366.

71. Hickel et al., "Plunder in the Post-Colonial Era: Quantifying Drain from the Global South Through Unequal Exchange, 1960–2018." *New Political Economy* 6 (2021), 1030.

72. Andrew Simms, *Ecological Debt: Global Warming & the Wealth of Nations (2e)* (Pluto, 2009), 90.

73. Hickel et al., "National Responsibility for Ecological Breakdown: A Fair-Shares Assessment of Resource Use, 1970–2017." *Lancet Planetary Health* 6(4), e342.

74. Ibid., e345.

75. Jason Hickel, Personal email. September 29, 2021.

76. *Allianz Research*, "Allianz Global Wealth Report 2022: The Last Hurrah." 2022, www.allianz.com/content/dam/onemarketing/azcom/ Allianz_com/economic-research/publications/specials/en/2022/october/12-10-2022-GlobalWealthReport.pdf, 10; *Credit Suisse Research Institute*, "Global Wealth Report 2023." UBS, 2023, www.allianz.com/content/dam/

onemarketing/azcom/Allianz_com/economic-research/publications/allianz-global-wealth-report/2023/2023-09-26-GlobalWealthReport.pdf.

77. Credit Suisse, "Global Wealth Report 2023," 28–29.
78. *Wisevoter*, "Billionaires by Country." https://wisevoter.com/country-rankings/billionaires-by-country.
79. Stefan Gössling and Andreas Humpe, "Millionaire Spending Incompatible with 1.5 °C Ambitions." *Cleaner Production Letters* 4 (2023).
80. *World Population Review*, Millionaires by Country 2024." https://worldpopulationreview.com/country-rankings/millionaires-by-country.
81. *Oxfam*, "Carbon Billionaires: The Investment Emissions of the World's Richest People." 2022, https://oxfamilibrary.openrepository.com/bitstream/handle/10546/621446/bn-carbon-billlionaires-071122-en.pdf, 2.
82. Jag Bhalla, "What's Your "Fair Share" of Carbon Emissions? You're Probably Blowing Way Past It." *Vox*, February 24, 2021, www.vox.com/22291568/climate-change-carbon-footprint-greta-thunberg-un-emissions-gap-report.
83. Americans for Tax Fairness, "Billionaires by the Numbers." 2023, https://web.archive.org/web/20230331064002/https://americansfortaxfairness.org/billionaires; Phoebe Liu, "The Richest American Tech Billionaires In 2023," *Forbes*, October 3, 2023, www.forbes.com/sites/phoebeliu/2023/10/03/the-richest-american-tech-billionaires-in-2023.
84. *Forbes*, "The World's Real-Time Billionaires." December 1, 2023, https://web.archive.org/web/20231201181420/www.forbes.com/real-time-billionaires/#5016c5553d78.
85. *RealLifeLore*, "The Insane Wealth of Jeff Bezos Visualized." September 27, 2020, https://nebula.tv/videos/real-life-lore-the-insane-wealth-of-jeff-bezos-visualized.
86. Ibid.
87. Beatriz Barros and Richard Wilk, "The Outsized Carbon Footprints of the Super-Rich." *Sustainability: Science, Practice and Policy* 17(1), 2021.
88. *Global Justice Now*, "69 of the Richest 100 Entities on the Planet are Corporations, Not Governments, Figures Show." October 17, 2018, www.globaljustice.org.uk/news/69-richest-100-entities-planet-are-corporations-not-governments-figures-show. Critically, that's measured by *revenue* (the amount of things sold by the entities in a given year) for both corporations *and* governments.
89. *Motley Fool Wealth Management*, "The Surprising Truth About the S&P 500 and the 'Magnificent 7' in 2024." January 30, 2024, https://foolwealth.com/insights/sp500-and-the-magnificent-7-in-2024.
90. Numbers were sourced from companiesmarketcap.com on November 9, 2023.
91. Paul Kunert, "Investor Tells Google: Cut Costs Now and Stop Paying Staff So Much." *The Register*, November 16, 2022, www.theregister.com/2022/11/16/tci_fund_google_cut_costs_waymo_compensation; Stephen J. Vaughan-Nichols, "What is Google Doing With its Open Source Teams?" *The Register*, January 27, 2023, www.theregister.com/2023/01/27/google_open_source.
92. *Levels.fyi*, "End of Year Pay Report 2022." 2022, www.levels.fyi/2022.

93. *Stack Overflow*, "2023 Developer Survey." 2023, https://survey.stackoverflow.co/2023.

94. According to *Crunchbase*, together with other (almost exclusively) US-based investors, Andela has received $381 million in seed funding to date.

95. Joseph Olaoluwa, "Ride-Hailing Drivers in Nigeria Begin Nationwide Strike as they ask Uber and Bolt to Increase Fares by 200%." *TechCabal*, June 7, 2023, https://techcabal.com/2023/06/07/ride-hailing-drivers-in-nigeria-begin-nationwide-strike-as-they-ask-uber-and-bolt-to-increase-fares-by-200; Abdul Jemilu, "Uber Drivers Earnings 2023: How Much Uber Drivers Make Weekly in Nigeria." *CAMP NG*, September 5, 2023, https://camp.com.ng/uber-drivers-earnings-2023-how-much-uber-drivers-make-weekly-in-nigeria.

96. Harrisberg et al., "Concerns Over Abuse and Exploitation as House-Cleaning Service Apps Take Off." *Sunday Times*, February 16, 2023, www.timeslive.co.za/news/africa/2023-02-16-concerns-over-abuse-and-exploitation-as-house-cleaning-service-apps-take-off.

97. *Andela*, "What is Andela?" *YouTube*, September 29, 2014, www.youtube.com/watch?v=vhJik9S9nxg.

98. *BrighterMonday*, "Andela Kenya: Shaping the Kenyan Tech Space." April 15, 2022, www.brightermonday.co.ke/discover/working-at-andela-kenya.

99. *Andela*, 2014; Jeremy Johnson, "This is Andela." https://web.archive.org/web/20230201133314mp_/https://andela.com/insights/this-is-andela.

100. Alex Kantrowitz, "'I'm Disturbed.' African Tech Workers Push Back on US Startup Built To Help Them." *Big Technology*, July 9, 2020, https://web.archive.org/web/20221225232746/www.bigtechnology.com/p/im-disturbed-african-tech-workers.

101. Andela recruits "don't relocate" but instead "work remotely." As of 2019, 90% of its alumni were still working in Nigeria. See Johny Cassidy and Lucky Hooker, "Engineered in Africa: 'We Knew the Talent was There.'" *BBC*, August 6, 2019, www.bbc.com/news/business-49207040.

102. Ian Carnevale, *LinkedIn*, February 25, 2024, https://archive.is/knIZO.

103. Susan Adams, "Andela Aims to Solve the Developer Shortage With Tech Workers From Africa." *Forbes*, January 12, 2018, www.forbes.com/sites/forbestreptalks/2018/01/12/andela-aims-to-solve-the-developer-shortage-with-tech-workers-from-africa.

104. Ha-Joon Chang, *Bad Samaritans: The Myth of Free Trade and the Secret History of Capitalism* (Bloomsbury Publishing, 2008), 210.

4. CLOUD COLONIALISM

1. Cited in Vickery, Kenneth, "South Africa—The Dutch Cape Colony." In *African Experience: From 'Lucy' to Mandela* (The Teaching Company, 2006).

2. Google Earth, https://earth.google.com/web/search/Observatory,+Cape+Town/@-33.93083433,18.47606299,4.74915499a,3129.83997447d,35y,0.0000000 1h,59.98047543t,0r/data=CigiJgokCVkPbnsxHjRAEV gPbnsxHjTAGe4aC6inZElAIe4aC6inZEnA; Royal Observatory Cape, *Face-*

book, April 22, 2021, www.facebook.com/Royal.Observatory.Cape/photos/a.489406317892863/1852844638215684.

3. Leslie London, "The River Club Development: What is Really at Stake?" *New Agenda* 79 (2021), https://obs.org.za/cms/wp-content/uploads/2021/05/Leslie-London-New-Agenda-No79-2021.pdf, 34.

4. Steve Kretzmann, "R4 Billion River Club Development Clears Major Obstacle." *GroundUp*, August 27, 2020, https://groundup.org.za/article/r4-billion-river-club-development-clears-major-obstacle.

5. Michael Kwet, "Amazon's Colonial Headquarters in South Africa." *YouTube*, November 16, 2021, www.youtube.com/watch?v=Y_S_J83W-3U.

6. Ibid.

7. London, "The River Club Development," 33.

8. Kwet, "Amazon's Colonial."

9. *City of Cape Town*, "City Welcomes Final Settlement of River Club Matter." June 27, 2023, www.capetown.gov.za/Media-and-news/City%20welcomes%20final%20settlement%20of%20River%20Club%20matter.

10. Steve Kretzmann, "Lawyer in Amazon Controversy Caught in Qualification Lie." *GroundUp*, August 29, 2023, https://groundup.org.za/article/lawyer-in-amazon-controversy-caught-in-qualification-lie.

11. Bulelwa Payi, "River Club Development Whistle-Blower Reveals Alleged Bribery." *IOL*, September 16, 2023, www.iol.co.za/weekend-argus/news/river-club-development-whistle-blower-reveals-alleged-bribery-65a2e540-e1f9-419b-af81-1b50fc9f1598; Trevor Sacks, "Whistle-Blowers Lay Out Amazon/River Club developers' Alleged 'Dirty Tricks.'" *Daily Maverick*, August 21, 2023, www.dailymaverick.co.za/opinionista/2023-08-21-whistle-blowers-lay-out-amazon-river-club-developers-alleged-dirty-tricks.

12. Jens Hosber, "Power, Money and PR—The River Club Development's Public Costs and Private Benefits." *Daily Maverick*, November 22, 2023, www.dailymaverick.co.za/article/2023-11-22-river-club-development-power-money-and-pr.

13. Michael Kwet and Tshiamo Malatji, "Amazon's Colonial HQ in Cape Town Must be Stopped." *Mail & Guardian*, January 26, 2022, https://mg.co.za/thought-leader/opinion/2022-01-26-amazons-colonial-hq-in-cape-town-must-be-stopped.

14. Kwet, "Amazon's Colonial."

15. Michael Kwet, "Digital Colonialism and Infrastructure-as-Debt." *University of Bayreuth African Studies Online*, 2022, https://papers.ssrn.com/sol3/papers.cfm?abstract_id=4004594.

16. Angus Loten, "AI-Ready Data Centers Are Poised for Fast Growth." *Wall Street Journal*, August 3, 2023, https://archive.is/RnyqE; Alex de Vries, "The Growing Energy Footprint of Artificial Intelligence." *Joule* 7(10), 2023, https://asociace.ai/wp-content/uploads/2023/10/ai-spotreba.pdf, 2; *Business Wire*, "Worldwide Server Market Revenue Declined 2.5% Year Over Year in the Second Quarter of 2021, According to IDC." September 9, 2021, www.businesswire.com/news/

home/20210909006193/en/Worldwide-Server-Market-Revenue-Declined-2.5-Year-Over-Year-in-the-Second-Quarter-of-2021-According-to-IDC.

17. Felix Richter, "Amazon Maintains Cloud Lead as Microsoft Edges Closer." *Statista*, February 5, 2024, www.statista.com/chart/18819/worldwide-market-share-of-leading-cloud-infrastructure-service-providers.

18. Emmanuel Oyedeji, "Intel Continues to Lead the Global Data Center CPU Market with 71% Share." March 1, 2023, www.techloy.com/global-data-center-cpu-market-share-2022. Of this, Intel claims to own 90% of the cloud computing market (*Intel*, "Cloud Policy." https://archive.is/tsfVZ). The distinction between cloud computing and data centers is a bit fuzzy, but for our purposes—establishing American the extent of American ownership—the numbers provided are sufficient.

19. Laura Dobberstein, "5% of the Cloud Now Runs on Arm as Chip Designer Plans 2023 IPO." *The Register*, February 8, 2023, www.theregister.com/2023/02/08/5_percent_cloud_arm.

20. Tae Kim, "Nvidia's AI Chips Are Pulling Ahead in the Cloud. Why the Stock Is a Buy." *Barron's*, August 17, 2023, www.barrons.com/amp/articles/nvidia-ai-chips-stock-buy-9755a69f; Kif Leswing, "Meet the $10,000 Nvidia chip powering the race for A.I." *CNBC*, www.cnbc.com/2023/02/23/nvidias-a100-is-the-10000-chip-powering-the-race-for-ai-.html.

21. *Semiconductor Industry Association*, "2023 Factbook," www.semiconductors.org/wp-content/uploads/2023/05/SIA-2023-Factbook_1.pdf

22. China has recently produced its own advanced chips that lag behind the US.

23. The US also owns 40.9% of the world's semiconductor manufacturing equipment—essential to manufacturing computer chips—followed by Japan (29.4%), South Korea (4.8%), China (2%), Taiwan (0.4%), and the rest of world (22.6%). Akhil Thadani and Gregory Allen, "Mapping the Semiconductor Supply Chain: The Critical Role of the Indo-Pacific Region." *Center for Strategic and International Studies (CSIS)*, May 30, 2023, www.csis.org/analysis/mapping-semiconductor-supply-chain-critical-role-indo-pacific-region.

24. Varas et al., "Strengthening the Global Semiconductor Supply Chain in an Uncertain Era." *Boston Consulting Group (BCG) and SIA*, 2021, https://web.archive.org/web/20210929023621/www.semiconductors.org/wp-content/uploads/2021/05/BCG-x-SIA-Strengthening-the-Global-Semiconductor-Value-Chain-April-2021_1.pdf.

25. *Seagate*, "Why HDDs Dominate Hyperscale Cloud Architecture." www.seagate.com/blog/why-hdds-dominate-hyperscale-cloud-architecture; Thomas Alsop, "Server Unit Shipments Worldwide from 2011 to 2021, by Quarter." *Statista*, November 6, 2023, www.statista.com/statistics/287005/global-server-shipments; Shehabi et al., "United States Data Center Energy Usage Report." *Berkeley Lab*, 2016, www.osti.gov/servlets/purl/1372902, 21; *Business Wire*, "Worldwide Server Market Revenue Declined 2.5% Year Over Year in the Second Quarter of 2021, According to IDC." September 9, 2021, www.businesswire.com/news/home/20210909006193/en/

Worldwide-Server-Market-Revenue-Declined-2.5-Year-Over-Year-in-the-Second-Quarter-of-2021-According-to-IDC.

26. See data at Thomas Alsop, "DRAM Manufacturers Revenue Share Worldwide from 2011 to 2023, by Quarter." *Statista*, January 8, 2024, www.statista.com/statistics/271726/global-market-share-held-by-dram-chip-vendors-since-2010.

27. See *Precedence Research*, "Semiconductor Market." https://archive.is/IxUl1; *Precedence Research*, "Cloud Computing Market." https://archive.is/8beLn; *Precedence Research*, "Hyperscale Data Center." https://archive.is/PxOmw; *Precedence Research*, "Microprocessor Market." https://archive.is/005t9; Market Growth Reports, "Servers Market Size in 2023." *LinkedIn*, September 13, 2023, www.linkedin.com/pulse/servers-market-size-2023-growth-status-revenue-industry; *Straits Research*, "Dynamic Random Access (DRAM) Market." https://archive.is/vRIWY; *Precedence Research*, "Graphic Processing Unit (GPU) Market Will Grow at CAGR of 33.8% By 2032." November 9, 2023, https://archive.is/EvJ6S; *Future Market Insights*, "Hard Disk Drive Market." https://archive.is/gNusb.

28. Emma Chervek, "Hyperscale Data Centers Will Triple Capacity to Meet Genai Demands." *SDxCentral*, October 23, 2023, www.sdxcentral.com/articles/analysis/hyperscale-data-centers-will-triple-capacity-to-meet-genai-demands/2023/10; *Fortune Business Insights*, "Hyperscale Cloud Market." https://archive.is/37i28.

29. Drew Robb, "Google, Azure and AWS battle for the hyperscale Data Center Market." *SDxCentral*, October 2, 2023, www.sdxcentral.com/articles/analysis/google-azure-and-aws-battle-for-the-hyperscale-data-center-market/2023/10.

30. *Business Standard*, "2012: Gartner." January 21, 2013, www.business-standard.com/article/companies/public-cloud-computing-market-to-be-109-bn-globally-in-2012-gartner-112091800202_1.html.

31. Rick et al., "Invisible Emissions: A forecast of Tech Supply Chain Emissions and Electricity Consumption by 2030." *Greenpeace*, 2023, www.greenpeace.org/static/planet4-eastasia-stateless/2023/04/620390b7-greenpeace_energy_consumption_report.pdf.

32. Petroc Taylor, "Volume of Data/Information Created, Captured, Copied, and Consumed Worldwide from 2010 to 2020, with Forecasts from 2021 to 2025." *Statista*, November 16, 2023, www.statista.com/statistics/871513/worldwide-data-created.

33. See, for example, Bender et al., "On the Dangers of Stochastic Parrots: Can Language Models Be Too Big?" *Proceedings of the 2021 ACM Conference on Fairness, Accountability, and Transparency*, 610–623.

34. Strubell et al., "Energy and Policy Considerations for Deep Learning in NLP." *arXiv preprint arXiv:1906.02243* (2019).

35. Payal Dhar, "The Carbon Impact of Artificial Intelligence." *Nature Machine Intelligence* 2 (2020); Roel Dobbe and Meredith Whittaker, "AI and Climate Change: How They're Connected, and What We Can Do About It." *Medium*, October 17, 2019, https://web.archive.org/web/20191017192003/https://

medium.com/@AINowInstitute/ai-and-climate-change-how-theyre-connected-and-what-we-can-do-about-it-6aa8d0f5b32c.

36. Stefan Gössling and Andreas Humpe, "The Global Scale, Distribution and Growth of Aviation: Implications for Climate Change." *Global Environmental Change* 65 (2020), 3.

37. Susanna Twidale, "Global Energy-Related CO2 Emissions Hit Record High in 2023—IEA." *Reuters*, March 1, 2024, www.reuters.com/business/energy/global-energy-related-co2-emissions-hit-record-high-2023-iea-2024-03-01.

38. *Physics World*, "CERN's Emissions Equal to a Large Cruise Liner, Says Report." September 19, 2020, https://physicsworld.com/a/cerns-emissions-equal-to-a-large-cruise-liner-says-report.

39. The IEA explicitly denounces degrowth; is silent on biodiversity, capitalism and inequality; and relies upon negative emissions technologies like BECCS for its projections on staying within the 1.5°C target.

40. *IEA*, "Data Centres and Data Transmission Networks." https://web.archive.org/web/20240202221747/www.iea.org/energy-system/buildings/data-centres-and-data-transmission-networks.

41. De Vries, 2.

42. Luccioni et al., "Power Hungry Processing: Watts Driving the Cost of AI Deployment?" *arXiv:2311.16863*, 2023.

43. Joshua Dávila, *Blockchain Radicals: How Capitalism Ruined Crypto and How to Fix It* (Repeater, 2023), 195.

44. John Markoff, "Data Centers' Power Use Less Than Was Expected." *New York Times*, July 31, 2011, www.nytimes.com/2011/08/01/technology/data-centers-using-less-power-than-forecast-report-says.html; Jonathan Koomey and Eric Massanet, "Does Not Compute: Avoiding Pitfalls Assessing the Internet's Energy and carbon Impacts." *Joule* 5(7) (2021). (Note that Koomey has taken money from Amazon.)

45. *CoinGecko*, "Global Cryptocurrency Market Cap Charts." https://archive.is/TVuGU; Ferreboeuf et al., "Environmental Impacts of Digital Technology: 5-Year Trends and 5G Governance." *The Shift Project*, 2021, https://theshiftproject.org/wp-content/uploads/2023/04/Environmental-impacts-of-digital-technology-5-year-trends-and-5G-governance_March2021.pdf, 10.

46. *World Population Review*, "Bitcoin Mining by Country 2024." https://archive.is/wip/cPVwC.

47. *The Shift Project*, "Climate Crisis: The Unsustainable Use of Online Video." 2019, https://theshiftproject.org/wp-content/uploads/2019/07/2019-02.pdf.

48. Rohit Shewale, "YouTube Statistics For 2024 (Users, Facts & More)." *Demandsage*, January 10, 2024, www.demandsage.com/youtube-stats; Abigail Bosze, "Google Revenue Breakdown (2024)." *Doofinder*, https://archive.is/yhzfD; Lai Lin Thomala, "Monthly Active Users of Leading Online Video Apps in China as of November 2023." *Statista*, February 6, 2024, www.statista.com/statistics/910676/china-monthly-active-users-leading-online-video-apps.

49. *Stock Analysis*, "Netflix, Inc. (NFLX)." https://archive.is/wip/3UfFK; *Statista*, "Video Streaming (SVoD)—Worldwide." https://web.archive.org/

web/20240207002554/www.statista.com/outlook/dmo/digital-media/vid-eo-on-demand/video-streaming-svod/worldwide#global-comparison; Brian Dean, "Amazon Prime User and Revenue Statistics (2024)." *Backlinko*, December 13, 2023, https://backlinko.com/amazon-prime-users; Mansoor Iqbal, "Disney Plus Revenue and Usage Statistics (2024)." *Business of Apps*, January 8, 2024, www.businessofapps.com/data/disney-plus-statistics; Amrita Khalid, "YouTube Now has More Than 100 Million Premium Subscribers." *The Verge*, February 1, 2024, www.theverge.com/2024/2/1/24058265/youtube-premi-um-music-100-million-subscribers; A. Guttmann, "Revenue of Warner Bros. Discovery Inc. from 2nd Quarter 2021 to 3rd Quarter 2023, by Segment." *Statista*, December 13, 2023, www.statista.com/statistics/1304796/war-ner-bros-discovery-revenue-segment; Phil Nickinson, "The 10 Most Popular Streaming Services, Ranked by Subscriber Count." *Digital Trends*, February 23, 2024, www.digitaltrends.com/home-theater/most-popular-streaming-ser-vices-by-subscribers; Georg Szalai and Etan Vlessing, "Peacock Quarterly Loss Narrows to $825M as Streamer Hits 31M Subscribers." *The Hollywood Reporter*, January 25, 2024, www.hollywoodreporter.com/business/business-news/com-cast-earnings-peacock-loss-2023-nbcuniversal-1235805822; Tencent, "2022 Annual Report." https://static.www.tencent.com/uploads/2023/04/06/214d-ce4c53122648oob2ocfab64861ba.pdf; Baidu, "Commission file number: 000-51469," 2023, https://ir.baidu.com/static-files/eb1b6454-b72d-4ba6-9836-67804e8a2ed9; *Macrotrends*, "IQIYI Revenue 2019–2023." https://archive.is/kq3RV; Sky Canaves, "Understanding China's Video Streaming Services: Part Two." *ChinaFilmInsider*, October 1, 2019, https://chinafilmin-sider.com/cbi-video-streaming-part-two.

50. Khalid, "YouTube Now has More"; Dean, "Amazon Prime User"; Canaves, "Understanding China's Video Streaming."

51. *Gitnux*, "Pornography Industry Statistics [Fresh Research]." January 9, 2024, https://gitnux.org/pornography-industry-statistics; *Semrush*, "Traffic Analytics: Pornhub.com." February 2024, www.semrush.com/analytics/traffic/overview/?searchType=domain&q=pornhub.com; Bradley Saacks, "Inside Pornhub's Finances." *Semafor*, July 27, 2023, www.semafor.com/article/07/27/2023/inside-pornhubs-finances; Todd Spangler, "OnlyFans Users Spent $5.6 Billion on Porn-Friendly Creator Site in Fiscal 2022, up 16%." *Variety*, August 24, 2023, https://variety.com/2023/digital/news/onlyfans-creator-earnings-fiscal-year-2022-1235703824; Drew Harwell, "Inside an OnlyFans Empire: Sex, Influence and the New American Dream." *Washington Post*, November 9, 2023, www.washingtonpost.com/technology/interactive/2023/onlyfans-bryce-adams-top-earners-creator-economy.

52. Tom Hollands, "The Economics of OnlyFans." *xsrus.com*, April 24, 2020, https://xsrus.com/the-economics-of-onlyfans; *Statista*, "Highest Paid OnlyFans Accounts Ever Worldwide as of August 2022." February 2, 2024, www.statista.com/statistics/1368874/highest-paid-onlyfans-accounts.

53. Ferreboeuf et al., "Environmental Impacts of Digital Technology," 29.

54. Ibid., 33; *TrendForce*, "Top Three Equipment Manufacturers Estimated to Account for 74.5% of Global Base Station Market in 2022, Says TrendForce." August 1, 2022, www.trendforce.com/presscenter/news/20220801-11324. html; Stu Woo and Dan Strumpf, "Huawei Loses Cellular-Gear Market Share Outside China." *Wall Street Journal*, March 7, 2021, https://archive.is/cEes6; *Precedence Research*, "5g Chipset Market," https://archive.is/B2qlF.

55. For starters, many outlets have reported, without direct reference, several studies by research firm International Data Corporation (IDC) claiming that there were 500,000 data centers worldwide in 2012 and 8 million in 2019, including almost 3 million in the United States as of *both* 2006 and 2012. In other words, the IDC numbers cited appear to contradict each other. The IDC's definition includes tiny server closets and small rooms, which account for at least a third (Shehabi, et al., 22). To label a "tiny server closet" a data "center" is misleading. Most people think of a data center as a facility full of server racks. There are about 33 million small businesses in the United States, so IDC data reported in the press would imply a data "center" for one out of every 11 businesses.

56. David Mytton and Masaō Ashtine, "Sources of Data Center Energy Estimates: A Comprehensive Review." *Joule* 6(9) (2022); Malmodin et al., "ICT Sector Electricity Consumption and Greenhouse Gas Emissions—2020 Outcome." *Telecommunications Policy* (2024); Sebastian Moss, "Extinction Rebellion Protest Amazon Data Centers and Warehouse Worker Conditions Outside Irish HQ." *DCD*, November 28, 2022, www.datacenterdynamics.com/en/news/extinction-rebellion-protest-amazon-data-centers-and-warehouse-worker-conditions-outside-irish-hq.

57. Mytton and Ashtine, "Sources of Data Center Energy Estimates." One study found between 2010 and 2018, there was a 550% increase of computational workload, but only a 6% increase in energy use; see Masanet et al., "Recalibrating Global Data Center Energy-Use Estimates." *Science* 367(6481), 985.

58. *DCD*, "US Data Centers Buy 40GW of Renewable Power—Two-Thirds of the Corporate Market." March 31, 2023, www.datacenterdynamics.com/en/news/us-data-centers-buy-40gw-of-renewable-power-two-thirds-of-the-corporate-market.

59. Daniel Oberhaus, "Amazon, Google, Microsoft: Here's Who Has the Greenest Cloud." *Wired*, December 10, 2019, www.wired.com/story/amazon-google-microsoft-green-clouds-and-hyperscale-data-centers; Nicole Loher, "What Makes a Data Center Sustainable?" *Meta*, April 17, 2023, https://sustainability.fb.com/blog/2023/04/17/what-makes-a-data-center-sustainable; Zeus Kerravala, "AWS Ups Its Sustainability Efforts at Re:Invent 2022." *No Jitter*, November 29, 2022, www.nojitter.com/industry-news/aws-ups-its-sustainability-efforts-reinvent-2022; Joe Burns, "How Google is Decarbonizing its Facilities." *Facilities Dive*, October 16, 2023, www.facilitiesdive.com/news/google-2023-environmental-sustainability-building-decarbonization-strategies/696681.

60. *Global Commission on the Economics of Water*, "Turning the Tide: A Call to Collective Action." 2023, https://watercommission.org/wp-content/uploads/2023/03/Turning-the-Tide-Report-Web.pdf.

61. David Mytton, "Data Centre Water Consumption." *npj Clean Water* 4(11) (2021).

62. Sebastian Moss, "Data Center Water Usage Remains Hidden." *DCD*, October 21, 2021, www.datacenterdynamics.com/en/analysis/data-center-water-usage-remains-hidden.

63. Marston et al., "High-Resolution Water Footprints of Production of the United States." *Water Resources Research* 54(3) (2018), 2300.

64. Siddik et al., "The Environmental Footprint of Data Centers in the United States." *Environmental Research Letters* 16(6) (2021); Mytton, 2021; Kenza Bryan, "Data Centres Curbed as Pressure Grows on Electricity Grids." *Financial Times*, February 12, 2024, www.ft.com/content/53accefd-eca7-47f2-a51e-c32f3ab51ad5.

65. Li et al., "Making AI Less "Thirsty": Uncovering and Addressing the Secret Water Footprint of AI Models." *arXiv preprint arXiv:2304.03271* (2023); for a skeptical take, see *David Mytton*, "Overestimating AI's Water Footprint." April 17, 2023, https://davidmytton.blog/overestimating-ai-water-footprint.

66. Dan Swinhoe, "Re-Use, Refurb, Recycle: Circular Economy Thinking and Data Center IT Assets." *DCD*, March 8, 2022, www.datacenterdynamics.com/en/analysis/re-use-refurb-recycle-circular-economy-thinking-and-data-center-it-assets.

67. Christopher Magee and Tessaleno Deveza, "A simple Extension of Dematerialization Theory: Incorporation of Technical Progress and the Rebound Effect." *Technological Forecasting & Social Change* 117 (2017).

68. *IDC*, "Datacenter Dilemma: Balancing Capacity Demand With Environmental Responsibility." July 7, 2023, https://blogs.idc.com/2023/07/07/datacenter-dilemma-balancing-capacity-demand-with-environmental-responsibility; Ferreboeuf et al., 2021; Javier Farfan and Alena Lohrmann, "Gone with the Clouds: Estimating the Electricity and Water Footprint of Digital Data Services in Europe." *Energy Conversion and Management* 290 (2023); De Vries, 2023.

69. Kate Crawford, "Generative AI's Environmental Costs are Soaring—and Mostly Secret." *Nature*, February 20, 2024, www.nature.com/articles/d41586-024-00478-x.

5. DIGITAL ECOCIDE

1. *USDA*, "Ag and Food Sectors and the Economy." February 12, 2024, https://archive.is/wip/G6qSw; *OECD*, "How we feed the world today," https://archive.is/wip/5oncP; *Feed the Future*, "Developing Countries and the Future of Small-scale Agriculture." https://archive.is/wip/tGjw8.

2. Feed the Future; Georgina Gustin, "Industrial Agriculture, an Extraction Industry Like Fossil Fuels, a Growing Driver of Climate Change." *Inside Climate News*, January 25, 2019, https://insideclimatenews.org/news/25012019/

climate-change-agriculture-farming-consolidation-corn-soybeans-meat-crop-subsidies; *USDA*, "Farming and Farm Income," February 7, 2024, https://archive.is/wip/mED3x.

3. *USAFacts*, "What is the Current State of Agriculture in the US?" https://archive.is/wip/erPLC.

4. Timothy A. Wise, *Eating Tomorrow: Agribusiness, Family Farmers, and the Battle for the Future of Food* (The New Press, 2019), 4–5.

5. Numbers sourced from Fatima Forooq, "Top 15 Agribusiness Companies in the World By Revenue." *Yahoo! Finance*, May 28, 2023, https://finance.yahoo.com/news/top-15-agribusiness-companies-world-131844717.html.

6. Shand et al., "Food Barrons 2022: Crisis Profiteering, Digitalization and Shifting Power." *ETC Group*, September 20, 2022, www.etcgroup.org/files/files/food-barons-2022-full_sectors-final_16_sept.pdf.

7. Nils-Gerrit Wunsch, "Leading Global Exporters of Agricultural Products in 2020, by Country." *Statista*, September 12, 2022, www.statista.com/statistics/1332329/leading-countries-worldwide-by-value-of-agricultural-products-exported.

8. *EDP*, "A2E Fund—aQysta Malawi." www.edp.com/en/EDP-YES/A2E-Fund/Aqysta; Salary.com, "J. R. Luciano." www1.salary.com/J-R-Luciano-Salary-Bonus-Stock-Options-for-ARCHER-DANIELS-MIDLAND-CO.html.

9. *OECD*, "Triadic Patent Families (indicator)." www.oecd-ilibrary.org/industry-and-services/triadic-patent-families/indicator/english_6a8d1of4-en.

10. Ibid.

11. Raj Patel, "The Long Green Revolution." *The Journal of Peasant Studies* 40(1) (2012), 5.

12. Patel, 6; *WHO*, "UN Report: Global Hunger Numbers Rose to as Many as 828 Million in 2021." July 6, 2022, www.who.int/news/item/06-07-2022-un-report—global-hunger-numbers-rose-to-as-many-as-828-million-in-2021; McKay et al., "Measuring Food Insecurity in India: A Systematic Review of the Current Evidence." *Current Nutrition Reports* 12(2) (2023), 349, 355; Saatvika Radhakrishna, "India's Triumphs Over Poverty Marred by an Alarming Hunger Crisis." *The Hindu*, July 21, 2023, https://frontline.thehindu.com/news/indias-triumphs-over-poverty-marred-by-an-alarming-hunger-crisis-as-niti-aayog-report-finds-that-majority-of-the-population-cannot-afford-healthy-food/article67101938.ece.

13. As Glenn Davis Stone observes, "on the eve of the Green Revolution in 1965, Indian farmers needed 17 pounds (8 kilograms) of fertilizer to grow an average ton of food. By 1980, it took 96 pounds (44 kilograms) ... Today, India remains the world's second-highest fertilizer importer, spending US$17.3 billion in 2022." Glenn Davis Stone, "The Green Revolution is a Warning, Not a Blueprint for Feeding a Hungry Planet." *The Conversation*, October 4, 2023, https://theconversation.com/the-green-revolution-is-a-warning-not-a-blueprint-for-feeding-a-hungry-planet-182269. See also, *Raj Patel*, "How to Be Curious About the Green Revolution." August 29, 2014, https://rajpatel.

org/2014/08/29/every-factoid-is-a-mystery-how-to-think-more-clearly-about-the-green-revolution-and-other-agricultural-claims.

14. Patel, "The Long Green Revolution," 16.

15. Haley Stein, "Intellectual Property and Genetically Modified Seeds: The United States, Trade, and the Developing World." *Northwest Journal of Technology and Intellectual Property* 3(2) (2005); Bartow J. Elmore, *Seed Money: Monsanto's Past and Our Food Future* (W.W. Norton & Company, 2021); ETC Group, 2022, 14.

16. Max Ajl, *A People's Green New Deal* (Pluto, 2021), 120.

17. This data point, first established in 2009 in a study by ETC Group, was recently challenged on spurious grounds, and parroted by the Bill & Melinda Gates-funded outlet, *Our World in Data*. For further explanation, see ETC Group, "Small-Scale Farmers and Peasants Still Feed the World," 2022.

18. Chril McGreal, "How America's Food Giants Swallowed the Family Farms." *Guardian*, March 9, 2019, www.theguardian.com/environment/2019/mar/09/american-food-giants-swallow-the-family-farms-iowa.

19. *UNCCD*, "Global Land Outlook: Second Edition." 2022, www.unccd.int/sites/default/files/2022-04/UNCCD_GLO2_low-res_2.pdf, x; Ray et al., "Crop Harvests for Direct Food Use Insufficient to Meet the UN's Food Security Goal." *Nature Food* 3(5) (2022), 367; Dan Blaustein-Rejto and Chris Gambino, "Livestock Don't Contribute 14.5% of Global Greenhouse Gas Emissions." *The Breakthrough Institute*, March 20, 2023, https://thebreakthrough.org/issues/food-agriculture-environment/livestock-dont-contribute-14-5-of-global-greenhouse-gas-emissions; *FAO*, "Pathways Towards Lower Emissions—A global Assessment of the Greenhouse Gas Emissions and Mitigation Options from Livestock Agrifood Systems." 2023, https://doi.org/10.4060/cc9029en, xi.

20. Crippa et al., "Food Systems are Responsible for a Third of Global Anthropogenic GHG Emissions." *Nature Food* 2(3) (2021); Xu et al., "Global Greenhouse Gas Emissions from Animal-Based Foods Are Twice Those Of Plant-Based Foods." *Nature Food* 2(9) (2021).

21. *FoodPrint*, "How Industrial Agriculture Affects Our Soil." January 18, 2024, https://foodprint.org/issues/how-industrial-agriculture-affects-our-soil.

22. Grantham Centre, "A Sustainable Model for Intensive Agriculture." 2015, https://grantham.sheffield.ac.uk/wp-content/uploads/A-sustainable-model-for-intensive-agriculture-Grantham-Centre-briefing-note-December-2015.pdf, 2.

23. *UNCCD*, 2, 149; Burrell et al., "Anthropogenic Climate Change has Driven over 5 Million km2 of Drylands Towards Desertification." *Nature Communications* 11(1), 1; *ClimateChangePost*, "Desertification: European Scale." February 19, 2024, https://archive.is/wip/XsyfZ.

24. *FAO*, "The 10 Elements of Agroecology: Guiding the Transition to Sustainable Food and Agricultural Systems." 2018, www.fao.org/3/i9037en/i9037en.pdf, 12.

25. See also European Coordination Via Campesina, "Peasant Agroecology is a Way of Life." 2022.

26. *FAO*, 2018, 5; on resiliency, see Kerr et al., "Can Agroecology Improve Food Security and Nutrition? A Review." *Global Food Security* 29 (2021).

27. Max Ajl, "The Hypertrophic City vs The Planet of Fields." *Implosions/Explosions: Towards a Study of Planetary Urbanization* (2014).

28. Max Ajl, "How Much Will the US Way of Life © Have to Change?" *Uneven Earth*, June 10, 2019, https://unevenearth.org/2019/06/how-much-will-the-us-way-of-life-have-to-change.

29. Pavageau et al., "Money Flows: What is Holding Back Investment in Agroecological Research for Africa?" *Biovision & IPES-Food*, 2020, www.ipes-food.org/_img/upload/files/Money%20Flows_Full%20report.pdf.

30. Alexander Zaitchik, "The New Colonialist Food Economy." *The Nation*, October 2023, www.thenation.com/article/world/new-colonialist-food-economy.

31. *Bill & Melinda Gates Foundation (BMGF)*, "Bill & Melinda Gates, Rockefeller Foundations Form Alliance to Help Spur "Green Revolution" in Africa." www.gatesfoundation.org/ideas/media-center/press-releases/2006/09/foundations-form-alliance-to-help-spur-green-revolution-in-africa.

32. Stacy Malkan, "Gates Foundation Agriculture Project in Africa Flunks Review." *U.S. Right to Know*, August 28, 2023, https://usrtk.org/bill-gates/gates-foundation-agriculture-project-in-africa-flunks-review; Timothy Schwab, *The Bill Gates Problem: Reckoning with the Myth of the Good Billionaire*, 160. Rockefeller had contributed $165 million to AGRA by September 2022.

33. Bartosz Brzeziński, "'Time's Up': Critics Call for End to Western-Funded Food Program in Africa." *Politico*, September 13, 2022, www.politico.eu/article/critic-call-end-western-fund-food-program-africa.

34. Mkindi et al., "False Promises: The Alliance for a Green Revolution in Africa (AGRA)." 2020, www.rosalux.de/en/publication/id/42635. See also Timothy A. Wise, "Failing Africa's Farmers: An Impact Assessment of the Alliance for a Green Revolution in Africa." *Tufts University*, 2020, https://sites.tufts.edu/gdae/files/2020/07/20-01_Wise_FailureToYield.pdf; Timothy A. Wise, "AGRA Update: Withheld Internal Documents Reveal No Progress for Africa's Farmers." *IATP*, February 25, 2021, www.iatp.org/blog/202102/agra-update-withheld-internal-documents-reveal-no-progress-africas-farmers.

35. *AFSA*, "Press Release: 200 organisations Urge Donors to Scrap AGRA." September 7, 2021, https://afsafrica.org/press-release-200-organisations-urge-donors-to-scrap-agra; Community Alliance for Global Justice, "1: The Foundation | Rich Appetites: How Big Philanthropy is Shaping the Future of Food in Africa." *YouTube*, September 24, 2021, www.youtube.com/watch?v=g9RFCmWmg98; Million Belay & Bridget Mugambe, "Bill Gates Should Stop Telling Africans What Kind of Agriculture Africans Need." *Scientific American*, July 6, 2021, www.scientificamerican.com/article/bill-gates-should-stop-telling-africans-what-kind-of-agriculture-africans-need1.

36. Raj Patel, "No More Green Revolutions," *New Internationalist*, September 21, 2021, https://newint.org/features/2021/08/09/no-more-green-revolutions-fjf.

37. *GRAIN*, "How the Gates Foundation is Driving the Food System, in the Wrong Direction." June 17, 2021, https://grain.org/en/article/6690-how-the-gates-foundation-is-driving-the-food-system-in-the-wrong-direction.

38. Pavageau et al., "Money Flows," 4; Pascal et al., "Corporate-Led Climate Adaptation: How the Gates Foundation, Microsoft, and AGRA are Enabling the Digital Capture of African Food Systems." *AGRA Watch*, 2023, https://cagj.org/wp-content/uploads/Digital-Ag-Report.pdf.

39. Microsoft doesn't have an acronym for this, but they use "DMA" on Azure for "Data Migration Assistant," so I decided on DMAg for short.

40. Miguel A. Altieri, "Agroecology, Small Farms, and Food Sovereignty." *Monthly Review* 61(3) (2009).

41. Cover crops enrich soil, reduce erosion, and sequester carbon.

42. Jason Davidson, "Following $10 Billion Roundup Settlement, Bayer Uses Climate Program as Front to Lock in Control of Farmer Data and Sell More Roundup." *Friends of the Earth*, 2020, https://foe.org/blog/bayer-climate-program-to-control-data; *GRAIN*, "The corporate agenda behind carbon farming," February 10, 2023, https://grain.org/en/article/6947-the-corporate-agenda-behind-carbon-farming.

43. *GRAIN*, "Digital control: How Big Tech Moves into Food and Farming (and What it Means)." January 21, 2021, https://grain.org/en/article/6595-digital-control-how-big-tech-moves-into-food-and-farming-and-what-it-means.

44. Kellsey Ruppel, "DigiFarm Creates a Sustainable Future for Agriculture and Achieves 30% Cost Savings with OCI." *Oracle*, October 11, 2023, www.oracle.com/customers/digifarm-case-study; Parlasca et al., "Use of Mobile Financial Services Among Farmers in Africa: Insights from Kenya." *Global Food Security* 32 (2022), 1. This comports with a press release that said 7,000 loans (for a population of 7 million farmers, or 0.1%) had been dispersed to Kenyan farmers 6 months after Digifarm's launch. The press reported 200,000 loan applications had been made by 2019. See *Capital Business*, "Safaricom's Digifarm Disburses 7,000 Loans to Farmers in Six Months." May 22, 2018, www.capitalfm.co.ke/business/2018/05/safaricoms-digifarm-disburses-7000-loans-farmers-six-months; *Mercy Corps*, "Building the DigiFarm Innovation Platform—The Journey to One Million Farmers." May 27, 2019, www.mercycorpsagrifin.org/building-the-digifarm-innovation-platform-the-journey-to-one-million-farmers.

45. Fiocco et al., "Agtech: Breaking Down the Farmer Adoption Dilemma." *McKinsey & Company*, February 7, 2023, www.mckinsey.com/industries/agriculture/our-insights/agtech-breaking-down-the-farmer-adoption-dilemma; *RELX*, "2021 RELX Emerging Tech Executive Report—Executive Summary." 2021, www.relx.com/~/media/Files/R/RELX-Group/documents/press-releases/2021/2021-relx-emerging-tech-exec-summary.pdf.

46. James Lowenberg-DeBoer and Bruce Erickson, "Setting the Record Straight on Precision Agriculture Adoption." *Agronomy Journal* 111(4) (2019), 1552.

47. Louise Story, "Anywhere the Eye Can See, It's Likely to See an Ad." *New York Times*, January 15, 2007, www.nytimes.com/2007/01/15/business/

media/15everywhere.html; *MDI*, "Adults Spend Almost 10 Hours Per Day with The Media, But Note Only 150 Ads." September 22, 2014, www.mediadynamicsinc.com/uploads/files/PR092214-Note-only-150-Ads-2mk.pdf.

48. Noam Chomsky, "Every Innocent Killed Creates Ten New Enemies." *DW*, June 17,2013,https://corporate.dw.com/en/every-innocent-killed-creates-ten-new-enemies/a-16962176.

49. Andrew Simms and Leo Murray, *Badvertising: Polluting Our Minds and Fuelling Climate Chaos* (Pluto, 2023), 39.

50. Ibid., 40.

51. Ibid.

52. *Statista*, "Companies With Largest Share of Digital Advertising Revenue Worldwide in 2023." August 29, 2023, www.statista.com/statistics/290629/digital-ad-revenue-share-of-major-ad-selling-companies-worldwide.

53. Simms and Murray, *Badvertising*, 40. Additional studies need to be conducted in the Global South. See, e.g., Jing Wang and Yongquan Huo, "Effect of Materialism on Pro-environmental Behavior Among Youth in China: The Role of Nature Connectedness," *Frontiers in Psychology* 13 (2022).

54. Muñoz-Villamizar et al., "The Environmental Impact of Fast Shipping Ecommerce in Inbound Logistics Operations: A Case Study in Mexico." *Journal of Cleaner Production* 283 (2021); Schöder et al., "The Impact of E-Commerce Development on Urban Logistics Sustainability." *Open Journal of Social Sciences* 4(3) (2016).

55. Jack Flynn, "21 Compelling Retail Statistics [2023]: How Many Retailers Are In The US?" *Zippa*, February 23, 2023, www.zippia.com/advice/retail-statistics; Yihan Ma, "E-commerce Share of Total Retail Sales in Consumer Goods in China from 2014 to 2023." *Statista*, February 2, 2024, www.statista.com/statistics/1129915/china-ecommerce-share-of-retail-sales.

56. Numbers compiled from *Statista*, "Global Parcel Shipping Volume in 2022, by Selected Country (in Million Parcels)*." September 21, 2023, www.statista.com/statistics/1140055/parcel-shipping-volume-worldwide-country.

57. Katharina Buchholz, "The Parcel Shipping Boom Continues." *Statista*, October 7, 2022, www.statista.com/chart/10922/parcel-shipping-volume-and-parcel-spend-in-selected-countries.

58. Jenna McNamee, "Mercado Libre Users in Brazil Can Now Pay For Purchases with Mercado Coin." *Insider Intelligence*, August 24, 2022, www.insiderintelligence.com/content/mercado-libre-mercado-coin.

59. Martin Armstrong, "No Match for Amazon." *Statista*, February 15, 2022, www.statista.com/chart/26846/ecommerce-brands-by-revenue-europe.

60. Sayan Chakraborty, "Amazon falls behind Walmart in battle for India's online shoppers," *Nikkei*, May 15, 2023, https://asia.nikkei.com/Business/Business-Spotlight/Amazon-falls-behind-Walmart-in-battle-for-India-s-online-shoppers.

61. Wang Zhuoqiong, "Walmart China's Q4 Points to Retail Health." *China Daily*, February 28, 2023, www.chinadaily.com.cn/a/202302/28/WS63fd4ab0a310 57c47ebb129a.html.

62. *GP. Bullhound*, "Q2 insights into Digital Commerce." July 20, 2023, www. gpbullhound.com/articles/q2-insights-into-digital-commerce, 11.

63. *Activate*, "Activate Technology & Media Outlook 2024." 2023, www.activate. com/insights-archive/Activate-Technology-and-Media-Outlook-2024.pdf, 53.

64. Matthew Johnston, "How Alibaba Makes Money." *Investopedia*, January 31, 2023, www.investopedia.com/articles/investing/121714/how-does-alibaba-make-money-simple-guide.asp.

65. Matsakis et al., "How Shein Beat Amazon at its Own Game—and Reinvented Fast Fashion," *Rest of World*, December 14, 2021, https://restofworld.org/2021/ how-shein-beat-amazon-and-reinvented-fast-fashion.

66. *Bloomberg*, "Temu's Win Over Shein in the US Is Hurting Its Bottom Line." *Business of Fashion*, October 24, 2023, www.businessoffashion.com/news/retail/ temus-win-over-shein-in-the-us-is-hurting-its-bottom-line; Zhou et al., "How China Took Over the World's Online Shopping Carts." *Rest of World*, November 14, 2023, https://restofworld.org/2023/china-shopping-shein-temu-global-rise, Jing Yang, "Shein's Revenue Surged More Than 40%, Likely Surpassing Zara." *The Information*, https://archive.is/idAbV; Julienna Law, "Battle of China's E-Commerce Titans: Temu Parent Emerges Ahead of Alibaba." *Jing Daily*, December 6, 2023, https://jingdaily.com/posts/ pinduoduo-temu-alibaba-ecommerce-market-value.

67. Some foreign investors benefit as well; Shein's investors include firms from China (IDG Capital, Sequoia Capital, HongShan), Singapore (JAFCO Asia), Hong Kong (Greenwoods Asset Management), the UAE (Mubadala), and the United States (Tiger Global, General Atlantic, SPARC Group). In November 2023, the company filed for a US IPO, which will be underwritten by Goldman Sachs, JPMorgan Chase, and Morgan Stanley. Underwriters typically make 2-7% of the total offering size. Pedro Longa, "Underwriting Your Underwriter (IPO)." *Forbes*, April 20, 2023, www.forbes.com/sites/ forbesfinancecouncil/2023/04/20/underwriting-your-underwriter-ipo. Shein hopes to debut at $90 billion.

68. *ECDB*, "Amazon & eBay: China-Based Sellers on Western Marketplaces Grow." January 17, 2024, https://ecommercedb.com/insights/china-based-sellers-increasingly-important-on-western-marketplaces/3986.

69. Chloe Cornish and Eleanor Olcott, "Reliance Seeks Retail Dominance in India with Comeback Deal for Shein." *Financial Times*, May 26, 2023, www. ft.com/content/a863317c-9baf-4a6f-9e72-1c976af7dfdd.

70. James Carbone, "Vietnam Becomes an Option for Low-Cost Electronics Manufacturing." *Supply Chain Connect*, April 27, 2017, www.supply chainconnect.com/supply-chain-technology/article/21866768/vietnam-becomes-an-option-for-low-cost-electronics-manufacturing.

71. Vauhini Vara, "Fast, Cheap, and Out of Control: Inside Shein's Sudden Rise." *Wired*, May 4, 2022, www.wired.com/story/fast-cheap-out-of-control-inside-rise-of-shein.

72. Timo Kollbrunner, "Toiling Away for Shein: Looking Behind the Shiny Façade of the Chinese 'Ultra-Fast Fashion' Giant." *Public Eye*, November 2021, https://stories.publiceye.ch/en/shein; Islam et al., "Impact of Global Retailers' Unfair Practices on Bangladeshi Suppliers During Covid-19." *University of Aberdeen*; Victoria Waldersee, "EXCLUSIVE Chinese Retailer Shein Lacks Disclosures, Made False Statements About Factories." *Reuters*, August 6, 2021, www.reuters.com/business/retail-consumer/exclusive-chinese-retailer-shein-lacks-disclosures-made-false-statements-about-2021-08-06.

73. Myunghee Lee and Emir Yazici, "China's Surveillance and Repression in Xinjiang." In Michael Kwet (ed.), *The Cambridge Handbook of Race and Surveillance* (Cambridge University Press, 2023), 166–189.

74. Sabrina Escobar, "Shein Could Capture 'Major Market Share' in Apparel. It's a Bad Sign for Other Retailers." *Barron's*, June 26, 2023, https://archive.is/9qfDX.

75. *European Parliament*, "Textiles and the Environment." 2022, www.europarl.europa.eu/RegData/etudes/BRIE/2022/729405/EPRS_BRI(2022)729405_EN.pdf.

76. Owen Mulhern, "The 10 Essential Fast Fashion Statistics." *Earth.org*, July 24, 2022, https://earth.org/fast-fashion-statistics; *World Bank*, "How Much Do Our Wardrobes Cost to the Environment?" September 23, 2019, www.worldbank.org/en/news/feature/2019/09/23/costo-moda-medio-ambiente.

77. Niinimäki et al., "The Environmental Price of Fast Fashion." *Nature Reviews Earth & Environment* 1(4) (2020).

78. World Bank, 2019; Mulhern; Majorie van Elven, "People Do Not Wear At Least 50 Percent of Their Wardrobes, Says Study." *Fashion United*, August 16, 2018, https://fashionunited.uk/news/fashion/people-do-not-wear-at-least-50-percent-of-their-wardrobes-according-to-study/2018081638356; Majorie van Elven, "Infographic: The Extent of Overproduction in the Fashion Industry." *Fashion United*, December 12, 2018, https://fashionunited.uk/news/fashion/infographic-the-extent-of-overproduction-in-the-fashion-industry/2018121240500; Vara; Matthieu Guinebault, "Microplastics: Fashion's Impact on the World's Oceans." *Fashion Network*, April 18, 2023, https://ww.fashionnetwork.com/news/Microplastics-fashion-s-impact-on-the-world-s-oceans,1507610.html; Karen Shedlock and Stephanie Feldstein, "At What Cost? Unraveling the Harms of the Fast Fashion Industry." *Center for Biological Diversity*, 2023, www.biologicaldiversity.org/programs/population_and_sustainability/pdfs/Unravelling-Harms-of-Fast-Fashion-Full-Report-2023-02.pdf; *FZN*, "Why Fashion Revolution Week Still Matters and How to Get Involved in 2021." April 19, 2021, www.fashionz.co.nz/why-fashion-revolution-week-still-matters-and-how-to-get-involved-in-2021; Tobin et al., "Here's What Actually Happens to All Your Online Shopping

Returns." *Rest of World*, February 14, 2022, https://restofworld.org/2022/shein-online-shopping-returns-what-happens.

79. Niinimäki et al., "The Environmental Price of Fast Fashion," 4.

80. Ibid., 4.

81. Parvez et al., "Health Consequences of Exposure to e-Waste: An Updated Systematic Review." *Lancet Planetary Health* 5(12) (2021), e905.

82. *WHO*, "Children and Digital Dumpsites: E-Waste Exposure and Child Health." 2021, https://iris.who.int/bitstream/handle/10665/341718/9789240023901-eng.pdf.

83. Ibid., vi.

84. Daniil Filipenco, "World Waste: Statistics by Country and Short Facts." *Development Aid*, March 7, 2023, www.developmentaid.org/news-stream/post/158158/world-waste-statistics-by-country; Emily Holden, "US Produces Far More Waste and Recycles Far Less of It Than Other Developed Countries." *Guardian*, July 3, 2019, www.theguardian.com/us-news/2019/jul/02/us-plastic-waste-recycling; Benedetta Cotta, "What Goes Around, Comes Around? Access And Allocation Problems in Global North–South Waste Trade." *International Environmental Agreements: Politics, Law and Economics* 20(2) (2020).

85. Kris De Decker, "How Circular is the Circular Economy?" *Resilience*, November 12, 2018, www.resilience.org/stories/2018-11-12/how-circular-is-the-circular-economy. These numbers comport with a 2020 report by *Circle Economy* finding that the global economy is only 8.6% circular (*Circle Economy*, "The Circularity Gap Report 2020." 2020, https://assets.website-files.com/5e185aa4d27bcf348400ed82/5e26ead616b6d1d157ff4293_20200120%20-%20CGR%20Global%20-%20Report%20web%20single%20page%20-%20210x297mm%20-%20compressed.pdf).

86. De Decker, "How Circular is the Circular Economy?"

87. Third World Network, "Toxic Waste Dumping in the Third World: Third World Network." *Race & Class* 30(3) (1989); Jennifer Clapp, *Toxic Exports: The Transfer of Hazardous Wastes from Rich to Poor Countries* (Cornell University Press, 2010); BaselAction, "Exporting Harm: The High-Tech Trashing of Asia." *YouTube*, May 16, 2013, www.youtube.com/watch?v=yDSWGV3jGek; Cassandra Profita and Jes Burns, "Recycling Chaos In U.S. As China Bans 'Foreign Waste.'" *NPR*, December 9, 2017, www.npr.org/2017/12/09/568797388/recycling-chaos-in-u-s-as-china-bans-foreign-waste; Brendan Lui, "US Waste Exporting Explained." *rePurpose*, April 16, 2019, https://repurpose.global/blog/post/us-waste-exporting-explained; *WHO*, 2021, xiii, 4.

88. *Basel Action Network*, "Secret Tracking Project Finds that Your Old Electronic Waste Gets Exported to Developing Countries." September 15, 2016, www.ban.org/news-new/2016/9/15/secret-tracking-project-finds-that-your-old-electronic-waste-gets-exported-to-developing-countries; Hiroko Tabuchi and Michael Corkey, "Countries Tried to Curb Trade in Plastic Waste. The U.S. Is Shipping More." *New York Times*, March 12, 2021, www.nytimes.com/2021/03/12/climate/plastics-waste-export-ban.html.

89. Tong et al., "Ecological Unequal Exchange: Quantifying Emissions of Toxic Chemicals Embodied in the Global Trade of Chemicals, Products, and Waste." *Environmental Research Letters* 17(4) (2022).

90. *ERI*, "10 Staggering Electronic Waste Facts in 2022." August 22, 2022, https://eridirect.com/blog/2022/08/10-staggering-electronic-waste-facts-in-2022; Tong et al., 1; Don Campbell, "More Developed Countries Dumping Toxic E-Waste in Global South, U of T Researchers Find." *University of Toronto*, April 13, 2022, www.utoronto.ca/news/more-developed-countries-dumping-toxic-e-waste-global-south-u-t-researchers-find. Global South countries recycle their electronics at an even lower rate than wealthy countries—not surprising, given their less developed state of logistics infrastructure.

91. *PACE and WEF*, "A New Circular Vision for Electronics: Time for a Global Reboot." 2018, www3.weforum.org/docs/WEF_A_New_Circular_Vision_for_Electronics.pdf, 14.

92. Asad Hamir, "Tech Waste Is a Danger to Us All." *Scientific American*, February 16, 2020, https://blogs.scientificamerican.com/observations/tech-waste-is-a-danger-to-us-all; WHO, 2021, vi, xiii; *PACE and WEF*, "A New Circular Vision for Electronics," 5.

93. Kang-Chun Cheng, "Scrappy Endeavor." *Earth Island Journal*, 2021, www.earthisland.org/journal/index.php/magazine/entry/scrappy-endeavor.

94. Hamir, "Tech Waste Is a Danger to Us All."

95. Cheng, "Scrappy Endeavor."

96. Owusu-Sekyere et al., "Assessing Data in the Informal E-Waste Sector: The Agbogbloshie Scrapyard." *Waste Management* 139 (2022); Daum et al., "Toward a More Sustainable Trajectory for E-Waste Policy: A Review of a Decade of E-Waste Research in Accra, Ghana." *International Journal of Environmental Research and Public Health* 142(2) (2017); Jo Kuper and Martin Hojsik, "Poisoning the Poor: Electronic Waste in Ghana." *Greenpeace*, 2008, https://wayback.archive-it.org/9650/20200513123835/http://p3-raw.greenpeace.org/international/Global/international/planet-2/report/2008/9/poisoning-the-poor-electonic.pdf.

97. Peter Yeung, "The Toxic Effects of Electronic Waste in Accra, Ghana." *Bloomberg*, May 29, 2019, www.bloomberg.com/news/articles/2019-05-29/the-rich-world-s-electronic-waste-dumped-in-ghana.

98. Yeung, "The Toxic Effects of Electronic Waste."; Chandra Steele, "Cleaning Up the E-Waste Mess: Big Tech Needs to Do More." *PCMag*, April 19, 2021, www.pcmag.com/news/cleaning-up-the-e-waste-mess-big-tech-needs-to-do-more.

99. Ibid.

6. THE BIG TECH MILITARY MACHINE

1. *Democracy Now!*, "The U.S. Has 750 Overseas Military Bases, and Continues to Build More to Encircle China." February 14, 2023, www.democracynow.org/2023/2/14/david_vine_us_bases_china_philippines; David Vine, *The*

United States of War: A Global History of America's Endless Conflicts, from Columbus to the Islamic State (California University Press, 2020), 138–184.

2. Akkerman et al., "Climate Collateral: How Military Spending Accelerates Climate Breakdown." *Transnational Institute*, 2022, www.tni.org/files/2022-11/Climate%20Collateral%20Report%20-%20TNI%20-%20final%20web.pdf.

3. Rich Whitney, "US Provides Military Assistance to 73 Percent of World's Dictatorships." *Truthout*, September 23, 2017, https://truthout.org/articles/us-provides-military-assistance-to-73-percent-of-world-s-dictatorships.

4. George Kennan, "Review Of Current Trends U.S. Foreign Policy." 1948, https://archive.is/xSd2a.

5. See Noam Chomsky, *What Uncle Sam Really Wants*.

6. Quoted in Walter Lafeber, *Inevitable revolutions: The United States in Central America* (W.W. Norton & Company, 2020), 107.

7. Elizabeth Becker, "Kissinger Tapes Describe Crises, War and Stark Photos of Abuse." *New York Times*, May 27, 2004, www.nytimes.com/2004/05/27/us/kissinger-tapes-describe-crises-war-and-stark-photos-of-abuse.html.

8. Alfred McCoy, "Imperial Mimesis: Migration of Surveillance from the Colonial Philippines to the United States." In Michael Kwet (ed.), *The Cambridge Handbook*, pp. 33–56.

9. Ibid.

10. Julian Assange, "The Banality of 'Don't Be Evil.'" *New York Times*, June 1, 2013, www.nytimes.com/2013/06/02/opinion/sunday/the-banality-of-googles-dont-be-evil.html.

11. *Reuters*, "NSA Infiltrates Servers of China Telecom Giant Huawei: Report." March 23, 2014, www.reuters.com/article/us-usa-security-china-nsa-idUSBREA2LoPD20140322.

12. In *Justice.gov*, "House Oversight and Government Reform Committee Holds Hearing on Terrorist Travel." December 17, 2015, www.justice.gov/oip/foia-library/general_topics/social_media_surveillance_06_11_20/download.

13. Quoted in Paul N. Edwards, *The Closed World: Computers and the Politics of Discourse in Cold War America* (MIT Press, 1997), 43.

14. Franklin Kramer, "The Sixth Domain: The Role of the Private Sector in Warfare." *Atlantic Council*, 2023, www.atlanticcouncil.org/wp-content/uploads/2023/10/The-sixth-domain-The-role-of-the-private-sector-in-warfare-Oct16.pdf.

15. Michael Kwet, "Google, Big Tech and the US War Machine in the Global South." *Counterpunch*, April 27, 2018, www.counterpunch.org/2018/04/27/google-big-tech-and-the-us-war-machine-in-the-global-south.

16. Jack Poulson, "Easy as PAI (Publicly Available Information)." *Tech Inquiry*, September 10, 2021, https://techinquiry.org/EasyAsPAI/resources/EasyAsPAI.pdf; Jack Poulson, "What We Know About Project Maven, Reapers, and Ukraine." *Tech Inquiry*, March 15, 2023, https://techinquiry.org/?article=maven-reapers-ukraine.

17. *Microsoft*, "Operation AI: Defense Digs into Data." 2019, https://web.archive.org/web/20200618023310/https://discover.microsoft.com/government-podcast-series-2-episode-3-defense-digs-into-data.

18. Michael Kwet, "The Big Tech Behind Israel's Digital Apartheid." *Truthdig*, October 26, 2023, www.truthdig.com/articles/the-big-tech-behind-israels-digital-apartheid.

19. Deborah Bach, "U.S. Army to Use Hololens Technology in High-Tech Headsets for Soldiers." *Microsoft*, June 8, 2021, https://news.microsoft.com/source/features/digital-transformation/u-s-army-to-use-hololens-technology-in-high-tech-headsets-for-soldiers.

20. Charles Riley and Samuel Burke, "Microsoft CEO Defends US Military Contract that Some Employees Say Crosses a Line." *CNN*, February 25, 2019, https://edition.cnn.com/2019/02/25/tech/augmented-reality-microsoft-us-military; Doug Richardson, "Sensors for Armoured Vehicles." *European Security & Defence*, 2018, 93.

21. Yarden Katz, "How Microsoft is Invested in Israeli Settler-Colonialism." *Mondoweiss*, March 15, 2021, https://mondoweiss.net/2021/03/how-microsoft-is-invested-in-israeli-settler-colonialism.

22. *Microsoft*, "Microsoft Combat Flight Simulator: WWII—Europe Series." 1998, www.scribd.com/document/556804684/Microsoft-Combat-Flight-Simulator-Manual-PC; Ross Wilkers, "Microsoft, Navy Sign $700M Software License Deal." *Govcon Wire*, July 6, 2012, www.govconwire.com/2012/07/microsoft-navy-sign-700m-software-license-deal; Edvard Pettersson, "Amazon Wins Ruling for $600 Million CIA Cloud Contract." *Bloomberg*, October 8, 2013, www.bloomberg.com/news/articles/2013-10-07/amazon-wins-ruling-for-600-million-cia-cloud-contract; Michael Peck, "Amazon Commercial Cloud Tapped for GEOINT." *DefenseNews*, December 10, 2014, www.defensenews.com/global/the-americas/2014/12/10/amazon-commercial-cloud-tapped-for-geoint; *Microsoft Europe*, "Microsoft at the Heart of NATO's Connected Forces Initiative." January 11, 2014, https://news.microsoft.com/europe/2014/11/01/microsoft-at-the-heart-of-natos-connected-forces-initiative; Europe Security & Defence, "Periscope," 4.

23. Christian Sorensen, Jack Poulson, Annie Jacobsen, and Roberto J. González are notable exceptions.

24. Outside of these four projects, academics have narrowly focused on automated warfare (e.g., "killer robots") and cyber warfare.

25. Thales, "The Connected Digital Battlespace with Thales and Microsoft." *YouTube*, February 18, 2022, www.youtube.com/watch?v=qSuO7hlpur8.

26. Gus MacGregor-Millar and Kate Maxwell, "Microsoft at Eurosatory: Modernizing and Enhancing the Defense Industry." *Microsoft*, June 2, 2022, www.microsoft.com/en-us/industry/blog/government/2022/06/02/microsoft-at-eurosatory-modernizing-and-enhancing-the-defense-industry.

27. *Defence24*, "Technologies in the Army. How Does Microsoft Cooperate with the Military?" *YouTube*, October 21, 2021, www.youtube.com/watch?v=-Sp6nYZM89g.

28. Ibid.
29. Microsoft, "Operation AI."
30. Northrop Grumman, "Northrop Grumman to Develop Enhanced Joint C4ISR and Mission Planning Capabilities Using Microsoft ESP." November 27, 2007, https://web.archive.org/web/20201026165520/https://news.northrop grumman.com/news/releases/northrop-grumman-to-develop-enhanced-joint-c4isr-and-mission-planning-capabilities-using-microsoft-esp.
31. Colin Demarest, "Lockheed and Microsoft Collaborating on 5G Military Tech." *DefenseNews*, February 28, 2022, www.defensenews.com/battlefield-tech/it-networks/5g/2022/02/28/lockheed-and-microsoft-collaborating-on-5g-military-tech.
32. *Aviation Pros*, "Lockheed Martin, Microsoft Announce Landmark Agreement On Classified Cloud, Advanced Technologies For Department Of Defense." November 16, 2022, www.aviationpros.com/aircraft/defense/press-release/21287408/lockheed-martin-lockheed-martin-microsoft-announce-landmark-agreement-on-classified-cloud-advanced-technologies-for-department-of-defense.
33. Colin Demarest, "Cloud-friendly Air Force has Eyes on Pentagon's JWCC Contract." *DefenseNews*, December 15, 2022, www.defensenews.com/smr/cloud/2022/12/15/cloud-friendly-air-force-has-eyes-on-pentagons-jwcc-contract.
34. *Intel*, "Federal and Aerospace Technology for Edge-to-Cloud." https://archive.is/wip/w8Gxe; *Cisco*, "Defense Agencies Modernizing Core IT Case Study." July 18, 2021, www.cisco.com/c/en/us/solutions/collateral/industries/government/military-defense-case-study.html; *Nvidia*, "Holistically Advancing AI within the Department of Defense to Meet the Challenges of Today and Tomorrow." 2021, www.nvidia.com/en-us/on-demand/session/gtcspring21-se2411.
35. Roberto J. González, "How Big Tech and Silicon Valley are Transforming the Military-Industrial Complex." April 17, 2024, https://watson.brown.edu/costsofwar/files/cow/imce/papers/2023/2024/Silicon%20Valley%20MIC.pdf.
36. Annie Jacobsen, *First Platoon: A Story of Modern War in the Age of Identity Dominance* (Dutton, 2021), 124–140.
37. Brown University, "Costs of War." https://archive.ph/wip/NDfYv.
38. See, for example, Jack Poulson's work at Tech Inquiry.
39. Barry Sanders, *The Green Zone: The Environmental Costs of Militarism* (AK Press, 2009), 22.
40. Ibid., 36.
41. Ibid., 41–55.
42. Ibid., 51–52.
43. Lorraine Mallinder, "'Elephant in the Room': The US Military's Devastating Carbon Footprint." *Al Jazeera*, December 12, 2023, www.aljazeera.com/news/2023/12/12/elephant-in-the-room-the-us-militarys-devastating-carbon-footprint.

44. Neta Crawford, "Pentagon Fuel Use, Climate Change, and the Costs of War." 2019, https://watson.brown.edu/costsofwar/files/cow/imce/papers/Pentagon%20Fuel%20Use%2C%20Climate%20Change%20and%20the%20Costs%20of%20War%20Revised%20November%202019%20Crawford.pdf, 20; Neta Crawford, *The Pentagon, Climate Change, and War: Charting the Rise and Fall of U.S. Military Emissions* (MIT Press, 2022), 15.

45. Stuart Parkinson, "The Carbon Boot-Print of the Military." *Responsible Science* 2 (2020).

46. Elizabeth Warren, "Our Military Can Help Lead the Fight In Combating Climate Change." *Warren for Senate*, May 15, 2019, https://elizabethwarren.com/plans/military-combat-climate-change.

47. Akkerman et al., "Climate Collateral."

48. Jorgenson et al., "Guns versus Climate: How Militarization Amplifies the Effect of Economic Growth on Carbon Emissions." *American Sociological Review* 88(3) (2023).

49. Ed McNally, "Green Empire?" *Sidecar*, February 2, 2023, https://newleftreview.org/sidecar/posts/green-empire.

50. Not that it would truly matter, but the Biden administration's Executive Order 14057 exempts the military and national security from its climate mitigation pledges.

51. Hanson et al., "Warfare in Biodiversity Hotspots." *Society for Conservation Biology* 23(3) (2009).

52. Jon Mitchell, *Poisoning the Pacific: The US Military's Secret Dumping of Plutonium, Chemical Weapons, and Agent Orange* (Rowman & Littlefield, 2020), 84.

53. Ibid., 130.

54. Ornstein et al., "The Children of Agent Orange." *ProPublica*, December 16, 2016, www.propublica.org/article/the-children-of-agent-orange. See also, Alexander Durie, "Agent Orange Case: After Defeat, Woman, 79, Vows to Keep Up Fight." *Al Jazeera*, May 12, 2021, www.aljazeera.com/news/2021/5/12/agent-orange-case-after-defeat-woman-79-vows-to-keep-up-fight.

55. De Klerk et al., "Climate Damage Caused by Russia's War in Ukraine." 2023, https://climatefocus.com/wp-content/uploads/2022/11/clim-damage-by-russia-war-12months.pdf; Guillot et al., "The Environmental Scars of Russia's War in Ukraine." *Politico*, February 21, 2023, www.politico.eu/article/environment-scars-russia-war-ukraine-climate-crisis; Emily Anthes, "A 'Silent Victim': How Nature Becomes a Casualty of War." *New York Times*, April 13, 2022, www.nytimes.com/2022/04/13/science/war-environmental-impact-ukraine.html; Brian Sabbe, "The Ukraine War, Environmental Destruction and the Question Of Ecocide." *IPIS*, October 17, 2023, https://ipisresearch.be/weekly-briefing/the-ukraine-war-environmental-destruction-and-the-question-of-ecocide; *UNEP*, "The Environmental Impact of the Conflict in Ukraine: A Preliminary Review." 2022, https://wedocs.unep.org/bitstream/handle/20.500.11822/40746/environmental_impact_Ukraine_conflict.pdf.

56. *Al Jazeera,* "How Much Environmental Damage is Israel's War on Gaza Causing?" December 14, 2023, www.youtube.com/watch?v=6OT8t1UGDdg.

57. Ahmed Abofoul, "Israel's Ecological Apartheid in the Occupied Palestinian Territory." *OpinioJuris,* October 22, 2021, http://opiniojuris.org/2021/10/22/israels-ecological-apartheid-in-the-occupied-palestinian-territory.

58. Hsiang et al., "Quantifying the Influence of Climate on Human Conflict." *Science* 341(6151) (2013); Mach et al., "Climate as a Risk Factor for Armed Conflict." *Nature* 571 (2019).

7. SURVEIL AND PUNISH

1. Njeri Wangari, "In Africa's First 'Safe City,' Surveillance Reigns." *Coda,* November 8, 2023, www.codastory.com/authoritarian-tech/africa-surveillance-china-magnum.

2. Malcolm Ray, *Free Fall: Why South African Universities are in a Race Against Time* (Bookstorm, 2017).

3. Laurel Wamsley, "In Reckoning With Confederate Monuments, Other Countries Could Provide Examples." *NPR,* August 22, 2017, www.npr.org/sections/thetwo-way/2017/08/22/545308125/in-reckoning-with-confederate-monuments-other-countries-could-provide-examples.

4. See Noam Chomsky, "The Soviet Union Versus Socialism." *Our Generation,* 1986, https://chomsky.info/1986____.

5. See Arnim Scheidel et al., "Environmental Conflicts and Defenders: A Global Overview." *Global Environmental Change* (63) (2020) finding that indigenous environmental defenders face disproportionately high rates of violence.

6. Jules Roscoe, "FBI Terrorism Docs Show Agency Investigated Greenpeace, Other Environmental Organizations." July 20, 2022, *VICE,* www.vice.com/en/article/3adbd8/fbi-terrorism-docs-show-agency-investigated-greenpeace-other-environmental-organizations.

7. Jenna Bitar, "6 Ways Government Is Going After Environmental Activists." *ACLU,* February 6, 2018, www.aclu.org/news/free-speech/6-ways-government-going-after-environmental-activists.

8. *Privacy International,* "How to Avoid Social Media Monitoring: A Guide for Climate Activists." December 9, 2022, https://privacyinternational.org/long-read/5000/how-avoid-social-media-monitoring-guide-climate-activists.

9. Brown et al., "Leaked Documents Reveal Counterterrorism Tactics Used at Standing Rock to 'Defeat Pipeline Insurgencies.'" *The Intercept,* May 27, 2017, https://theintercept.com/2017/05/27/leaked-documents-reveal-security-firms-counterterrorism-tactics-at-standing-rock-to-defeat-pipeline-insurgencies; Brown et al., "Standing Rock Documents Expose Inner Workings of 'Surveillance-Industrial Complex.'" *The Intercept,* June 3, 2017, https://theintercept.com/2017/06/03/standing-rock-documents-expose-inner-workings-of-surveillance-industrial-complex.

10. Levi Rickert, "Standing Rock Water Protector Red Fawn Fallis Released from Federal Prison." *Native News Online,* September 11, 2020, https://

nativenewsonline.net/currents/standing-rock-water-protector-red-fawn-fallis-released-from-federal-prison.

11. Quoted in Ali Hines, "Decade of Defiance." *Global Witness*, May 10, 2023, www.globalwitness.org/en/campaigns/environmental-activists/decade-defiance.

12. *Sida*, "Environmental Defenders Under Attack: The Threats Facing People Who Protect Nature." 2021, https://cdn.naturskyddsforeningen.se/uploads/2021/05/11102844/environmental_defenders_under_attack_eng.pdf, 35.

13. Publications and activism around border patrol tends to take a more integrated approach. See, e.g., works by Mijente, Todd Miller, and the Transnational Institute. On the history of police tech in the US, see Brian Jefferson, *Digitize and Punish: Racial Criminalization in the Digital Age* (University of Minnesota Press, 2020).

14. See Michael Kwet, "Apartheid in the Shadows: The USA, IBM and South Africa's Digital Police State." *Counterpunch*, May 3, 2017, www.counterpunch.org/2017/05/03/apartheid-in-the-shadows-the-usa-ibm-and-south-africas-digital-police-state.

15. Ibid.

16. I attempted to publish the expose in South African press outlets *Mail & Guardian* and *Daily Maverick*, but they turned me down.

17. Michael Kwet, "People's Tech for People's Power: A Guide to Digital Self-Defense and Empowerment." *Right2Know*, 3; *Drive with John Perlman*, "Vumacam and the JMPD." October 24, 2023, https://omny.fm/shows/afternoon-drive-702/vumacam-and-the-jmpd-the-key-partner-in-the-integr.

18. Michael Kwet, "Smart CCTV Networks Are Driving an AI-Powered Apartheid in South Africa." *Motherboard*, November 22, 2019, www.vice.com/en/article/pa7nek/smart-cctv-networks-are-driving-an-ai-powered-apartheid-in-south-africa.

19. Martin Murray, *The Infrastructures of Security: Technologies of Risk Management in Johannesburg* (University of Michigan Press, 2022).

20. Kwet, "Smart CCTV."

21. *Microsoft*, "SafeCity Public Space Cameras, Powered by Vumacam." https://archive.is/wip/HDz9I.

22. Lesufi previously championed tech-fixes via Gauteng's "paperless classrooms" initiative which resulted in the reception of devices at a handful of schools (dubbed "Classrooms of the Future"), which have thus far amounted to little, if not a decline in test scores (Michael Kwet, "Digital Colonialism: South Africa's Education Transformation in the Shadow of Silicon Valley." PhD dissertation, 2019, https://papers.ssrn.com/sol3/papers.cfm?abstract_id=3496049; Tebogo Monama, "Trails, Tribulations of Paperless Classrooms." *IOL*, February 12, 2016, www.iol.co.za/news/south-africa/gauteng/trails-tribulations-of-paperless-classrooms-1983931). Nevertheless, Lesufi is also pursuing a project to make the Gauteng a "cashless province."

23. Michael Kwet, "The Microsoft Police State: Mass Surveillance, Facial Recognition, and the Azure Cloud." *The Intercept*, July 14, 2020, https://theintercept.com/2020/07/14/microsoft-police-state-mass-surveillance-facial-recognition.

24. *NYPD*, "Technology." https://archive.is/T5ZlQ.

25. *NYPD*, "Domain Awareness System: Impact and Use Policy." April 11, 2022, www.nyc.gov/assets/nypd/downloads/pdf/public_information/post-final/domain-awareness-system-das-nypd-impact-and-use-policy_4.9.21_final.pdf, 4. Some of the NYPD's claims, e.g., that it doesn't use artificial intelligence and or machine learning, have been contradicted by available evidence. See Michael Sisitzky and Ben Schaefer, "The NYPD Published Its Arsenal of Surveillance Tech. Here's What We Learned." *NYCLU*, February 24, 2021, www.nyclu.org/en/news/nypd-published-its-arsenal-surveillance-tech-heres-what-we-learned.

26. Levine et al., "The New York City Police Department's Domain Awareness System." *Interfaces* (2017).

27. George Joseph and Kenneth Lipp, "IBM Used NYPD Surveillance Footage to Develop Technology That Lets Police Search by Skin Color." *The Intercept*, September 6, 2018, https://theintercept.com/2018/09/06/nypd-surveillance-camera-skin-tone-search; Chris Gelardi, "Inside D.C. Police's Sprawling Network of Surveillance." *The Intercept*, June 18, 2022, https://theintercept.com/2022/06/18/dc-police-surveillance-network-protests.

28. Kirk Arthur, "Supporting Law Enforcement Resources With Predictive Policing." *Microsoft*, January 1, 2014, https://web.archive.org/web/2015011111650/www.microsoft.com/en-us/government/blogs/supporting-law-enforcement-resources-with-predictive-policing/default.aspx; Richard Zak, "Predictive Policing is Empowering Law Enforcement." *Microsoft*, September 26, 2017, https://web.archive.org/web/20180107013930/https://enterprise.microsoft.com/en-us/articles/industries/government/public-safety/predictive-policing-is-empowering-law-enforcement.

29. Ensign et al., "Runaway Feedback Loops in Predictive Policing." *Conference on fairness, accountability and transparency* (2018).

30. Michael Kwet, "ShadowDragon: Inside the Social Media Surveillance Software That Can Watch Your Every Move." *The Intercept*, September 21, 2021, https://theintercept.com/2021/09/21/surveillance-social-media-police-microsoft-shadowdragon-kaseware.

31. Kwet, "The Microsoft Police State." In 2017, Microsoft advertised its MAPP patrol solution in the US city of Atlanta, where it also provides its Aware DAS (*Microsoft*, "Helping Empower Atlanta's Smart-City Transformation." September 18, 2017, www.microsoft.com/en-us/industry/blog/government/2017/09/18/helping-empower-atlantas-smart-city-transformation). It's not clear if Atlanta cops use MAPP in its vehicles.

32. *Ring*, "Select Your Country." https://web.archive.org/web/20240229010908/https://ring.com/country-selector.

33. Sylvia Hui and Huizhong Wu, "China is Hardening Against Dissent, Rights Groups Say as they Mark International Human Rights Day." *AP*, December 10, 2023, https://apnews.com/article/china-human-rights-day-019854630542c24

1cb48447fc0435e6d; Ben Westcott and Yong Xiong, "Young Marxists are Going Missing in China After Protesting for Workers." *CNN*, November 14, 2018, www.cnn.com/2018/11/13/asia/china-student-marxist-missing-intl/index.html.

34. Myunghee Lee and Emir Yazici, "China's Surveillance and Repression in Xinjiang." In Michael Kwet (ed.), *Cambridge Handbook*, 166–189; Darren Byler, *In the Camps: China's High-Tech Penal Colony* (Columbia Global Reports, 2021).

35. *IPVM*, "Hikvision Uyghur Recognition, NVIDIA-Powered, Sold to PRC China Authorities." July 25, 2023, https://ipvm.com/reports/hikvision-uyghur-nvidia?code=fsdcyedb321.

36. Beraja et al., "Exporting the Surveillance State via Trade in AI." *Brookings*, December 24, 2022, www.brookings.edu/wp-content/uploads/2023/01/Exporting-the-surveillance-state-via-trade-in-AI_FINAL-1.pdf, 13.

37. Dumisani Ndela, "Creating a Surveillance State: ED Govt Zooms in for Critics with Chinese Help." *The Standard*, March 1, 2020, www.thestandard.co.zw/2020/03/01/creating-surveillance-state-ed-govt-zooms-critics-chinese-help.

38. Hagar Shezaf and Jonathan Jacobson, "Revealed: Israel's Cyber-spy Industry Helps World Dictators Hunt Dissidents and Gays." *Haaretz*, October 20, 2018, https://archive.is/ogQYS; *Amnesty International*, "Massive Data Leak Reveals Israeli NSO Group's Spyware Used to Target Activists, Journalists, and Political Leaders Globally." July 19, 2021, www.amnesty.org/en/latest/press-release/2021/07/the-pegasus-project; Michael Levenson, "F.B.I. Secretly Bought Israeli Spyware and Explored Hacking U.S. Phones." *New York Times*, January 28, 2022, www.nytimes.com/2022/01/28/world/middleeast/israel-pegasus-spyware.html; Jurgita Lapienytė, "NSO Group Sold Spyware to 14 EU Governments." *Cybernews.com*, November 15, 2023, https://cybernews.com/news/nso-group-sold-spyware-to-14-eu-governments.

39. The term, "tech-to-prison pipeline" was first used in a petition to describe predictive policing technology (Coalition for Critical Technology, "Abolish the #TechToPrisonPipeline." *Medium*, June 23, 2020, https://medium.com/@CoalitionForCriticalTechnology/abolish-the-techtoprisonpipeline-9b5b14366b16). The article was well-researched, but incomplete as far as a "pipeline" concept goes, as it didn't cover the other technologies across the carceral pipeline, e.g., other police tech, prison tech, legal tech, e-carceration, etc.

40. Michael Kwet, "Microsoft's Iron Cage: Prison Surveillance and E-Carceration." *Al Jazeera*, December 21, 2020, www.aljazeera.com/features/2020/12/21/microsofts-iron-cage-prison-surveillance-and-e-carceral-state.

41. Kwet, "Microsoft's Iron Cage."

42. Ibid.

43. Ibid.

44. Ibid.

45. See references in Kwet, "Microsoft's Iron Cage."

46. Sajith Karikkandathil, "How Digital Justice Is Transforming the Justice System." *Microsoft*, October 30, 2016, https://news.microsoft.com/en-xm/2016/10/30/how-digital-justice-is-transforming-the-justice-system.

47. Kwet, "Microsoft's Iron Cage."

48. Ibid.

49. Ibid.

50. Candace Whitney-Morris, "After Spending Time Behind Bars, This Employee Set No Bars On His Own Success." *Microsoft*, August 10, 2016, https://news.microsoft.com/life/spending-time-behind-bars-employee-set-no-bars-success.

51. Rajan Chandra Ghosh and Caroline Orchiston, "A systematic Review of Climate Migration Research: Gaps in Existing Literature." *SN Social Sciences* 2(47) (2022), 47.

52. *UNHCR*, "Climate Change and Conflict Pursue Displaced Burkinabes." January 25, 2021, www.unhcr.org/us/news/stories/climate-change-and-conflict-pursue-displaced-burkinabes.

53. Linke et al., "Dry Growing Seasons Predicted Central American Migration to the US from 2012 to 2018." *Scientific Reports* 13(1) (2023); *AP*, "24 charged with forcing migrants into 'modern-day slavery,'" December 10, 2021, https://apnews.com/article/business-georgia-slavery-forced-labor-migrant-workers-0e0d7235e79a4e216307e007a7aa716b; Hannah Dreier, "Alone and Exploited, Migrant Children Work Brutal Jobs Across the U.S." *New York Times*, February 25, 2023, www.nytimes.com/2023/02/25/us/unaccompanied-migrant-child-workers-exploitation.html.

54. *Mijente*, "The War Against Migrants: Trump's Tech Tools Powered by Palantir." 2019, https://mijente.net/wp-content/uploads/2019/08/Mijente-The-War-Against-Immigrants_-Trumps-Tech-Tools-Powered-by-Palantir_.pdf, 8.

55. Ayyan Zubair, "Domain Awareness System." *Surveillance Technology Oversight Project*, September 26, 2019, www.stopspying.org/latest-news/2019/9/26/domain-awareness-system.

56. Kwet, "Microsoft's Iron Cage."

57. Center for Biological Diversity, "No Border Wall." https://archive.is/wip/MvHz1.

58. Todd Miller with Nick Buxton and Mark Akkerman, "Global Climate Wall: How the World's Wealthiest Nations Prioritise Borders Over Climate Action." *Transnational Institute*, 2021, www.tni.org/files/publication-downloads/global-climate-wall-report-tni-web-resolution.pdf, 1.

59. Ainhoa Ruiz Benedicto et al., "A Walled World: Towards a Global Apartheid." *Centre Delàs d'Estudis per la Pau*, 2020, www.tni.org/files/publication-downloads/informe46_walledwolrd_centredelas_tni_stopwapenhandel_stopthewall_eng_def.pdf.

60. Ian Urbina, "The Secretive Prisons That Keep Migrants Out of Europe." *New Yorker*, November 28, 2021, www.newyorker.com/magazine/2021/12/06/the-secretive-libyan-prisons-that-keep-migrants-out-of-europe.

61. Michael Kwet, "Cmore: South Africa's New Smart Policing Surveillance Engine." *Counterpunch*, January 27, 2017, www.counterpunch.org/2017/01/27/cmore-south-africas-new-smart-policing-surveillance-engine.

62. Ibid.

63. Kagee, Tariq. Personal interview, May 14, 2020.

64. Engelbrecht, "Projections of Future Climate Change in Southern Africa and the Potential for Regional Tipping Points." *Sustainability of Southern African Ecosystems under Global Change: Science for Management and Policy Interventions* (2024).

65. Michael Kwet, "The Big Tech Behind Israel's Digital Apartheid." *Truthdig*, October 26, 2023, www.truthdig.com/articles/the-big-tech-behind-israels-digital-apartheid; Michael Kwet, "How US Big Tech supports Israel's AI-powered genocide and apartheid." *Al Jazeera*, May 12, 2024, www.aljazeera.com/opinions/2024/5/12/how-us-big-tech-supports-israels-ai-powered-genocide-and-apartheid.

66. Sam Biddle, "Documents Reveal Advanced AI Tools Google Is Selling to Israel." *The Intercept*, July 24, 2022, https://theintercept.com/2022/07/24/google-israel-artificial-intelligence-project-nimbus.

67. Yarden Katz, "How Microsoft is Invested in Israeli Settler-Colonialism." *Mondoweiss*, March 15, 2021, https://mondoweiss.net/2021/03/how-microsoft-is-invested-in-israeli-settler-colonialism.

68. *Who Profits*, "IBM: A Major Facilitator of Israel's Surveillance and Security Apparatus." 2022, www.whoprofits.org/publications/report/158?ibm-a-major-facilitator-of-israels-surveillance-and-security-apparatus.

69. Todd Miller, "The Bipartisan Border Machine: Biden Never Really Stopped Building the Wall." *Counterpunch*, October 18, 2023, www.counterpunch.org/2023/10/18/the-bipartisan-border-machine-biden-never-really-stopped-building-the-wall.

70. Antony Loewenstein, *The Palestine Laboratory: How Israel Exports the Technology of Occupation Around the World* (Verso, 2023).

71. Farhad Majoo, "Biden Just Clobbered China's Chip Industry." *New York Times*, October 20, 2020, www.nytimes.com/2022/10/20/opinion/biden-china-semiconductor-chip.html.

72. Martin Luther King, Jr. "Beyond Vietnam—A Time to Break Silence." April 4, 1967, www.americanrhetoric.com/speeches/mlkatimetobreaksilence.htm.

8. PEOPLE'S TECH AND A DIGITAL TECH DEAL

1. Michael Kwet, "People's Tech for People's Power: A Guide to Digital Self-Defense and Empowerment." *Right2Know*.

2. *GNU.org*, "What is Free Software?" www.gnu.org/philosophy/free-sw.en.html.

3. Casey Newton, "The Battle Inside Signal." *Platformer*, January 25, 2021, www.platformer.news/-the-battle-inside-signal.

4. *Signal Technology Foundation*, "Form 990." 2022, https://projects.propublica.org/nonprofits/organizations/824506840/202342569349300244/full.

5. Ibid. Its President, Meredith Whittaker, takes about $200,000 per year.
6. *FSF India*, "Better than WhatsApp: Try these Free Software Apps and Services." January 23, 2021, https://fsf.org.in/article/better-than-whatsapp.
7. See Kwet, "People's Tech," 79.
8. *FSF India*, "Better than WhatsApp."
9. *Mozilla Foundation*, "Return of Organization Exempt From Income Tax [Form 990]." 2022, https://projects.propublica.org/nonprofits/organizations/200097189/202313199349323576/full.
10. For an overview, see Michael Kwet, "Fixing Social Media: Toward a Democratic Digital Commons." *Markets, Globalization & Development Review* 5(1), 2020; Michael Kwet, "Dawn of the Fediverse," *Truthdig*, March 2, 2023, www.truthdig.com/articles/dawn-of-the-fediverse.
11. Widder et al., "Open (For Business): Big Tech, Concentrated Power, and the Political Economy of Open AI." *SSRN*, https://papers.ssrn.com/sol3/papers.cfm?abstract_id=4543807.
12. Hickel et al., "Urgent Need for Post-Growth Climate Mitigation Scenarios." *Nature Energy* 6 (2021).
13. Adam Lucas, "Risking the Earth Part 2: Power Politics and Structural Reform of the IPCC and UNFCCC." *Climate Risk Management* 31 (2021).
14. Michael Kwet, "The Digital Tech Deal: A Socialist Framework for the Twenty-First Century." *Race & Class* 63(3) (2022); Michael Kwet, "Digital Ecosocialism: Breaking the power of Big Tech." *Transnational Institute*, May 31, 2022, www.tni.org/en/article/digital-ecosocialism. The rest of this chapter draws from these two works. For an earlier version of these, see Michael Kwet, "A Digital Tech Deal: Digital Socialism, Decolonization, and Reparations for a Sustainable Global Economy." *Global Information Society Watch*, 2020, https://giswatch.org/node/6225.
15. See Aissa Dearing, "Cochabamba People's Agreement: Annotated." *JSTOR Daily*, September 1, 2023, https://daily.jstor.org/cochabamba-peoples-agreement-annotated. Quotes in the following paragraphs are derived from here.
16. In Ibid.
17. Ajl, *A People's*; The Red Nation, *The Red Deal: Indigenous Action to Save Our Earth* (Common Notions, 2021); *Climate Justice Charter Movement*, https://cjcm.org.za. Other radical "deals" are a bit shorter on detail, but include the Red, Black and Green New Deal (by the Movement for Black Lives), a Feminist Agenda for a Green New Deal, and A Feminist and Decolonial Global Green New Deal). The first doesn't explicitly problematize capitalism.
18. The Red Deal only focuses on carbon debt.
19. See Robin Hahnel, *A Participatory Economy* (AK Press, 2022); Michael Albert, *No Bosses: A New Economy for a Better World* (Zero Books, 2021).
20. See Eben Moglen, "A History of the GPLv3 Revision Process." *Software Freedom Law Center* (2013) www.softwarefreedom.org/resources/2013/A_History_of_the_GPLv3_Revision_Process.pdf.

21. Rana Foroohar, "Digital Tools Can Be a Useful Bolster to Democracy." *Financial Times*, February 16, 2020, www.ft.com/content/5a9fad90-4f0a-11ea-95a0-43d18ec715f5.

22. Dean Baker, "Working Paper: Is Intellectual Property the Root of All Evil? Patents, Copyrights, and Inequality." 2018, https://cepr.net/images/stories/reports/ip-2018-10.pdf.

23. Eben Moglen, "The dotCommunist Manifesto: How Culture Became Property and What We're Going to Do About It." *YouTube*, 2021, www.youtube.com/watch?v=BgCKRN_Bzzs.

24. Dan Hind, "The British Digital Cooperative: A New Model Public Sector Institution." *The Next System Project*, September 19, 2019, https://thenextsystem.org/bdc.

25. James Wohr, "Ad Blocking: What It Is and Why It Matters to Marketers and Advertisers." *Insider Intelligence*, October 11, 2023, www.insiderintelligence.com/insights/ad-blocking; *Statista*, "Companies with Largest Share of Digital Advertising Revenue Worldwide in 2023." August 29, 2023, www.statista.com/statistics/290629/digital-ad-revenue-share-of-major-ad-selling-companies-worldwide.

26. *Fairphone*, "Fair Materials 101: Why Recycling Isn't Enough." February 12, 2021, www.fairphone.com/en/2021/02/12/recycling-is-not-enough.

27. Kris De Decker, "How Circular is the Circular Economy?" *Resilience*, November 12, 2018, www.resilience.org/stories/2018-11-12/how-circular-is-the-circular-economy.

28. Arroyos et al., "A Tale of Two Mice: Sustainable Electronics Design and Prototyping." *CHI Conference on Human Factors in Computing Systems Extended Abstracts* (2022).

9. FIGHTING BACK

1. By my count, there are about 40 journal articles even somewhat connecting degrowth to computing, but they all depart from the contemporary, global approach that connects colonialism and the North-South divide to Big Tech. To the best of my knowledge, my publications, dating back to 2020 (Kwet, "A Digital Tech Deal"), are the only to do so to date—a reflection of how the field of digital studies is on the wrong track.

2. For a detailed overview of the media analysis below, see Michael Kwet, "Our World In Denial," forthcoming.

3. See e.g., Peter Coy, "An Economic Case Against Environmental Doomsayers." *New York Times*, September 13, 2023, www.nytimes.com/2023/09/13/opinion/degrowth-superabundance-climate-change.html; Paul Krugman, "Wonking Out: Why Growth Can Be Green." *New York Times*, February 17, 2023, www.nytimes.com/2023/02/17/opinion/economic-growth-green-degrowth.html.

4. For a critique of Daly's position, see Frederick Blauwhof, "Overcoming Accumulation: Is a Capitalist Steady-State Economy Possible?" *Ecological Economics* 84 (2012).

5. Robinson Meyer, "How Many Stories Do Newspapers Publish Per Day?" *The Atlantic*, May 26, 2016, https://archive.is/sieVJ.

6. Bayard Rustin, "No Growth Has to Mean Less Is Less." *New York Times*, May 2, 1976, www.nytimes.com/1976/05/02/archives/no-growth-has-to-mean-less-is-less-growth.html.

7. Whitney Webb, "Corporations See a Different Kind of 'Green' in Ocasio-Cortez's 'Green New Deal.'" *Mint News*, February 8, 2019.

8. See Vijay Kolinjivadi and Ashish Kothari, "No Harm Here is Still Harm There: The Green New Deal and the Global South (I)." *Jamhoor*, May 20, 2020, www.jamhoor.org/read/2020/5/20/no-harm-here-is-still-harm-there-looking-at-the-green-new-deal-from-the-global-south; Ajl, *A People's*.

9. Naomi Klein, *On Fire: The Burning Case for a Green New Deal* (Simon & Schuster, 2019).

10. Ajl, *A People's*, 86–87.

11. Klein, *On Fire*.

12. *The Intercept*, "Form 8879-E." https://web.archive.org/web/20230608022947/https://theintercept.com/wp-content/uploads/2023/05/FLMW-2021-990.pdf.

13. Mark Ames and Yasha Levine, "The Extraordinary Pierre Omidyar." *NFSW*, November 15, 2013, https://web.archive.org/web/20131130161037/www.nsfwcorp.com/dispatch/extraordinary-pierre-omidyar.

14. *The Intercept*, "Corporate Advertisers Won't Fund This Reporting. Can You Donate \$5 by Tonight's Deadline?," Subscriber Email, December 31, 2023.

15. Naomi Klein, "An Explanation of Speaking Fees." *This Changes Everything*, 2015, http://thischangeseverything.org/an-explanation-of-speaking-fees.

16. Nick Couldry and Ulises Mejias, "Data Colonialism: Rethinking Big Data's Relation to the Contemporary Subject." *Television & New Media* 20(4) (2019), 2.

17. Sean Starrs offers some evidence on general US tech dominance (referenced in Chapter 1). See also Cecilia Rikap and Bengt-Åke Lundvall, *The Digital Innovation Race: Conceptualizing the Emerging New World Order* (Palgrave MacMillan, 2021), where they evaluate the US vs China in AI and find American dominance. (In my view, they overstate China's capacity to narrow the gap.)

18. Elsewhere I've called this "tech hegemony." See Michael Kwet, "Digital Colonialism: US Empire and the New Imperialism in the Global South." *Race & Class* 60(4), 3–26 (2019).

19. Mark Achbar and Peter Wintonick, *Manufacturing Consent: Noam Chomsky and the Media*, 1992.

20. For what follows, see Michael Kwet, "Big Tech Antitrust: A Critique from the Left," forthcoming, including references.

21. 21 Cong. Rec. 2457 (1890).

22. Ibid.

23. Gabriel Kolko, *The Triumph of Conservatism: A Reinterpretation of American History, 1900–1916* (Free Press, 1963), 1.

24. Cited in Roxanne Dunbar-Ortiz, *An Indigenous Peoples' History of the United States* (Beacon Press, 2014), 9–10.
25. Gilbert King, "Where the Buffalo No Longer Roamed." *Smithsonian Magazine*, July 17, 2012, www.smithsonianmag.com/history/where-the-buffalo-no-longer-roamed-3067904.
26. Similar monstrous positions were held by subsequent antitrust figures, including Louis Brandeis, who railed against socialism, was silent about Jim Crow racism, led the American Zionist movement for a Jewish state in Palestine, and endorsed scientific management. See Kwet, "Big Tech Antitrust."
27. Spencer Y. Kwon, Yeuran Ma and Kasper Zimmerman, "100 Years of Rising Corporate Concentration." 2023, https://bfi.uchicago.edu/wp-content/uploads/2023/02/BFI_WP_2023-20.pdf. The authors note that antitrust can be effective addressing *specific* products and services, a far cry from the *general* powers of antitrust to rein in corporate concentration alleged by neo-Brandeisians.
28. Michael Kwet, "The Farce of Microsoft's Anti-Racism and the Capture of Academia." *Truthdig*, April 17, 2023, www.truthdig.com/articles/the-farce-of-microsofts-anti-racism-and-the-capture-of-academia.
29. Yarden Katz, *Artificial Whiteness* (Columbia University Press, 2020), 80.
30. Rodrigo Ochigame, "The Invention of 'Ethical AI': How Big Tech Manipulates Academia to Avoid Regulation." *The Intercept*, December 20, 2019, https://theintercept.com/2019/12/20/mit-ethical-ai-artificial-intelligence. This article, while decent at the time, missed a more general anti-capitalist, anti-colonial critique of these think tanks. See Katz, *Artificial Whiteness*; Michael Kwet, "The Microsoft Police State: Mass Surveillance, Facial Recognition, and the Azure Cloud." *The Intercept*, July 14, 2020, https://theintercept.com/2020/07/14/microsoft-police-state-mass-surveillance-facial-recognition.
31. Microsoft Research, "Computing Technology as Racial Infrastructure: A History of the Present & Blueprint for Black Future." *YouTube*, August 4, 2021, https://youtu.be/g7WcCjL14iQ?t=3400.
32. Sarah Myers West et al., "Discriminating Systems: Gender, Race, and Power in AI." *AI Now*, 2019, https://ainowinstitute.org/wp-content/uploads/2023/04/discriminatingsystems.pdf, 6–7, 33.
33. See e.g., Aziz Choudry and Dip Kapoor (eds.), *NGOization: Complicity, Contradictions and Prospects* (Zed Books, 2013); INCITE!, *The Revolution Will Not Be Funded* (Duke University Press, 2017); Edward Berman, *The Influence of Carnegie, Ford, and Rockefeller Foundations on American Foreign Policy: The Ideology of Philanthropy* (Suny Press, 1983).
34. Jamey Essex, *Development, Security, and Aid: Geopolitics and Geoeconomics at the U.S. Agency for International Development* (University of Georgia Press, 2013).
35. Rajiv Shah, "Embracing Enlightened Capitalism." *Geo. J. Int'l Aff.* 13(7) (2012).
36. Kristin Myers, "Ford Foundation President: 'We Need a New Form of Capitalism' to 'Level the Playing Field.'" *Yahoo! Finance*, May 28, 2021, https://finance.yahoo.com/news/ford-foundation-president-we-need-a-new-form-of-capitalism-to-level-the-playing-field-204433759.html.

37. *Pensions & Investments*, "Global foundation Assets Reach $1.5 Trillion." May 8, 2018, www.pionline.com/article/20180508/INTERACTIVE/180509883/global-foundation-assets-reach-1-5-trillion.

38. Joy James, "Airbrushing Revolution for the Sake of Abolition." *Black Perspectives*, July 20, 2020, https://aaihs.org/airbrushing-revolution-for-the-sake-of-abolition.

39. Black Power Media, "Myth: Angela Davis was a Black Panther Pt. 2." *YouTube*, August 25, 2021, www.youtube.com/watch?v=27AfxsCQwIo&t=4007s.

40. Brand et al., "From Planetary to Societal Boundaries: An Argument for Collectively Defined Self-Limitation," *Sustainability: Science, Practice and Policy* 17(1), 2021.

41. Yarden Katz and Ulrich Matter, "Metrics of Inequality: The Concentration of Resources in the U.S. Biomedical Elite." *Science as Culture* 29(4) (2020).

42. Michael Kwet, "Flying the KITE High against Digital Colonialism: FOSS in the Era of EdTech." *Bot Populi*, June 27, 2023, https://botpopuli.net/flying-the-kite-high-against-digital-colonialism-foss-in-the-era-of-edtech.

43. The project received a small amount of attention in the Western academy about a decade ago, but they lost interest fast.

44. Richard Knight, "US Computers in South Africa." *The Africa Fund*, 1986, https://projects.kora.matrix.msu.edu/files/210-808-10823/al.sff.document.afoo0219.pdf.

45. Ibid., 1.

46. Michael Kwet, "The Digital Tech Deal: A Socialist Framework for the Twenty-First Century." *Race & Class* 63(3) (2022), 79.

47. See e.g., Kuhnhenn et al., "A Societal Transformation Scenario for Staying Below 1.5°C." *Heinrich Böll Stiftung*, 2020, www.boell.de/sites/default/files/2020-12/A%20Societal%20Transformation%20Scenario%20for%20Staying%20Below%201.5C.pdf; Olk et al., "How to Pay for Saving The World: Modern Monetary Theory for a Degrowth Transition." *Ecological Economics* 214 (2023); Richard Bärnthaler and Ian Gogh, "Provisioning for Sufficiency: Envisaging Production Corridors." *Sustainability: Science, Practice and Policy* 19(1) (2023).

48. Ahmed White, *Under the Iron Heel: The Wobblies and the Capitalist War on Radical Workers* (University of California Press, 2022).

Index